T0183425

More information about this series at http://www.springer.com/series/7408

Sami Yangui · Athman Bouguettaya ·
Xiao Xue · Noura Faci ·
Walid Gaaloul · Qi Yu ·
Zhangbing Zhou · Nathalie Hernandez ·
Elisa Y. Nakagawa (Eds.)

Service-Oriented Computing – ICSOC 2019 Workshops

WESOACS, ASOCA, ISYCC, TBCE, and STRAPS
Toulouse, France, October 28–31, 2019
Revised Selected Papers

 Springer

Editors
Sami Yangui (ID)
LAAS-CNRS
Toulouse, France

Xiao Xue
Tianjin University
Tianjin, China

Walid Gaaloul
Télécom SudParis
Évry, France

Zhangbing Zhou
University of Geosciences in Beijing
Beijing, China

Elisa Y. Nakagawa
University of São Paulo
São Paulo, Brazil

Athman Bouguettaya
University of Sydney
Sydney, NSW, Australia

Noura Faci
University of Lyon
Villeurbanne, France

Qi Yu
Rochester Institute of Technology
Rochester, NY, USA

Nathalie Hernandez
University of Toulouse 2
Toulouse, France

ISSN 0302-9743   ISSN 1611-3349   (electronic)
Lecture Notes in Computer Science
ISBN 978-3-030-45988-8   ISBN 978-3-030-45989-5   (eBook)
https://doi.org/10.1007/978-3-030-45989-5

LNCS Sublibrary: SL2 – Programming and Software Engineering

This Springer imprint is published by the registered company Springer Nature Switzerland AG
The registered company address is: Gewerbestrasse 11, 6330 Cham, Switzerland

Preface

This volume presents the proceedings of the scientific satellite events that were held in conjunction with the 17th International Conference on Service-Oriented Computing (ICSOC 2019), held in Toulouse, France, during October 28–31, 2019.

The satellite events provide venues for specialist groups to meet, generate focused discussions on specific sub-areas within service-oriented computing, and engage in community-building activities. These events significantly helped enrich the main conference by both expanding the scope of research topics and attracting participants from a wider community. As is customary, these satellite events were organized around three main tracks, including a workshop track, a PhD symposium track, and a demonstration track. The ICSOC 2019 workshop track consisted of five workshops covering a wide range of topics that fall into the general area of service computing:

- The 15th International Workshop on Engineering Service-Oriented Applications and Cloud Services (WESOACS 2019)
- The 4th International Workshop on Adaptive Service-Oriented and Cloud Applications (ASOCA 2019)
- The 4th International IoT Systems Provisioning & Management for Context-Aware Smart Cities (ISYCC 2019)
- The first edition of Towards Blockchain-Based Collaborative Enterprise (TBCE 2019)
- The first edition of Smart daTa integRation And Processing on Service based environments (STRAPS 2019)

The workshops were held on October 28, 2019. ASOCA 2019 and ISYCC 2019 were held over a common one-day session. Similarly, WESOACS 2019 and STRAPS 2019 were held over a common one-day session. Finally, TBCE 2019 was held over a half-day session.

The PhD symposium is an international forum for PhD students to present, share, and discuss their research in a constructive and critical atmosphere. It also provides students with fruitful feedback and advice on their research approach and thesis. The PhD symposium track was held over a half-day session.

The demonstration track offers an exciting and highly interactive way to show research prototypes/work in service-oriented computing and related areas. The demonstration track was held over a two-hour session with all the demonstrations running in parallel.

We would like to thank the workshop, PhD symposium, and demonstration authors, as well as the Organizing Committees, who together contributed to these important events of the conference. We hope that these proceedings will serve as a valuable reference for researchers and practitioners working in the service-oriented computing domain and its emerging applications.

November 2019   Sami Yangui

Submission and Review Information

Each published paper in this proceedings was reviewed by at least two anonymous reviewers.

Concerning the workshops, 14 papers were accepted of the 32 received papers. In addition, 6 selected papers were invited. ISYCC 2019 accepted 3 papers of the 5 received submissions. Moreover, 3 invited papers were presented in this workshop. ASOCA 2019 accepted 2 papers of the 4 received submissions. Moreover, 2 invited papers were presented in this workshop. WESOACS 2019 accepted 4 papers of the 6 received submissions. STRAPS 2019 accepted 3 papers of the 7 received submissions. An additional invited paper was presented in this workshop. Finally, TBCE 2019 accepted 2 papers of the 3 received submissions.

Conerning the PhD symposium, the track co-chairs accepted the 4 received submissions to give the PhD students the chance to present and discuss their work, and benefit from audience feedback.

Finally, concerning the demonstration track, 12 proposals were received in total. The demonstration co-chairs selected 5 demonstrations.

Organization

Workshop Chairs

Sami Yangui	LAAS-CNRS, France
Athman Bouguettaya	The University of Sydney, Australia
Xiao Xue	Tianjin University, China

Demonstration Chairs

Noura Faci	University of Lyon, France
Qi Yu	Rochester Institute of Technology, USA
Walid Gaaloul	Télécom SudParis, France

PhD Symposium Chairs

Zhangbing Zhou	University of Geosciences in Beijing, China
Nathalie Hernandez	University of Toulouse 2, France
Elisa Y. Nakagawa	University of São Paulo, Brazil

Finance Chair

Bernd Krämer	Fern University, Germany

Publication Chair

Ismael Bouassida Rodriguez	University of Sfax, Tunisia

Publicity Chairs

Nicolas Seydoux	LAAS-CNRS, France
Ilhem Khlif	University of Sfax, Tunisia
YiWen Zhang	Anhui University in Hefei, China
Manel Abdellatif	École Polytechnique de Montréal, Canada

Web Chairs

Nour El-Houda Nouar	LAAS-CNRS, France
Fatma Raissi	LAAS-CNRS, France
Josue Castañeda Cisneros	LAAS-CNRS, France

Workshop on Engineering Service-Oriented Applications and Cloud Services

Willem-Jan van den Heuvel	Tilburg School of Economics and Management, The Netherlands
Andreas S. Andreou	Cyprus University of Technology, Cyprus
George Feuerlicht	Prague University of Economics, Czech Republic
Winfried Lamersdorf	University of Hamburg, Germany
Guadalupe Ortiz	University of Cádiz, Spain
Christian Zirpins	Karlsruhe University of Applied Sciences, Germany

Workshop on Adaptive Service-Oriented and Cloud Applications

Ismael Bouassida Rodriguez	University of Sfax, Tunisia
Ghada Gharbi	Sensinov, Toulouse, France

Workshop on IoT Systems Provisioning and Management for Context-Aware Smart Cities

Mohamed Mohamed	Cupertino, USA
Khouloud Bouakadi	University of Sfax, Tunisia

Workshop on Towards Blockchain-Based Collaborative Enterprise

Layth Sliman	EFREI, France

Workshop on Smart daTa integRation And Processing on Service Based Environments

Chirine Ghedira Guegan	IAE Lyon School of Management, University Lyon 3, LIRIS Lab, France
Nadia Bennani	INSA Lyon, LIRIS Lab, France
Genoveva Vargas-Solar	CNRS, LIG-LAFMIA, France

Contents

TBCE: Towards Blockchain-Based Collaborative Enterprise

**STRAPS: Smart daTa integRation And Processing on Service
Based Environments**

PhD Symposium

Demonstrations

WESOACS: Engineering Service-Oriented Applications and Cloud Services ˎ

Introduction to the 15th International Workshop on Engineering Service-Oriented Applications and Cloud Services (WESOACS 2019)

The International Workshop on Engineering Services-Oriented Applications and Cloud Services (WESOACS) is a long-established forum (formerly known as WESOA) for innovative ideas from research and practice in the field of software engineering for modern service-oriented application systems. This year, the 15th meeting took place on October 28, 2019, in Toulouse, France.

Service-oriented systems play an important role in many areas, such as enterprise computing, cloud/fog computing, and the Web. While there is agreement on the main principles for designing and developing application systems based on distributed software services, methods and tools that support the development of such applications are still the subject of intense research. These research topics include software service life cycle development methodologies, service-oriented enterprise architectures, service-oriented analysis and design, and in particular service engineering technologies for cloud computing environments in general, and more specifically for current trends in cloud-based applications such as intelligent cyber-physical systems.

Currently, there is a shift in this area to so-called "DevOps" approaches of software development in which software service development and operations are continuously and inextricably linked to achieve faster application delivery with automated release and deployment. Agile processes, microservices, continuous delivery, containers and cluster management technologies are just some of the popular topics that contribute to the current IT transformation in this context.

For the workshop event, WESOACS 2019 joined forces with the First Workshop on Smart Data Integration and Processing on Service-based Environments (STRAPS 2019) to present an attractive workshop program including a keynote presentation together with two technical sessions and discussion.

The keynote was presented by Finjan Shi from Groupe PVCP, and gave industry insights into "Constructing a secured, reactive & scalable data platform for a better exploitation of rich data assets in the tourism industry."

The first technical session on smart data featured a WESOACS 2019 contribution by Philippe Lalanda et al. on "Service-oriented pervasive platform supporting machine learning applications in smart buildings."

The second technical session on service engineering featured WESOACS 2019 contributions from Denis Wolters et al. on "Specifying Web Interfaces for Command-line Applications Based on OpenAPI", Claas Keller et al. "Towards understanding adaptation latency in self-adaptive systems," and Antonio Brogi et al. on "Freshening the air in microservices: Resolving architectural smells via refactoring."

In the course of the workshop, the participants had ample opportunity for professional exchange and networking, so that the 15th edition of the event can once again be regarded as a complete success.

Organization

Workshop Organizers

Andreas S. Andreou	Cyprus University of Technology, Cyprus
George Feuerlicht	Prague University of Economics, Czech Republic
Winfried Lamersdorf	University of Hamburg, Germany
Guadalupe Ortiz	University of Cádiz, Spain
Willem-Jan van den Heuvel	Tilburg School of Economics and Management, The Netherlands
Christian Zirpins	Karlsruhe University of Applied Sciences, Germany

Program Committee

Marco Aiello	University of Stuttgart, Germany
Danilo Ardagna	Politechnico Milano, Italy
David Bermbach	TU Berlin, Germany
Juan Boubeta-Puig	University of Cádiz, Spain
Alena Buchalcevova	Prague University of Economics, Czech Republic
Sotirios P. Chatzis	Cyprus University of Technology, Cyprus
Chi-Hung Chi	CSIRO, Australia
Javier Cubo	University of Malaga, Spain
Florian Daniel	Politechnico Milano, Italy
Efstratios Georgopoulos	TEI of Kalamata, Greece
Laura Gonzalez	Universidad de la Republica, Uruguay
Paul Greenfield	CSIRO, Australia
Patricia Lago	University of Amsterdam, The Netherlands
Frank Leymann	University of Stuttgart, Germany
Spyros Likothanassis	University of Patras, Greece
Mark Little	Red Hat, USA
Massimo Mecella	University Roma La Sapienza, Italy
George Pallis	University of Cyprus, Cyprus
Mike Papazoglou	University of Tilburg, The Netherlands
Pierluigi Plebani	Politechnico Milano, Italy
Wolfgang Reisig	Humboldt-University Berlin, Germany
Ioannis Stamelos	Aristotle University of Thessaloniki, Greece
Erik Wittern	IBM Watson Research, USA

Acknowledgements

We wish to thank all authors for their contributions, the Program Committee members for their expert input and the ICSOC 2019 workshop co-chairs for the organization.

Service-Oriented Pervasive Platform Supporting Machine Learning Applications in Smart Buildings

Philippe Lalanda[1]([⊠]), Dan Wang[2], German Vega[1],
Humberto Cervantes[3], and Moustapha A. Khalid[1]

[1] Grenoble University (UGA), 38058 Grenoble, France
`{philippe.lalanda,german.vega,`
`moustapha.khalid}@imag.fr`
[2] The Hong Kong Polytechnic University,
Hong Kong, Hong Kong
`dan.wang@polyu.edu.hk`
[3] Universidad Autónoma Metropolitana Iztapalapa, Mexico City, Mexico
`hcm@xanum.uam.mx`

Abstract. Following the success of image recognition, machine learning approaches have recently been proposed to improve the efficiency for such systems as industry operation and maintenance, smart buildings, and smart homes. These applications are beginning to be deployed in pervasive environments. This poses greater stress in maintaining the quality of the applications. To date, there is no architecture and tools developed that can automatically support application quality maintenance. Even worse, there is no clear definition on the requirements. In this paper, we present initial experiments that we conducted with real use cases pertaining to Industry 4.0 and discuss a set of requirements that should be met by pervasive platforms to better support AI-based applications running in the edge.

Keywords: Smart building · Machine learning · Service-oriented pervasive platform · Industry 4.0

1 Introduction

Pervasive computing [1, 2] promotes the integration of connected electronic devices in our living spaces in order to assist us in our daily activities, be they professional or private. These devices can pick up a wide variety of signals in the environment and transmit them to computers of various sizes and capacities in order to run services. Devices can be blended in the environment, inserted into everyday objects, or integrated into already existing electronic equipment like smartphones or embedded control systems. Clearly, pervasive computing is playing an increasingly important role in civil and professional society. Several factors account for this strong enthusiasm like the falling of device prices, the increased computing power and storage capabilities, the widespread availability of the Internet and, of course, the strong demand for added-value services. As a consequence, whether at home, in commute, or at work, we

S. Yangui et al. (Eds.): ICSOC 2019 Workshops, LNCS 12019, pp. 5–16, 2020.
https://doi.org/10.1007/978-3-030-45989-5_1

already enjoy a variety of simple, unobtrusive services that enhance our quality of life or allow companies to optimize resource management.

Pervasive computing already has, and will continue to have, profound effects on entire industries. This applies for instance to the manufacturing domain where the notion of Industry 4.0, proposed in 2011 by a government-funded German project, is gaining increasing attention. This initiative promotes the generalized adoption of digital technologies [3, 35] to favor the emergence of smart, connected plants. Similar ideas are also applied to the popular domains of smart buildings or smart cities.

The smart building domain is an interesting and highly symbolic example that touches our daily lives. A smart building is filled with electronic devices collecting data and managing major functions like heating, ventilation, air conditioning, lighting, or security. It provides multiple, unobtrusive services to the building occupants, making them more comfortable and productive. Smart buildings also help operators improve asset reliability and performance, which reduces energy use, optimizes space usage and minimizes the environmental impact. A number of services, in particular related to energy management, are in place today. However, given the many bold visions of pervasive computing applications, services available today are still limited and often restricted to off-line analysis and reporting.

Two developments, which are likely to change the whole picture, have gained significant momentum recently. The first one is the move from cloud computing to edge, or fog, computing [4]. Most pervasive applications are currently based on cloud infrastructures. This, unfortunately, limits the number and type of services that can be implemented because of unpredictable delays, lack of security and privacy preservation, and sometimes insufficient bandwidth or excessive costs. The use of edge resources will make it possible to envisage a greater variety and quality of services. Another major change is the urge for AI-based services. Machine learning has been very successful to solve complex problems where traditional algorithmic approaches cannot be applied like, for instance, in computer vision or speech processing. It is then not surprising that there is today an increasing demand to apply AI techniques in pervasive domains, like smart buildings, where again traditional solutions cannot be used for lack of modeling tools and excessive algorithmic complexity.

These two evolutions put together generate great expectations but also raise major scientific and technical challenges.

The purpose of this paper is to present some first experiments we have conducted in the smart building domain and a set of requirements that have been inferred, essentially regarding fog-level platforms. The paper is structured as it follows. First, some background about our driving use-case is provided. In Sect. 3, we discuss the limits of the current solution and present a list of requirements that should be met by pervasive platforms to effectively support AI-based applications running in the edge. We also detail experiments based on a service-oriented pervasive platform called iCasa that has been extended to that end. Section 5 discusses some related work and Sect. 6 deals with conclusion and coming work.

2 Use Case

2.1 Description and Early Results

As introduced, the concept of smart building has been in existence for some time and a number of services, mainly related to energy and assets management, have been implemented. Chillers are the most energy consuming components of buildings. Note that the amount of electricity consumed by a chiller is not only determined by the total cooling load but also by its energy-efficiency. Intuitively, if this efficiency is low (e.g. due to poor maintenance), then more electricity will be consumed to support a required cooling demand.

Chiller sequencing refers to operating the most efficient combination of chillers in a building in real-time in order to meet time-varying cooling demands. For example, sequencing a building with two chillers [0.5, 0.7] implies that chiller 1 and chiller 2 are operating at 50% and 70% of their maximum rated capacity, respectively. The sequencing problem is to allocate the cooling load at any given time to the chillers in the most energy efficient manner so that the overall cooling demand of the building is satisfied while at the same time the electricity consumed by the chillers is kept at a minimum [5]. The efficacy of chiller sequencing control relies heavily on the run-time performance profile of the chillers, namely the COP under different cooling load regimes. COP is a measure of the energy efficiency of a chiller and captures the cooling power that it can output for a certain input power consumption.

Recently, we have developed a data-driven approach, named Chiller AIOps, and applied it successfully to Hong-Kong high rise buildings. Here, a machine learning model is trained using data collected in the Hong-Kong buildings BMS during four years and used for COP prediction [8]. Our approach is to develop individualized COP for each chiller by applying machine learning techniques using historical chiller data. A private cloud is established to store the historical data from the BMS. Plant-floor gateways act as intermediaries between physical environments and the cloud. When a cooling demand D arrives, the cloud can perform chiller sequencing assisted by our data-driven COP prediction schemes. To do so, one needs to be wary of the following: (1) The cooling demand changes over time, so chiller sequencing must be performed repeatedly in order to continuously meet the varying cooling demand. The common practice is to trigger chiller sequencing in a periodic manner [9]. (2) To ensure cooling performance, chiller sequencing needs time for feedback control until the system regains stability when switching from one sequence to another. There is also a minimum start-stop-start time (called deadband) for every chiller. (3) The chiller sequencing for each period must be completed before the start of the next sequencing period. Otherwise, the system can be unstable and return inaccurate data which can be detrimental to subsequent COP prediction and sequencing operations, as well as for the overall performance of the chillers.

The proposed solution has demonstrated its interest. Authors of [8] evaluated the performance of the solution by applying it to BMS data, spanning 4 years, obtained from multiple chillers across 3 large commercial buildings in Hong Kong. It has been showed that the proposed solution can save over 30% of HVAC electricity consumption compared to the current mode of chiller operation in the buildings.

Deploying this solution and bringing it to production is however very challenging. In fact, cloud-based architectures do not meet these requirements, essentially those related to security, performance, and cost. First, cloud-based solutions are exposed to unpredictable delays or insufficient bandwidth due to the Internet-based connection. Security also seriously challenges current architectures for several reasons.

2.2   Approach

Generally speaking, it is admitted that an elastic use of a mixture of device-to-device, fog, and cloud coordination is necessary to implement complex pervasive services that integrate multiple data sources, must be responsive at human time scales, but may demand significant computing and memory capacities in some situations [13]. Our approach is then aiming for an optimal usage of the computing infrastructure, from devices to cloud, and the meeting of fundamental requirements related to accuracy, privacy, performance and cost.

Precisely, we advocate a solution where an initial training is performed in the cloud. Then the computed model (also called application in our case) and some selected data are sent to the pervasive gateways installed in buildings for additional training and execution. Re-training is then an important and key issue. This approach is sometimes called federated learning [32]. Prediction and retraining are performed on a client machine, and this client sends local model updates to a server that performs a global model update. This global model is then sent back to the clients. There are multiple criteria for deciding where to perform predictions, an important one being privacy: local predictions do not require sensitive information to be sent to a server. On the contrary, remote prediction allows the model, which can be an important asset, to remain protected from access. Local predictions do not require information to be sent over the network, and thus can be performed with lower latency. Depending on the serving environment, however, local predictions may be limited in terms of computing or power resources, so complex models may need more powerful hardware on the server side to make predictions.

A common approach is to introduce an execution platform that provides a development model and a set of technical services. This can be done at the operating system level, or at a higher level. In the latter case, the term middleware is generally introduced. Making a distinction between the execution platform and the hosted services lowers complexity in terms of code, debug, configuration, and administration operations. Decades of research in pervasive computing have led to many solutions for individual components of such middleware [13].

3   Requirements for AI-Based Pervasive Platforms

Performances of current industrial gateways and networking capabilities are sufficient to support the timely execution of many AI applications. However, developing and administrating these applications is marked by a high degree of technical complexity. Advanced, hard to find skills are necessary. It is known that streamlining the production of such applications will require developers and system administrators to be equipped with new software engineering tools. Current pervasive platforms have been designed to run "traditional" applications, not learning based applications. The dominant paradigm today is to conceive pervasive devices as loci of simple services, e.g., a service for uploading sensed data or one for executing a simple actuation command. These services are managed and monitored as traditional components. As a consequence, running AI based applications requires a lot of additional complex, tricky code. In many domains, for instance pertaining to Industry 4.0, there is clearly a shortage of skills in software engineering. It is then hard to develop and administrate too complex solutions.

We then believe that current pervasive platforms have to be extended. In particular, specific technical services supporting AI (machine learning) singularities have to be provided. Requirements for such platforms must be carefully established. This means that it is necessary today to determine the technical services that can be provided by a supporting platform and then, as a second step, to implement them in a usable way for application developers.

Let us detail here a set of requirements that have been identified based on our first experiments:

1. Deployment support. Deployment is an essential step in software development, which purpose is to transform passive code into an active entity. Code to be deployed is more and more located in remote repositories and has to be transferred, often with communication middleware, to execution platforms. In our case, deployment is concerned with the installation, activation and update of learning models in a potentially huge number of gateways. There is a clear need for automation tools that continuously deploy models into execution, push updates or adapt existing software regarding contextual and business changes [14].
2. Heterogeneity in the capabilities of fog devices. In a pervasive environment, the fog devices, e.g., gateways, can have different capacities regarding processing speed, storage, communication bandwidth, etc. Masking such differences in capability is necessary so that developers do not need to put efforts on manually handling the heterogeneity of fog devices and gateways.
3. Data collection support. Collecting data in pervasive computing is a major and complex activity, which purpose is to build contextual information and feed running pervasive applications with relevant data. Getting relevant data is especially important for learning-based applications. To provide meaningful predictions, those applications need the right data distribution, coherent with data used during the learning phase. In pervasive environments, data generally come from heterogeneous devices and platforms. Specific mechanisms to deal with interoperability are then needed to access as much data as possible. In particular, mediation mechanisms are needed to align business data, business services and communication protocols.
4. Model execution support. Machine learning models are coded in different languages, usually in Python, C++ or Java. This result in technical heterogeneities at the platform level, especially when applications are developed by different parties, and therefore in complex engineering work. Here again, there is a need to provide automatic support to make adaptation to diverse languages as transparent as possible.

5. Model retraining support. Trained models are data dependent, making it necessary to retrain them when data change. The key to retraining is to observe data distribution changes, so as to determine the best timing to perform that operation. Once again, there is here a clear need for automated tools integrated in a supporting platform to facilitate the problem detection. Thus, the role of the applications programmers is not anymore to track deviations but rather to specify how to react when some kind of deviation is detected by the platform.

6. Model monitoring support. It is important to monitor the performance of a model, which may degrade because of a changing environment or, in extreme case, of evolving tasks. A usual approach is to use a set of prediction models, instead of a single prediction model which might be over fitting. Using several models is likely to be more robust since final results are based on the output of several models. Here again, automatic support is highly relevant to realize those functions.

7. Incremental training support. In a distributed environment, the data are imbalanced both spatially and temporally. Therefore, it is necessary to transfer knowledge, e.g., a partial of the model between different gateways. An automatic service support in knowledge transfer due to spatial or temporal data imbalance will help developers to emphasize on application requirements.

8. Human in the loop. It is of major importance to include human, essentially experts, in the applicative loops. A simple solution is to monitor the applications behavior and switch to a human mode when some tasks (data collection, model predictions, and so on) are uncertain. Here, visualization tools are definitively needed to assist the domain experts in reviewing the current tasks and in providing help. It is also needed to define a global process making explicit the situations and moments where human can be included.

In this paper, we focus on the first four points (deployment, heterogeneity, data collection, model execution) through the extended iCasa platform. We also provide architectural basis to deal with the remaining issues. Let us note here that dynamicity is a cross-cutting issue that has to be considered for all the mentioned requirements.

4 Developments

4.1 The iCasa Pervasive Platform

The gateway is based on the iCasa pervasive middleware, an industrial strength fog-level platform [16] supporting the development and management of dynamic, context-aware applications. ICasa is based on a service-oriented component model called iPOJO [17] that has been extended to support machine learning applications. The iCasa platform has been entirely implemented and installed in a dedicated industrial gateway. This gateway takes the form of an industrial box that is easily pluggable in existing industrial environments, in particular with Modbus. Specifically, the gateway is based on Schneider Electric Magelis G5U, a highly configurable and robust hardware using an Intel X86 processor (1.3 GHz) with 16 Gigabytes of data storage (CF Card) and a memory of 2 Gigabytes (RAM). It is equipped with network interfaces, including Ethernet and the most common fieldbuses.

In its first version, represented in "blue" in Fig. 1, iCasa focused on the integration of heterogeneous and dynamic devices (data providers) as services. Precisely, as soon as a device is detected by the communication layer, an iPOJO proxy is created and published in the local registry. Applications could then use the devices as services, opportunistically and transparently. Similarly, when a device disappears, its corresponding proxy is destroyed. Applications using that service are automatically bound to alternative services or frozen. This provides runtime flexibility with a fairly simple code.

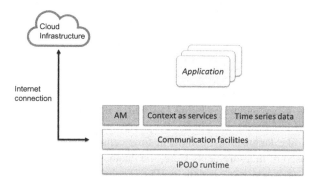

Fig. 1. iCasa overview. (Color figure online)

In its current version, iCasa includes new modules, represented in "orange" in Fig. 1. Our purpose was to provide more advanced capabilities regarding data collection and context building. In doing so, the platform relieves developers building complex applications like those based on machine learning modules. The context module here is a key element. It serves as an abstraction layer between physical environment and applications. Its goal is to present contextual information captured in the environment in a format usable by applications.

Precisely, iCasa has been extended in order to allow both real-time accesses to devices (as services) and query-based accesses to stored temporal data. This typically corresponds to the needs of machine-learning-based applications.

Precisely, iCasa has been enhanced with the following three complementary modules (Fig. 2): a context module, a time-series database and an autonomic manager. The purpose of the context module is to present a dynamic set of services providing contextual information. It contains proxies providing transparent access to devices and more elaborated services, generally built on top of other contextual services. If needed, mediation operations are applied for syntactic or semantic alignment (or for monitoring purposes). This context is implemented with iPOJO components and thus benefits from dependency resolution mechanisms to deal with dynamism. Applications use contextual services transparently as they would use any service.

A time-series database containing time-stamped data has also been integrated in iCasa. These data actually come from data flows provided by devices. They are numerous, and generally simple and unstructured. Time series databases are optimized

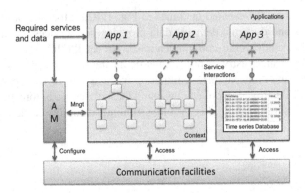

Fig. 2. Contextual information in iCasa.

for handling time-sensitive data and support applications requests about time varying data. Specifically, iCasa integrates Influx DB which turned out to be very efficient to store unstructured IoT-based data, indexed by time. It also provides very fast access through an SQL-like language with built-in time-centric functions for querying data structures composed of measurements Here, the database is presented to application as a service thanks to a wrapper written in IPOJO which forwards SQL requests (for storage or access).

Finally, an Autonomic Manager (AM) [18] managing these two modules depending on the running applications demands. Precisely, its purpose is to present the applications with the needed services and data. Depending on the sources availability and the applications evolving needs, different services and data are computed and stored in the context or in the time-series database. The AM then creates/deletes/updates components in the context module and triggers the creation/deletion/update of database recordings.

4.2   Implementation of the Chiller Use Case

As stated before, initial training is performed in the cloud. It is based on data collected in the BMS of Hong-Kong Pacific buildings. The total data collected from the BMS is more than 1 TB. We configure a private cloud to process the data for our experiments, with 16 cores of 2.6 GHz CPU and a total memory of 64 GB. We train the models with three-year data and predict with one-year data, which is a common setting in time-series data mining [19] and multi-task learning [20].

Technically speaking, we used scikit-learn, a library exposing concise and consistent interfaces to the common machine learning algorithms. We have used several algorithms, including linear regression, support Vector Regression, and AdaBoost. We found that the ensemble approach like AdaBoost (1) can better capture the non-linearity than linear regression, and (2) are less likely to become over-fitted other than support vector regression on large datasets, due to the model combination nature of AdaBoost.

Then the computed models (also called application in our case) and some selected data are sent to the iCasa gateways for additional training and execution. In order to run

AIOps on iCasa, we had to insert the Python code and the collected data in a Java bundle and to integrate a Python interpreter. Precisely, a bundle is both a deployment unit and a composition unit. Regarding deployment, bundles are used to package classes and resources so that they can be deployed on one or more execution platforms. Bundles are thus tangible artefacts that can be copied or transferred by software administrators. Execution of the python code is performed using the Jep (Java Embedded Python) library (see https://github.com/ninia/jep). Jep embeds a native Cpython interpreter in the JVM using JNI (Java Native Interface). The main benefit of this approach is that Python scripts packaged in bundles are run by a native Python interpreter, which is faster than using existing Python implementations in Java (like Jython for instance), and that they can access high quality optimized modules like scikit-learn without restrictions.

Currently, the Python scripts packaged in iCasa work in isolation, with little interaction with other Java services of the platform. The main limitation comes from the different type systems of the JVM and the python interpreter, which restricts the exchange of data to primitive types and simple data structures like maps. We are working to improve the integration to allow the efficient exchange of the data structures commonly used by the scikit-learn library.

Regarding performances, between 500 and 1000 measures can be collected every second depending on the needs of the machine-learning applications. A similar number of items is also written in the time series database every second. This range is conservative: we made sure that the architecture could support ten times more data. The amount of data sent back to the cloud is of course way smaller. The performance of the prediction model meets the requirements of the target application (calculating the COP and updating the chillers sequencing). Let us remind here that the goal of pervasive applications is not to replace existing control systems, often based on PLCs, but to provide additional services based on secondary sensing, with relaxed demands in term of real-time requirements.

5   Related Work and Discussion

As said, Industry 4.0 builds on generalized connectivity. However, its purpose is not to replace existing PLCs (Programmable Logic Controllers) with new Internet-based technology but rather to provide additional added-value services. In the industry, today, these services mainly rely on cloud solutions. Plant floor gateways can be seen as network bridges. Their main purpose is indeed to collect data, perform simple mediation operations and send the great majority of the gathered data to a cloud. Gateways need to get smarter to meet new requirements related to security, performance or cost.

As discussed above, most current middleware systems for pervasive computing and the IoT assume a service-oriented perspective [21]. That is, their primary goal is to coordinate and combine the execution of services and contextual events. Thus, the question of what additional (and possibly different) features a middleware should integrate to properly support learning-based applications arises. A number of platforms have been built on top of the OSGi framework. Various extensions have been developed to simplify the OSGi development model and to deal with pervasive specific features like context modeling. For instance, GatorTech [22] extends the OSGi framework with context representation and heterogeneous device access services. It also provides touch points required to build autonomic behavior. SOCAM [23] uses ontologies to model the context and effectively simplifies the development of context-aware applications. Other platforms introduced autonomic features [24, 25] and proposed specific component models to build autonomic applications. PCOM proposes a component model based on the BASE middleware [26].

But, to our knowledge, no support for machine learning applications has been deployed so far in the pervasive world. Most efforts are today dedicated to the distribution of traditional machine learning applications like image or voice recognition in the cloud, with Google TensorFlow for instance (see www.tensorflow.org).

Regarding data management, to the best of our knowledge, no previous work has incorporated time-series principles on service-oriented pervasive platforms so far. Our first approach was to use in-memory data [27] but it could not scale properly. An alternative investigated in this paper is to use embedded databases. In the pervasive domain, time series management systems (TSMS) are highly considered because they can scale out through distributed computing and are able to cache the most recently collected or queried data in-memory for efficient processing [28]. Williams et al. [29] proposed a distributed system based on an in-memory data grid to deal with time series from sensors monitoring industrial installations. TSDS [30] has a specific component of its architecture used primarily for caching time series from disk, reducing query response time. Gorilla [31] is a distributed in-memory TSMS built as a caching layer on top of an existing system for monitoring the infrastructure at Facebook in particular.

6   Conclusion

Pervasive computing has invested a number of industrial domains, including smart buildings where many applications are concerned with energy management. Most current services however do not meet essential requirements related to security, privacy and sometimes performance. New architectures reconsidering the cloud-to-fog continuum are expected in order to better balance computing and storage between devices, fog and cloud resources. AI techniques are also awaited to deal with many situations where classic algorithmic solutions are not possible.

A well-proven solution to run applications close to devices is to use supporting pervasive platforms. This approach lowers the overall complexity of these solutions, freeing developers and administrators from complicated, low-level technical code. Current platforms, however, have not been thought for AI-based applications. In this paper, we have listed a set of requirements that, if met by pervasive platforms, would bring us back to lower level of complexity. We have also shown that service-oriented platforms like iCasa can meet part of these requirements and be used to host machine learning based applications. With some extensions, they can deal with issues like deployment, heterogeneity, data collection, model execution, security [33, 34]. More work, however, is needed to deal with data distribution, model monitoring, and model retraining.

References

1. Weiser, M.: The computer for the 21st century. In: Human-Computer Interaction, pp. 933–940. Morgan Kaufmann Publishers Inc. (1995)
2. Satyanarayanan, M.: Fundamental challenges in mobile computing. In: Proceedings of the Fifteenth Annual ACM Symposium on Principles of Distributed Computing, pp. 1–7. ACM, New York (1996)
3. Acatech (ed.): Recommendations for implementing the strategic initiative INDUSTRIE 4.0. Final report of the Industrie 4.0 Working Group (2013)
4. Shi, W., Cao, J., Zhang, Q., Li, Y., Xu, L.: Edge computing: vision and challenges. IEEE Internet Things J. **3**(5), 637–646 (2016)
5. Liu, Z., Tan, H., Luo, D., Yu, G., Li, J., Li, Z.: Optimal chiller sequencing control in an office building considering the variation of chiller maximum cooling capacity. Energy Build. **140**, 430–442 (2017)
6. Powell, K.M., Cole, W.J., et al.: Optimal chiller loading in a district cooling system with thermal energy storage. Energy **50**, 445–453 (2013)
7. Firdaus, N., et al.: Chiller: performance deterioration and maintenance. Energy Eng. **113**(4), 55–80 (2016)
8. Zheng, Z., et al.: Data driven chiller sequencing for reducing HVAC electricity consumption in commercial buildings. In: ACM e-Energy 2018, Karlsruhe, Germany, June 2018
9. Sun, Y., Wang, S., Xiao, F.: In situ performance comparison and evaluation of three chiller sequencing control strategies in a super high-rise building. Energy Build. **61**, 333–343 (2013)
10. Chen, Z., Liu, B.: Lifelong Machine Learning. Morgan & Claypool Publishers, San Rafael (2018)
11. Hu, C., Bao, W., Wang, D., Qian, Y., Zheng, M., Wang, S.: sTube+: an IoT communication sharing architecture for smart after-sales maintenance in buildings. In: Proceedings ACM Buildsys 2017, Delft, The Netherland, November 2017
12. Zhang, M.C.T.: Fogandiot: an overview of research opportunities. IEEE Internet Things J. **3**(6), 854–864 (2016)
13. Becker, C., Julien, C., Lalanda, P., Zambonelli, F.: Pervasive computing middleware: current trends and emerging challenges. CCF Trans. Pervasive Comput. Interact., 1–14 (2019)
14. Gunalp, O., Escoffier, C., Lalanda, P.: Rondo: a tool suite for continuous deployment in dynamic environments. In: IEEE International Conference on Services Computing, pp. 720–727 (2015)
15. Zheng, A., Casari, A.: Feature Engineering for Machine Learning. Principles and Techniques for Data Scientists. O'Reill, Sebastopoly (2018)
16. Lalanda, P., Gerber-Gaillard, E., Chollet, S.: Self-aware context in smart home pervasive platforms. In: IEEE ICAC 2016, Columbus (2017)
17. Escoffier, C., Hall, R.S., Lalanda, P.: iPOJO: an extensible service oriented component framework. In: IEEE International Conference on Services Computing, SCC 2007, pp. 474–481. IEEE (2007)
18. Lalanda, P., McCann, J.A., Diaconescu, A.: Autonomic Computing - Principles. Design and Implementation. Undergraduate Topics in Computer Science. Springer, London (2013). https://doi.org/10.1007/978-1-4471-5007-7
19. Tong, Y., et al.: The simpler the better: a unified approach to predicting original taxi demands based on large-scale online platforms. In: Proceedings ACM SIGKDD 2017, pp. 1653–1662 (2017)

20. Carbonell, J., Murugesan, K.: Self-paced multitask learning with shared knowledge. In: Proceedings of the Twenty-Sixth International Joint Conference on Artificial Intelligence, IJCAI 2017, pp. 2522–2528 (2017)
21. Razzaque, M.A., Milojevic-Jevric, M., Palade, A., Clarke, S.: Middleware for internet of things: a survey. IEEE Internet Things J. 3(1), 70–95 (2016)
22. Helal, S., Mann, W., El-Zabadani, H., King, J., Kaddoura, Y., Jansen, E.: The Gator Tech Smart House: a programmable pervasive space. Computer 38(3), 50–60 (2005)
23. Gu, T., Pung, H.K., Zhang, D.Q.: Toward an OSGi-based infrastructure for context-aware applications. IEEE Pervasive Comput. 3(4), 66–74 (2004)
24. Lupu, E., et al.: AMUSE: autonomic management of ubiquitous e-Health systems. Concurrency Comput. Pract. Experience 20(3), 277–295 (2008)
25. Liu, H., Parashar, M., Hariri, S.: A component-based programming model for autonomic applications. In: Autonomic Computing (2004)
26. Becker, C., Handte, M., Schiele, G., Rothermel, K.: PCOM - a component system for pervasive computing. In: Proceedings International Conference on Pervasive Computing and Communications, pp. 67–76. IEEE (2004)
27. Lalanda, P., Mertz, J., Nunes, I.: Autonomic caching management in industrial smart gateways. In: IEEE Industrial Cyber-Physical Systems, pp. 26–31 (2018)
28. Jensen, S.K., Pedersen, T.B., Thomsen, C.: Time series management systems: a survey. IEEE Trans. Knowl. Data Eng. 29(11), 2581–2600 (2017)
29. Williams, J.W., Aggour, K.S., Interrante, J., McHugh, J., Pool, E.: Bridging high velocity and high volume industrial big data through distributed in-memory storage & analytics. In: Proceedings International Conference Big Data, pp. 932–941 (2014)
30. Weigel, R.S., Lindholm, D.M., Wilson, A., Faden, J.: TSDS: high-performance merge subset and filter software for time series-like data. Earth Sci. Inform. 3(1/2), 29–40 (2010)
31. Pelkonen, T., et al.: Gorilla: a fast scalable in-memory time series database. VLDB Endowment 8(12), 1816–1827 (2015)
32. Konečný, J., Brendan McMahan, H., Yu, F.X., Richtárik, P., Suresh, A.T., Bacon, D.: Federated learning: strategies for improving communication efficiency. arXiv:1610.05492 (2017)
33. Chollet, S., Lalanda, P.: Security at the process level. In: International Conference on Service-Oriented Computing (SCC), pp. 165–172 (2008)
34. Chollet, S., Lalanda, P.: An extensible abstract service orchestration framework. In: International Conference on Web Services (ICWS), pp. 831–838 (2009)
35. Morand, D., Garcia, I., Lalanda, P.: Autonomic enterprise service bus. In: IEEE 16th Conference on Emerging Technologies & Factory Automation (2011)

Freshening the Air in Microservices: Resolving Architectural Smells via Refactoring

Antonio Brogi, Davide Neri, and Jacopo Soldani[✉]

University of Pisa, Pisa, Italy
{antonio.brogi,davide.neri,jacopo.soldani}@unipi.it

Abstract. The adoption of microservice-based architectures is becoming common practice for enterprise applications. Checking whether an application adheres to the main design principles of microservices, and —if not— understanding how to refactor it, are two key issues in that context. In this paper, we present a methodology to systematically identify the architectural smells that possibly violate the main design principles of microservices, and to select suitable architectural refactorings to resolve them. We also present a prototype implementing the methodology, based on a novel representation of microservices in TOSCA.

Keywords: Microservices · SOA · Architectural principles · Architectural smells · Architectural refactoring

1 Introduction

Microservice-based architectures are increasingly considered an enabling technology to shorten the lead time in software development and to effectively scale software application deployments [19,22]. The interest in microservice-based architectures is witnessed by their adoption by the major IT companies (like Amazon, Facebook, Google, Netflix and Spotify, just to mention some).

Microservice-based architectures can be seen as service-oriented architectures that satisfy some key principles [32]. These include shaping services around business concepts, adopting a culture of automation, decentralising all aspects of microservices (from governance to data management), ensuring their independent deployability and high observability, and isolating failures [22]. As the adoption of microservices is becoming common practice for enterprise applications, checking whether an application adheres to the main design principles of microservices, and —if not— understanding how to refactor it, are two key issues [3,27].

In this paper, we present a methodology to systematically identify architectural smells possibly violating key design principles of microservices, and to select architectural refactorings allowing to resolve such smells. We take as starting point the industry-driven review presented in [3], which singled out a set of architectural smells possibly violating some main principles of microservices, by also eliciting the architectural refactorings allowing to resolve each smell. In particular, we consider four of the architectural smells in [3], each with the architectural refactorings that permit resolving it.

© Springer Nature Switzerland AG 2020
S. Yangui et al. (Eds.): ICSOC 2019 Workshops, LNCS 12019, pp. 17–29, 2020.
https://doi.org/10.1007/978-3-030-45989-5_2

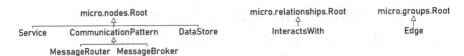

Fig. 1. The node types, relationship types and group types defining μTOSCA.

Our proposal is to model the architecture of a microservice-based application with the OASIS standard TOSCA [23]. We hence introduce μTOSCA, which allows to specify service-based architectures as typed directed graphs. Based on such representation, we formally define the conditions to identify the occurrence the considered architectural smells in a microservice-based application, and we illustrate how to refactor its architecture to resolve identified smells.

We also present μFRESHENER, a prototype showcasing our methodology. We believe that our methodology and its prototype implementation can provide a valuable decision support for designing microservice-based architectures.

The rest of the paper is organized as follows. Section 2 introduces μTOSCA. Sections 3 and 4 illustrate our methodology to identify/resolve architectural smells and its prototype implementation, respectively. Finally, Sect. 5 discusses related work and Sect. 6 draws some concluding remarks.

2   Modelling Service-Based Architectures with μTOSCA

TOSCA [23] allows to represent service-based architectures as typed directed graphs, where nodes represent software components, and arcs represent the interactions occurring among such components. We hereby present the μTOSCA type system[1], providing building blocks for such a representation (Fig. 1).

Nodes can be services, communication patterns or data stores. A `Service` is a component running some business logic, e.g., a service managing users' orders in an e-commerce application. A `CommunicationPattern` is a component implementing a messaging pattern decoupling the communication among two or more components. Figure 1 contains two communication patterns from [16]: `Message-Router` (e.g., load balancers, API gateways) and `MessageBroker` (e.g., message queues). Finally, a `DataStore` is a component storing the data pertaining to a certain domain, e.g., a database of orders in an e-commerce application.

Nodes can be interconnected via `InteractsWith` relationships, to model that a source node invokes functionalities offered by a target node. Such relationships can be enriched by setting the boolean properties `circuit_breaker`, `timeout` and `dynamic_discovery`. The first two properties allow to indicate whether the source node is interacting with the target node via a circuit breaker or by setting proper timeouts, to avoid that the source fails/gets stuck waiting for an answer from the target when the latter is unresponsive (e.g., because it failed). Property `dynamic_discovery` allows to specify whether the endpoint of the target of the interaction is dynamically discovered (e.g., by exploiting a discovery service).

---

[1] https://di-unipi-socc.github.io/microTOSCA/microTOSCA.yml.

Nodes can also be placed in an **Edge** group, to define the subset of application components directly accessed from outside of the application.

Formally, the architectures represented with μTOSCA are triples, whose elements are (i) the typed nodes and (ii) the relationships forming the graph representing the architecture of an application, and (iii) the group of nodes defining the edge of the architecture.

Definition 1 (Architecture). *The* architecture *of an application is represented by a triple* $A = \langle N, R, E \rangle$, *where*

(i) N is a finite set of typed nodes representing application components,
(ii) R is a finite multiset[2] of pairs of nodes representing the relationships occurring among application components, and
(iii) $E \subseteq N$ is a non-empty set of nodes defining the edge of the architecture.

Definition 1 allows to describe an architecture where (a) a node interacts with itself. It also allows to specify that (b) a data store is invoking functionalities offered by another component or being accessed by something different from a service internal to the application, Finally, Definition 1 allows to indicate that (c) a message broker is invoking functionalities offered by other components or that no component is placing messages in a broker, and that (d) a message router is not routing messages towards other components or that it is never invoked. To avoid such undesirable situations, we hereafter consider an architecture to be *well-formed* when none of cases (a–d) is occurring.

Notation 1 (Types). *We write x.type to denote the* type *of a node x, and we write* $\bigcirc$, $\boxed{\text{mB}}$, $\boxed{\text{mR}}$ *and* $\square$ *to visually denote the μTOSCA types* Service, MessageBroker, MessageRouter *and* DataStore, *respectively. Given two types t and* t', *we also write* $t \geq t'$ *iff t extends or is equal to* t'.

Definition 2 (Well-formedness). *An architecture* $A = \langle N, R, E \rangle$ *is well-formed iff*

(a) $\forall \langle x, y \rangle \in R : x \neq y$,

(b) $\forall x \in N : x.\text{type} \geq \square \Rightarrow$
$$((\nexists \langle x, y \rangle \in R) \wedge x \notin E \wedge (\forall \langle y, x \rangle \in R : y.\text{type} \geq \bigcirc)),$$

(c) $\forall x \in N : x.\text{type} \geq \boxed{\text{mB}} \Rightarrow ((\nexists \langle x, y \rangle \in R) \wedge (\exists \langle y, x \rangle \in R))$, *and*

(d) $\forall x \in N : x.\text{type} \geq \boxed{\text{mR}} \Rightarrow ((\exists \langle x, y \rangle \in R) \wedge (x \in E \vee \exists \langle y, x \rangle \in R))$.

We hereafter assume architectures to be well-formed.

---

[2] Multiple relations from component x to component y indicate that x interacts with y in different ways (e.g., directly in one case, via a circuit breaker in another case).

3   Discovering and Resolving Architectural Smells

The architectural smells violating the *horizontal scalability, isolation of failures* and *decentralisation* of microservice-based applications, as well as the architectural refactorings allowing to resolve them, have been classified in [3]. An excerpt of the resulting taxonomy is reported in Fig. 2.

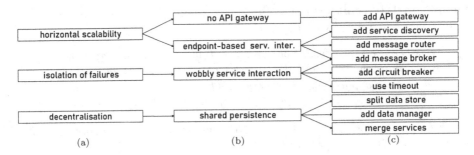

Fig. 2. A taxonomy for (a) design principles of microservices, (b) architectural smells, and (c) architectural refactorings [3].

Starting from such taxonomy, we hereby formalise the conditions allowing to automatically determine the occurrence of smells in architectures modelled with μTOSCA, and we illustrate how to refactor an architecture to resolve each identified smell. In doing so, we exploit the graphical support provided by Fig. 3.

Architectural Smells Possibly Violating Horizontal Scalability. The possibility of adding/removing replicas of a microservice is a direct consequence of the independent deployability of microservices. To ensure its horizontal scalability, all the replicas of a microservice m should be reachable by the microservices invoking m [17]. In [3], two architectural smells emerged as possibly violating the horizontal scalability of microservices, i.e., *no API gateway* and *endpoint-based service interactions*, which we discuss hereafter.

The *no API gateway* smell occurs whenever the external clients of an application directly interact with some internal services. If one of such services is scaled out, the horizontal scalability of microservices may get violated because external clients may still keep invoking the same instance, without reaching any replica.

To identify the occurrence of a no API gateway smell, we should hence check whether some application components are accessed without passing through an API gateway, i.e., whether the edge of the architecture contains something that is not a message router.

Definition 3 (No API gateway). *Let* $A = \langle N, R, E \rangle$ *be an architecture. A node* $x \in N$ *indicates a* no API gateway *smell iff*

$$x \in E \wedge x.\text{type} \not\succeq \boxed{\text{mR}}$$

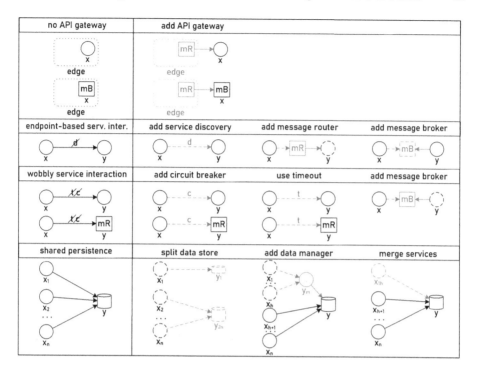

Fig. 3. Visual representation of the architectural smells (left column) and refactorings (right column) in Fig. 2, with the Edge group denoted by a dotted line and interactions depicted as arrows. Labels d, c and t represent that properties dynamic_discovery, circuit_breaker and timeout are true, while d̸, c̸ and t̸ represent that they are false. Updates due to refactorings are in grey, with mandatory updates being dashed. Solid grey lines indicate updates that may be implemented by reusing existing components.

Figure 3 illustrates the possible no API gateway smells, due to a component x (either a service or a message broker) being placed at the edge of an architecture. The figure also shows the architectural refactorings resolving the occurrence of no API gateway smells. In both cases, the refactoring consists in introducing a message router (e.g., a gateway or a load balancer), or reusing one already available in the application. Such a message router will act as an API gateway, hence avoiding x to get directly accessed from outside of the application.

The *endpoint-based service interaction* smell occurs in an application when a service x directly invokes another service y (e.g., because the location of y is hardcoded in the source code of x, or because no message router is used). If this is the case, when scaling out service y by adding new replicas, these cannot be reached by x, hence only resulting in a waste of resources [3]. Formally, this happens whenever there is a direct interaction from x to y, where x is not using any support for dynamically discovering the actual endpoint of y.

Notation 2 (Properties of relations). *Given an architecture $A = \langle N, R, E \rangle$, we write $\langle x, y \rangle$.p to denote the property p of a relationship $\langle x, y \rangle \in R$.*

Definition 4 (Endpoint-based service interaction). *Let $A = \langle N, R, E \rangle$ be an architecture. A relation $\langle x, y \rangle \in R$ indicates an* endpoint-based service interaction *smell iff*

$$x.\mathsf{type} \geq \bigcirc \wedge y.\mathsf{type} \geq \bigcirc \wedge \langle x, y \rangle.\mathsf{dynamic\_discovery} = \mathsf{false}$$

A visual representation of an endpoint-based service interaction is in Fig. 3, where a service x is directly invoking another service y. The figure also illustrates the architectural refactorings allowing to resolve the occurrence of an endpoint-based service interaction smell, all sharing the same goal, i.e., decoupling the interaction between two services by introducing an intermediate integration pattern. Such refactorings predicate only on the value of property dynamic_discovery of the relationship outgoing from x.

The most common solution is to add a service discovery mechanism to dynamically resolve the endpoint of the service targeted by the interaction [24]. The other possible solutions instead consist in decoupling the interaction between two services by exploiting a message router or a message broker, respectively. In all cases, the interaction outgoing from x must necessarily be updated, while the message router/broker used to decouple the interaction may also be already available and reused to implement the architectural refactoring.

Architectural Smell Possibly Violating Isolation of Failures. Microservice-based architectures should be designed to isolate failures, meaning that each microservice should tolerate the failure of any invocation to the microservices it depends on [19]. In [3], the *wobbly service interaction* smell emerged as possibly violating the isolation of failures in microservices.

The interaction between two microservices is "wobbly" when a failure in the microservice targeted by the interaction can result in triggering a failure also in the source, potentially starting a cascade of failures [18]. This typically happens when a microservice x is consuming functionalities offered by another microservice (directly or through a message router), and x is not provided with any solution for handling the possibility of the target microservice to fail and be unresponsive, such as a circuit breaker or a timeout.

Definition 5 (Wobbly service interaction). *Let $A = \langle N, R, E \rangle$ be an architecture. A relation $\langle x, y \rangle \in R$ indicates a* wobbly service interaction *smell iff*

$$x.\mathsf{type} \geq \bigcirc \wedge (y.\mathsf{type} \geq \bigcirc \vee y.\mathsf{type} \geq \boxed{\mathsf{mR}}) \wedge$$

$$\langle x, y \rangle.\mathsf{circuit\_breaker} = \mathsf{false} \wedge \langle x, y \rangle.\mathsf{timeout} = \mathsf{false}.$$

The possible wobbly service interactions are illustrated in Fig. 3, which shows that such a kind of interactions occurs when a service x is interacting with another service or with a message router (dispatching the messages outgoing from x to other microservice), and such interaction are not equipped with a support for tolerating failures, i.e., no circuit breaker or timeout is used.

Figure 3 also illustrates the architectural refactorings allowing to resolve wobbly service interaction smells. Such refactorings predicate only on the value of the properties `circuit_breaker` and `timeout` of the relationship outgoing from x.

The easiest solutions consist replacing the wobbly service interaction between x and y with one exploiting a circuit breaker to wrap the invocations outgoing from service x or using a timeout. Both solutions allow x not to get stuck waiting for an answer from y. Another possible solution is to decouple the interactions between x and y through a message broker, with the latter being a new one, or one already available in the application. The usage of a broker allows x to send its requests to the broker, with y processing such requests when it is available, hence avoiding x to get stuck or fail when y fails.

It is worth noting that, when x and y are both services, applying the refactoring based on the usage of a message broker allows to also resolve the occurrence of an endpoint-based service interaction smell, if any. At the same time, when x is a service and y is a message router, such a refactoring would not be local to x and y, but rather it would involve acting on the rest of the architecture. It would indeed require to apply a solution like the one for the situation where x and y are both services to *all* services that can be reached through the message router y, by exploiting a single message broker or multiple brokers depending on the actual application needs.

Architectural Smell Possibly Violating Decentralisation. Decentralisation should occur in every aspect of microservice-based architectures, including data management [22]. In this perspective, each data store should be directly accessed by only one service [3]. The *shared persistence* smell hence occurs whenever multiple services interact with the same data store y.

Definition 6 (Shared persistence). *Let $A = \langle N, R, E \rangle$ be an architecture. A set of relations $R(y) = \{\langle x, y \rangle \in R\}$ indicates a* shared persistence *smell iff*

$$y.\mathsf{type} \geq \square \wedge (\exists \langle x_1, y \rangle, \langle x_2, y \rangle \in R(y) : x_1 \neq x_2).$$

A visual representation of the shared persistence smell is in Fig. 3, where $x_1 \ldots x_n$ are all the services accessing the data store y. The figure also shows the three architectural refactorings for reducing the amount of services accessing the same data store, hence ultimately allowing to resolve the occurrence of a shared persistence smell. Although their goal is the same, such refactorings are very diverse in spirit, and apply to different situations, highly depending on the services accessing the same data store.

If a service x_1 is the only service accessing a portion of the data stored in the data store y, then y can be split in two different data stores y_1 and y_{2n}, with y_1 only storing the portion of data accessed by x_1, and with y_{2n} storing the rest of the data. The service x_1 then becomes the only accessing y_1, while y_{2n} is accessed by the other services $x_2 \ldots x_n$.

Other possible solutions to reduce the amount of services accessing the same data store y are exploiting a data manager or merging some of the services accessing the data store. Exploiting a data manager consists in adding a service y_m, or reusing one already available, to proxy the access of services $x_1 \ldots x_h$ (with $h \leq n$) to the data store y. The other refactoring instead consists in merging the services $x_1 \ldots x_h$ (with $h \leq n$) into a single service x_{1h}. The rationale behind this last refactoring is that, when multiple services access the same data store, this may be indicating that the application has been split too much, by obtaining too fine-grained services processing the same data [28].

Some Important Remarks. Our approach focuses on the *architecture* of an application, by identifying smells based on the interactions among the components forming an application, and by suggesting refactorings of the architecture itself. The concrete implementation of an architectural refactoring (i.e., the actual updates of the application sources) are left to the application owner, in a similar way as the concrete implementation of a design pattern is left to developers. Hence, the application owner can decide which refactoring to apply also based on the cost for actually implementing it.

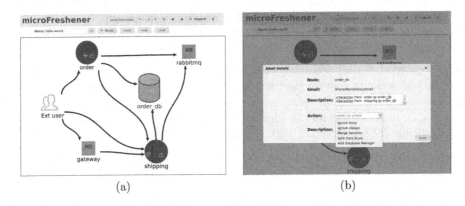

Fig. 4. Snapshots of (a) the editing/analysis and (b) refactoring views of μFRESHENER.

Also, the architectural smells discussed in this section indicate *potential* violations of design principles of microservices. This means that the occurrence of an architectural smell does not mean that a design principle is necessarily violated, hence not necessarily needing to be resolved by applying a corresponding architectural refactoring. Even if an architectural smell is denoting an actual violation of a design principle, the application owner may still decide to not apply any refactoring as well, e.g., because updating the application sources in accordance with an architectural refactoring is too expensive. Another possible reason for choosing to not resolve an architectural smell can be that an application architect intentionally structured the corresponding part of the application as that, due to some contextual requirement. For instance, she may have decided to share a same data store among multiple services for overriding reasons. If this is the case, she will ignore the corresponding shared persistence smell, otherwise she would break her contextual requirements.

In any case, manually identifying architectural smells, deciding whether to resolve them and which refactoring to apply is not easy. It would be helpful to have a support system automatically identifying the smells affecting the architecture of an application and allowing to explore among multiple possible refactorings to resolve them. One such support system is presented in the following section.

4 μFreshener: A Prototype Implementation

To illustrate the feasibility of our approach and support the design of microservice-based applications, we implemented a prototype tool (called μFRESHENER) publicly available on GitHub[3]. μFRESHENER provides a web-based graphical user interface for (i) editing μTOSCA specifications, (ii) automatically identifying architectural smells in specified applications and (iii) exploring/applying architectural refactorings for resolving the identified smells.

Figure 4 provides two snapshots of the GUI of μFRESHENER. Figure 4(a) shows the editing and analysis view, where one can add/remove nodes and relationships from an architecture, and where automatically identified smells are displayed with icons on top of corresponding nodes. By clicking on one of such icons, one can open the view in Fig. 4(b), which permits selecting the architectural refactoring to apply to resolve the selected smell. Once selected, the architecture modelling is updated in accordance with the architectural refactoring. Note that the refactoring is only applied to the μTOSCA specification of an application (and not on its sources), and that one can go back and forth in architectural refactorings, by undoing/redoing them by clicking on the corresponding buttons.

5   Related Work

Even if there exists studies classifying various architectural smells for microservices (e.g., [3,6,28]), to the best of our knowledge, ours is the first systematic approach for identifying *and* resolving architectural smells possibly violating the design principles of microservices in existing microservice-based applications.

[2,12] report on design patterns and decision models to design microservice-based applications (from scratch, or by migrating from monoliths to microservices). [2] also illustrates different possible solutions to resolve potential design issues. In both cases, this is done by retrieving information from practitioners or industry-scale projects, and by organising such information in informal guidelines, which can be used for driving the design of microservice-based application. Our approach tries to further support the design of microservices, by providing

---

[3] https://github.com/di-unipi-socc/microFreshener.

a systematic solution to identify and resolve the architectural smells affecting an already existing application, also providing a tool support.

Systematic solutions for modelling and analysing microservice-based architectures anyway exist, even if conceived for different purposes. For instance, [29] presents *MicroDSL*, a domain-specific language for modelling microservice-based architectures, where microservices interact through RESTish protocols, and models are then used to generate an executable deployments of specified applications. [4] instead proposes a Petri net-based solution for the runtime verification of the orchestration of microservice-based application on top of Netflix's Conductor. Even if conceived for different purposes, [4,29] share our baseline idea of eliciting all interactions among microservices to analyse an architecture. They however differ in the goals of the proposed approachs, due to which they focus on modelling specific types of applications (microservices interacting with REST in [29], Conductor-based applications in [4]).

[5,7] present two other existing tools for analysing of microservices, which exploit a modelling closer to ours. Indeed, they both model a microservice-based architecture as a graph, whose nodes represent components and whose arcs represent interactions. They however do not support modelling the edge of an architecture, nor distinguishing whether a component is a service, communication pattern or a data store. This, along with our willingness to exploit a standard to model microservice-based architectures, is the reason why developed μTOSCA instead of reusing the modelling in [5] or [7].

Another tool worth mentioning is [26], which provides an approach to automate the testing of microservice-based applications. [26] relates to our approach as it allow to systematically check whether the interfaces of running microservices adhere to a given specification. It however requires to run the microservice-based application to be tested, while ours is a design-time support not needing to actually run an application.

[9,25] instead present solutions for detecting smells in the design of a single service (specified in UML and ARCHERY, respectively). [1,8,31] focus on identifying smells in the structuring of the sources of a service, and propose refactorings for resolving detected smells. All such approaches however differ from ours, as they focus on the design of a single service, while our approach focuses on the architectural smells due to the interactions among all components forming a microservice-based application. In other words, such approaches and ours can complement each other, to permit identifying both the architectural smells affecting a single service and those due to the interactions among the components in an application.

Similar considerations apply to [13,14]. Even if with different approaches (self-adaptation in [13], aspect-oriented ambients in [14]), they both focus on analysing a single microservice to determine whether the its granularity is optimal, or whether it needs some adaptation to rightsize its granularity. We instead focus on analysing the interactions among all microservices forming an application to identify and resolve architectural smells.

Finally, it is also worth relating our work with [10,11,20,21]. Starting from the idea that service interactions are the main mechanism to program the microservices forming an application, [11] proposes to develop microservice-based applications with Jolie, a language for developing service compositions by programming their interactions. Our approach follows the same idea, as we consider service interactions as the basis for identifying architectural smells.

[10,20,21] instead propose different solutions for microservice-based architecture recovery, i.e., identifying the microservices forming an application and the interactions among them. [10,20] also show how automatically recovered architectures can be analysed for identifying issues (i.e., unnecessary service interactions in [10], dependency cycles in [20]). [10,20,21] could then be used in conjunction with our approach, to first derive the architecture of a microservice-based application, and then identify and resolve the architectural smells affecting such application.

6   Conclusions

We have presented a methodology to identify the architectural smells possibly violating design principles of microservices, and to apply architectural refactorings to resolve them. We have also presented the μFRESHENER, implementing our methodology to support the design of microservice-based applications.

While our methodology and the μFRESHENER prototype can be actually applied to analyse and improve existing microservice-based applications, users must currently define (with the GUI of μFRESHENER) or provide a μTOSCA description of the architecture of their applications. To increase the usability of our prototype, we plan to develop plug-ins to automatedly extract the μTOSCA description of the architecture of an application (from its code structure like in [15,20,30] and/or from its runtime behaviour like in [10,21]).

We also plan to extend the architectural smells that can be identified and resolved with our methodology (and with μFRESHENER), by starting from the smells and refactoring classified in [3,6,28]. As a concrete example, we plan to extend μTOSCA with a type for grouping nodes to represent team assignment (i.e., which components are assigned to which team), to formalise the team-related architectural smells available in [3], to correspondingly extend μFRESHENER to identify and resolve such smells, and to feature team-wise usage of μFRESHENER.

Finally, we plan to extend μFRESHENER to account for the container orchestrator (e.g., Docker Compose, Kubernetes) used to deploy the application, as the container orchestration layer can resolve some smells possibly present at the architecture layer. We also intend to validate the effectiveness of our methodology and the usability μFRESHENER against real-world microservice-based applications (possibly involving hundreds of interconnected services).

Acknowledgements. Work partly funded by the projects *AMaCA* (POR-FSE, Regione Toscana) and *DECLware* (PRA_2018_66, University of Pisa).

References

1. Arcelli, D., Cortellessa, V., Pompeo, D.D.: Automating performance antipattern detection and software refactoring in UML models. In: 2019 International Conference on Software Analysis, Evolution and Reengineering, pp. 639–643. IEEE (2019)
2. Balalaie, A., Heydarnoori, A., Jamshidi, P., Tamburri, D.A., Lynn, T.: Microservices migration patterns. Softw. Pract. Exper. **48**(11), 2019–2042 (2018)
3. Brogi, A., Neri, D., Soldani, J., Zimmermann, O.: Design principles, architectural smells and refactorings for microservices: a multivocal review. Softw. Intensive Cyber Phys. Syst. (2019). https://doi.org/10.1007/s00450-019-00407-8
4. Camilli, M., Bellettini, C., Capra, L., Monga, M.: A formal framework for specifying and verifying microservices based process flows. In: Cerone, A., Roveri, M. (eds.) SEFM 2017. LNCS, vol. 10729, pp. 187–202. Springer, Cham (2018). https://doi.org/10.1007/978-3-319-74781-1_14
5. Cardarelli, M., Iovino, L., Di Francesco, P., Di Salle, A., Malavolta, I., Lago, P.: An extensible data-driven approach for evaluating the quality of microservice architectures. In: 34th Symposium on Applied Computing, pp. 1225–1234. ACM (2019)
6. Carrasco, A., Bladel, B., Demeyer, S.: Migrating towards microservices: migration and architecture smells. In: 2nd International Workshop on Refactoring, pp. 1–6. ACM (2018)
7. Cockroft, A.: Spigo. https://github.com/adrianco/spigo
8. Fontana, F.A., Pigazzini, I., Roveda, R., Tamburri, D., Zanoni, M., Nitto, E.D.: Arcan: a tool for architectural smells detection. In: 2017 International Conference on Software Architecture Workshops, pp. 282–285. IEEE (2017)
9. Garcia, J., Popescu, D., Edwards, G., Medvidovic, N.: Identifying architectural bad smells. In: 13th European Conference on Software Maintenance and Reengineering, pp. 255–258. IEEE (2009)
10. Granchelli, G., Cardarelli, M., Di Francesco, P., Malavolta, I., Iovino, L., Salle, A.D.: MicroART: a software architecture recovery tool for maintaining microservice-based systems. In: 2017 International Conference on Software Architecture Workshops, pp. 298–302. IEEE (2017)
11. Guidi, C., Lanese, I., Mazzara, M., Montesi, F.: Microservices: a language-based approach. In: Mazzara, M., Meyer, B. (eds.) Present and Ulterior Software Engineering, pp. 217–225. Springer, Cham (2017). https://doi.org/10.1007/978-3-319-67425-4_13
12. Haselböck, S., Weinreich, R., Buchgeher, G.: Decision models for microservices: design areas, stakeholders, use cases, and requirements. In: Lopes, A., de Lemos, R. (eds.) ECSA 2017. LNCS, vol. 10475, pp. 155–170. Springer, Cham (2017). https://doi.org/10.1007/978-3-319-65831-5_11
13. Hassan, S., Bahsoon, R.: Microservices and their design trade-offs: a self-adaptive roadmap. In: 2016 International Conference on Services Computing, pp. 813–818. IEEE (2016)
14. Hassan, S., Ali, N., Bahsoon, R.: Microservice ambients: an architectural meta-modelling approach for microservice granularity. In: 2017 International Conference on Software Architecture, pp. 1–10. IEEE (2017)
15. Headway Software Technologies: Structure 101. https://structure101.com
16. Hohpe, G., Woolf, B.: Enterprise Integration Patterns: Designing, Building, and Deploying Messaging Solutions. Addison-Wesley, Boston (2003)

17. Indrasiri, K.: Microservices in practice: from architecture to deployment. https:// dzone.com/articles/microservices-in-practice-1
18. Jamshidi, P., Pahl, C., Mendonca, N., Lewis, J., Tilkov, S.: Microservices: the journey so far and challenges ahead. IEEE Softw. **35**(3), 24–35 (2018)
19. Lewis, J., Fowler, M.: Microservices. https://www.martinfowler.com/articles/ microservices.html
20. Ma, S., Fan, C., Chuang, Y., Lee, W., Lee, S., Hsueh, N.: Using service dependency graph to analyze and test microservices. In: 42nd Annual Computer Software and Applications Conference, vol. 02, pp. 81–86. IEEE (2018)
21. Mahlen, P.: Modelling microservices at Spotify. In: jFokus Developer Conference (2016)
22. Newman, S.: Building Microservices, 1st edn. O'Reilly Media Inc., Newton (2015)
23. OASIS: TOSCA Simple Profile in YAML Version 1.2 (2018)
24. Richardson, C.: Microservices Patterns, 1st edn. Manning Publications, New York (2018)
25. Sanchez, A., Barbosa, L.S., Madeira, A.: Modelling and verifying smell-free architectures with the Archery language. In: Canal, C., Idani, A. (eds.) SEFM 2014. LNCS, vol. 8938, pp. 147–163. Springer, Cham (2015). https://doi.org/10.1007/ 978-3-319-15201-1_10
26. Savchenko, D., Radchenko, G., Taipale, O.: Microservices validation: mjolnirr platform case study. In: 38th International Convention on Information and Communication Technology, Electronics and Microelectronics, pp. 235–240. IEEE (2015)
27. Soldani, J., Tamburri, D.A., Van Den Heuvel, W.J.: The pains and gains of microservices: a systematic grey literature review. J. Syst. Softw. **146**, 215–232 (2018)
28. Taibi, D., Lenarduzzi, V.: On the definition of microservice bad smells. IEEE Softw. **35**(3), 56–62 (2018)
29. Terzić, B., Dimitrieski, V., Kordić, S., Milosavljević, G., Luković, I.: Development and evaluation of microbuilder: a model-driven tool for the specification of rest microservice software architectures. Enterp. Inf. Syst. **12**(8–9), 1034–1057 (2018)
30. Tessier, J.: DependencyFinder. https://github.com/jeantessier/dependency-finder
31. Vidal, S., Vazquez, H., Diaz-Pace, J.A., Marcos, C., Garcia, A., Oizumi, W.: JSpIRIT: a flexible tool for the analysis of code smells. In: 34th International Conference of the Chilean Computer Science Society, pp. 1–6. IEEE (2015)
32. Zimmermann, O.: Microservices tenets. Comp. Sci. Res. Dev. **32**(3–4), 301–310 (2017)

Specifying Web Interfaces for Command-Line Applications Based on OpenAPI

Dennis Wolters[✉], Jonas Kirchhoff, and Gregor Engels

Department of Computer Science, Paderborn University, Paderborn, Germany
{dennis.wolters,jonas.kirchhoff,engels}@uni-paderborn.de

Abstract. Command-line applications help to deal with various different tasks, reaching from automation, text manipulation or document conversion to administrating databases or firewalls. Powerful orchestrations of those applications can be created, e.g., to build Continuous Delivery or decision support pipelines. If the functionality of those applications and their orchestrations shall be used within a service-oriented architecture or as a backend of a web application, a web-compatible interface is necessary, which is usually not provided. Thus, those applications need to be retrofitted with a web interface. In this paper, we present CL2HTTP, an approach to map command-line interfaces to HTTP interfaces using an extended form of the OpenAPI service description format. The extensions specify how HTTP requests are mapped to command-line invocations and how the command-line responses are mapped back to HTTP responses. Our approach does not require any programming to specify a web interface for command-line applications, is available for public use and supports deployment as a container or lambda function in cloud environments.

Keywords: Web services · Interface adaptation · Command-line · OpenAPI

1 Introduction

Command-line applications play an important role in modern computing. A large repository of powerful command-line applications exists, providing functionality that reaches from automation, text manipulation or document conversion to administrating databases or firewalls. The orchestration of command-line applications enables businesses to quickly react to continuous and rapid changes in market needs. For instance, Continuous Integration/Delivery principles embodied in DevOps [14] require the orchestration of command-line applications to pipelines that automatically assemble, test and deploy software [13,16]. Also, to support decision making processes, model management systems [1] can orchestrate decision making models provided as command-line applications [15] to gain new insights and transform them into recommendations for actions.

The increasing complexity in the environment and consequently in the products themselves [3] requires orchestrations not only on individual machines but across multiple distributed systems in a web-based service-oriented manner, as it can for instance be seen in [2–4] for decision making. While such a web service-oriented approach enables businesses to cope with the increasing complexity, it also comes with the downside that

© Springer Nature Switzerland AG 2020
S. Yangui et al. (Eds.): ICSOC 2019 Workshops, LNCS 12019, pp. 30–41, 2020.
https://doi.org/10.1007/978-3-030-45989-5_3

the previously used and proven command-line applications can no longer be used due to a lack of a web-compatible communication interface. We experienced this problem when wanting to reuse command-line conversion tools in a web service orchestration to enable the linkage of services to websites based on embedded semantic data [18].

While remote execution of command-line applications via SSH is possible, using them within a service-oriented architecture or as a backend for web applications requires a web-compatible interface like an HTTP interface or support of a WebSocket connection. If this is not given, either the source code of those application needs to be extended so that they also provide a web interface or adapters need to be developed that adapt the command-line interface to a web interface. While this might work for individual applications, doing this repetitively for multiple command-line applications is cumbersome, especially since all of this new code needs testing and maintenance.

In this paper, we present CL2HTTP, an approach which enables the mapping of command-line interfaces of applications to HTTP interfaces in a non-invasive, descriptive and secure way. CL2HTTP consists of an extension of the OpenAPI specification [8] to describe web interfaces for command-line applications as well as an interpreter for this extension that provides the actual interfaces and delegates between web interface and command-line interface. Thereby, it circumvents the need for individual web service implementations tailored to specific command-line applications. In fact, no programming is necessary to provide the HTTP interface and since our approach is defined as an extension to the OpenAPI specification, the resulting service is descriptive enough to be used by service consumers. Furthermore, the web interface can be independently maintained and is not limited to the evolution cycles of the used command-line applications.

The usage scenarios for CL2HTTP include, but are not limited to, integrating (legacy) command-line applications into web service orchestrations, aggregating multiple command-line applications into a single coherent web service offering and rapidly prototyping backends for web applications by building up on command-line applications. CL2HTTP is implemented, open source and available for public use[1].

Following the design science research method presented by Peffers et al. [10], the remainder of this paper is structured as follows: In Sect. 2, we formulate concrete and verifiable requirements for the CL2HTTP interface adapter motivated in this section. In Sect. 3, we explain the solution in detail and demonstrates its technical feasibility by showing how a web service for document conversion can be built using our adapter. In Sect. 4, we discuss when to use our approach and what constraints apply. In Sect. 5, we present related work, and in Sect. 6, we summarize the main insights and give an outlook on future work.

2   Requirements

Before we explain CL2HTTP in detail in Sect. 3, we discuss the requirements for our approach to define web interfaces for command-line applications in this section. The rationale behind every requirement is given in its description.

---

[1] http://cl2http.dwolt.de.

R1 Non-intrusive Approach: Access to the source code of a certain command-line application is not always given. Hence, it is not feasible to add a web interface directly to an application's source code. Instead, providing a web interface for an existing command-line application shall be done in a non-intrusive manner based on the provided command-line interface.

R2 Descriptive Interface: Creating web interfaces for command-line applications is only helpful if service consumers know how to use the newly created interfaces. Therefore, descriptions of the resulting web interface are needed. Various languages to describe web interfaces exist, e.g., the Web Service Description Language (WSDL) or the OpenAPI specification. If the resulting service shall be integrated into a service-oriented architecture, this interface description must be machine-readable.

R3 Independent Interface Design: The web interface design shall be independent of the command-line interface. Thereby, we can follow best practices for interface design, hide interna of command-line interfaces, and create export interfaces that match import interfaces of requestors. This requirement can be further split into two sub-requirements:

> **R3.1 Parameter Value Transformation:** Parameter values of the web interface and command-line interface might need transformation, e.g., if a command-line application provides human-readable output but a JSON object is expected from the web interface. Hence, parameter value transformation shall be supported.

> **R3.2 Input/Output Mapping:** The input and output parameters of web interfaces are not the same as those of a command-line interface. For instance, the structure of an HTTP request with header values in addition to the request body is very different to a command-line call with parameters and referenced files. Therefore, a mapping between the input and output parameters of web and command-line interfaces is needed.

R4 Security: Since a web interface has a broader accessibility than a command-line interface, it has additional security requirements. Communication shall be encrypted and authentication means shall be supported for access restriction. Injection of custom command-line calls must be prohibited.

R5 Flexible Deployment: Command-line applications can be bound to a specific machine, i.e., because the used data resides with this machine, or they can be unbound and independently deployed, e.g., to leverage load balancing. Hence, flexible deployment options are needed for both command-line applications as well as the web interfaces defined for the respective applications.

3   Adapting Command-Line to HTTP Interfaces

This section explains how CL2HTTP can be used to enrich command-line applications with an HTTP interface. We start by giving a general overview over our approach. Afterwards, we explain how the HTTP interface is described and how parameters are being mapped between the web interface and the command-line interface. We illustrate this mapping using an example, discuss security characteristics and deployment options.

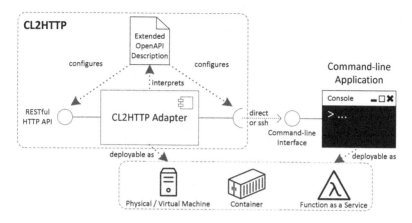

Fig. 1. Structural overview of the CL2HTTP approach

3.1   Solution Overview

Various forms of web interfaces exist. CL2HTTP focuses on adding HTTP interfaces to command-line applications. While SOAP-based interfaces described via WSDL are still relevant in some domains, HTTP interfaces are the de facto standard. Furthermore, the advantages of describing interfaces with WSDL and having tools, e.g., for client stub generation or testing, now also hold for HTTP interfaces since documentation standards with comparable tool support exist. WebSockets are not taken into account, because they just provide means of communication and a protocol has to be used on top.

A structural overview of CL2HTTP in relation to its environment is given in Fig. 1. CL2HTTP consists of two main parts: The first part is an extension of the OpenAPI specification [8], a widely-used documentation standard for describing HTTP interfaces. The standard specification is used to describe a new HTTP interface and our CL2HTTP OpenAPI extension allows to map this HTTP interface to a command-line application. Hence, the creation of the HTTP interface is documentation-driven, which ensures a descriptive interface, thereby satisfying Requirement R2. Furthermore, the CL2HTTP OpenAPI extension is defined using OpenAPI's extension mechanism, which requires that any custom properties added to the specification start with "x-". The standard defines that these properties are ignored by OpenAPI-based tools if they are unknown. Thus, the created interface description is directly usable by existing OpenAPI tools used for testing or creating interactive documentations and client stubs.

The second part, the CL2HTTP adapter, is the interpreter for our extended OpenAPI specification. The adapter provides an HTTP interface as specified by a given OpenAPI description and interacts with command-line applications as defined via our CL2HTTP OpenAPI extension. By having an adapter as a separate entity instead of integrating it into the command-line application, providing an HTTP interface can be done in a non-intrusive manner (see Requirement R1) and does not require altering a command-line application. Command-line applications can be called locally by the adapter or remotely via SSH. This allows a joint or independent deployment of adapter and the command-line application on a physical/virtual machine, as a container or as a function as a service.

Table 1. Available input and output parameters of HTTP and command-line interfaces. This table only lists the parameters of the different interfaces and does not imply a correspondence.

	HTTP interface	Command-line interface
Input parameters	Method	Executable
	Path	Command-line options
	Query	Environment variables
	Header fields	Standard input (STDIN)
	Cookies	Input files
	Request body	
Output Parameters	Status code	Exit code
	Header fields	Standard output (STDOUT)
	Response body	Standard error (STDERR)
		Output files

3.2 Describing the HTTP Interface Using OpenAPI

CL2HTTP is a documentation-driven approach, since the first step is to describe the HTTP interface using OpenAPI. This includes the definition of all input and output parameters. A listing of all available input and output parameters of HTTP and command-line interfaces is given in Table 1. This subsection explains how to describe input and output parameters of the new HTTP interface. The upcoming subsections explain how to establish a mapping between the input and output parameters of both interfaces.

To explain how input and output parameters are documented using OpenAPI and as a running example for the remainder of this paper, we explain how to create an HTTP interface for the command-line application *pandoc*[2], a universal document converter. A simplified example for an interface description using OpenAPI for pandoc is given in Listing 1. Lines 2 to 5 give general information on the service, such as title, description and version. Lines 6 to 7 define the server where the service can be reached and the protocol that needs to be used.

The `paths` property in Line 20 marks the start of the definition of the HTTP endpoints. In this example, just the single path /pandoc with support for the HTTP method POST is defined. The parameters for this method are declared in Lines 26 to 42. The document to be converted by pandoc is given in the request body, the header field Content-Type describes the type of document given in the body and the header field Accept defines the target type. Unless stated otherwise, CL2HTTP assumes that body consist of binary data, whereas for all other parameters we assume the data type string. Thus, the schema defining the header field Content-Type in Lines 31 to 36 of Listing 1 is redundant and just given to indicate how data types can be defined. In this case, the schema object just defines the data type string, however, more specific types like date or email or elaborate type descriptions via JSON Schema can be used.

---

[2] https://pandoc.org.

The OpenAPI specification also allows the definition of possible responses based on different HTTP status code, like it can be seen in Lines 46 to 53. For the responses, important header fields and a schema for the response's body can be specified.

Listing 1. Simplified OpenAPI description that uses our extension to create a service for document conversion based on the command-line application pandoc

```
1  openapi: 3.0.2
2  info:
3    title: Pandoc
4    description: Pandoc Universal Document Converter.
5    version: '1.0'
6  servers:
7    - url: https://example.com
8  x-transforms:
9    toPandocType:
10     text/html: html
11     text/markdown: markdown
12 components:
13   securitySchemes:
14     basic_auth:
15       type: http
16       scheme: Basic
17       x-connector:
18         type: csv
19         file: /secure-directory/username-hashedpwd.csv
20 paths:
21   "/pandoc":
22     post:
23       summary: Pandoc Conversion
24       security:
25         - basic_auth: []
26       requestBody:
27         description: Document to be converted
28         content:
29           "*/*": {}
30       parameters:
31         - name: Content-Type
32           in: header
33           required: true
34           schema:
35             type: string
36           x-transform: toPandocType
37         - name: Accept
38           in: header
39           required: true
40           schema:
41             type: string
42           x-transform: toPandocType
43       x-cli:
44         command: pandoc ${:inputFile} -t ${:accept} -f
               ↪ ${:contentType}
45         bodyToFile: true
46       responses:
47         "200":
48           description: Successful conversion
49           headers:
50             Content-Type:
51               schema:
52                 type: string
53               x-value: ${=accept}
```

3.3 Parameter Value Transformation

The input parameters defined for HTTP interfaces are not necessarily directly usable as input parameters for command-line applications. For instance, to be HTTP compliant, the header field `Content-Type` should contain media types like `text/html` or `text/markdown`. If the command-line application does not directly accept these media types but instead expects `html` or `markdown`, these values have to be transformed. Thus, in addition to the standard way of defining parameters using OpenAPI, we added a property called `x-transform`, which can either refer to a key-value map or a serialized JavaScript function which performs this transformation. This addresses the data conversion and manipulation Requirement R3.1.

The transformation map or function can be specified in the `x-transform` property or it can refer to a globally defined declaration. An example for the latter is given in Listing 1, where the `x-transform` properties in Lines 36 and 42 both refer to the transformation map `toPandocType` defined globally in the Lines 8 to 11. Even though not shown in the example, `x-transform` can also be defined for responses to transform the output of the command-line application as required for the HTTP response.

3.4 Input/Output Mapping

For each HTTP method defined for a path, the `x-cli` object is required to declare which command-line applications need to be called. This object contains various properties to specify the mapping between the HTTP and the command-line interface and addresses Requirement R3.2. The property `command` defines which command is executed on the command-line. This command can be parameterized using input parameters of the HTTP interface (see Line 44 of Listing 1).

For all parameters, the original values are accessible using `${=ParameterName}`, whereas `${:ParameterName}` gives you the transformed value (cf. the previous Sect. 3.3). By default, we assume that the request body is used as standard input for the command-line application. This behavior can be overridden is two ways: (1) If `bodyToFile` is set to `true`, like in Line 45, then the request's body is written to a file which can be referred to using `${:inputFile}`. (2) Alternatively, similar to defining the command, a parameterized standard input for the command-line application can be specified using the property `input`.

We also assume that the standard output of the executed command shall be used as the response body. This can be overridden in a similar fashion, either by setting `fileToBody` to `true` and then the response's body is read from the `${:outputFile}`, or defining a parameterized response's body using property `x-value` in OpenAPI's response descriptions.

Treating parameter values as a whole hinders the independent design of the HTTP interface (see Requirement R3). For instance, HTTP interface designers may want to encode all relevant values for the input parameter of a command-line application as a JSON object, as it is typical for HTTP-based APIs. However, if the command-line application does not accept JSON object directly, but rather requires the values of the

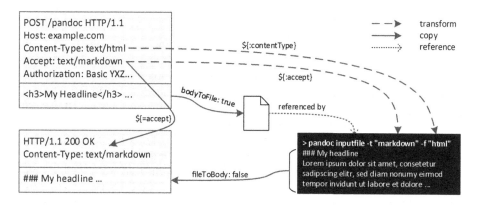

Fig. 2. Mapping example for the document conversion tool pandoc

individual properties, we need a more fine-grained access. To support this, we allow that parameter values cannot only be mapped one-to-one but can also be queried.

For JSON objects, we support JSON Path queries[3], e.g., `${:body.name}` would return the value of the property name or `${:body..item}` would return a comma-separated list all values of properties called `item`. A separator to join the values can be defined after a pipe. For instance, `${:body..item|\n}`, would provide a string with each item in a new line. To get a JSON array instead, `${=body..item}` can be used. For text values, regular expressions can be used to extract specific information. For instance, `${:body/[0-9]{5}/}` would return the first 5 digit number in the body. Standard regular expression flags for returning all occurrences or case insensitive or multi-line search can be added. Multiple results are provided as a comma-separated list or joined using an explicit separator as for multiple JSON Path results. Support for further query language for other content types can be added, like XPath for XML.

Figure 2 shows an example translation between HTTP request and response and input and output of the command-line application according to the example description provided in Listing 1. When a request is received, it is translated into the specified command-line calls. For this, the values of parameters `Content-Type` and `Accept` are transformed, i.e., to the values `markdown` and `html`, and inserted as arguments. Since `bodyToFile` is set to `true` (see Line 45 of Listing 1), the body of the request is stored in a file, which is then referenced in the command-line call. If not specified otherwise using the properties `inputFilename` and `outputFilename` in the `x-cli` object, random filenames are generated for the input and output files. These file names are accessible using `${:inputFile}` and `${:outputFile}`. An example for this can be seen in Line 44 of Listing 1. In the HTTP response, the body is filled directly with the content of standard output, because no transformation has been defined for the response and it has not been stated that the output should be read from a file. As defined in Lines 46 to 53, the original value for the `Accept` header field in the request is taken as the value for the `Content-Type` header field in the response.

---

[3] https://github.com/s3u/JSONPath.

3.5 Security

As mentioned in Requirement R4, exposing command-line applications to the web bares a security risk which needs to be addressed. The resulting service needs to support secure communication, in our case HTTPS, and must be able to validate that service consumers are authenticated. For using HTTPS, the extended OpenAPI specification allows to specify the paths of certificate information. For authentication, the CL2HTTP adapter supports all authentication methods definable in OpenAPI 3.0. These include HTTP basic authentication (cf. Lines 13 to 19 of Listing 1), bearer tokens used by OAuth as well as API keys. The credentials (user, password, token or keys) do not need to be defined within the extended OpenAPI specification, instead we introduce connector objects to check credentials (cf. Lines 17 to 19 of Listing 1). These connector objects enable the validation of credentials against external data sources such as CSV files or databases. Additionally, developing custom connector objects is supported to tailor authentication capabilities to specific needs.

Since parameters given in HTTP requests are forwarded either in original or transformed form, there is a risk of injecting custom commands, e.g., to manipulate the executed command or execute additional commands. To circumvent this problem, data types of parameters need to be specified and are checked by the CL2HTTP adapter. Strings are by default enclosed in quotes and any quotes in the parameters values are escaped. As mentioned in Subsection 3.2, more specialized type definitions can be specified. If a value in a request does not fit the specified data type, the request immediately leads to a "400 Bad Request" HTTP error.

3.6 Deployment

To comply with Requirement R5, different deployment options exist for the CL2HTTP adapter as well as the command-line application, as illustrated in Fig. 1. Both can be deployed together on the same physical/virtual machine or container or as a Function as a Service (FaaS). Alternatively, both can be deployed independently. In this case, the CL2HTTP adapter can invoke the command-line application via SSH.

Whether a joint or independent deployment is feasible and/or more beneficial depends on the command-line applications which are being used. In case of our example, deploying pandoc alongside the adapter is feasible, since the application is stateless. Stateful command-line applications, however, are often bound to specific (physical or virtual) machines. The adapter could be deployed on these machines as well, or separately as a container or as a FaaS, e.g., if no additional software should be installed on the machine or container offering a command-line application. Concrete support for specifying Docker images and deploying on AWS Lambda is implemented.

4 Discussion

The previous section already explains how the requirements of Sect. 2 are addressed. In this section, we discuss what kind of mappings of command-line interfaces to HTTP interfaces are possible with our approach and which are not. Furthermore, we discuss maintainability, runtime overhead and usage of OpenAPI alternatives.

We decided to create a manual approach for creating HTTP interfaces for command-line applications. While automated mappings could be created, deciding which command-line options are relevant and need to be combined cannot properly be automated. Hence, an automatic approach exposes the full command-line interface over HTTP, which leads to a tight coupling to the command-line interface. CL2HTTP allows an interface design independent of the command-line interface's structure. Since we support mapping of input/output parameters as well as value transformation, we even allow different data types than those supported by the command-line interface, e.g., JSON objects could be used by the HTTP interface and individual properties can be passed to the command-line application.

The approach is limited to non-interactive applications that terminate. Hence, command-line applications that require user input beyond initial input parameters or do not terminate, e.g., because they continuously monitor changes, are not supported, yet. Supporting interactive command-line applications does not align well with HTTP interfaces because it would require maintaining a client state on the service side. If those applications require a web interface, individual adapters need to be developed. Future work gives an outlook on how non-terminating applications can be supported.

The maintenance of the new interface consists of two parts: the extended OpenAPI description and the CL2HTTP adapter. The latter is just the interpreter for the former and maintained globally for all services built with our approach. Unless there is a problem with the interpretation, only the maintenance of the extended OpenAPI description is relevant for users of our approach. If a problem occurs with the interpreter, it can be solved globally. Making the adapter available through package managers, allows the distribution of updates and communication of potential (security) problems.

Implementing functionality directly can lead to a faster response time than reusing command-line applications, because there is a runtime overhead for creating processes and mapping inputs and outputs. The individual overhead depends of the complexity of the mappings and transformations. For our test sets covering the different mappings concepts, the overhead is roughly 100 ms on a Intel Core i7. However, custom implementations can be costly and require testing and maintenance effort. Our approach can be used to rapidly create backends for web applications if required functionality is available through command-line applications. This shortens the time-to-market. Due to the independent HTTP interface design, a more efficient implementation can later on replace the command-line application without needing to change the HTTP interface.

Several alternatives to OpenAPI for describing HTTP interfaces are available, like RAML or API Blueprint. CL2HTTP is based on OpenAPI because it is widely supported and a large tool base exists. We currently support OpenAPI specification v2 and v3. If a service description in a different format is needed, tools for converting OpenAPI descriptions to other formats can be used[4].

5   Related Work

Related work for the paper is twofold: Approaches concerned with the adaptation of command-line interfaces and approaches leveraging OpenAPI descriptions.

---
[4] https://apimatic.io/transformer.

The Common-Gateway Interface (CGI)[5] enables web servers to delegate the received requests to command-line applications and return the response of the application back to the client. For this to work, the called applications need to understand HTTP requests and must be able to provide HTTP responses. This, however, is not the case for most command-line applications. Wohlstadter et al. [17] enable mapping command-line applications to the CORBA interoperability standard and thereby offer them to external requesters. The resulting external interfaces are, however, not usable by web applications and there is no description of the resulting interface. Soaplab [11] offers external access to command-line applications via SOAP. The need for Soaplab originated in the bioinformatics domain where most analysis programs only offer command-line interfaces. Soaplap requires more specification effort, the specification is far more technical and not as flexible as CL2HTTP w.r.t. to mapping and transformation. Gannod et al. [6] also developed an approach to convert command-line applications into services. Their approach is based on the ACME architecture description language (ADL). In contrast to our approach, they generate glue code instead of interpreting their ACME specification and they do not create an HTTP interface but enable integration with Jini, a framework for developing distributed applications. In [9], Pautasso and Alonso show how a service composition tool can abstract from the service type and support various kinds of services, including command-line applications. They also enable mapping of input and output parameters, but their approach is limited enabling a specific composition tool to use command-line applications as individual services.

Koren and Klamma [7] present an approach to use OpenAPI specification in combination with the Interaction Flow Model Language (IFML) to synthesize web frontends. Instead, our approach focusses on defining an HTTP interface for command-line applications that could be used by frontends. Ed-douibi et al. [5] enable the translation of OpenAPI specification into UML models. Their approach could also be used on our extended OpenAPI specification to increase the comprehensibility of the defined HTTP interface. In [12], a model-driven approach to build web services based on OpenAPI specifications is presented. In contrast to our approach, they focus on developing new services and not adapting interfaces of existing command-line applications.

6 Conclusion

In this paper, we present CL2HTTP, an approach to rapidly specify web interfaces for command-line applications. For this approach, the OpenAPI specification has been extended so that it can be defined which command-line application shall be executed for a specific HTTP request and how the input and outputs are being mapped and transformed. We explained the extended specification by providing an example defining a web interface for a command-line document conversion tool. Web interfaces are added in a non-intrusive manner via the CL2HTTP adapter, a component separate from the command-line application. It interprets the extended service description, calls the command-line applications, and performs transformations and mappings as specified. Using CL2HTTP, command-line applications can be used to build backends for web applications or within web service orchestrations.

---

[5] https://tools.ietf.org/html/rfc3875.

For the future, the approach shall be extended to support multipart bodies in both requests and responses. Furthermore, dealing with command-line applications that do not terminate but instead frequently output information, like file changes or log data, shall be supported by allowing streams as a response. One option for this is the support of server-sent events.

References

1. Blanning, R.W.: Model management systems: an overview. Decis. Support Syst. **9**(1), 9–18 (1993)
2. Delen, D., Demirkan, H.: Data, information and analytics as services. Decis. Support Syst. **55**(1), 359–363 (2013)
3. Demirkan, H., Delen, D.: Leveraging the capabilities of service-oriented decision support systems: putting analytics and big data in cloud. Decis. Support Syst. **55**(1), 412–421 (2013)
4. Deokar, A.V., El-Gayar, O.F., Aljafari, R.: Developing a semantic web-based distributed model management system: experiences and lessons learned. HICSS **2010**, 1–10 (2010)
5. Ed-douibi, H., Cánovas Izquierdo, J.L., Cabot, J.: OpenAPItoUML: a tool to generate UML models from OpenAPI definitions. In: Mikkonen, T., Klamma, R., Hernández, J. (eds.) ICWE 2018. LNCS, vol. 10845, pp. 487–491. Springer, Cham (2018). https://doi.org/10.1007/978-3-319-91662-0_41
6. Gannod, G.C., Mudiam, S.V., Lindquist, T.E.: Automated support for service-based software development and integration. J. Syst. Softw. **74**(1), 65–71 (2005)
7. Koren, I., Klamma, R.: The exploitation of OpenAPI documentation for the generation of web frontends. In: Companion Proceedings of WWW 2018, pp. 781–787 (2018)
8. OpenAPI Initiative: OpenAPI Specification (2018). http://spec.openapis.org/oas/v3.0.2
9. Pautasso, C., Alonso, G.: From web service composition to megaprogramming. In: Shan, M.-C., Dayal, U., Hsu, M. (eds.) TES 2004. LNCS, vol. 3324, pp. 39–53. Springer, Heidelberg (2005). https://doi.org/10.1007/978-3-540-31811-8_4
10. Peffers, K., Tuunanen, T., Rothenberger, M.A., Chatterjee, S.: A design science research methodology for information systems research. J. Manage. Inf. Syst. **24**(3), 45–77 (2007)
11. Senger, M., Rice, P., Oinn, T.: Soaplab - a unified sesame door to analysis tools. In: In UK e-Science All Hands Meeting, pp. 509–513 (2003)
12. Sferruzza, D., Rocheteau, J., Attiogbé, C., Lanoix, A.: A model-driven method for fast building consistent web services from OpenAPI-compatible models. In: Hammoudi, S., Pires, L.F., Selic, B. (eds.) MODELSWARD 2018. CCIS, vol. 991, pp. 9–33. Springer, Cham (2019). https://doi.org/10.1007/978-3-030-11030-7_2
13. Spinellis, D.: Being a DevOps developer. IEEE Softw. **33**(3), 4–5 (2016)
14. Virmani, M.: Understanding DevOps & bridging the gap from continuous integration to continuous delivery. In: INTECH 2015, pp. 78–82. IEEE (2015)
15. Voss, A., Voss, J.: Fast-dm: a free program for efficient diffusion model analysis. Behav. Res. Methods **39**(4), 767–775 (2007)
16. Wettinger, J., Andrikopoulos, V., Leymann, F.: Automated Capturing and systematic usage of DevOps knowledge for cloud applications. In: IC2E 2015, pp. 60–65 (2015)
17. Wohlstadter, E., Jackson, S., Devanbu, P.: Generating wrappers for command line programs: the Cal-Aggie Wrap-O-Matic project. In: ICSE 2001, pp. 243–252 (2001)
18. Wolters, D., Heindorf, S., Kirchhoff, J., Engels, G.: Linking services to websites by leveraging semantic data. In: ICWS 2017, pp. 668–675. IEEE (2017)

Towards Understanding Adaptation Latency in Self-adaptive Systems

Claas Keller and Zoltán Ádám Mann[✉]

University of Duisburg-Essen, Essen, Germany

Abstract. An important feature of service-based and cloud-based systems is their ability to perform self-adaptation. Through self-adaptation, such systems can automatically react to changes and thus ensure the continued satisfaction of their functional and non-functional requirements. Self-adaptation may take non-negligible time (which we term adaptation latency), and during this period the self-adaptive system may exhibit degraded performance or other negative impact. Hence, it is important to understand how long self-adaptations take and what influences the adaptation latency. However, we are not aware of a systematic study of this question in the literature. This paper is a first step in this direction. We present (i) a model of adaptation latency that breaks it down into four components and (ii) a preliminary survey, limited to one conference series and to service-based and cloud-based systems, to analyze information about adaptation latency in the available literature on self-adaptive systems. According to the findings from this preliminary survey, although some components of the adaptation latency are studied in some publications, the whole adaptation delay is seldom considered.

1 Introduction

Modern software systems must operate in highly dynamic environments. To effectively cope with changes of the environment, the concept of self-adaptation has been proposed [31]. A self-adaptive system reacts to changes in the environment by adapting its own structure or behavior at run time, so that the system continues to satisfy its requirements [5]. For example, in a service-based application, if one of the used services becomes unavailable, an alternative service can automatically be involved instead to ensure that the service-based application remains functional [14]. As another example, a cloud-based application can react to an increasing workload by automatically scaling out to use more virtual machines [21].

From the moment the change in the environment happens, it takes some time until the self-adaptive system resolves the issue. We call this time *adaptation latency*. The amount of the adaptation latency can be very different, depending on the type of change of the environment, the type of adaptation used by the self-adaptive system etc. During the period of the adaptation latency, the self-adaptive system may be in a transient state in which its performance may be

© Springer Nature Switzerland AG 2020
S. Yangui et al. (Eds.): ICSOC 2019 Workshops, LNCS 12019, pp. 42–53, 2020.
https://doi.org/10.1007/978-3-030-45989-5_4

degraded and some requirements may be temporarily violated [23]. For example, if a cloud-based application scales out to support an increased number of user requests, it takes some time until this adaptation action takes effect, and in the meantime, the application's response time may be too high (e.g., higher than stipulated in the service level agreement) [24].

The adaptation latency is important for multiple reasons. First, it is a fundamental goal of self-adaptation to reach a new system state in which the requirements are again satisfied as soon as possible, i.e., with minimum adaptation latency, so as to minimize the negative impact of the transient state during the adaptation process [12]. Second, if the new state is reached with a high delay, this increases the likelihood that in the meantime the environment has changed again, so that the ongoing adaptation will not be effective anymore. In other words, the speed of adaptation should be commensurate with the speed of change in the environment [23]. Third, the self-adaptive system may be able to make better adaptation decisions if it is aware of the latency associated with the possible adaptation actions. For example, knowing how long it takes to spin up a new virtual machine, a cloud-based application can start the scale-out in a proactive way, early enough [25,26].

Despite the importance of adaptation latency for self-adaptation, we are not aware of a systematic study about adaptation latency, the factors influencing adaptation latency, or the implications of adaptation latency. In fact, there is not even consensus about the name and the exact scope of adaptation latency. For example, Tamura et al. call it "settling time" and include the time for making an adaptation decision and executing it [35]. On the other hand, Gambi et al. consider what they call "actuation delay", which includes the time for executing an adaptation and the time it takes for the adaptation to show its effect [13]. Cámara et al. use the terms "adaptation latency"[1] and synonymously "adaptation tactic latency" to refer to the time it takes to execute an adaptation action [8].

Therefore, this paper makes two contributions towards a better understanding of adaptation latency in self-adaptive systems. First, we present a simple model of adaptation latency that breaks it down into four components. This model makes it easier to compare different notions of adaptation latency used by different authors. Second, we present preliminary results of a literature survey, so far limited to one relevant conference series (Software Engineering for Adaptive and Self-Managing Systems, SEAMS[2]) and to the topics of service-based and cloud-based systems. In the survey, we identified the papers that contain specific information about adaptation latency and mapped them on our model of adaptation latency. According to the preliminary findings, most of the relevant papers address only some components of the adaptation latency.

---

[1] It should be noted that this is different from the meaning of "adaptation latency" in this paper. The adaptation latency considered by Cámara et al. is only a part of the adaptation latency considered in this paper.

[2] http://self-adaptive.org/seams/.

The rest of the paper is organized as follows. Section 2 presents our model of adaptation latency and the components of adaptation latency. Section 3 describes the methodology and the results of our preliminary literature survey. Section 4 discusses the findings, and Sect. 5 concludes the paper.

2   A Model of Adaptation Latency

As already mentioned in Sect. 1, different authors consider different latencies when evaluating the speed of adaptation. To make a meaningful comparison between different approaches, we provide a simple model of adaptation latency that we believe to be a good basis for capturing different temporal aspects of adaptation.

Our model is related to the well-known MAPE model of self-adaptive systems [19]. According to the MAPE model, a self-adaptive system monitors (M) its environment to detect changes, analyzes (A) the changes to decide if adaptation is necessary, plans (P) adaptations if necessary, and executes (E) the adaptations.

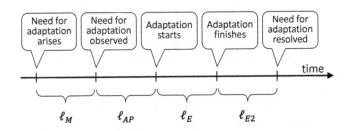

Fig. 1. Model of adaptation latency

The proposed model for adaptation latency is shown in Fig. 1. As can be seen, there are five key points in time:

1. First, the need for adaptation arises, typically in the form of a change in the environment. For example, the number of users of a cloud-based application starts to increase.
2. After some time ℓ_M, which is related to the monitoring activity, the self-adaptive system recognizes the change. For example, the cloud-based application observes that the queue length of user requests grew over a threshold.
3. This is followed by the analysis and planning activities, taking altogether ℓ_{AP} time, leading to the decision to perform a specific adaptation. For example, the cloud-based application decides to turn on a new virtual machine for the purpose of scale-out.
4. The execution of the adaptation takes ℓ_E time. In our example, this is the time until the new virtual machine is turned on and registered with the load balancer.

5. Finally, it takes further ℓ_{E2} time until the adaptation shows its effect. In our example, this is the time until the queue length is normalized again as a result of the increased processing power.

There are two main differences between our model and the MAPE model. First, we do not differentiate between the analysis and planning activities. The differentiation between analysis and planning is a purely internal concern of the self-adaptive system; moreover, there are a number of approaches to self-adaptation that do not have separate analysis and planning activities [3,31]. The other difference is that our model also includes ℓ_{E2} which does not have an equivalent in the MAPE model, but it is important for understanding the overall temporal behavior of self-adaptive systems.

We define the *adaptation latency* as $L = \ell_M + \ell_{AP} + \ell_E + \ell_{E2}$. The individual delays $\ell_M, \ell_{AP}, \ell_E, \ell_{E2}$ are called the *components* of the adaptation latency.

3 Preliminary Literature Study

Using the model introduced above, we performed a (limited) literature survey. We first describe the methodology of this survey in Sect. 3.1, followed by the main results in Sect. 3.2. Finally, in Sect. 3.3, we mention some further papers excluded during the literature survey which could nevertheless provide interesting impetuses to further research.

3.1 Methodology

In the long run, we plan to perform a comprehensive literature review on the topic of adaptation latency in self-adaptive systems. As a first step, we systematically reviewed all papers published in the SEAMS (Software Engineering for Adaptive and Self-Managing Systems) conference series from 2009 to 2019. We filtered the papers according to the following criteria:

- We only included papers that contain some information about adaptation latency. This also includes papers in which information about adaptation latency is only present in diagrams about experiments.
- We only included papers that are related to the field of service-based or cloud-based systems.

We performed this limited literature study manually, i.e., looking at each paper published in SEAMS in the given period. Although it is more common to perform a literature survey using a set of search strings applied to a set of databases, we opted for the manual approach focused on one conference series because of the difficulties associated with finding the appropriate search terms. This way, we do not run the risk of missing whole classes of relevant papers because of a poorly chosen search string. In fact, the papers found with the help of the manual search can serve in the future as baseline for identifying appropriate search terms, which can then be applied in a database search in the future. For now, we manually went through all 225 papers published in SEAMS between 2009 and 2019 and applied the above filter criteria.

Table 1. Relevant publications

Paper	ℓ_M	ℓ_{AP}	ℓ_E	ℓ_{E2}	Time	Notion
[9]	✓	✓	✓	✓	≈300 s	None explicitly mentioned
[34]		✓			118–389 ms	Time to find a reconfiguration
[20]		✓			≥9 min	Planning time
[32]		✓			≥1513 ms	Time for generating a workflow
[1]		✓	✓		0.2–1.02 ms	Performance of adaptation
[35]		✓	✓		1.85–2.34 ms	Performance, settling time
[36]		✓	✓		12 s–15 min	Redeployment time
[29]			✓	✓	125–625 μs	Transition time
[13]			✓	✓	115–420 s	Actuation delay
[7]				✓	∅19.74 s	Time to recovery
[38]		✓	✓			Execution time
[8]			✓			Adaptation (tactic) latency
[28]		*	✓			Tactic latency

3.2 Results

The papers identified as relevant according to the above criteria are summarized in Table 1. For each of the relevant papers, the components of the adaptation latency covered by the paper are indicated, as well as the name that the authors of the paper used to call the considered part of the adaptation latency. In the first half of the table, also the specific duration measured in the paper (corresponding to the sum of the marked components of the adaptation latency) is given; the papers in the second half of the table did not contain such values.

As can be seen from Table 1, only [9] considers the whole adaptation latency. However, that paper does not make any specific statement about the adaptation latency. The quoted information about adaptation latency can only be read off from a diagram of an experiment within the paper. The experiment shows how a self-adaptive web application can manage the slashdot effect by appropriate adaptations, so that the response time of the web application goes after an initial increase back to its normal values.

Several papers focus on the ℓ_{AP} component of the adaptation latency. This may be attributed to the fact that analysis and planning exhibit the most interesting challenges algorithmically, leading to high research attention. In particular, [34] proposes a sophisticated planning algorithm using Pseudo-Boolean constraints; the performance of the planning algorithm was also in the focus of the evaluation using the Heroku platform-as-a-service environment. Similarly, [20] proposes a planner using genetic programming, and makes statements about the time it takes to create a plan by their planner and a baseline planner based on an existing model checker. [32] considers the problem of generating a workflow for dynamically changing the configuration of a self-adaptive system by integrating and testing new components at run time. This problem is a part of the general planning activity of a self-adaptive system (e.g., it does not include the choice of components to add), but the authors formulate it as a planning problem on its own and evaluate the time needed for this planning.

Some papers take, beside ℓ_{AP}, also ℓ_E into account. [1] considers the proactive adaptation of service compositions. In evaluating their approach, they measure the time of determining the need for adaptation (analysis), the time to determine the necessary changes to the service composition (planning) and the time to actually change it (execution). An interesting finding is that problems occurring early in the workflow of composed services lead to higher adaptation latency than problems occurring later. This is because the space of possible solutions is larger if the problem occurs early. [35] considers the adaptation of the monitoring infrastructure for an adaptive web application. In their experimental evaluation the authors measure the time from detecting a change until the adaptation is finished. [36] addresses the problem of dynamically redeploying service-oriented systems, also measuring latency from detecting a change until the adaptation is finished.

[29] presents an approach for the dynamic change between pre-compiled variants of a software at run time. In the experimental evaluation, the time of transitioning from one variant to another is measured, corresponding to $\ell_E + \ell_{E2}$ in our model. Similarly, also [13] considers the time $\ell_E + \ell_{E2}$ and calls it actuation delay. In contrast to most other found papers which only make statements about the adaptation latency in the context of their empirical evaluation, [13] focuses explicitly on the problem of estimating the actuation delay.

We also found one paper that focuses specifically on the ℓ_{E2} component of the adaptation latency. [7] investigates to what extent and how quickly self-adaptive systems can recover after changes. The authors define the metric Mean Time To Recover and measure it for an adaptive web service.

The second part of Table 1 lists papers that do not contain specific duration information, but still explicitly address (some components of) the adaptation latency. [38] presents a simulator of a self-adaptive system in which different adaptation engines can be evaluated, and the simulator measures the execution time of the adaptation engine. [8] shows that taking into account the latency associated with the execution of different adaptation tactics leads to better adaptation decisions. [28] also takes into account the latency of adaptation tactics (ℓ_E); in addition, it aims to speed up decision-making (ℓ_{AP}, denoted by a * in the table to make clear that this duration is not part of the tactic latency).

In addition to the papers in Table 1, also [16] should be mentioned. This paper is not about the latency of specific adaptations, but about overall metrics to quantify the performance of cloud elasticity solutions, thus aggregating the effect of a series of adaptations.

3.3 Adaptation Latency in Other Papers

Although our present study was limited to papers about service-based and cloud-based systems, we also found papers published in SEAMS that are unrelated to these domains but contained interesting information about adaptation latency. For example, [10] addresses the problem of reverting short-term remediation actions. The suggested approach is evaluated using an example from the smart homes domain, which is not relevant to the domains covered here. However, the evaluation contains information about all four components of the adaptation latency. [2] proposes an adaptive approach for the mitigation of Denial-of-Service attacks; the experimental results also showcase the full adaptation latency with all its four components. [39] addresses adaptations in networked embedded systems under real-time constraints, where the adaptation latency must remain within given bounds even in the worst case. [6] improves the self-adaptation behavior of an industrial data acquisition and control system using architecture-based self-adaptation and shows that the re-engineered system can recover from disturbances faster.

Other works contain information about specific components of the adaptation latency. [30] investigates the application of genetic algorithms to find optimal adaptations for mobile applications and is specifically concerned with the time taken by the algorithm (ℓ_{AP}). [33] devises an approach for the self-adaptation of access control policies, and measures the execution time of the proposed approach (ℓ_{AP}). [4] proposes an approach which can adapt the requirements if the available resources are not sufficient to satisfy the requirements, applies this approach in meal planning to reduce food waste, and measures the processing time ($\ell_{AP} + \ell_{E}$). [27] presents an exemplar for self-adaptation approaches for cyber-physical systems, and emphasizes the importance of timing in this domain. In particular, the exemplar explicitly supports tactic latencies (ℓ_{E}). Also in the domain of cyber-physical systems, [17] investigates how offline machine learning can reduce the time needed for online planning (ℓ_{AP}).

[15] presents a systematic literature study about self-adaptation in mobile apps. Regarding timing, the result of the study was that all found approaches were best-effort, i.e., without any guarantees for the adaptation latency.

[18] is domain-independent and defines a large set of metrics for the evaluation of self-adaptive systems. The metric that comes closest to our adaptation latency is "Time for Adaptation" which is defined as the "time to return to a nominal behavior after a perturbation". Similarly, [37] defines a set of properties and metrics for the evaluation of self-adaptive systems. That paper uses "settling time", defined as "the time required for the adaptive system to achieve the desired state", but it is mentioned that several other terms are used in the literature (recovery time, reaction time, healing time).

[11] proposes a control-theoretic approach to self-adaptation, which allows to derive an upper bound on the settling time. The resulting estimate is actually the number of iterations of the control loop, after which the investigated system property will be within given proximity of the goal.

4   Discussion

Regarding the model of adaptation latency proposed in Sect. 2, some details may require further elaboration. For example, it is not always clear when exactly the "need for adaptation arises" (which is the point in time from which ℓ_M is measured). Like any model, also our model of adaptation latency abstracts from some details of reality and thus may leave some room for interpretation when being applied to a specific scenario. We found this level of uncertainty acceptable when analyzing the literature, and we could determine in each case which components of the adaptation latency are involved. Also the question of how appropriate the model is can be answered in this context: we found the model very useful for structuring the literature relating to adaptation latency. For other purposes, it may or may not be appropriate, depending on the required level of detail.

Regarding the results of the survey presented in Sect. 3, several observations can be made:

- In most of the found papers, information about adaptation latency was only presented in the context of an experimental evaluation. In most cases, the proposed approaches were not adaptation-latency-aware themselves, i.e., they did not perform any reasoning on latency-related information. Such reasoning, however, could be very useful [25]. Also those papers that did reasoning about adaptation latency, were only concerned with the latency of the execution of adaptation tactics. Hence we expect to see more research on adaptation-latency-aware self-adaptation approaches in the future.
- Information about adaptation latency was limited in most papers to ℓ_{AP} and/or ℓ_E, which are the parts of the adaptation latency that are mostly internal to the self-adaptive system. The other parts of the adaptation latency, which are more strongly related to the environment (ℓ_M and ℓ_{E2}) are considered less frequently. On the one hand, this is understandable since we can better control the system-related components (ℓ_{AP} and ℓ_E). However, the effectiveness of self-adaptation is ultimately determined by the adaptation latency as a whole, in which the environment-related components (ℓ_M and ℓ_{E2}) can be just as important as the system-related components. Hence, more research may be needed on the environment-related components of the adaptation latency.
- The specific timing information collected in the penultimate column of Table 1 has huge variance. Obviously, timing measurements stemming from different technical environments cannot be directly compared to each other, but there could be some trends at least concerning the orders of magnitudes (especially since the considered papers are all from similar domains). However, not even such trends are observable: for each component of the adaptation latency for which we have multiple measurements, these vary by several orders of magnitude.
- As shown in the last column of Table 1, there is no generally accepted name for adaptation latency. Rather, the authors usually resort to different, longer expressions to describe adaptation latency. Naming is also challenging because of the ambiguity with the base functionality of the self-adaptive system (e.g., latency for processing web page requests versus latency of an adaptation).

Unfortunately, the lack of a generally accepted term for adaptation latency makes it difficult to search for relevant work using keyword search.

Of course, these observations are based on the limited literature survey presented in this paper, and should hence be seen as preliminary. It remains an important task for future research to check whether the observations are supported also by a comprehensive survey of the relevant literature.

5   Conclusions and Future Work

This paper is a first step towards a better understanding of adaptation latency in self-adaptive systems. In particular, we have presented a model of adaptation latency that identifies its main components. Furthermore, we conducted a literature survey on information about adaptation latency, for the time being restricted to the SEAMS conference series and to service-based and cloud-based systems, and used our model of adaptation latency to categorize the found papers. The results of the literature survey show that there is some awareness of the importance of adaptation latency in the research community, but this awareness is limited. One of the identified limitations is that most of the relevant papers only consider some components of the adaptation latency and ignore other components that could also be important. Another limitation is that most of the relevant papers deal with adaptation latency only in their experimental evaluation, which means that most of the presented approaches are not adaptation-latency-aware. On the other hand, adaptation-latency-aware approaches can be very powerful, even if limited to awareness of a component of the adaptation latency, like the latency of adaptation execution [25] or the latency of planning [22]. Hence we expect to see more research in this direction in the future.

The next step in our research is to extend the literature survey to other publication venues and to other domains of self-adaptive systems. This way, we expect to collect a larger body of related papers, allowing us to do a more comprehensive qualitative and quantitative analysis, also comparing different research communities in terms of their relation to adaptation latency. We are particularly interested in (i) insights into the aspects influencing adaptation latency, (ii) experience about the consequences of adaptation latency, and (iii) approaches that explicitly take into account adaptation latency, either reactively (e.g., taking into account ongoing adaptations while planning new ones) or proactively (e.g., preferring quick planning algorithms or quick adaptation tactics in cases of urgency). In the long run, we hope to contribute to building better self-adaptive systems by raising the awareness of adaptation latency in the research community, and incorporating such aspects in approaches to self-adaptation.

Acknowledgments. Research leading to these results received funding from the European Union's Horizon 2020 research and innovation programme under grant agreement no. 731678 (RestAssured). Useful comments of Javier Cámara on an earlier version of the paper are gratefully acknowledged.

References

1. Aschoff, R.R., Zisman, A.: Proactive adaptation of service composition. In: Proceedings of the 7th International Symposium on Software Engineering for Adaptive and Self-Managing Systems, pp. 1–10. IEEE Press (2012)
2. Barna, C., Shtern, M., Smit, M., Tzerpos, V., Litoiu, M.: Model-based adaptive DoS attack mitigation. In: Proceedings of the 7th International Symposium on Software Engineering for Adaptive and Self-Managing Systems, pp. 119–128. IEEE Press (2012)
3. Bartók, D., Mann, Z.Á.: A branch-and-bound approach to virtual machine placement. In: Proceedings of the 3rd HPI Cloud Symposium "Operating the Cloud", pp. 49–63 (2015)
4. Bennaceur, A., Zisman, A., McCormick, C., Barthaud, D., Nuseibeh, B.: Won't take no for an answer: resource-driven requirements adaptation. In: Proceedings of the 14th International Symposium on Software Engineering for Adaptive and Self-Managing Systems, pp. 77–88 (2019)
5. Calinescu, R., Ghezzi, C., Kwiatkowska, M., Mirandola, R.: Self-adaptive software needs quantitative verification at runtime. Commun. ACM **55**(9), 69–77 (2012)
6. Cámara, J., et al.: Evolving an adaptive industrial software system to use architecture-based self-adaptation. In: Proceedings of the 8th International Symposium on Software Engineering for Adaptive and Self-Managing Systems, pp. 13–22. IEEE Press (2013)
7. Cámara, J., de Lemos, R.: Evaluation of resilience in self-adaptive systems using probabilistic model-checking. In: Proceedings of the 7th International Symposium on Software Engineering for Adaptive and Self-Managing Systems, pp. 53–62. IEEE Press (2012)
8. Cámara, J., Moreno, G.A., Garlan, D.: Stochastic game analysis and latency awareness for proactive self-adaptation. In: Proceedings of the 9th International Symposium on Software Engineering for Adaptive and Self-Managing Systems, pp. 155–164. ACM (2014)
9. Cheng, S.W., Garlan, D., Schmerl, B.: Evaluating the effectiveness of the Rainbow self-adaptive system. In: ICSE Workshop on Software Engineering for Adaptive and Self-Managing Systems, pp. 132–141. IEEE (2009)
10. Faccin, J., Nunes, I.: Cleaning up the mess: a formal framework for autonomously reverting BDI agent actions. In: Proceedings of the 13th International Conference on Software Engineering for Adaptive and Self-Managing Systems, pp. 108–118. ACM (2018)
11. Filieri, A., et al.: Software engineering meets control theory. In: Proceedings of the 10th International Symposium on Software Engineering for Adaptive and Self-Managing Systems, pp. 71–82. IEEE Press (2015)
12. Filieri, A., et al.: Control strategies for self-adaptive software systems. ACM Transactions on Auton. Adapt. Syst. (TAAS) **11**(4), 24 (2017)
13. Gambi, A., Moldovan, D., Copil, G., Truong, H.L., Dustdar, S.: On estimating actuation delays in elastic computing systems. In: Proceedings of the 8th International Symposium on Software Engineering for Adaptive and Self-Managing Systems, pp. 33–42. IEEE Press (2013)
14. Ghezzi, C., Pinto, L.S., Spoletini, P., Tamburrelli, G.: Managing non-functional uncertainty via model-driven adaptivity. In: 35th International Conference on Software Engineering (ICSE), pp. 33–42. IEEE (2013)

15. Grua, E.M., Malavolta, I., Lago, P.: Self-adaptation in mobile apps: a systematic literature study. In: Proceedings of the 14th International Symposium on Software Engineering for Adaptive and Self-Managing Systems, pp. 51–62 (2019)

16. Herbst, N.R., Kounev, S., Weber, A., Groenda, H.: BUNGEE: an elasticity benchmark for self-adaptive IaaS cloud environments. In: Proceedings of the 10th International Symposium on Software Engineering for Adaptive and Self-Managing Systems. pp. 46–56. IEEE Press (2015)

17. Jamshidi, P., Cámara, J., Schmerl, B., Kästner, C., Garlan, D.: Machine learning meets quantitative planning: enabling self-adaptation in autonomous robots. In: Proceedings of the 14th International Symposium on Software Engineering for Adaptive and Self-Managing Systems, pp. 39–50 (2019)

18. Kaddoum, E., Raibulet, C., Georgé, J.P., Picard, G., Gleizes, M.P.: Criteria for the evaluation of self-* systems. In: Proceedings of the 2010 ICSE Workshop on Software Engineering for Adaptive and Self-Managing Systems, pp. 29–38. ACM (2010)

19. Kephart, J.O., Chess, D.M.: The vision of autonomic computing. Computer **36**(1), 41–50 (2003)

20. Kinneer, C., Coker, Z., Wang, J., Garlan, D., Goues, C.L.: Managing uncertainty in self-adaptive systems with plan reuse and stochastic search. In: Proceedings of the 13th International Conference on Software Engineering for Adaptive and Self-Managing Systems, pp. 40–50. ACM (2018)

21. Mann, Z.Á.: Resource optimization across the cloud stack. IEEE Trans. Parallel Distrib. Syst. **29**(1), 169–182 (2017)

22. Mann, Z.Á.: Two are better than one: an algorithm portfolio approach to cloud resource management. In: De Paoli, F., Schulte, S., Broch Johnsen, E. (eds.) ESOCC 2017. LNCS, vol. 10465, pp. 93–108. Springer, Cham (2017). https://doi.org/10.1007/978-3-319-67262-5_8

23. Mann, Z.Á., Metzger, A.: Auto-adjusting self-adaptive software systems. In: IEEE International Conference on Autonomic Computing (ICAC), pp. 181–186. IEEE (2018)

24. Mao, M., Li, J., Humphrey, M.: Cloud auto-scaling with deadline and budget constraints. In: 11th IEEE/ACM International Conference on Grid Computing, pp. 41–48. IEEE (2010)

25. Moreno, G.A., Cámara, J., Garlan, D., Schmerl, B.: Proactive self-adaptation under uncertainty: a probabilistic model checking approach. In: Proceedings of the 10th Joint Meeting on Foundations of Software Engineering, pp. 1–12. ACM (2015)

26. Moreno, G.A., Cámara, J., Garlan, D., Schmerl, B.: Efficient decision-making under uncertainty for proactive self-adaptation. In: IEEE International Conference on Autonomic Computing (ICAC), pp. 147–156. IEEE (2016)

27. Moreno, G.A., Kinneer, C., Pandey, A., Garlan, D.: DARTSim: an exemplar for evaluation and comparison of self-adaptation approaches for smart cyber-physical systems. In: Proceedings of the 14th International Symposium on Software Engineering for Adaptive and Self-Managing Systems, pp. 181–187 (2019)

28. Moreno, G.A., Strichman, O., Chaki, S., Vaisman, R.: Decision-making with cross-entropy for self-adaptation. In: Proceedings of the 12th International Symposium on Software Engineering for Adaptive and Self-Managing Systems, pp. 90–101. IEEE (2017)

29. Neamtiu, I.: Elastic executions from inelastic programs. In: Proceedings of the 6th International Symposium on Software Engineering for Adaptive and Self-Managing Systems, pp. 178–183. ACM (2011)

30. Pascual, G.G., Pinto, M., Fuentes, L.: Run-time adaptation of mobile applications using genetic algorithms. In: Proceedings of the 8th International Symposium on Software Engineering for Adaptive and Self-Managing Systems, pp. 73–82. IEEE Press (2013)

31. Salehie, M., Tahvildari, L.: Self-adaptive software: landscape and research challenges. ACM Trans. Auton. Adapt. Syst. **4**(2), 14 (2009)

32. da Silva, C.E., de Lemos, R.: Dynamic plans for integration testing of self-adaptive software systems. In: Proceedings of the 6th International Symposium on Software Engineering for Adaptive and Self-Managing Systems, pp. 148–157. ACM (2011)

33. da Silva, C.E., da Silva, J.D.S., Paterson, C., Calinescu, R.: Self-adaptive role-based access control for business processes. In: Proceedings of the 12th International Symposium on Software Engineering for Adaptive and Self-Managing Systems, pp. 193–203. IEEE Press (2017)

34. Sousa, G., Rudametkin, W., Duchien, L.: Extending dynamic software product lines with temporal constraints. In: Proceedings of the 12th International Symposium on Software Engineering for Adaptive and Self-Managing Systems, pp. 129–139. IEEE Press (2017)

35. Tamura, G., Villegas, N.M., Muller, H.A., Duchien, L., Seinturier, L.: Improving context-awareness in self-adaptation using the DYNAMICO reference model. In: 8th International Symposium on Software Engineering for Adaptive and Self-Managing Systems (SEAMS), pp. 153–162. IEEE (2013)

36. Van Der Burg, S., Dolstra, E.: A self-adaptive deployment framework for service-oriented systems. In: Proceedings of the 6th International Symposium on Software Engineering for Adaptive and Self-Managing Systems, pp. 208–217. ACM (2011)

37. Villegas, N.M., Müller, H.A., Tamura, G., Duchien, L., Casallas, R.: A framework for evaluating quality-driven self-adaptive software systems. In: Proceedings of the 6th International Symposium on Software Engineering for Adaptive and Self-Managing Systems, pp. 80–89. ACM (2011)

38. Vogel, T.: mRUBiS: An exemplar for model-based architectural self-healing and self-optimization. In: Proceedings of the 13th International Conference on Software Engineering for Adaptive and Self-Managing Systems, pp. 101–107. ACM (2018)

39. Zeller, M., Prehofer, C.: Timing constraints for runtime adaptation in real-time, networked embedded systems. In: Proceedings of the 7th International Symposium on Software Engineering for Adaptive and Self-Managing Systems, pp. 73–82. IEEE (2012)

ASOCA: Adaptive Service-Oriented and Cloud Applications

Introduction to the 4th Edition
of the International Workshop on Adaptive
Service-Oriented and Cloud Applications
(ASOCA 2019)

The ASOCA 2019 workshop was held in conjunction with the 17th International Conference on Service Oriented Computing (ICSOC 2019) on October 28, 2019, in Toulouse, France.

The workshop addressed the adaptation and reconfiguration issues of the service-oriented and cloud applications and architectures. ASOCA session gathered about 20 attendees. Discussions followed the presentations. We accepted 4 papers presented in this edition. The ASOCA program was merged with the program of the 4th Workshop on IoT Systems Provisioning & Management for Context-Aware Smart Cities (ISYCC 2019). The presentations of the two workshops were held during the same session.

We would like to thank the authors for their submissions, the Program Committee for their reviewing work, and the organizers of the ICSOC 2019 conference for their support which made this workshop possible.

Organization

Workshop Organizers

Ismael Bouassida Rodriguez   ReDCAD, University of Sfax, Tunisia
Ghada Gharbi   Sensinov, Toulouse, France

Representing Multicloud Security and Privacy Policies and Detecting Potential Problems

Anthony Opara[1($\boxtimes$)], Youngsang Song[2], Seong-je Cho[2], and Lawrence Chung[1]

[1] University of Texas at Dallas, Richardson, TX 75080, USA
{anthony.opara,chung}@utdallas.edu
[2] Dankook University, Yongin, South Korea
{yssong,sjcho}@dankook.ac.kr

Abstract. As more organizations adopt cloud computing, they are increasingly moving towards a mixture of public, private, and hybrid cloud services and infrastructure. These organizations turn to multi-cloud, which involves the use of two or more public clouds, to avoid vendor lock-in, overcome latency, mitigate risks, and control costs. The use of multicloud does have some advantages, such as flexibility and redundancy, but comes with some management, security, and privacy challenges as well. To overcome some of the security challenges, orga-nizations would have to capture and analyze security and privacy poli-cies across multiple clouds to ensure the policies are free from errors and enforce them at runtime independent of the cloud provider. In this paper, we present CERBERUS, a framework for representing multicloud security and privacy policies and detecting potential problems in the policies. CERBERUS adopts an object-oriented approach and consists of an ontology and notation, policies, guidelines and rules, and a tool for capturing and detecting policy errors. Using CERBERUS, policies can be analyzed for potential problems, including policy conflicts, inconsis-tencies, ambiguities, and incompleteness. An application of CERBERUS shows that it indeed helps discover policy errors, that would otherwise go undetected, or in many cases would be detected a posteriori at runtime.

Keywords: Cloud security and privacy · Multicloud · Cloud security policy

1 Introduction

Cloud computing presents unique privacy and security implications. Limited visibility and control of data, the inability to maintain regulatory compliance, theft of data stored in the cloud, and a lack of data isolation for multi-tenant customers, all of these contributing to the new sources of security and privacy risks associated with the cloud [1]. Cloud service providers (CSPs) treat security and privacy in cloud computing as a shared responsibility between itself and the

© Springer Nature Switzerland AG 2020
S. Yangui et al. (Eds.): ICSOC 2019 Workshops, LNCS 12019, pp. 57–68, 2020.
https://doi.org/10.1007/978-3-030-45989-5_5

customer. In the shared responsibility model, the CSP is responsible for securing the underlying infrastructure that supports and powers the cloud, while the cloud customer is responsible for anything it deploys in the cloud or connects to the cloud [2].

Increasingly, organizations are finding that a single cloud deployment model could lead to vendor lock-in, a lack of flexibility through choice, hidden costs, latency issues, and a lack of options to overcome security and privacy challenges. Hence, they are beginning to adopt a multicloud strategy to enjoy best of breed services across multiple cloud providers. A multicloud strategy involves the use of various cloud services from more than one public cloud provider. For instance, a health care provider may decide to use the AWS platform for its application deployment, while leveraging on the infrastructure from Azure for its disaster recovery and then performing its development and testing on the IBM-backed PaaS platform. This shift in cloud strategy comes with its security and management challenges, especially given the fact that different cloud stakeholders may have different security and management requirements [3]. In addition to the existing single cloud-related challenges, which are further exacerbated in a multicloud, there are new security and privacy challenges associated with a multicloud strategy. One such new challenge is the management of heterogeneous policies across multiple cloud service providers consistently across numerous CSPs, where heterogenous policies could lead to policy errors during policy integration [4].

Management of security and privacy policies becomes a significant challenge when multiple cloud providers are involved. A security (or privacy) policy is a set of rules that guides the principles and procedures to enforce and manage security (or privacy) on cloud computing services, where each rule consists of a set of conditions with a corresponding set of actions. Security and privacy policies are often defined at a high level of abstraction by policy administrators and then later refined into fine-grained, implementable policies. In a multicloud environment, defining security and privacy policies in a vendor-agnostic manner is challenging, and is often done in an informal and ad-hoc manner leading to policy errors.

In this paper, we propose CERBERUS, a framework for representing multicloud security and privacy policies and detecting potential conflicts, inconsistencies, and ambiguities in the policies. CERBERUS consists of the CERBERON ontology and notation, with key ontological concepts for managing multicloud security and privacy policies, CERBAC policies, CERBERUS guidelines and rules and the CERBERUX prototype tool for capturing and detecting policy errors.

The rest of this paper is organized as follows. Section 2 presents the CERBERON ontology for modeling cloud security and privacy policies and notation for representing the policies. Section 3 describes general rules and guidelines for representing and detecting cloud security and privacy policy errors. Section 4 describes CERBERUX, a prototype tool for capturing and detecting cloud security and privacy policy errors. Section 5 describes related work together with discussion. In the end, a summary of the paper is given with some future research direction.

2   Multicloud Security and Privacy Policy Ontology and Notation

In this section, we introduce a running example, our ontology and notation for modeling multicloud security and privacy policies.

2.1   Running Example

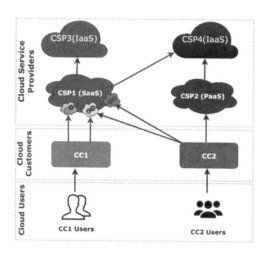

Fig. 1. Multicloud health care running example

To illustrate the problem and motivate our approach, we will use an example of a health care service provider, which adopts a multicloud strategy to offer services to its customers. Figure 1 shows a multicloud setting, involving multiple cloud stakeholders. CSP1, a cloud service provider, provides software as a service (SaaS), which enables patient's remote consulting with doctors, home delivery pharmacy prescription ordering service, and home laboratory services, to its network of customers (doctors, hospitals, and pharmacies). To meet its latency requirements, it leverages compute and storage services provided by CSP3 (IaaS Provider), while relying on CSP4 (IaaS provider) for its development and testing environment. CSP2 is another cloud service provider that offers a DevOps platform backed by the infrastructure provided by CSP4. CC1 and CC2 are two cloud customers that both subscribe to the services provided by CSP1. CC1 is a community hospital with a pharmacy unit that provides telehealth services to its users as well as a mobile service to request mail-to-home prescription service. CC2 is a hospital-chain offering telehealth services as well as a mobile app-based home laboratory service. CC2 also provides a development environment to its developers through the service and platform provided by CSP2 (PaaS provider).

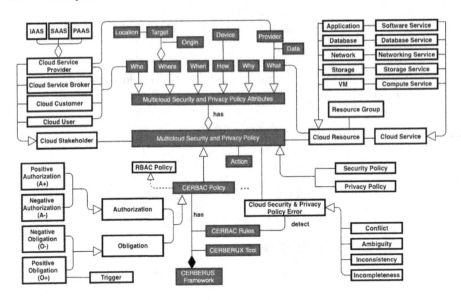

Fig. 2. CERBERON: Cloud security and privacy ontology

2.2 Multicloud Security and Privacy Policy Ontology

In our model, subjects are either individual users or mapped to appropriate roles (e.g., pharmacy technician) and roles are mapped to access rights or actions (e.g., CREATE, USE). In this paper, we shall be concerned with two categories of security policies [6,7]. Authorization policies are security policies, which specify what actions a user or role is allowed (positive authorizations or A+ policies) or not allowed (negative authorizations or A− policies) to perform on a set of target objects or resources (e.g, VM, Data). Obligation policies specify what actions a role or user must (positive obligations or O+ policies) or must not (negative obligations or O− policies) perform on a set of target objects or resources. An obligation policy requires authorization policies to enable the roles of the obligation policies to fulfill their obligations. A cloud customer or enterprise may adopt one of the following policy management strategies. (a) Closed policy, which allows access if there exists a corresponding positive authorization else access is denied. (b) Open policy, which denies access if there exists a corresponding negative authorization else access is allowed. The use of negative authorization is often associated with enterprises that adopt an open policy, but we consider both positive and negative authorization policies important for capturing security and privacy policies at a higher level of abstraction. We allow the specification of both positive and negative authorization and obligation policies. Figure 2 shows our ontology for multicloud security and privacy policies, which illustrates the relationship between cloud stakeholders, cloud resources and cloud security & privacy policies. Elements in green represent our contributions.

CERBAC (Cloud Extended Role Based Access Control) policies are described in terms of Cloud Stakeholder, Cloud Security & Privacy policy, and Cloud Resource. A multicloud security and privacy policy consists of policy attributes (Who, Where, How, When, Why and What) and is associated with one or more Actions. A cloud stakeholder represents one of infrastructure provider, service provider, cloud customer, cloud broker, or cloud user and is associated with a subject (Who) in our ontology. We identify four classes of security and privacy policy errors. Conflicts are errors, which may occur whenever there is an interaction between positive and negative security policies of similar types (i.e., O+/O− or A+/A− applying to the same subject (who) or target (what)). Inconsistencies are errors, which may occur when there is a mix of positive and negative policies of different types (i.e., A+/O− or A−/O+ applying to the same subject (who) or target (what)). Incompleteness errors occur when there is a positive obligation (O+) policy without a corresponding positive authorization (A+) policy to enable the execution of the obligation policy. Ambiguity errors occur when two policies with the same modality signs contradict each other (i.e., A+/A+ or A−/A− or O+/O+ or O−/O−). CERBERUS framework is composed of CERBAC Policy (Realization of RBAC framework), CERBERUX tool, and a set of rules and guidelines for validating CERBAC policies. A CERBAC policy is the base class of Positive Authorization, Negative Authorization, Positive Obligation and Negative Obligation. The CERBERON policy notation allows the expression of cloud security and privacy policies in the JSON format with the possibility of defining a policy document that includes multiple policies.

2.3   CERBERON Policy Notation

```
PolicyStatement:[
    {
        Id:        <policy_id_string> ,
        Type:      A+ | A- | O+ | O- ,
        Who:       * | <principal_string> | <resource.tag>,
        Action:    * | [action1, action2, ...],
        What:      { Provider: * | [providers...], Data: * | <data>, Service: * | <service> },
        Trigger?:  <trigger.event>,
        Why?:      <why.reason>,
        How?:      <how.value>,
        When?:     {time.at | time.after | time.before | time.between:{start, end} },
        Where?:    {(Origin: *| [origin1, origin2, ...]) | (Target: *| [target1, target2, ...]) }
    }
]
```

Fig. 3. CERBERON policy notation

Figure 3 shows the general format of our security and privacy policy notation [6–9]., which can be used to express both identity-based policies and resource-based policies. Identity-based policies are policies attached to a user or role, while resource-based policies are policies attached to a cloud resource, identified by a resource name. A PolicyStatement consists of an array of one or more policies. Each policy block is enclosed in braces, with comma used to separate multiple policies. A question mark (?) next to an attribute (e.g., How?) indicates that the attribute is optional, while a vertical line between attributes indicates options. The Id attribute is a unique identifier for a policy and is used to refer to the policy. The Type of the policy is one of positive authorization (A+), negative authorization (A−), positive obligation (O+), or negative obligation (O−). Who is the subject of a policy and represents the user or role for which a policy applies. A user is an agent, user, role or process in the cloud. The attribute What is the target of a policy and it represents the cloud service for which a set of actions are to be performed or the platform provider, responsible for cloud infrastructure (e.g. Azure). The Action attribute is used to specify what must be performed (obligations) and what is permitted or allowed (authorizations). Multiple actions are separated with a comma (e.g. [READ, WRITE]. The optional attributes *When, Where, Why* and *How* represents CERBAC constraints, which limits the applicability of the policy. The *When* attribute is used to specify the time in which the policy is applicable. The attribute *Where* is used to specify a constraint on the origin for a request to a cloud resource or the physical location(target) where data may be stored. The attribute *Why* specifies the reason for the access to the cloud resource, while the attribute *How* specifies the device used to access a cloud resource. The default value for the constraints is ALL (*). The optional keyword trigger is used to specify an event trigger for positive obligations. Consider the following policies from the running example described in Sect. 2.1:

Id: P1, **Type:** A−, **Who:** Pharmacy Technicians, **Action:** [CREATE], **What: Provider:** CSP3, **Data:** PHI, **Where:** {**Target:** [Location/Europe]}

P1 is a negative authorization policy by cloud customer CC1, that forbids pharmacy technicians from creating protected health information (PHI) in any location in Europe provided by CSP3.

Id: P2, **Type:** A+, **Who:** Physicians, **Action:** [ACCESS], **What: Provider:** CSP2, **Service:** Software Service/Telehealth

Id: P3, **Type:** A−, **Who:** Lab Technicians, **Action:** [ACCESS], **What: Provider:** CSP2, **Service:** Software Service/Telehealth

P2 and P3 are two policies by cloud customer CC2. P2 (Positive Authorization) allows Physicians access to the Telehealth software hosted by CSP2, while P3 (Negative Authorization) denies Lab Technicians access to the Telehealth application

Id: P5, **Type::** O−, **Resource::** VM/DevOps, **Action:** [PROVISIONED], **What:** {**Provider:** CSP2}

Id: P6, **Type::** O+, **Resource::** Storage/Prescription, **Action:** [ARCHIVED], **What:** {**Provider:** CSP4}, **Trigger:** ArchiveEvent

p5 and p6 are two resource-based policies. P5 is a negative obligation policy, which states that VMs with DevOps tag must not be provisioned on the CSP platform. P6 is a positive obligation policy, which states that the Prescription storage must be archived on CSP4 platform when the archive event trigger is raised. This type of policy should have a corresponding authorization policy.

3 Multicloud Security and Privacy Policy Rules and Error Detection

In this section, we explore a UML-based, visual mechanism for displaying and reasoning about policy errors [8]. We also provide general rules for identifying conflicts, inconsistencies and ambiguities in security and privacy policies.

Fig. 4. Base case of authorization and obligation conflict.

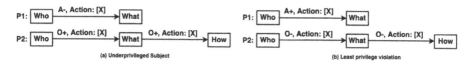

Fig. 5. Underprivileged subject and Least privileged violation.

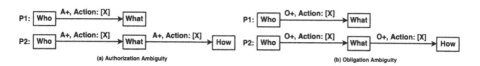

Fig. 6. Base case of authorization and obligation ambiguities.

Figure 4(a) and (b) show base conflict cases between negative and positive authorization and obligation policies. In Fig. 4(a), P2 states that a subject is allowed to perform an action on a target with a specified device type (How), while P1 does not permit the subject to perform the same action on the target. Figure 4(b) shows another obvious conflict scenario, in which a subject must perform an action on a target using a specified device type (P2), while at the same time, the subject must not perform the action on the target (P1).

Figure 5(a) shows a case of the underprivileged subject, who does not have the required authorization to perform an action on the target but at the same time must perform the action on the target. Figure 6(a) and (b) are two cases of policy ambiguity, involving two policies with the same policy types. Figure 6(a) states that a subject must perform an action on a target; while P2 states that the subject must perform the action on the target with the use of the specified device type (How). Similarly, Fig. 6(b) shows a scenario where a subject must perform an action on the subject but must also perform the same action on the target with a specified device type. The base cases of conflicts, inconsistencies and ambiguities shown in Figs. 4, 5 and 6 can be extended to other policy attributes by replacing *How* with *Why*, *When* and *Where*. Next, we take a look at inheritance and aggregation cases.

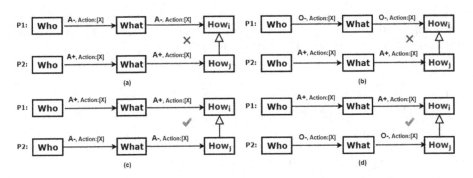

Fig. 7. Inheritance relationship between policy attributes (How).

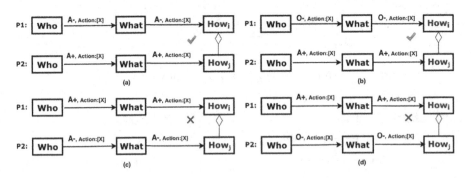

Fig. 8. Aggregation relationship between policy attributes (How).

Figures 7 (Inheritance relationship) and 8 (Aggregation relationship) illustrate relationships between subjects, targets and policy attributes, and the conflicts that may arise as a result of these relationships. Figure 7(a) shows that a subject (Who) is authorized to perform an action on a target (What) with a child How$_j$ but forbidden to perform the same action from the parent How$_i$ attribute. These two policies will be in conflict since the relationship between the How attributes is an Is-a relationship. As indicated by the tick, Fig. 7(c) and (d) are error-free scenarios. In Fig. 8, we examine aggregation relationships between subjects, targets and policy attributes (Why, Where, How, and When). It shows the different scenarios when two How attributes (How$_i$, How$_j$) are related by composition. Figure 8(a) and (b) turn out to be error-free, while Fig. 8(c) and (d) contains policy errors. Figure 9(a) and (b) illustrate concrete cases of inheritance and aggregation conflicts among policy subjects, targets and attributes. In Fig. 9(a), a nurse is allowed to update a patients health information record for the purpose of writing a prescription (why), while at the same time not allowed to update the patients health information record for the purpose of treatment.

(a) Concrete case of inheritance conflict   (b) Concrete case of aggregation conflict

Fig. 9. Concrete case of policy conflict.

Basic Rules	
Rule Id	**Rule**
PA1	~ {Id: P1, Type: A-, Who$_i$, Action: [x], What$_i$} ∧ {Id: P2, Type: A+, Who$_i$, Action: [x], What$_i$, How$_i$} ∨
PA2	~ {Id: P1, Type: O-, Who$_i$, Action: [x], What$_i$} ∧ {Id: P2, Type: O+, Who$_i$, Action: [x], What$_i$, How$_i$ } ∨
PA3	! {Id: P1, Type: O-, Who$_i$, Action: [x], What$_i$} ∧ {Id: P2, Type: A+, Who$_i$, Action: [x], What$_i$, How$_i$ } ∨
PA4	! {Id: P1, Type: A-, Who$_i$, Action: [x], What$_i$} ∧ {Id: P2, Type: O+, Who$_i$, Action: [x], What$_i$, How$_i$ } ∨
PA5	? {Id: P1, Type: O+, Who$_i$, Action: [x], What$_i$} ∧ {Id: P2, Type: O+, Who$_i$, Action: [x], What$_i$, How$_i$ } ∨
PA6	? {Id: P1, Type: A+, Who$_i$, Action: [x], What$_i$} ∧ {Id: P2, Type: A+, Who$_i$, Action: [x], What$_i$, How$_i$ } ∨
Inheritance Rules: Is-A (How$_j$, How$_i$)	
Rule Id	**Rule**
PB1	~ {Id: P1, Type: A-, Who$_i$, Action: [x], What$_i$, How$_i$ } ∧ {Id: P2, Type: A+, Who$_i$, Action: [x], What$_i$, How$_j$} ∨
PB2	~ {Id: P1, Type: O-, Who$_i$, Action: [x], What$_i$, How$_i$ } ∧ {Id: P2, Type: O+, Who$_i$, Action: [x], What$_i$, How$_j$} ∨
PB3	! {Id: P1, Type: O-, Who$_i$, Action: [x], What$_i$, How$_i$ } ∧ {Id: P2, Type: A+, Who$_i$, Action: [x], What$_i$, How$_j$} ∨
PB4	! {Id: P1, Type: A-, Who$_i$, Action: [x], What$_i$, How$_i$ } ∧ {Id: P2, Type: O+, Who$_i$, Action: [x], What$_i$, How$_j$} ∨
Aggregation Rules: Has-A (How$_i$, How$_j$)	
Rule Id	**Rule**
PC1	~ {Id: P1, Type: A+, Who$_i$, Action: [x], What$_i$, How$_i$ } ∧ {Id: P2, Type: A-, Who$_i$, Action: [x], What$_i$, How$_j$} ∨
PC2	~ {Id: P1, Type: O+, Who$_i$, Action: [x], What$_i$, How$_i$ } ∧ {Id: P2, Type: O-, Who$_i$, Action: [x], What$_i$, How$_j$} ∨
PC3	! {Id: P1, Type: O+, Who$_i$, Action: [x], What$_i$, How$_i$ } ∧ {Id: P2, Type: A-, Who$_i$, Action: [x], What$_i$, How$_j$} ∨
PC4	! {Id: P1, Type: A+, Who$_i$, Action: [x], What$_i$, How$_i$ } ∧ {Id: P2, Type: O-, Who$_i$, Action: [x], What$_i$, How$_j$}

Fig. 10. CERBAC rules

Since policies are often specified in a hierarchical manner, prescription would be defined as a treatment; thus, the concrete policy would lead to a conflict. In Fig. 9(b), a Administrator (Who) is authorized to backup patients health information record to a location in Europe (Where: Location) but forbidden from backing up the same data to a region in Europe (region1).

Next, we describe general rules (Fig. 10) for identifying conflicts, inconsistencies and ambiguities in cloud security policies. The scenarios provided above result in some interesting generalization of rules for identifying conflicts and inconsistencies in cloud security policies. We will use the '~' symbol to represent a policy conflict, while the ! symbol will be used to represent a policy inconsistency and the ? symbol to represent an ambiguity. The Is-a predicate will be used to represent an inheritance relationship and the Has-a predicate will be used to represent an aggregation association.

4   CERBERUX: A Prototype Tool

Our prototype tool for modeling and detecting errors in security and privacy policies, known as CERBERUX is based on the Papyrus Eclipse Platform [10]. The Papyrus platform can be extended with (1) Profiles and stereotypes based on standard UML profile extensibility (2) Symbol appearance controlled with CSS and SVG (3) Customizable toolbars, menus, property views, etc. (4) Code plugins/ program logic that adds new features and integrations and (5) Hiding existing functionality. Figure 11 shows an example of a positive authorization policy modeled using the CERBERUX tool.

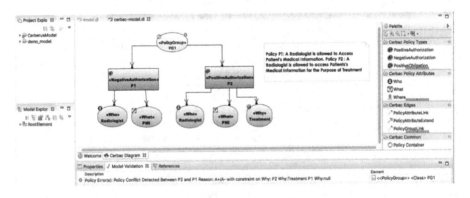

Fig. 11. An Example of a positive authorization policy using the CERBERUX tool

The model validation window shows a policy violation between the two policies (P1 and P2). The CERBERUX tool is developed as an Eclipse plugin that includes a wizard for creating a new project based on our UML profile and a UML diagram for modelling CERBAC policies. In addition to the UML models been elaborated using OCL (Object constraint language) for validation of stereotypes, we add extra validations on the policy grammar. Our UML profile, which can be found in [13]., extends the UML Meta model with stereotypes for modeling cloud computing security and privacy policies. A Policy type requires one or more action attributes, a Subject (Who) stereotype, a target (What) stereotype and optional policy attributes of *Why, When, When* and *How*.

5 Related Work and Discussion

Our work focuses on the expression of single and multi-cloud security and privacy policies with the ability to detect policy errors. In contrast, existing work mostly involves general on-premise security specification with limited support for policy error detection and expression of privacy rules. Our policy notation can be used to express policies in a vendor-neutral manner, which could avoid errors during policy integration across multiple cloud providers. In general, logic-based languages have a well-understood formalism, which makes them amenable to analysis; however, they are challenging to use and to translate into efficient implementations [11]. Rei [12] is an example of a policy language for a pervasive computing environment, modeled on deontic concepts of rights, prohibitions, obligations and dispensations. It allows the specification of role-based policies. However, a separate rule must be specified for each action and there is no explicit way to capture privacy rules. The Ponder Policy Specification Language [3] is a declarative, strongly typed, object-oriented language for specifying security and management policies for distributed object systems. We find the ponder language both simple and effective at capturing both security and management policies and also detecting some conflicts in security policies both statically as well as at runtime. However, we believe the language is still limited in its expressive power, especially for privacy rules as well as cloud-related security policies. While the ponder policy language can detect some conflicts in security and management policies, we believe it has some limitations with regards to policy conflict detection (e.g., ambiguity errors with A+/A+ and O+/O+). Our policy notation includes multicloud-specific extensions to handle cloud security and privacy policy constraints. The addition of these policy attributes reveals additional modality conflicts not considered by the ponder specification. Our notation goes beyond the capability of major cloud vendors in their expressive power as shown. However, our result should be considered as preliminary and our framework will have to be applied to a real-world, large size multicloud software system with advanced multi-tenancy policy requirements.

6 Conclusion and Future Work

In this paper, we propose a framework for modeling multicloud security and privacy policies and detecting policy errors. The main contributions of this paper include: (1) an ontology for modeling multicloud security and privacy policies; (2) a notation for representing multicloud security and privacy policies; (3) a set of guidelines and rules for detecting errors of incompleteness, inconsistencies, conflicts and ambiguities among cloud security and privacy policies, and (4) a tool for visually modeling, and discovering problems with, multicloud security and privacy policies. Using our framework, we were able to detect policy errors in a multicloud-based health care system, which otherwise would have gone undetected or more likely would have been detected later at execution time, thereby offering the user little or no opportunity for determining the outcome of the policy impact on the system. There are several lines of future research. One involves extending the CERBERUS framework to include more rules and generalize the rules for policy errors. Another line of future work will involve adding dynamic policy error detection capabilities and traceability of policies. Investigation of ways to automatically convert cloud provider policy statements (e.g. AWS policies) into CERBAC policies and vice-versa will also be useful. Future work will also focus on the use of the tool as a cloud-broker security and privacy policy tool. To determine both the strengths and weaknesses of our framework, we plan to apply it to a wide variety of applications.

References

1. Takabi, H., Joshi, J.B.D., Ahn, G.-J.: Security and privacy challenges in cloud computing environments. IEEE Secur. Priv. **8**(6), 24–31 (2010)
2. Baron, J., et al.: AWS Certified Solutions Architect Official Study Guide, 1st edn. Wiley, Indianapolis (2017)
3. Tianfield, H.: Security issues in cloud computing. In: 2012 IEEE International Conference on Systems, Man, and Cybernetics (SMC), COEX, Seoul, Korea, pp. 1082–1089 (2012)
4. Singhal, M., et al.: Collaboration in multicloud computing environments: framework and security issues. Computer **46**(2), 76–84 (2013)
5. Verma, D., Beigi, M., Jennings, R.: Policy based SLA management in enterprise networks. In: Sloman, M., Lupu, E.C., Lobo, J. (eds.) POLICY 2001. LNCS, vol. 1995, pp. 137–152. Springer, Heidelberg (2001). https://doi.org/10.1007/3-540-44569-2_9
6. Moffett, J., Sloman, M.: Policy conflict analysis in distributed systems management. J. Organ. Comput. **4**, 1–22 (1993)
7. Lupu, E.C., Sloman, M.: Conflicts in policy-based distributed systems management. IEEE Trans. Software Eng. **25**, 852–869 (1999)
8. Oladimeji, E.A., Chung, L.: Representing security goals, policies and objects. In: Proceedings of the 5th IEEE/ACIS International Conference on Computer and Information Science, Honolulu, Hawaii, pp. 160–167 (2006)
9. AWS. https://docs.aws.amazon.com/. Accessed 27 May 2019
10. Papyrus Modeling environment. https://www.eclipse.org/papyrus/. Accessed 27 May 2019
11. Damianou, N., Bandara, A., Sloman, M. and Lupu, E.: A survey of policy specification approaches, pp. 142–156. Department of Computing, Imperial College of Science Technology and Medicine, London (2002)
12. Kagal, L., Finin, T., Joshi, A.: A policy language for pervasive systems. In: Fourth IEEE International Workshop on Policies for Distributed Systems and Networks (2003)
13. Opara, A., Song, Y., Cho, S. and Chung, L.: Representing multicloud security and privacy policies and detecting potential problems (2019, in preparation)

Survey and Evaluation of Blue-Green Deployment Techniques in Cloud Native Environments

Bo Yang[1]([✉]), Anca Sailer[2], and Ajay Mohindra[3]

[1] IBM Research – China, IBM, Beijing, China
yangbbo@cn.ibm.com
[2] IBM Research, IBM, New York, USA
ancas@us.ibm.com
[3] IBM Watson Health, IBM, New York, USA
ajaym@us.ibm.com

Abstract. Today, the cloud computing customers assume that the services or applications consumed from the cloud are always on, highly available for uninterrupted utilization. The requirement then for the service providers becomes to minimize the planned maintenance windows duration in order to reduce their repercussions on the service availability for the consumers. We evaluate in this paper the continuous deployment methodology called Blue/Green deployment which aims to support zero maintenance windows, and consequently to avoid any interruption to the end users. Our experiments analyze the most common Blue/Green deployment techniques in the industry, measure and normalize their behavior, and aim to identify the approach with the best performing continuous delivery as compared to the available technologies.

Keywords: Continuous delivery · Blue/Green deployment · High availability · Service discovery

1 Introduction

The Blue/Green deployment technology provides support for DevOps continuous delivery [1–3] with zero or near zero-downtime. This technology uses two different environments hosting two different versions of the service. The goal is to shift the incoming traffic from the environment hosting the current service version to the environment hosting the new service version. In most implementations, only one of the environments is live and thus serving all the production traffic. The live environment is typically considered "Blue", while the idle "to be" production environment is called "Green", as shown in Fig. 1. The key challenge of the Blue/Green deployment is the cut-over phase, when taking the service from its Green final stage of testing to Blue to handle the live production traffic. The zero or near-zero maintenance downtime comes down to how efficient the Blue/Green switch is performed.

In this paper, we first evaluate the state-of-art and current practices, and report on key performance results identified. We summarize in Sect. 2 the most prevalent Blue/Green deployment techniques and detail in Sect. 3 two example implementations

© Springer Nature Switzerland AG 2020
S. Yangui et al. (Eds.): ICSOC 2019 Workshops, LNCS 12019, pp. 69–81, 2020.
https://doi.org/10.1007/978-3-030-45989-5_6

of Blue/Green based on service discovery framework which is the most advanced technique. Section 4 presents the outline of our experiments for each implementation of Blue/Green deployment described in Sect. 2 and detailed in Sect. 3. We describe in Sect. 5 the experimental results and their analysis, pointing out the features and relevant scenarios for each implementation of the Blue/Green deployment techniques investigated. Finally, we summarize the paper and discuss the challenges and potential future work in Sect. 6.

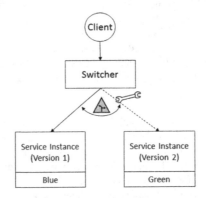

Fig. 1. Overall architecture of migration system with compliance validation

2   Blue/Green Deployment Related Work

The Blue/Green (BG) terminology was first introduces by Fowler [4] and it is just a way to distinguish between the two separate environments hosting the current (Blue) and new (Green) service releases. Other references call it A/B deployment [5], or Red/Black [6] deployment. Although there are slight differences between their overall goals of the upgrade, the common denominator is the key challenge of switching efficiently between the two environments. The various techniques that implement the switch from the service's Blue current version to its Green new version, impact in specific ways the performance of the B/G deployment. Before detailing the metrics we considered for comparing the various existing implementations, we summarize below the most prevalent implementations of B/G deployment.

2.1   Domain Name System (DNS)

These techniques rely on the DNS record update for the B/G switch and thus can be implemented with any of the leading DNS service providers, such as Cloudflare [7], DigitalOcean [8], Google Cloud DNS [9]. For example in Tutum and Cloudflare based implementation [10], CloudFlare cli is used to edit DNS CNAME entry for the B/G switch. The Amazon DNS based B/G technique is the DNS Routing Update with Amazon Route 53 [11]. This technique applies to single instances switch, swapping the environment of an Elastic Beanstalk application, cloning a stack in AWS OpsWorks and updating DNS with alternative environment's IP address [11].

2.2 Software Reconfiguration

These techniques rely on software reconfiguration for the B/G switch. Cloud Foundry (CF) leverages a CF Router [12]. Once a new service release is ready for production traffic, the CF Router is updated to remap the route to the new release. Virtual IP based solutions such as Floating IP [13] in Digital Ocean and Elastic IP [14] in AWS are used for single node.

B/G switch, where in the association of the virtual IP is changed. The AWS techniques which fall into this category are swapping the Auto Scaling group behind Elastic Load Balancer and updating Auto Scaling Group launch configurations [14]. This technique is not as granular as the DNS technique, but the traffic switch is more efficient.

2.3 Load Balancer

These techniques leverage a load balancer to trigger the change of routing configuration. For example, IBM Urban Code Deploy [15] works with Blue and Green environments hosted on the same machines, but different ports. The switching is achieved by changing the port in the load balancer routing rules. Examples of load balancers leveraged in this type of B/G deployments are HAProxy and nginx. The B/G deployment technique for docker uses nginx [16, 17], where nginx runtime configuration reload feature is used for the B/G switch. In the B/G deployment with HAProxy [18], the HAProxy health check is used for the B/G switch.

2.4 Service Discovery

These implementations use a level 7 service discovery framework to switch to a new service release. The service discovery is the automatic detection of services offered in an environment. One such framework example is the Netflix Eureka service discovery [19] which works together with the Zuul dynamic routing [20] to support zero-downtime rolling deployments [21]. Another example is Kubernetes [22] and the ISTIO intelligent router [23] which allows to configure service-level properties like circuit breakers, timeouts, and retries, for B/G deployments as detailed in the next section.

3 Blue/Green Deployment with Service Discovery

To route a request to its destination, we need to know the network location (IP address and port) of the targeted service instance. In a traditional application the network locations of the service instances are relatively static and could be retrieved from a configuration file that is occasionally updated. In a cloud native environment, however, this is a much more difficult problem to solve since the service instances have dynamically assigned network locations and the instance itself changes dynamically because of auto-scaling, migration, and upgrades. Thus, in most implementations of B/G deployment there are two main challenges: (1) the routing rules update requires additional efforts to collect the new service instances IP hosts information, particularly in a dynamic auto-scaling environment; (2) the routing rules update on the router/load balancer service takes a significant amount of time to become effective because of cache on each node in routing path, thus affecting the service's version overlap or availability. To address these challenges, solutions like Netflix and Kubernetes use service discovery-based solutions (Zuul and Eureka [19, 20], ISTIO [23]) for VM and container deployments, as illustrated in Fig. 2.

In this paper, we use a test service named hereafter "My-Service", which registers its release version 1 for Blue and version 2 for Green. It uses node 1 and node 2 for the current, Blue service instance and node 3 and node 4 for the new, Green service instance. The incoming traffic reaches our Blue environment via a secure gateway, e.g., IBM DataPower for VMs and Kubernetes Ingress for the Kube cluster, which validates the applications calls credentials for My-Service and routes the calls to the dynamic router. My-Service is deployed on a cluster with multiple nodes. In order to support the automated service lifecycle management, and hence automatic deployment and switching of release versions, we leverage automation pipelines such as IBM Urban Code Deploy (UCD) [15] and IBM Cloud Delivery Pipeline [24]. In the pipeline, all the deployment locations are managed through the cloud management API, e.g., SoftLayer API for VMs and Kubectl API for Kubernetes. We first deploy two service instances in the target environments (Blue and Green), then we trigger the version switching process by invoking the pipeline as detailed hereafter.

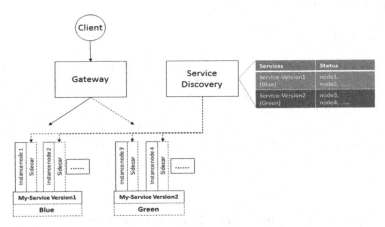

Fig. 2. Implementation for service discovery based Blue/Green Deployment. (Color figure online)

3.1 Blue/Green Deployment with Eureka and Zuul

We implemented this technique for VM based environments where a node in Fig. 2 indicates a VM hosting a service instance. Zuul, as the dynamic router, queries the service registry, Eureka, by using the service name from each incoming call, to retrieve the actual Blue IP hosts where to load balance the calls. To enable My-services' nodes to register with Eureka, Netflix uses a sidecar agent on each node to communicate with the service registry server. Hence, we need to install the sidecar agent on each node and manage the sidecar's configuration file to detect the service registry server, register itself and start sending the health check heartbeats necessary to preserve the registration.

Zuul is continuing to route the traffic to those nodes tagged "My-Service-BLUE-ENV" in Eureka, during the backend nodes being replaced with those installed with the new service version. For the end user, this is a black box of traffic shifting from the old service version to the new one. The traffic switch is controlled via a pipeline orchestration tool (e.g. UCD or Jenkins). This approach does not require load balancer rule updates, nor DNS updates, nor router reboot, aiming for a real zero downtime switch.

3.2 Blue/Green Deployment with Kubernetes and ISTIO

We implemented this technique for the container based deployments. The container cluster environment is set up using the IBM Cloud Kubernetes service. In this case, a node in Fig. 2 indicates a pod which runs a service instance. ISTIO is the dynamic router that parses the uri of each incoming call for the service name, queries based on the service name to retrieve the hosts registered for the service and routes then the call to the retrieved Blue hosts load balancing the calls. To enable My-Service' pod to register with ISTIO, an istio-sidecar is used on each pod to communicate with ISTIO. Hence, we need to manage the pod deployment configuration to make it inject the istio-sidecar with the service instance and register itself to ISTIO. All the requests to the targeted service will be routed by ISTIO according to the predefined routing policies.

Similar to the automation for VM based environment, we leveraged the IBM Cloud Delivery Pipeline to enable the automation for service instance deployment and traffic routing configuration update.

4 Blue/Green Experimental Setup and Evaluation Metrics

4.1 Experimental Setup

We implement with Node.js for My-Service as test service API which returns when called its version information, and deploy it in two identical environments as instances of the service configured with different version information, i.e., "version1" for Blue and "version2" for Green. Moreover, we use a Switcher to shift the request traffic from one service instance (Blue) to the other (Green). In this paper, we implement the Switcher using five B/G deployment techniques: (1) AWS R53 DNS [11], (2) AWS Load Balancer-Auto Scaling Group (LB-ASG) [11], (3) Cloud Foundry Route Remapping (CF-RR) [12], (4) Netflix Service Discovery (NSD) based solution, and (5) Kubernetes Service Discovery (KSD) based solution. We also implement and deploy a Tester which sends curl requests every second and records the response routed from the Switcher. The response includes the request time, the response time, and the replied version information for each request.

To evaluate the selected Blue/Green deployment techniques performance, we setup five experiment environments for My-Service deployments as described in following.

For the AWS R53 DNS based B/G deployment [11], we created two EC2 instances on AWS for service deployment, one for Blue and another one for Green., and configured a DNS (e.g., bgtest.res-lab.ibm.biz) with the public IP of the Blue EC2 instance.

For the AWS LB-ASG based B/G deployment [11], we created two AMI images with two different versions of service. And we also created a Launch Template, an auto scaling group (ASG) instance and a load balancer (LB) instance as required to work with the ASG instance to route the request at the unique (LB) access endpoint when the backend EC2 instance is changed.

For the CF-RR based B/G deployment [12] on a container-based architecture, we published two Node.js applications (Blue and Green) on Cloud Foundry with two different versions of the service, and developed a switch script on the client side using the CF CLI to trigger the route remapping.

For the Eureka and Zuul based B/G deployment, we created two VMs on Soft-Layer, one serving as Zuul server, and another one serving as Eureka server. We also created two more VM, deployed the Eureka sidecar on each of them, and then deployed the service with two different versions on each VM. We developed an UCD process to manage the sidecar's configuration and operation as described in Sect. 3.2, including the "update registration" process.

For the Kube and ISTIO based B/G deployment, we deployed ISTIO (v1.0) within istio namespace (it is used to isolate and manage a set of resource group in Kube) in Kubernetes, and created another two namespaces "BlueBox" and "GreenBox" to deploy container with different service version. In a routing rule of ISTIO, we predefined two destination environment for BlueBox and GreenBox, and control the request traffic routing with managing the workload weight in the destination rules.

In order to reduce the impact of noise data in our experiment environments, we run the experiments ten times for each use case in each environment, and used the arithmetic mean to get the average performance metrics as detailed in the next section.

4.2   Blue/Green Deployment Performance Metrics

Ideally, the switch from Blue to Green should be effective immediately, as shown in Fig. 3(A), i.e., when the switch is activated, all incoming traffic requests are immediately routed to the new service release (version 2) without delay or error. However, in reality, the switch is always followed by a period of inconsistency as shown in Fig. 3 (B) when some incoming traffic requests are routed to the current service release (version 1) while other incoming traffic requests are routed to version 2. The reason for this inconsistency dwells within the distributed nature of the information identifying a service instance deployed in the environment. The propagation of the switch from the Blue service version to the Green service version is specific to each implementation of the B/G deployment techniques. To compare the performance of each B/G techniques, we define four analysis metrics, illustrated in Fig. 3(C) and described here after.

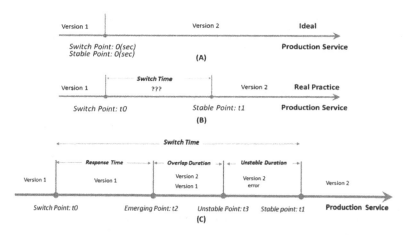

Fig. 3. Comparison between Ideal (A) and real (B) lifecycle of Blue/Green deployment traffic switch; and (C) performance indexes definition for switching Traffic. (Color figure online)

Let t0, called the Switch Point, be the activation time of switching the service versions, i.e., the moment when the information related to the new service version, is made available in the production environment. Let t1, called the Stable Point, be the time corresponding to a consistent successful response to the incoming traffic from the new service version without any response from the original service version. The time difference between t1 and t0, called the Switch Time as Eq. (1), indicates the duration of the B/G deployment and it is our first comparison metric.

$$Switch\,Time = t1 - t0 \tag{1}$$

In the ideal case, the *Switch Time* is zero given that no delay or error occurred when switching the releases. In the real case, we aim to minimize this value.

Let t2, called the *Emerging Point*, be the time when the new service version is observed for the first time in reply to the incoming traffic. The time difference between t2 and t0 indicates the *Response Time* as Eq. (2), to the activation of the switch to the new service version. This is the second comparison metric.

$$Response\,Time = t2 - t0 \tag{2}$$

Let t3, called the *Unstable Point*, indicate the time when the new service version becomes unavailable resulting in an error reply to the incoming traffic. We call the *Unstable Duration* as Eq. (3), the time interval when the new service version is unavailable during the switch period. This is our third comparison metric.

$$Unstable\,Duration = t1 - t3 \tag{3}$$

Finally, our forth comparison metric is the *Overlap Duration* as Eq. (4) which indicates the time interval when the service's two versions are both observed in reply to the incoming traffic. This is the error free time between the *Emerging Point t2* and the *Stable Point t1*, as follows:

$$Overlap\,Duration = t1 - t2 - Unstable\,Duration \tag{4}$$

The aim of all the B/G deployment techniques is to minimize the *Switch Time*:

$$Min\,(Switch\,Time) = Min\,(Response\,Time,\,Overlap\,Duration,\,Unstable\,Duration) \tag{5}$$

5   Experimental Results and Analysis

In the experiments for AWS R53 DNS based B/G deployment, we observed that the Response Time is about 3 min (178 s), while the *Overlap Duration* is about 10 s, as shown in Fig. 4. The root cause for such a large delay on the *Response Time* is due to the DNS functionality, i.e., its caching mechanism used to speeds up the process by storing information for periods of time and re-using it for future DNS queries.

Besides the cache on the nodes in the routing path towards the target service instance, the client and the browser could also use local cache for the target domain name. Thus, there is a long period to update all cache systems on the routing path when the DNS configuration is updated to point to another service instance (i.e., version 2).

Additionally, if the original service instance is still up, the requests will observe an overlap of service response as version 1 or version 2 randomly on different routing path due to the cache.

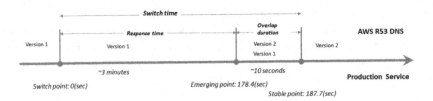

Fig. 4. Experiment result & analysis for AWS R53 DNS based Blue/Green Deployment. (Color figure online)

The experimental results for AWS LB-ASG based B/G deployment are illustrated in Fig. 5 and show a shorter *Response Time* than those in the previous DNS based solution. This is due to the requests being routed to the same endpoint of the Load Balancer (LB). The LB is configured with the internal routing rule to forward the requests to a working node in the target group which is integrated with ASG [11]. However, there is delay for the scale-in/scale-out nodes in AWS ASG, which causes an overlap when both version 1 node and version 2 node are present at the same time in the group. This confuses the LB into sending requests to version 1 node which impacts the *Overlap Duration* in this B/G deployment. Moreover, even when the version 1 node is removed from ASG, the LB could still send request to the removed service instance due to health status update delay, which will lead to a response error (when the service is unavailable). Therefore we observe an *Unstable Duration* in these experiments.

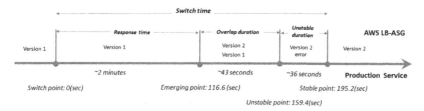

Fig. 5. Experiment result & analysis for AWS LB-ASG based Blue/Green Deployment. (Color figure online)

In the experiments for CF-RR based B/G deployment, the *Switch Time* is smaller than in the previous experiments (DNS based and LB-ASG based), as shown in Fig. 6. The *Response Time* is only about 18 s when another version (version 2) in Green environment is emerging in the request responses. As in the previous solutions, a version overlap is again observed (~ 7 s) when we switch the traffic from version 1 to version 2. After analyzing this technique [12], we found the root cause being the sequence of the CF CLI execution for mapping and unmapping the route between the Blue and Green service instances. The CLI execution takes time to make the mapping/unmapping operational. If we change the sequence of the CF CLI execution, to execute first "unmapping blue.example.com from blue", and then "mapping green to blue.example.com", we could remove the overlap. However, the risks is to render the service unavailable when the route of blue.example.com would be requested without an instance mapping.

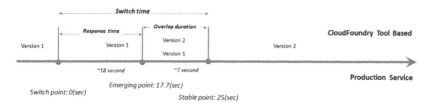

Fig. 6. Experiment result & analysis for CF route remapping based Blue/Green Deployment

In the experiments for our Eureka and Zuul based B/G deployment, we got similar performance results on the Switch Time with those in the CF-RR based B/G deployment. Additionally, no overlap or unstable duration was observed, as illustrated in Fig. 7. It is the service discovery direct configurations and its cache update mechanism which are different from the methods used in the AWS EC2 services and CF tools. In the Eureka and Zuul based B/G deployment implementation, there are multiple configurations we can customize.

Fig. 7. Experiment result & analysis for Eureka and Zuul based Blue/Green Deployment. (Color figure online)

As presented in Sect. 4, we optimized the time for service registry and cache update. Those optimizations are used to make sure the service instances in the Blue and Green environments register and de-register from the service registration and discovery server (Eureka) synchronously to minimize the switch time, while informing the router (Zuul) of those registry service instances expediently. To minimize the *Switch Time*, besides minimizing the *Response Time* (i.e., discover registry service update in time), we are also trying to minimize the *Overlap Duration* and *Unstable Duration*. This is achieved by controlling the cache content and the cache update interval for the Zuul server, since Zuul manages all the requests routing to the backend service instances. Given that we keep only one service instance (Blue or Green) in the service registry server, the ambiguity for the response (the service version in our experiments) is eliminated in this technique. Additionally, since the service instances are kept running in both the Blue and the Green environments, the risk for service unavailability is avoided even when we keep one service instance in the service cache of Zuul.

The experiments for Kube and ISTIO based B/G deployment, resulted in the best performance results on the *Switch Time* comparing with other B/G deployment solutions, with less than 1 s for switching as illustrated in Fig. 8. The traffic shifting is achieved with updating ISTIO routing policy as described in Sect. 4. Similar to the Netflix Eureka and Zuul solution, the Kube and ISTIO based B/G deployment shows no overlap or unstable duration. The traffic switch takes place immediately within 1 s which only causes a longer response time for the requests in transaction with from new version.

Fig. 8. Experiment result & analysis for KUBE and ISTIO based Blue/Green deployment. (Color figure online)

Table 1 summarizes the performance metrics values of our comparison between the five solutions of B/G deployment. It shows the average results of the performance across 10 sets of experiments for each solution, and the standard deviation values for those experiments in each solution.

Table 1. Blue/Green switch performance comparison summary

Metric (sec)	Switch traffic solutions				
	AWS R53-DNS based	AWS LB-ASG based	CF RR based	Zuul & Eureka	Kube & ISTIO
Response time	178.4	116.6	17.7	22.9	0.087
Standard deviation of RT	36.6	9.8	4.8	5.5	0.025
Overlap duration (OD)	9.3	42.8	7.3	0	0
Standard deviation of RT	6.1	8.6	6.3	0	0
Unstable duration (UD)	–	35.8	–	–	–
Standard Deviation of UD	–	9.8	–	–	–
Switch time (ST)	187.7	195.2	25	22.9	0.087
Standard deviation of ST	32.3	18.5	3.8	5.5	0.025

The DNS based solution which is a simple and general solution for switching traffic to a new service instance, takes the longest time to switch the traffic due to its usage of cache, and introduces service version response ambiguity on the application/client side. Moreover, this method exhibits the maximum standard deviation for its metrics, which means its performance is the most unstable.

For the LB-ASG based solution, it is the service instance initialization from the Launch Template which takes very long during the response time interval. The performance could be improved if the Launch Template can support containers. Moreover, the AMI images creation for each service instance in the template is an extra load for the B/G deployment, which also limits the agility of the new version release.

The Service Discovery based method shows the best performance for switching traffic due to is minimal *Overlap Duration* time cost. This approach also solved the issue of the service unavailability, although it requires customized configurations and sidecar installation on the nodes of the B/G environments, which is an extra load that we addressed via automation pipeline (e.g. UCD). All service instances are running via Kube DNS while ISTIO provides traffic routing in the service mesh for our container environment on the Kube special "VPN" (virtual private network) without outside network routing path. This is key to eliminate the cache on the routing path shown in other solutions and which impacts the overlap duration performance.

6 Conclusion

In this paper, we discussed a continuous delivery methodology, Blue/Green deployment. The most prevalent solutions for implementing Blue/Green deployments were investigated and their performance compared and analyzed. The DNS based solution provides a simple approach that can be used in environments equipped with DNS servers. However, it performs very poor when it comes to switching over traffic between service releases. AWS Load Balancer & Auto-Scaling-Group (ASG) based solution can achieve cost efficiency continuous delivery by keeping only one environment running. However, it takes a relatively long time to initialize a new service instance update. CloudFoundry Remapping Router (CF-RR) is an approach to update a service's route mapping which showed a good response time. CF-RR switches traffic from a service's old version to the new version once the new version becomes available. However, an overlap was observed when using this approach because there is a delay for client commands to take effect. CF-RR and AGS share the same weakness, this is they both work only for services running in their respective platforms. Lastly, the Service Discovery solution exhibited a better overall switch over performance by removing the overlap and unstable periods. The Eureka and Zuul solution however spends more time on the response phase than the CF-RR solution. Kube and ISTIO solution shows the best performance for the switch time, with the caveat that it only works for Kubernetes based environments. Eureka and Zuul approach provides a general way to support any services.

Based on the analysis of the characteristics of each solution, it is important to choose a suitable Blue/Green deployment for service continuous delivery according to the run-time conditions. Getting services up and running quickly while achieving upgradeability and easy to manage deployments with minimized risk, are key to delivering fast and reliable deployments of new technology investments.

Our future work will focus on investigating the more complex scenario of upgrade on hybrid cloud. In such case, the challenge will be the cache synchronization among nodes on different clouds with different service discovery instances, while minimizing the overlap duration and service instance conflict.

References

1. Humble, J., Farley, D.: Continuous Delivery: Reliable Software Releases Through Build, Test, and Deployment Automation (Adobe Reader). Pearson Education, London (2010)
2. Chen, L.: Continuous delivery: huge benefits, but challenges too. IEEE Softw. **32**(2), 50–54 (2015)
3. Soni, M.: End to end automation on cloud with build pipeline: the case for DevOps in insurance industry, continuous integration, continuous testing, and continuous delivery. In: IEEE Cloud Computing in Emerging Markets (CCEM), pp. 85–89, 25 November 2015
4. Fowler, M.: Blue Green Deployment (2010). https://martinfowler.com/bliki/BlueGreen-Deployment.html
5. https://searchitoperations.techtarget.com/definition/blue-green-deployment
6. https://medium.com/netflix-techblog/deploying-the-netflix-api-79b6176cc3f0
7. Cloudflare global managed DNS: https://www.cloudflare.com/dns
8. How to set up a host name with DigitalOcean. https://www.digitalocean.com/community/tutorials/how-to-set-up-a-host-name-with-digitalocean
9. Google Cloud DNS. https://cloud.google.com/dns/docs/
10. Ellis, N.: An example Blue/Green deployment using Tutum and Cloudflare (for DNS) (2016). https://gist.github.com/neilellis/2d25f0ade3d6cae6f7c9
11. Amazon: Blue/Green deployments on AWS. Whitepaper, August 2016. https://d0.awsstatic.com/whitepapers/AWS_Blue_Green_Deployments.pdf
12. Cloud Foundry: Using Blue-Green deployment to reduce downtime and risk. https://docs.cloudfoundry.org/devguide/deploy-apps/Blue/Green.html#map-green
13. Digital Ocean: How to use Blue-Green deployments to release software safely. https://www.digitalocean.com/community/tutorials/how-to-use-Blue/Green-deployments-to-release-software-safely
14. Danial S.: Thought Works, Implementing Blue-Green deployments with AWS (2013) https://www.thoughtworks.com/insights/blog/implementing-Blue/Green-deployments-aws
15. IBM UrbanCode Deploy. https://developer.ibm.com/urbancode/products/urbancode-deploy/
16. Klusak, V.: Klokan Technologies, Blue-Green Deployment with Docker and Nginx (2016). https://blog.klokantech.com/2016/08/Blue/Green-deployment-with-docker-and.html
17. Pérez, I.S.: Simple Blue/Green deployments with Docker and Nginx (2016). http://dukebody.com/?p=511
18. Holý, J.: DZone/Devops Zone, WebApp Blue/Green Deployment Without Breaking Sessions (2016). https://dzone.com/articles/webapp-bluegreen-deployment
19. Netflix Eureka. https://github.com/Netflix/eureka/wiki
20. Netflix Zuul. https://github.com/Netflix/zuul/wiki
21. Zero-Downtime Rolling Deployments With Netflix's Eureka and Zuul, March 2019. https://www.credera.com/blog/technology-solutions/zero-downtime-rolling-deployments-netflixs-eureka-zuul/
22. Janakiram, M.S.V.: Blue/Green Deployments with Kubernetes and Istio, October 2018https://thenewstack.io/tutorial-blue-green-deployments-with-kubernetes-and-istio/
23. Istio. https://istio.io
24. IBM Cloud Toolchain. https://cloud.ibm.com/devops/create?bss_account=49f48a067ac-4433a911740653049e83d&ims_account=167466

AutoCADep: An Approach for Automatic Cloud Application Deployment

Saddam Hocine Hiba[(✉)] and Meriem Belguidoum

LIRE Laboratory, Constantine 2 University, Constantine, Algeria
{saddam.hiba,meriem.belguidoum}@univ-constantine2.dz

Abstract. One of the key aspects related to cloud application deployment is its automatic and flexible management. However, existing solutions are ad-hoc and do not deal with dynamic reconfiguration and scaling as well as is expected. In this work, we propose AutoCADep, an approach to automatically manage the deployment, reconfiguration and elasticity aspects of cloud applications. It provides a higher level of abstraction from modelling to specify the deployment process. Therefore, we use MDA approach, MAPE-K loop and ECA rules in order to automate the deployment process of parametrized component based applications. We introduce an external DSL based on an extended metamodel gathering all relevant deployment concepts and architecture description of applications. Finally, we illustrate the automatic deployment management through a case study.

Keywords: Cloud computing · Automatic deployment · MDA · DSL · MAPE-K · ECA rules

1 Introduction

Cloud computing [16] is one of the emerging technology that attracted more and more attention from the industry. However, its implementation remains very complicated due to the diversity of providers, platforms, languages and standard technologies. Moreover, the company's strategies involve several requirements concerning the reliability and flexibility of their provided services.

Therefore, in order to deliver all this variety of services, the cloud application deployment should be automatic and flexible. The current way to deploy an application is highly dependent on cloud providers, in which most of the deployment process is done manually or based on specific company tools and proprietary APIs. Moreover, the diversity of cloud providers requires learning their deployment tools as well as reimplementing parts of the application in some cases, and consequently, changing from one provider to another is too expensive and time-consuming.

In this work, we aim to propose a generic, reusable and structured approach to automatically manage cloud application deployment, on one hand by reducing the time and effort and having the freedom to choose services from different

© Springer Nature Switzerland AG 2020
S. Yangui et al. (Eds.): ICSOC 2019 Workshops, LNCS 12019, pp. 82–94, 2020.
https://doi.org/10.1007/978-3-030-45989-5_7

vendors and organizations. On the other hand, to have a dynamic deployment that can take into account the internal architecture of component-based applications. For this, we use the MDA approach [14], MAPE-K control loop [10] and ECA rules [8] to propose an external Domain-Specific Language [19] allowing automatic deployment of component-based applications including automatic reconfigurations on demand according to the description of its internal architecture. The DSL has modelling capabilities to represent the structure of cloud applications in terms of components and their deployment. The benefits of the language are to take into account the diversity of features provided by cloud environments and to support different application scenarios, such as migrating existing applications to the cloud, developing, deploying, new cloud applications, or optimizing them. It allows automating the code generation following the principle of the MDA approach which includes the CIM and PIM model (representing the abstract and concrete DSL syntax) towards the PSM model DSL code generation). Therefore, we apply the MDA approach together with the DSL to provide high-level modelling capabilities for better representation of the deployment and elasticity domain.

We intend to achieve the objectives mentioned above by defining an extended metamodel for deployment management, offering a DSL for Automatic Cloud Application Deployment (AutoCADep), and developing a platform that uses the DSL to provide an execution runtime engine for the deployment process.

The rest of the paper is structured as follows. Section 2 reviews some related work and gives a comparative study. In Sect. 3, we describe our proposed architecture and define a DSL for the AutoCADep approach. Section 4 illustrates the proposal through a case study. In Sect. 5, we conclude the paper and outline our future work.

2 Related Work

Several approaches have been proposed for modelling and managing automatically cloud application deployment. Libraries and configuration management tools are one of these deployment mechanisms, the liberties such as DeltaCloud [7], jClouds [13], and LibCloud [15], they provide abstraction layers to facilitate the provisioning and the deployment of cloud application through a single interface. The configuration management tools such as Chef [6], Puppet [20] and CFEngine [24] are DevOps tools for automation of deployment, they share the same idea of automating configuration tasks by providing their own DSL. However, these tools are available at the code level and do not provide a general abstraction layer or application architecture to be used by the deployment designer to properly model and deploy the application.

The European projects such as Reservoir [21], mOSAIC [17], PaaSage [18], MODAClouds [2] and others, they provide platforms, APIs, languages, and models for the development, description and deployment of application at IaaS or PaaS levels, some of these projects support elasticity of applications through different techniques. MODAClouds is based on a model-driven approach to provide methods, a decision support system (DDS), an Integrated Development Environment (IDE) and an execution environment for high-level design and automatic deployment of applications in a multi-cloud with guaranteed QoS. In general, European projects represent a middleware solution that intermediate between cloud applications and cloud providers, covering all three phases of the cloud application lifecycle: the development, the deployment, and the execution. This projects lack a complete covering of the deployment phases and do not specify the application architecture.

Some academic works have been proposed to address this area. For example TOSCA, CloudML, Pim4Cloud-DSL, VAMP and CoMe4ACloud. TOSCA [4]stands for Topology and Orchestration Specification for Cloud Applications, it is an XML-based language used to describe cloud applications and their automated deployment and management. TOSCA conceptually consists of two different parts: (i) application topologies provide the structural description of the applications, its components and their interdependency relationships. (ii) management plans are the standardized description of the application's management by plans. The plans combine these management capabilities to create management tasks, which can be executed to deploy the application.

CloudML [5] is proposed as a cloud modelling language according to MDE techniques and methods, to provide a DSML for modelling the provisioning, deployment, monitoring, and adaptation of multi-cloud systems at design-time and their enactment at runtime. Pim4Cloud-DSL [12] is a component-based approach to model software deployment. This approach is provided as a DSL, which is given to the software designer. The language is based on a reduced component metamodel and supports the modelling of the deployment relationship between components. VAMP (Virtual Applications Management Platform) [22] ensures an autonomous and a generic deployment of any distributed application in the cloud. VAMP offers a formalism based on Open Virtualization Format (OVF) to describe the virtual machines and the distributed application using an architecture description language (ADL). Also, it provides a protocol for self-configuration and auto-activation of applications. CoMe4ACloud [1] Constraints and Model Engineering for Autonomic Clouds, is a generic model-based architecture to provide autonomous runtime management of heterogeneous cloud systems. The approach uses constraint programming as a decision-making tool to automatically obtain system configurations respecting specified SLA contracts.

2.1 Summary

The Table 1 compares the closest works to our proposal according to some criteria related to the application deployment

- Mechanism: describes how the deployment is assured, it can be: manual, language-based, script-based or model-based
- Deployment automation: represents the automation strategy used for the deployment
- Deployment phases: represent the covered deployment phases

Table 1. Comparison with some related work

Work	Mechanism	Deployment automation	Deployment phases	Application architecture	Elasticity management	Input	Output	Runtime support
DevOps tools [6, 20, 24]	Language, script	Control system	Installation, reconfiguration	-	-	Configuration plans	Execution plans	+
MODAClouds [2]	Language, model	-	Installation, uninstallation, update	-	-	Model representation	Code representation	+
TOSCA [4]	Language, script	Management plans	Release, installation, uninstallation	Topologies	-	Graph	Container of TOSCA	+
Cloudml [5]	Language, model	-	Installation, adaptation	-	-	Metamodel	Environment of models@runtime	+
VAMP [9]	Language, model	Protocol for auto-configuration and activation	Release, installation, activation, reconfiguration	-	-	Formalism on OVF and ADL for the applications description	Virtual images, protocol for auto-configuration and activation	+
Pim4Cloud DSL [12]	Language	-	Installation, update	-	-	Metamodel	Deployment descriptors	-
CoMe4A-Cloud [1]	Model, language	MAPE-K	Reconfiguration	TOSCA topologies	+	Topology metamodel	Configuration model	+
AutoCADep	Language, model	MAPE-K	Release, installation, activation, reconfiguration, deactivation, uninstallation	Based on a formal intra-dependeny language	+	Metamodel	Java code generation, API	+

- Application architecture: represents the description of the application architecture
- Elasticity management: represents the management of elasticity strategies.
- Input: represents the input deployment solution
- Output: the result obtained after the deployment process
- Runtime support: represents a set of mechanisms that supports the runtime aspect.

We noticed that the aforementioned works did not completely cover all the deployment phases, doesn't have a generic deployment model that includes all relevant deployment aspects. These deployment solutions dealt with the cloud application as a black box and do not provide a clear description of the application architecture (intra-dependencies descriptions) and deployment phases. Indeed, an automatic cloud application deployment approach should (i) provides an abstract description level of deployment concepts; (ii) provides a language that describes the application internal architecture and deployment management; (iii) carries out cloud application deployment in an automatic way. For this, the novelty of our approach to offer an automatic, parametrized, and dynamic deployment depending on the intra-dependency architecture of the application to provide high-level modelling capabilities for a better representation of the deployment domain.

3   AutoCADep Approach

To address the issues outlined in Sect. 2, we present our approach named Auto-CADep for Automatic Cloud Application Deployment. AutoCADep provides a higher level of abstraction for modelling and specifying the deployment process of applications at the SaaS layer (design time), and a PaaS platform to manage the deployment and elasticity of cloud applications automatically (runtime). AutoCADep includes an external DSL based on a generic metamodel gathering all relevant application deployment and elasticity concepts, it is also based on a formal intra-dependency language [3] used to describe the internal application architecture. This section describes the AutoCADep approach and the proposed DSL.

3.1   AutoCADep Architecture

Figure 1 presents the architecture of the proposed approach. In step (1), the application producer creates the application and prepares its installable packages, then sends them to the deployment designer. In step (2), the deployment designer creates the application description and its deployment constraints using the proposed DSL. In step (3), the deployment operator uses the platform to manage the deployment by adding new deployment entities or performing reconfigurations using the deployment runtime engine. It groups the components used to automate the deployment management such as MAPE-K components and ECA rules. These components (monitor, analyser, planner, executor) are responsible for monitoring the system (using sensors), analyzing metrics, planning actions and executing them (using actuators). In the last step (4), the administrator supervises the application resources, while the users have access to the application, they can add requirements and preferences during the deployment process.

3.2   AutoCADep DSL

AutoCADep DSL is a textual language used to describe cloud application and deployment concepts. It is developed with Xtext Framework [23], it is an Eclipse framework for implementing programming languages and DSLs. Xtext covers all aspects of a complete language infrastructure, starting from the parser, code generator, or interpreter, up to a complete Eclipse IDE integration (with all the typical IDE features).

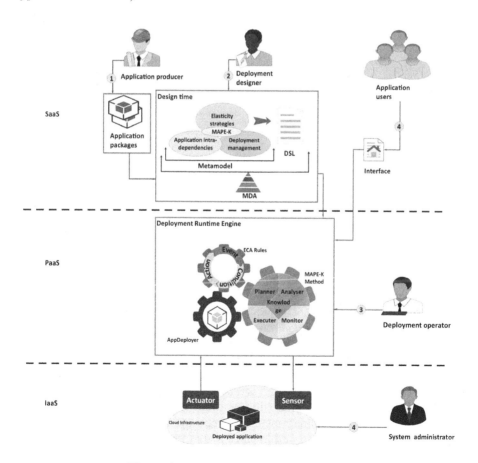

Fig. 1. AutoCADep architecture overview

Abstract Syntax. the conceptual metamodel presented in this part describes the proposed DSL abstract syntax which extends the model proposed in [11] to cover the intra-dependency application architecture. So, in this paper we present the cloud deployment models with the cloud application architecture (Fig. 2).

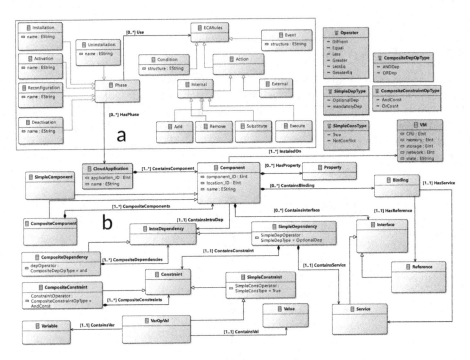

Fig. 2. (a) the deployment metamodel, (d) the application Intra-dependencies metamodel

Deployment management metamodel is based on automatic rules to take into account the dynamic aspect of the deployment, we have extended to the metamodel with the ECA concept (i.e. Event, Condition and Action) to allow the automatic management of cloud application deployment phases such as: *Installation, Activation, Reconfiguration, Deactivation, Uninstallation*. The ECA rules are based on the MAPE-K mechanism (Fig. 1) to specify deployment or elasticity rules in a declarative way. When an *event* is triggered, a *condition* (a logical expression) have to be checked and then an *action* will be performed. There are two kinds of action: the first is related to the internal architecture of the component based application (e.g. add, remove, substitute, etc.), the second one is related to the elasticity management (e.g. replication, migration, resizing, etc.) [11]. The internal actions are: *add/remove* a component or a service, *substitute* (replace) a component or a service with another and *execute* a shell scripts inside service VMs or containers.

Concrete Syntax. based on the Ecore metamodel (Fig. 2), the concrete syntax of our proposed language is generated. This grammar is expressed in Backus Normal Form (BNF). Listing 1.1 presents the principal rule named CloudApplication, with its hierarchical subcomponents.

```
CloudApplication returns CloudApplication:
'CloudApplication' name=ID
('components' '{' ContainsComponent+=Component
ContainsComponent+=Component)* '}' )
('phases' '{' hasDeploymentPhase+=Phase
(hasDeploymentPhase+=Phase)*'}' )? '}';
```

Listing 1.1. The application rule grammar

The Semantic Rules. some aspects of the implementation of the language have an impact on what is required for a semantic model to be validated. The semantics gives meaning to the syntactic elements of the language. In the proposed DSL, the semantics is verified through the following concepts:

- Scope: this term refers to the calculation of elements of the model that can be referenced by a particular reference. For example, listing 1.2 shows the binding rule grammar that contains two references: HasService, HasReference.

```
Binding returns Binding:
'bind'HasService=[Service]   'to'HasReference=[Reference];
```

Listing 1.2. The binding rule grammar

- Validator: Xtext and Xtend automatically support these types of validations: syntax, cross-reference, and concrete syntax validation. In addition, we specify more constraints specific to our model.

4   Case Study

In this section, we illustrate our proposed approach through the E-learning cloud deployment. E-learning is an online learning system based on formalised teaching, it provides educational services and electronic resources. The end-users of this application are students, teachers, and administrators. E-learning must be installed on a web server, which is a cloud provider service. As shown in Fig. 3, this application consists of the following components:

- Assembly is composed of four components: Database, WebServer, Extention, Databasebackup.
- Database offers *mysqls* service that represents MySQL Server.
- WebServer provides *ws* service which is the application server, this service requires the *dbmysqls* service of the Database component, and other constraints.

– Extension provides *ssls* service for establishing an encrypted link between the WebServer and browsers of users.
– Databasebackup: refers to the process of having copies that are recoverable when data is lost during an unfortunate event.

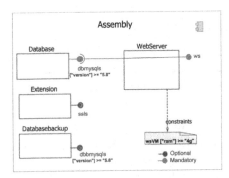

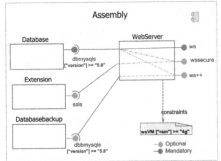

Fig. 3. E-learning components   **Fig. 4.** E-learning reconfiguration

Based on the AutoCADep architecture, we have developed a platform that includes a DSL web editor and execution/validation runtime engine. This is used by the deployer to automatically develop, deploy and manage applications (following the MAPE-k loop and ECA rules). The proposed DSL web editor is an IDE with powerful features such as immediate feedback, auto-completion, suggested corrections and syntax-aware editor (highlight DSL keywords). Furthermore, it allows the analysis, code generation and semantic validation. A DSL description of E-learning application is presented in Listing 1.3. Table 2 shows how do we apply the proposed DSL to describe the application internal architecture and analyse automatic deployment. Therefore, we present four scenarios, install the E-learning application, perform reconfigurations to adapt to the changes (increased on memory usage) and execute two reconfiguration rules according to the application user requirements (add services). Figure 4 captures new intra-dependencies added on the application architecture according to the reconfigurations rules that added services.

The runtime engine component is responsible for deploying the applications created by the web DSL editor on the AutoCADep platform (left side of Fig. 5). First, once the creation of DSL description is completed, the runtime engine will automatically generate the java code (right side of Fig. 5). Then, the engine creates an instance of the application class from the java file generated to read the application information: name, properties, components, and phases. Next, it builds the dependency graph of the components to establish the order in which they must be deployed and activated with their respective services. After that, the services of components will be deployed at the corresponding cloud provider (by the engine). Finally, it activates the applications in the following

```
CloudApplication Elearning {
components
compositeComponent Assembly {
subComponents
optional component Extension {
interfaces
service ssls
intraDeps (true => ssls) },
component Database {
interfaces
service dbmysqls
intraDeps (true => dbmysqls) },
component Databasebuckup {
interfaces
service dbbmysqls
intraDeps (true => dbbmysqls) },
component WebServer {
interfaces
service ws,
reference dbmysqlr, dbbmysqlr,sslr
intraDeps (dbmysqls["version"]>="5.8" => ws)
AND optional(ssls => wssecure)}
bindings
bind dbmysqls to dbmysqlr,
bind dbbmysqls to dbbmysqlr,
bind ssls to sslr   } }
```

Listing 1.3. Elearning DSL description

order: installation, configuration, activation, reconfiguration, deactivation, and uninstallation. Each phase is run in a limited period of time, except for the reconfiguration phase that takes longer (the elasticity rules will be executed in this phase), start after the Activation phases, and end when the application is uninstalled.

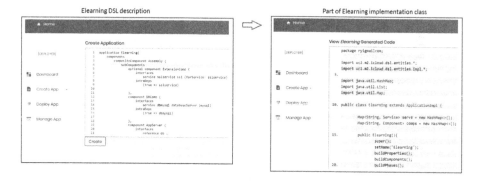

Fig. 5. AutoCADep platform

Table 2. DSL rules of some deployment phases

DSL code	Description

`installation setupElearning {`
`execute(`
`executeCmd(service:ws,cmd:["link1"]),`
`executeCmd(service:dbmysqls,cmd:["link2"])}`
	execute some shell scripts to activate the application.

`reconfiguration resizing {`
`on(service ws )`
`when(ws consume >= 80% of memory in 5 min)`
`execute(resizing memory 2)}`
	when the VM is increased to 80 % in 5 minutes, the monitor treats the event and the analyser verifies the condition. Then, the planner schedules the execution of the action received by the analyser (resizing). The new reconfiguration will be carried out by the executor.

`reconfiguration add_ssls{`
`on(app "Elearning")`
`when(this[activate_ssls] == false)`
`execute(addComponent Extension)}`
	the rule adds SSL service (ssls) provided by Extension component to the WebServer.

`reconfiguration add_dbbmysqls{`
`on(app "Elearning")`
`when(this[activate_dbbmysqls] == false)`
`execute(`
`addComponent Databasebackup)}`
	the rule adds database backup service (dbbmysqls) of Databasebackup component to the WebServer.

5   Conclusion and Future Work

In this paper, we have described our approach AutoCADep for the automatic deployment of cloud applications. The proposed solution is based on MDA, MAPE-k loop and the ECA rules. The deployment constraints and cloud application architecture (intra-dependencies) are described using a DSL from an elaborated metamodel. The reconfiguration is based on the application description which is represented by a parametrized couples of provided services and requirements. This reconfiguration can be represented by adding, removing or substituting components and/or services within an application). The external view of reconfiguration is represented by cloud elasticity management (resizing, replication, migration, etc). As future work, we plan to verify formally the automatic cloud application deployment, therefore, we have to use MDA transformation tools from the proposed metamodel and DSL to a formal method for system level modelling and analysis like event-B.

References

1. Al-Shara, Z., Alvares, F., Bruneliere, H., Lejeune, J., Prud'Homme, C., Ledoux, T.: CoMe4ACloud: an end-to-end framework for autonomic cloud systems. Future Gener. Comput. Syst. **86**, 339–354 (2018). https://doi.org/10.1016/j.future.2018. 03.039. https://hal.archives-ouvertes.fr/hal-01762716
2. Ardagna, D., et al.: Modaclouds: a model-driven approach for the design and execution of applications on multiple clouds. In: Proceedings of the 4th International Workshop on Modeling in Software Engineering, pp. 50–56. IEEE Press (2012)
3. Belguidoum, M., Dagnat, F.: Dependency management in software component deployment. Electron. Notes Theor. Comput. Sci. **182**, 17–32 (2007). https://doi. org/10.1016/j.entcs.2006.09.029
4. Binz, T., Breitenbücher, U., Kopp, O., Leymann, F.: TOSCA: portable automated deployment and management of cloud applications. In: Bouguettaya, A., Sheng, Q., Daniel, F. (eds.) Advanced Web Services, pp. 527–549. Springer, New York (2014)
5. Brandtzæg, E., Mosser, S., Mohagheghi, P.: Towards CloudML, a model-based approach to provision resources in the clouds. In: 8th European Conference on Modelling Foundations and Applications (ECMFA), pp. 18–27 (2012)
6. Chef - Automate Your Infrastructure, February 2019. https://www.chef.io/chef/
7. deltacloud, January 2018. http://deltacloud.apache.org
8. Dittrich, K.R., Gatziu, S., Geppert, A.: The active database management system manifesto: a rulebase of ADBMS features. In: Sellis, T. (ed.) RIDS 1995. LNCS, vol. 985, pp. 1–17. Springer, Heidelberg (1995). https://doi.org/10.1007/3-540-60365-4_116
9. Etchevers, X., Coupaye, T., Boyer, F., De Palma, N.: Self-configuration of distributed applications in the cloud. In: 2011 IEEE International Conference on Cloud Computing (CLOUD), pp. 668–675. IEEE (2011)
10. Group, I., et al.: An Architectural Blueprint for Autonomic Computing. IBM White paper, June 2006

11. Hiba, S.H., Belguidoum, M.: A DSL for elastic component-based cloud application. Int. J. High Perform. Comput. Network. **15**(1–2), 58–71 (2019). https://doi.org/10.1504/IJHPCN.2019.103543. https://www.inderscienceonline.com/doi/abs/10.1504/IJHPCN.2019.103543

12. IKT S.: Towards a domain-specific language to deploy applications in the clouds. In: Cloud Computing 2012, p. 225 (2012)

13. jclouds: The Java Multi-Cloud Toolkit, February 2019. http://jclouds.apache.org/

14. Kleppe, A.G., Warmer, J.B., Bast, W.: MDA Explained: The Model Drivenarchitecture: Practice and Promise. Addison-Wesley Professional, Boston (2003)

15. libcloud: One Interface To Rule Them All, February 2019. http://libcloud.apache.org

16. Mell, P., Grance, T., et al.: The NIST definition of cloud computing (2011)

17. Moscato, F., Aversa, R., Di Martino, B., Fortiş, T.F., Munteanu, V.: An analysis of mosaic ontology for cloud resources annotation. In: 2011 Federated Conference on Computer Science and Information Systems (FedCSIS), pp. 973–980. IEEE (2011)

18. A Model-based cross cloud development and deployment platform, February 2019. https://paasage.ercim.eu/

19. Pastor, O., Molina, J.C.: Model-Driven Architecture in Practice: A Software Production Environment Based on Conceptual Modeling. Springer, Heidelberg (2007). https://doi.org/10.1007/978-3-540-71868-0

20. Puppets: Deliver better software, faster Make software discovery, management, and delivery automatic and pervasive with Puppet, February 2019. https://puppet.com/

21. Rochwerger, B., et al.: The reservoir model and architecture for open federated cloud computing. IBM J. Res. Dev. **53**(4), 4:1–4:11 (2009)

22. Salaün, G., Etchevers, X., De Palma, N., Boyer, F., Coupaye, T.: Verification of a self-configuration protocol for distributed applications in the cloud. In: Cámara, J., de Lemos, R., Ghezzi, C., Lopes, A. (eds.) Assurances for Self-Adaptive Systems. LNCS, vol. 7740, pp. 60–79. Springer, Heidelberg (2013). https://doi.org/10.1007/978-3-642-36249-1_3

23. Xtext: Xtext Home Page, February 2019. https://eclipse.org/Xtext

24. Zamboni, D.: Learning CFEngine 3: Automated System Administration for Sites of Any Size. O'Reilly Media, Inc., Sebastopol (2012)

Microservices Management on Cloud/Edge Environments

André Carrusca, Maria Cecília Gomes$^{(\boxtimes)}$, and João Leitão

NOVA LINCS & DI/FCT/UNL, Costa da Caparica, Portugal
a.carrusca@campus.fct.unl.pt, {mcg,jcleitao}@fct.unl.pt

Abstract. The microservices architecture is a promising approach for application development, deployment, and evolution, both on cloud and emerging fog/edge platforms. Microservices' single functionality, small size, and independent development/deployment support faster and cheaper scaling of pressing functionalities on cloud systems. They support applications' evolution via service reuse and smooth service modification/inclusion. Individual or sets of inter-related services may also be dynamically deployed onto resource-restricted nodes closer to end devices and data sources, which are typical of fog/edge computational platforms. The resulting system is very complex and impossible to be adequately managed manually. This work presents an automatic solution for microservices' deployment/replication in the fog/edge, adapting the system according to the runtime evaluation of client accesses and resource usage. The evaluation validates the adaptability and performance gains.

Keywords: Microservices architecture · Cloud and fog/edge computing · Self-adaptable applications

1 Introduction

The microservices architecture [7,10] presents several advantages for application development, deployment and evolution, in the accelerating omnipresent and omniscient digital world. Traditional monolithic architectures represent a single large application composed of tightly interdependent and non reusable components. In contrast, microservices applications combine small, single functionality, loosely coupled services, to implement more complex functionalities. Each microservice accesses its own private database, displays a well defined API, and may communicate with others directly (e.g. via RPC/REST protocols) or indirectly (e.g. via messaging/event systems). This allows their independent development with diverse technologies and their individual scaling, simplifying applications' reliability and continuous delivery responding to new requirements [1].

The constant need for evolving systems is intensified by the surge of both mobile and Internet of Things (IoT)/terminal devices, e.g. in the domain of

© Springer Nature Switzerland AG 2020
S. Yangui et al. (Eds.): ICSOC 2019 Workshops, LNCS 12019, pp. 95–108, 2020.
https://doi.org/10.1007/978-3-030-45989-5_8

Smart Cities/Health [27]. Traditionally, these types of applications are supported by services running on cloud platforms [20]. Yet such high number of client devices produce a large number of requests towards the *backend* services and generate huge amounts of data, requiring novel solutions adaptable to systems' evolution. Many of these services correspond to bandwidth intensive and increasingly popular applications like video-on-demand, streaming, or real time TV [3]. Also, the predicted huge number of IoT devices [9] will collect data needing to be mined and analysed (e.g. sensors dispersed over wide areas) and often with time restrictions (e.g. drone applications). It is so necessary to avoid latency degradation and guarantee the applications' QoS.

Hybrid Cloud/Edge Computing. Emerging solutions capitalise on the microservices architecture both as *cloud-native* applications [17] and applications distributed on novel hybrid cloud/edge platforms [32]. Applications rely on services in *cloud computing* [24] providing ubiquitous and on-demand access to shared resources perceived as unlimited (e.g. computational, storage, and network resources). Novel solutions capitalise on lighter, faster, and cheaper scaling of microservices in the cloud to support applications' variable geographical accesses and incremental evolution. This is the case of interactive applications with constant updates and performance/availability constraints [2, 21]. Novel solutions also may capitalise on cloud technologies' expansion to the periphery of the network. Namely, edge/fog computing [18, 34, 37] represent the usage of diverse heterogeneous computational resources on the continuum from the cloud datacenters to end devices. The resources range from routers, base stations, to microdatacenters/cloudlets. The result is a computational platform of highly heterogeneous nodes, geographically dispersed at large numbers, closer to end users and data sources, and that typically present reduce computational capabilities in comparison to cloud datacenters [3, 6, 8]. The microservices architecture is also adequate to exploit such capability restricted nodes since small services may be migrated/replicated in a faster way, according to user/application needs. This allows reducing the latency on accessing services, lowering the amount of data on transit in the communication infra-structure (e.g. by filtering/pre-processing data closer to data sources) and exploring an adequate usage of the computational infrastructure.

Problem and Goals. Computing in heterogeneous platforms composed by cloud nodes and a large number of highly heterogeneous edge resources presents several challenges for application development and management [19, 35]. Also, microservices applications are composed of a large number of services (and their replicas), each one with diverse functionalities, possibly a database, and diverse hardware/software needs. Services may have different levels of interaction (e.g. frequent/sporadic invocation of other services depending on the workload), which aggravates the overall management and debugging [11]. The services may have to be upscale and their databases replicated to improve the applications' performance and energy efficiency. In this setting, examples of challenges are adequate and flexible resource management solutions with service location/deployment depending on the origin/volume of user accesses and on the computing nodes' total/current resources and their cost; eventual dynamic migration/replication of microservices' databases following services' replicas; service coordination in a distributed context; the guarantee of security and privacy issues; etc.

Due to such management complexity, our long-term goal is to build an autonomic solution [14,18,28] for these systems. We envision a self-management solution composed of three dimensions for decoupled functionality/management:

(a) a service management component, discussed here, to deploy and scale individual and inter-related services (e.g. necessary for a particular functionality);
(b) a database management component responsible for the dynamic replication of microservices' databases whose replica instances may be widely dispersed;
(c) a monitoring component responsible for observing services (e.g. load/ location of accesses) and infrastructure nodes (e.g. current consumed resources) and timely providing the necessary information to the other two components.

Each dimension is self-adaptable on fulfilling its objective and cooperates with the other two towards establishing a global self-managing solution. The database component guarantees the consistency model of (the existing/newer replicas of) a particular microservice's database. The monitoring component flexibly collects and delivers a variable set of metricas with diverse time intervals and without incurring unaffordable overheads over the infrastructure's nodes and network.

Whereas we have already presented solutions advancing the database and monitoring dimensions, this work presents an automatic solution for microservice migration/replication contributing to a self-adaptable service management and, in the future, to an autonomic solution able to learn from applications' evolution and previous decisions and to predict adaptation requirements.

Document Organisation. The following section describes the proposed solution and it is followed by Sect. 3 that discusses the implementation and evaluation results. Section 4 presents the related work and Sect. 5 concludes the paper.

2   Proposed Solution

We present an automatic management approach for node allocation and service migration/replication within the emergent cloud/edge platforms. The objective is to improve the application's performance and the clients' perceived latency, and to adequately operate the infra-structure's resources. This in spite of the system's inherent complexity and dynamics both in terms of the infra-structure volatility (with failing/new nodes) and the dynamic application requirements. Namely, many cloud applications experience a high variability of accesses, and other applications rely on the large volumes of data generated from end devices at diverse locations, at variable times.

To respond to such variability, we propose a self-adaptable mechanism with a decision process based on an modifiable set of user defined constraints and

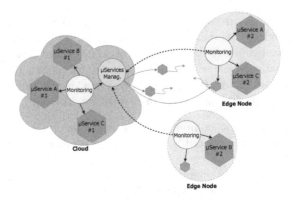

Fig. 1. A simplified view of the solution.

rules. The system's state is continuously monitored within an evaluation/decision feed-back loop, typical of self-adaptable systems [30] and autonomic systems [28]. At each iteration it evaluates (*a*) which services should be migrated or replicated, when, and to where, or be otherwise eliminated; and (*b*) which nodes need to be dynamically created/activated or eliminated, from a computational platform providing virtual nodes. The decisions in the loop are tuned to improve the applications' performance while avoiding possible system's destabilisations caused by too frequent updates. This means that some evaluations have to be confirmed in a few consecutive iterations before the corresponding decisions are applied. Figure 1 presents a simplified version of the solution's architecture with microservices' replicas deployed at the cloud and two edge nodes. A single (centralised) microservices management component, *uServices Manag.*, is located at the cloud and communicates with the monitoring components, one at each edge node. These are responsible to collect the relevant services' and nodes' metrics. In the continuous feedback loop, the *uServices Manag.* decides upon service scalability level and location, and the number and location of computational nodes.

2.1 The Architecture Components and Their Operation

The main architecture components in Fig. 1 include *microservices (uServices)* and their replicas, *computational nodes* in the cloud/edge, and the *service management component* and associated components e.g. a *monitoring component*. The uServices (typed as *frontend/backend*) and their interactions comprise the user application to be optimised. Each uService instance is placed in a container for its faster/lighter deployment on the nodes [26,29]. Each node is a *virtual machine* (VM), a basic resource management unit in cloud providers, where one or more containers may be deployed to [20]. The monitoring component collects the relevant service/node metrics as required by the service manager. The latter needs also the pre-configuration of services' and nodes' execution requirements, and the specification of the constraints/decision rules that guide the decision process. The manager allows pre-scheduled events and relies on the *service registry* and *load balancing* components/patterns [29]. All this is described next.

Specification of Execution Requirements for Microservices and Nodes.

Types of information specification for services:

- First execution: service type (frontend/backend, database); service image repository; service access ports; start command (e.g. parameter's initialization values); services' dependencies (e.g. service communication).
- Operational: running service's lowest/highest number of replicas; parameters/ metrics limits for a replica's correct operation (e.g. minimum RAM).
- Monitoring: service latency; service access (number and source of accesses); bandwidth; service's used resources (CPU, RAM, ...).

Information requirements for cloud/edge nodes:

- Operating data requirements: parameters/metrics constraints (e.g. RAM); location information for edge nodes (from continent to city);
- Monitoring data:used resources (CPU, RAM, ...), and bandwidth.

Decision Process.

To perform decisions, the microservices manager uses a rule mechanism with *Event Condition Action (ECA) rules* [13,22]. Each rule encodes the conditions and the consequent actions to be performed, accepts multiple values (parameters) representing the current state of the system, and may have a priority level. The rules express the set of constraints on services and nodes, and the modification operations. A rules engine (see Sect. 3) performs their evaluation in the *analysis phase* of the adaptation feedback loop based on the current system state captured by the *monitoring phase* (Fig. 2b and Sect. 2.2).

Rules Related with Services and Their Replicas: The parameters may include %CPU, %RAM, transferred bytes, etc., and the actions are *replicate, migrate, stop, nothing*. Rules capture situations such as (*i*) if the argument values exceed the ones expressed in the rules, a service needs to be replicated or migrated; (*ii*) if the arguments are less than the defined minimum, a replica is marked to be removed; (*iii*) nothing is done, otherwise. The priority level of the fired rules define the final decision. For instance, the service replication/migration rules may privilege a (closer) edge node than the cloud for placing a replica. Nonetheless, the new replica is always located in the cloud in case no edge node is available.

Rules Associated with Nodes: The parameters are %CPU, %RAM, and the actions are *add, stop, nothing*. The rules encode (*i*) a node's creation, if the containers' execution resources are scarce; (*ii*) a node's removal, if its resources are underutilised; (*iii*) nothing is done, otherwise. A node's placement onto the edge vs cloud may also have a priority. In case an edge node's creation/activation is not possible, the node is allocated from the cloud's resources seen as unlimited.

To allow a more precise tuning of the adaptation actions in response to the current system state, both service and edge rules allow diverse parameter configurations: *precise/effective parameter value*, uses exactly the read value of a particular metric; *average value*, the evaluation process considers the average value of a set of particular metrics; *mean deviation percentage*, considers the deviation percentage of the current value in comparison to a given metric's average; *last value deviation percentage*, considers the current value's deviation percentage in relation to a specific metric's last read value. *Event Scheduling:* The definition of *pre-scheduled events* aims to improve the overall system performance by allocating a set of resources at some particular places and times. E.g., increasing the minimum number of replicas needed for a popular social network application expected to have high access volumes, at the time and place of a particular football game or pop music concert. Similarly, a pre-scheduled reduction of no longer needed resources is also possible.

Service Manager's Necessary Components and Functionalities. To dynamically create/destroy nodes and migrate/replicate microservices, the service manager relies on a few external components to support its operation:

- *Container manager*, to detect nodes' and services' failures and support the creation of services and nodes whereto services may be deployed (see Sect. 3).
- *Monitoring component*, to collect fresh metrics from services/nodes defining the system state, allowing its evaluation and necessary adjustments (see Sect. 3).
- *Service registry*, to record new services and replicas, including their location. When a service is created, replicated/moved, it has to be reachable/communicate with other services. This demands a more general communication process than a point-to-point one, which includes a *Register and discover services* component to bridge individual microservices' interaction.
- *Load balancer*, to adequately distribute service accesses to existing replicas deployed at diverse locations, improving the system's performance/efficiency.

Service Communication: The components *Service Registry* and *Register and discover services*, shown in Fig. 2a, support communication decoupling and some level of inter-service load balancing. The communication from a *uService A* to *uService B* is based on the target's type/name (i.e. *B*) and not on a fixed communication endpoint. This is fundamental to carry out service migration or replica selection, e.g. to access a *uService B*'s replica located on the same node as *A*.

The *Service Registry* extends the *service registry pattern* [29] to support migration and replication. It allows service registration and discovery by service name/type via the organisation of running services' endpoints according to service type. It also stores the location of services and their replicas, and if they are active. Whenever a microservice is migrated or replicated, the registry has to be notified to update the service's information. The registry is deployed in its own container and can be replicated to enable faster queries.

The *Register and discover services* component is essential to microservices' migration/replication and supports basic load balancing towards backend

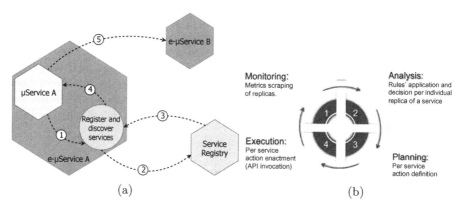

Fig. 2. (a) Service communication via the *Register and discover services* subcomponent and the *Service Registry* component. (b) Service reconfiguration; adapted from [14].

services. It has some contact points to the function of *sidecars* in the recent *service mesh pattern* [29], since it is coupled to a particular microservice to bridge its accesses. Namely, to support the use of the Service Registry features described above, each microservice in the adaptability system has to exist within an *extended microservice* wrapper container that also includes a *Register and discover services* component. For instance, in Fig. 2a, the *e-uService A* contains the *uService A* and a *Register and discover services* component. This latter component has the following functionalities: (*a*) registers its microservice creation/deletion in the service registry and updates the registry periodically to inform that the service is still active; (*b*) queries the endpoints of other services taking into account the location of its service, and in case of several equal possibilities (e.g. same edge node) chooses one endpoint at random, e.g. service *A* may access a local replica of *B*. The numbers in Fig. 2a illustrates the process when *uService A* wants to communicate with a service named *B*: to obtain an endpoint for *B*, *A* contacts the *Register and discover services* (1); the latter requests the (all possible) endpoint(s) from the *Service Registry* (2, 3), selects the best endpoint and sends it microservice *A* (4) that uses it to communicate with *B* (5).

Load Balancing Service Requests: The *Load Balancer* component distributes client requests towards a microservice's replicas to adjust their load. Clients access a load balancer preferably in their own region and only the calls to a *frontend* microservice are balanced. Yet the load balancer can be replicated to the same *regions* as the frontend replicas to level the load at each location. All load balancers' replicas have access to all service replicas regardless their location, allowing them to redirect accesses when a region has no replicas or the local ones are overloaded. Figure 3a represents an extended microservice *e-uS A* with a single replica and a single load balancer in the cloud. Figure 3b shows a scenario with the *e-uS A* and the load balancer replicated in two regions. The *Load Balancer #1* serves the clients in the USA and gives priority to the *e-uS A* replicas #1 and #2 in the same region. However, it redirects the requests to the replica #3 located at an edge node, in case the first two microservices become overloaded. The replica selection algorithm uses (*i*) the *Least Connections* method and (*ii*) a weight assigned to each replica to privilege replicas in the same region/location as the load balancer. The choice was tuned based on the number of each replica's active connections and its weight, to access less loaded replicas but also to reduce clients' communication with remote replicas. E.g. the closest replica may still be chosen if its connections' number is just slightly higher than a farther one.

2.2   Adaptation Process and Migration/Replication Scenarios

To respond to services' and nodes' overload and comply to the applications' QoS requirements, the adaptation process uses migration and horizontal scalability of services/nodes for the system's dynamic reconfiguration, instead of vertical scalability (increase a VM's capacity). The creation of multiple service/node replicas allows a simpler and faster management process, e.g. replicating a pre-existing service with the same resources, and, above all, supports large-scale scalability via replica deployment onto geographically dispersed edges devices.

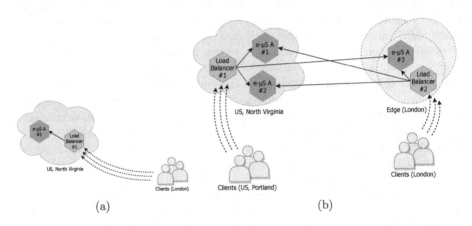

Fig. 3. Function of the load balancer: (a) cloud only, (b) replicas in cloud/edge.

The adaptation process consists of a four stage feedback loop inspired on [14,30], as shown in Fig. 2b for service management (similar for nodes): (*i*) *service replicas' monitoring*, to collect relevant metrics (e.g. data transfer, CPU usage); (*ii*) *analysis per service replica*, to evaluate the action to apply to each particular service (e.g. migrate or replicate/eliminate if overloaded/underused); (*iii*) *planning for all services*, considers the overall system state to decide the action for each service; (*iv*) *plan's execution*. The system follows a set of rules like previously discussed and that may be configured by the application administrator. To avoid a constant system reconfiguration causing its instability, a problem well known in self-adaptability, there is a time gap between the first indication for reconfiguration and its effective execution. For instance, the indication to remove a edge node has to be confirmed in three consecutive loop cycles before the node is effectively deactivated. This allows that in case of sudden changes in nearby client accesses meanwhile, the decision may be to keep the node active.

The migration of microservices to respond to local latency variations diverges from the usual meaning within the cloud domain (e.g. migration of VMs). The *migration process* is based on replication to keep the service available but also in a way to promote further flexibility depending on the perceived ongoing changes in the system state. Its steps may be: 1. create a local replica of an overloaded service; 2. eventually move the replica to e.g. a edge node with higher service accesses, in the next loop cycles; 3. eliminate the original service if underused in the next cycles, e.g. all client requests are now better served by the replica at the edge. Although taking a few (parametrisable) iteration cycles of the adaptation loop, the service eventually migrates to a new location.

Discussion on the Adaptation Solution and Scenarios. Microservices applications executing on Cloud/edge systems have to deal with [11] inter-service communications and dependencies that may cause network overheads and a cascade of QoS violations; microservices' diversity, with different bottlenecks that may change as the load increases; or cloud applications' latency variability. When considering live migration/replication of microservices, an adequate decision on which ones to migrate/replicate, when, and where to, becomes even more pressing to guarantee a good application QoS and efficient resource usage. Our solution, via its self-adaptable management with a gradual replication/reduction of nodes/services according to the ongoing system modification expressed via diverse metrics/conditions in rules, aims to address the concerns above. Our system detects when services/nodes exceed some resources' threshold and need to be replicated

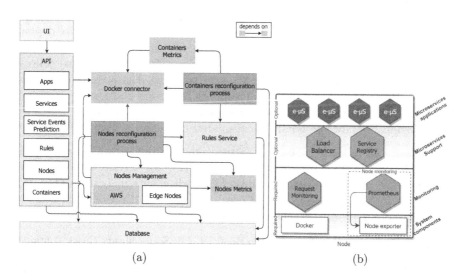

Fig. 4. (a) Detailed view of the uS management component. (b) Node architecture.

and decides where to based on the collected metrics. A service may so move to an edge node closer to a high number of clients to reduce their perceived access time and the communication traffic. In case the service performs some additional local data filtering, the data on transit volume may be reduced even further, and if it has predictable peak loads its resources can be provisioned a priori. The decision process also has to assess the type of metrics underlying the decisions, if the service has a database which impacts transfer costs, or if there are dependencies between services. For instance, the evaluation in section Sect. 3 focus on a frontend service communicating frequently with a backend catalog service upon clients' accesses. When the clients view the full catalog the whole database is transferred. The migration/replication of both services to a nearby edge node reduces hence the communication traffic.

3   Prototype and Evaluation

The service management's modules are detailed in Fig. 4a[1]: *User Interface (UI)*, APIs for e.g. container/node/service creation, rules definition, etc.; *Docker container manager*, e.g. to start/stop containers and resource usage data; *Rules module*, an engine for ECA rules' management e.g. creation/deletion and analyses i.e. which rules to trigger based on current nodes' and services' metrics; the application administrator uses the UI to manage ECA rules, e.g. defining a rule's triggering conditions and affected entities (services or nodes); *Node management*, integrates the management for cloud (in AWS) and edge nodes, e.g creates/suspends VMs, and uses the *node metrics module* (*Prometheus*) to get each node's resource usage; *reconfiguration process*, it is subdivided into containers and nodes, and periodically decides the actions to perform on services/nodes.

Figure 4b shows the necessary management components to support service deployment in a node. A node is a VM that is created in the context of a cloud platform or fog/edge device, and a set of nodes forms a cluster for service deployment. *Docker* manages the node's containers, e.g. identifies a container's resource usage (CPU, RAM) and failures. The *Node exporter* (from Prometheus) collects the node's resource usage (CPU/RAM), e.g. to know if is possible to deploy another service. The components that support microservices, i.e. the load balancers and the service registry, are only present in some nodes, which is decided by the system. Finally, the uS are encapsulated into extended uS (Sect. 2.1).

Evaluation. To allocate VMs from data centers in different regions we used the EC2 service from AWS. The evaluation setting for service deployment on the cloud uses nodes in North Virginia, US, with clients in London (Fig. 3a). The setting for cloud/edge execution uses the same cloud region with users in Portland, and edge nodes and clients in London, UK (Fig. 3b). The load tests use

---

[1] Sw used: uS management, Java/Spring Boot; UI, JavaScript library React; container manager, https://www.docker.com; rules engine, https://www.drools.org/; monitoring, https://prometheus.io; AWS cloud, https://aws.amazon.com; Load tests, https://docs.k6.io/docs & https://loadimpact.com/insights/; Sock shop https://microservices-demo.github.io/.

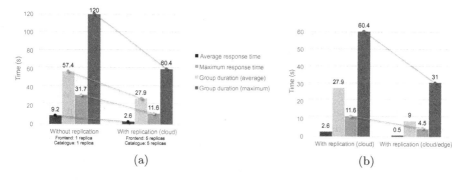

Fig. 5. (a) Cloud execution results without (left) and with replication (right). (b) Comparison of cloud only (left) and cloud/edge (right) replication; clients in London.

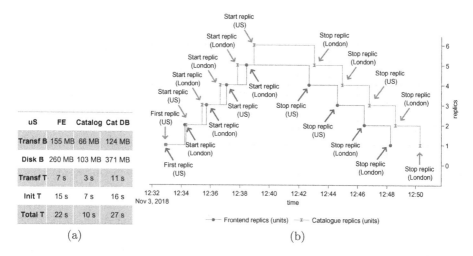

Fig. 6. (a) Microservices' replication costs. (b) Catalog test cloud/edge replica variation.

the *Weaveworks' Sock Shop* demo composed of one *front end* (FE) microservice that communicates with seven back end microservices. One is the *Catalog* service managing the socks' catalog data and images stored in its database. The test for the *Catalog* access to retrieve the products' data is an example of inter-service dependency (the test targeting *Login and Registration* had similar results [4]). When a user communicates with the FE service, it contacts the Catalog service which responds with the required data (metadata or the full socks' database). The FE then resends this data to the user. The *evaluation points* were (a) the application's response times; (b) the replication mechanism, i.e. the replicas' number per service, the replicas' execution place, the replication cost; (c) the replication removal mechanism. Figure 5 shows the evaluation results considering the settings in Fig. 3 for obtaining the catalog's metadata (*response time*) and the full catalog (*group duration*), for an increasing number (until fifty) of virtual users. Figure 5a shows the results for the Catalog in the Cloud only with/without replication. Figure 5b shows the reduction times when the FE and the Catalog are replicated at both cloud and edge nodes. In this case, the applied rules use the *transmitted bytes per second* rate: *uS replication*: replicate when the rate is $>= 2.5\,MB/s$ for two consecutive loop iterations; *uS removal*: stop the uS when its rate for three consecutive loop iterations is $<0.5\,MB/s$. Figure 6a presents the transfer bytes (*Transf B*) for the FE and the catalog metadata (*Catalog*) and with its database (*Cat DB*), and their replication costs as transfer time (*Transf T*) and initialisation time (*Init T*) at the target edge node. These seem adequate for a fast replication towards the edge. Figure 5b shows the system's evolution on self-adapting the replicas' number according to the execution conditions. First the replicas are located in the cloud/US but due to client accesses in the London edge node are replicated here and later removed.

4   Related Work

This work follows the concepts of computation offloading and *Osmotic computing* [33] on automatic deploy of microservices in containers into the cloud/edge, for efficient resource usage and service access. This concept admits edge nodes' highly diverse and restricted capacity, whereas existing container managers (e.g. Kubernetes) include too heavy modules for those nodes and target cloud environments. Our work implements microservice replication with the vision that diverse microservices have different requirements and dependencies [4,11,18] and, along with edge resource management needs, require an adaptable tripartite solution on data, monitoring and service management. E.g. selecting a service to migrate/replicate needs adaptable monitoring for evaluating the dynamic evolution of its dependencies/communication and its dynamic database replication [23]. Coexisting solutions like *Caus* and *Enorm* [16,36] offered single-parameter configuration for microservices' auto-scaling on the cloud. *Caus* has no automatic node management nor dynamic uS placement on the edge. *Enorm* supports dynamic uS placement but on a single edge node. Other works offer interesting multi-variable auto-scaling solutions but only in cloud environments or FaaS [5,12,15]. Recent work [31] also uses a MAPE loop [14] for uS adaptive scaling and nodes' saving based on affinity. Another [25] uses an unsupervised learning approach to automatically decompose an application into uS and select the adequate resource type. Both do not consider fog/edge platforms.

5   Conclusions and Future Work

This work defends the autonomic management of microservices applications deployed on hybrid cloud/edge infra-structures relying on three dimensions, service, data, and monitoring self-management, to cope with these systems' complexity. It focuses on the service component based on an automatic microservice migration and replication solution. The approach is evaluated in the context of a demo application deployed in the Amazon AWS. The results show the adaptability of the system in the presence of varied client access scenarios and present promising values in terms of lower latencies and the system's efficiency. In future the solution will be extended with a hierarchical service managing system and integrated with the adaptable database and monitoring components in progress and a novel security component. The autonomic service will also include machine learning mechanisms to better analyse and predict access patterns.

References

1. Balalaie, A., Heydarnoori, A., Jamshidi, P.: Microservices architecture enables devops: migration to a cloud-native architecture. IEEE Softw. **33**(3), 42–52 (2016)
2. Bucchiarone, A., Dragoni, N., Dustdar, S., Larsen, S.T., Mazzara, M.: From monolithic to microservices: experience from the banking domain. IEEE Softw. **35**(3), 50–55 (2018)
3. Carlini, S.: The drivers and benefits of edge computing. APC white paper 226
4. Carrusca, A.: Gestão de micro-serviços na Cloud e Edge. Master's thesis, UNL (2018). http://hdl.handle.net/10362/59505
5. Danayi, A., Sharifian, S.: PESS-MinA: a proactive stochastic task allocation algorithm for FaaS edge-cloud environments. In: ICSPIS, pp. 27–31 (2018)
6. Dastjerdi, A.V., Buyya, R.: Fog computing: helping the internet of things realize its potential. IEEE Comput. **49**(8), 112–116 (2016)
7. Dragoni, N., et al.: Microservices: yesterday, today, and tomorrow. Present and Ulterior Software Engineering, pp. 195–216. Springer, Cham (2017). https://doi.org/10.1007/978-3-319-67425-4_12
8. Edge, O.: Open edge computing. http://openedgecomputing.org/
9. Evans, D.: The internet of things. Technical report, cisco Systems (2011)
10. Fowler: Microservices. https://martinfowler.com/microservices/
11. Gan, Y. et al.: An open-source benchmark suite for microservices and their HW-SW implications for cloud & edge systems. In: ASPLOS 2019. ACM (2019)
12. Guerrero, C., Lera, I., Juiz, C.: Resource optimization of container orchestration: a case study in multi-cloud us-based applications. J. Supercomput. **74**(7) (2018)
13. Huebscher, M.C., McCann, J.A.: A survey of autonomic computing: degrees, models, and applications. ACM Comput. Surv. **40**(3), 7:1–7:28 (2008)
14. IBM: An architectural blueprint for autonomic computing. Technical report, IBM (2005)
15. Jindal, A., Podolskiy, V., Gerndt, M.: Performance modeling for cloud microservice applications. In: Proceedings of ICPE 2019. ACM, New York (2019)
16. Klinaku, F., Frank, M., Becker, S.: CAUS: an elasticity controller for a containerized microservice. In: Companion of ICPE 2018, pp. 93–98. ACM (2018)
17. Kratzke, N., Quint, P.: Understanding cloud-native applications after 10 years of cloud computing. J. Syst. Softw. **126**, 1–16 (2017)
18. Leitão, J., Costa, P.Á., Gomes, M.C., Preguiça, N.M.: Towards enabling novel edge-enabled applications. CoRR abs/1805.06989 abs/1805.06989 (2018)
19. Mahmud, R., Kotagiri, R., Buyya, R.: Fog computing: a taxonomy, survey and future directions. In: Di Martino, B., Li, K.-C., Yang, L.T., Esposito, A. (eds.) Internet of Everything. IT, pp. 103–130. Springer, Singapore (2018). https://doi.org/10.1007/978-981-10-5861-5_5
20. Marinescu, D.C.: Cloud Computing: Theory & Practice. Morgan Kaufmann, Boston (2013)
21. Mauro, T.: Adopting microservices at netflix. NGiNX (2015)

22. McCarthy, D., Dayal, U.: The architecture of an active database management system. SIGMOD Rec. **18**(2), 215–224 (1989)
23. Mealha, D., Preguiça, N., Gomes, M.C., Leitão, J.A.: Data replication on the cloud/edge. In: PaPoC 2019 Eurosys Workshop. ACM, New York (2019)
24. Mell, P.M., Grance, T.: The NIST definition of cloud computing. NIST (2011)
25. Abdullah, M., Iqbal, W., Erradi, A.: Unsupervised learning approach for web application auto-decomposition into microservices. J. Syst. Softw. **151** (2019)
26. Newman, S.: Building Microservices, 1st edn. O'Reilly Media Inc., Sebastopol (2015)
27. OpenFog: Size & impact of fog computing market. Technical report, OpenFog (2017)
28. Parashar, M., Hariri, S.: Autonomic computing: an overview. In: Banâtre, J.-P., Fradet, P., Giavitto, J.-L., Michel, O. (eds.) UPP 2004. LNCS, vol. 3566, pp. 257–269. Springer, Heidelberg (2005). https://doi.org/10.1007/11527800_20
29. Richardson, C.: Microservices patterns (2017). http://microservices.io/index.html
30. Salehie, M., Tahvildari, L.: Self-adaptive software: landscape and research challenges. ACM Trans. Auton. Adapt. Syst. **4**(2), 14:1–14:42 (2009)
31. Sampaio, A.R., Rubin, J., Beschastnikh, I., Rosa, N.S.: Improving microservice-based applications with runtime placement adaptation. J. Internet Serv. Appl. **10**(1), 1–30 (2019). https://doi.org/10.1186/s13174-019-0104-0
32. Satyanarayanan, M.: The emergence of edge computing. Computer **50**(1), 30–39 (2017)
33. Sharma, V., Srinivasan, K., Jayakody, D.N.K., Rana, O.F., Kumar, R.: Managing service-heterogeneity using osmotic computing. CoRR abs/1704.04213 (2017)
34. Shi, W., Cao, J., Zhang, Q., Li, Y., Xu, L.: Edge computing: vision and challenges. IEEE Internet Things J. **3**(5), 637–646 (2016)
35. Varghese, B., Wang, N., Barbhuiya, S., Kilpatrick, P., Nikolopoulos, D.S.: Challenges and opportunities in edge computing. In: IEEE SmartCloud, NY (2016)
36. Wang, N., Varghese, B., Matthaiou, M., Nikolopoulos, D.S.: ENORM: a framework for edge node resource management. IEEE Trans. Serv. Comput. (2017)
37. Yi, S., Li, C., Li, Q.: A survey of fog computing: concepts, applications and issues. In: Mobidata 2015 Workshop Proceedings. ACM, New York (2015)

ISYCC: IoT Systems Provisioning and Management for Context-Aware Smart Cities

Introduction to the 4th Workshop on IoT Systems Provisioning and Management for Context-Aware Smart Cities (ISYCC 2019)

The ISYCC 2019 workshop was held in conjunction with the 17th International Conference on Service Oriented Computing (ICSOC 2019) on October 28, 2019, in Toulouse, France.

ISYCC 2019 session gathered about 30 attendees. The discussions following the presentations and the closing showed a big interest on the novel and emerging research fields such as fog computing, data analytics, smart agriculture, and healthcare in IoT.

For this edition, we received 7 submissions, out of which 3 papers were accepted. In addition, we invited 3 papers co-authored by experts in IoT and smart agriculture. Similarly to ISYCC 2018, The ISYCC 2019 program was merged with the program of the 4th edition of the International Workshop on Adaptive Service-oriented and Cloud Applications (ASOCA 2019). The presentations of the two workshops were held during the same session (full-day session).

We would like to thank the authors for their submissions, the Program Committee for their reviewing work, and the organizers of the ICSOC 2019 conference for their support which made this workshop possible.

Organization

Workshop Program Chairs

Khouloud Boukadi   University of Sfax, Tunisia
Mohamed Mohamed   Cupertino, USA

Workshop Committee

Mohamed Abu-Lebdeh   Concordia University, Canada
Sami Bhiri   University of Monsatir, Tunisia
Carla Mouradian   Concordia University, Canada
Amira Mouakher   University of Burgundy Franche-Comté, France
Sami Yangui   LAAS-CNRS, France
Zhangbing Zhou   China University of Geosciences in Beijing, China
Takoua Abdellatif   University of Carthage, Tunisia

Towards Geo-Context Aware IoT Data Distribution

Jonathan Hasenburg$^{(\boxtimes)}$ and David Bermbach

TU Berlin & Einstein Center Digital Future, Mobile Cloud Computing Research
Group, Berlin, Germany
{jh,db}@mcc.tu-berlin.de

Abstract. In the Internet of Things, the relevance of data often depends
on the geographic context of data producers and consumers. Today's data
distribution services, however, mostly focus on data content and not on
geo-context, which would benefit many scenarios greatly. In this paper,
we propose to use the geo-context information associated with devices to
control data distribution. We define what geo-context dimensions exist
and compare our definition with concepts from related work. By example,
we discuss how geo-contexts enable new scenarios and evaluate how they
also help to reduce unnecessary data distributions.

Keywords: Geo-context · IoT · Data distribution

1 Introduction

A long term vision of the Internet of Things (IoT) is to make sensor data available across applications and devices [13] to enable new and better services. For instance, exchanging information between cars, bikes, and other road users could improve road safety [15].

There are many data distribution services that are specifically tailored for IoT devices, e.g., AWS IoT[1] or Google Cloud IoT[2]. These services enable a selective distribution of messages as clients can define criteria [2,13] so that they only receive messages based on their respective interests. Compared to distributing data to all possible clients, this reduces bandwidth consumption and the amount of data processed by the clients which often operate in environments with constrained computational resources or bandwidth limitations.

Today's data distribution services, however, mostly focus on data content and not on the associated geo-context, which would benefit many IoT scenarios greatly. For example, a car that aims to avoid red traffic lights needs to process data from traffic lights within its current neighborhood only in order to determine an optimal route and velocity. Therefore, from the perspective of data consumers, it is often desirable not to receive data originating outside an area of interest

---

[1] https://aws.amazon.com/iot/.
[2] https://cloud.google.com/solutions/iot/.

© Springer Nature Switzerland AG 2020
S. Yangui et al. (Eds.): ICSOC 2019 Workshops, LNCS 12019, pp. 111–121, 2020.
https://doi.org/10.1007/978-3-030-45989-5_9

to reduce computational efforts and cope with bandwidth limitations. A data producer, on the other hand, might already know that provided data is only relevant for data consumers in a certain area, and thus prevent others from receiving it. E.g., only drivers in the immediate vicinity of a particular car need to know when it brakes. Furthermore, if a data producer trusts the location provided by a data consumer, the geo-context can be used as an alternative to credentials-based authentication for data access control in some scenarios.

In the past, other researchers have been successful in using spatial data for various reasons (e.g., [5–7,10–12,14]). Every group of authors, however, has its own interpretation of the term geo-context and corresponding use cases. Thus, no standardized definition of geo-context exists, yet, and none of the related works consider the entire geo-context of data producers and consumers for their proposals. Therefore, we make the following contributions:

- We propose a definition of the geo-contexts associated with IoT devices.
- We compare our geo-context definition with concepts found in related work.
- We introduce three scenarios that benefit from using geo-context information and discuss how this reduces unnecessary data transmissions.

The remainder of this paper is structured as follows. We first present our motivation and three IoT scenarios that benefit from using geo-context information (Sect. 2). We then discuss related work and present our definition for the geo-context of IoT devices (Sect. 3). Next, we evaluate how using this additional information reduces unnecessary message transmissions (Sect. 4). Finally, we draw a conclusion and present an outlook on future work (Sect. 5).

2   Motivation

To better understand our motivation for using geo-contexts, we first need to highlight the difference between content and context. We do this by explaining these terms with the help of a topic-based pub/sub system. In such a system, publishers are the data producers and subscribers are the data consumers. Subscribers define which **content** they are interested in by subscribing to topics, e.g., when a subscriber creates a subscription to the topic *sensor/temperature*, he will receive temperature sensor measurements published to the same topic.

Dey defines **context** as "any information that can be used to characterize the situation of an entity" [8]. Thus, the context of IoT devices comprises many things such as other nearby devices, the type of power source, etc. In this paper, we only look at the geo-context which we consider to comprise (1) the location of the device and (2) special areas that are of interest/relevance to the device.

So why is it necessary to distinguish between content and geo-context? Both producers or consumers may have moved in between sending and receiving two data items. This, however, is not reflected in the content-related interests (e.g., the subscription) but affects the context-related interests. Hence, location information is not related to content.

Distinguishing content and geo-context information also has many practical benefits. For example, while it is possible to encode some geo-context information in topics, this requires clients to agree on such a structure and leads to very complicated and bloated topic trees. E.g., one could agree that the first topic level is always the country and the second topic level is always the city a given message refers to. Then, the topic *france/paris/sensor/temperature* would refer to all temperature sensors in Paris, while the topic *germany/berlin/sensor/temperature* would refer to all temperature sensors in Berlin. Besides the disadvantages mentioned above, this approach is very coarse-grained and it is not possible to distinguish between the location of a device and its area of interest.

We propose to consider the associated geo-context of IoT devices when distributing their messages for two reasons. First, with the geo-context additional information can be used to control data distribution. This can significantly reduce the amount of transmitted messages for scenarios where geo-context matters, thus reducing the load on data distribution services, the bandwidth consumption, and the amount of messages that need to be processed by clients. Especially in the IoT, such scenarios are quite common as IoT devices operate in a specific physical environment. Therefore, data collected by sensors such as temperature measurements or actions provided by actuators like moving a robotic arm are most relevant for other things in physical proximity. Such scenarios are the reason why Bellavista et al. [2] argue that geographical co-location should be taken into account. More domains with applications in which the value of information depends on the location of data producers and recipients include the Internet-of-Vehicle [10,20], Smart Cities [19] or Mobile Health [1].

Second, filtering data based on content and geo-context supports new (IoT) scenarios. In the following, we present three such scenarios from which two will also be used in our evaluation (Sect. 4).

2.1 Scenario 1: Local Messaging and Information Sharing

In this scenario, clients travel on individual routes and send data to other clients in close proximity on a regular basis. Data can be of any kind, e.g., information concerning a client's current surroundings (e.g., the condition of the road), as well as simple text messages. Data should not be sent to clients too far away so that information is kept local; this prevents data from being mined by third parties. Furthermore, clients consume data based on their content interests, but also based on their individual geo-context. For example, a hiker might be interested in text messages (content) from clients in close proximity (geo-context), while a biker might be interested in road condition information (content) of a trapezoidal area in front of him (geo-context).

Other examples for the use of such a data distribution service are the real-time messaging service Jodel[3] or the location-based chats of Telegram[4].

---

[3] https://jodel.com.
[4] https://telegram.org/blog/contacts-local-groups.

2.2 Scenario 2: Open Environmental Data

Today's IoT sensor data is often not available directly to users, instead, it is common to create data dumps that are released once per day[5]. Such a procedure renders all IoT applications that require real time data impossible. Connecting the IoT sensors directly to a data distribution service, however, could easily lead to situations in which the service (and its potential clients) become overloaded, e.g., if a client accidentally consumes all data produced by temperature sensors at once by expressing interest for data labeled with *temperature*. While such a situation could be prevented by having the sensors use more diverse labels such as *temperature/regionA*, *temperature/regionB*, etc., considering the geo-context of data producers and consumers is more effective.

Data producers, for example, could restrict access based on arbitrarily shaped areas, e.g., only consumers in a certain geographic area can access data of said producer. On the other hand, data consumers often only have an interest in data of nearby sensors. For example, a tourist might want to receive weather data (content) only from the city he is visiting (geo-context) or a smart home application might only be interested in barometric pressure values (content) of sensors that are at most 20 km away (geo-context) in order to identify approaching storms so that windows can be closed. Besides these more advanced application use cases, prohibiting the consumption of data from large areas at once can prevent accidental overload of services and clients.

2.3 Scenario 3: Context-Based Data Distribution

Often, data needs to be distributed to clients in certain geographic areas. A prominent example for this is the Wireless Emergency Alerts system that is used to warn US citizens about dangerous weather or other critical situations[6]. The current system is not very accurate; only after November 30, 2019 it will reach an accuracy of below one-tenth of a mile overshoot [9] which is still rather imprecise.

A more accurate approach, however, in which messages are delivered based on the content interests of data consumers and the additional domain knowledge of data producers enables additional and better kinds of services. E.g., citizens interested in traffic information need to specify such a content interest only once and are then able to travel between districts (and even cities or states) while still receiving only relevant information as data producers know in which geographic area their messages are of relevance.

Many similar scenarios are possible in which data producers use their domain knowledge about the relevant geo-context to control the distribution of data, e.g., in the context of smart parking, advertisement, or smart buildings.

---

[5] E.g., this is done by the open data initiative of the German Meteorological Office: https://opendata.dwd.de/.

[6] Wireless Emergency Alerts - https://www.fcc.gov/consumers/guides/wireless-emergency-alerts-wea.

3 Geo-Context Dimensions

Previous work has already proposed to use geo-context information for a more advanced control of data distribution. Their focus, however, is not developing a general view on IoT device geo-contexts. Instead, the authors typically design a system for a very specific use case in which location-based data needs to be processed.

Chen et al. [7] propose a spatial middleware service that delivers messages to clients when they enter "zones" defined by data producers. While this allows data producers to control data distribution based on areas they consider as relevant, data consumers cannot control data distribution based on their own areas of interest.

Guo et al. [11, 12] also propose a location-aware pub/sub service that delivers messages based on zones. In contrast to the service above, data consumers can control data distribution based on their areas of interest. The data producers, however, cannot use areas to control data distribution.

Frey and Roman [10] propose a protocol to bring context to a publish/subscribe system. They allow publishers to define a "context of relevance", and subscribers to define a "context of interest". When both contexts overlap, a message is delivered to the subscriber. While their context definition is very general, it can also be used for geo-context information, i.e., the (1) location of a device and (2) areas that are of interest/relevance to the device. However, they understand these two dimensions as one, so if a client moves he needs to update his subscriptions even if his area of interest did not change.

Li et al. [16] propose to use an R-tree index structure to efficiently identify which data producers are located in areas defined by data consumers. Again, this group of authors only looks at geo-context from one perspective so their approach does not work for areas defined by data producers and consumer locations.

Chapuis et al. [5, 6] propose a horizontally scalable pub/sub architecture that supports matching based on a circular area around publishers and around subscribers. If the area of a publisher and subscriber overlap, messages are delivered. As these areas are not independent of client locations, this setup does not allow subscriptions to areas independently of the current location or subscriptions to multiple areas for different topics, e.g., as needed for the scenario in Sect. 2.1.

Bryce et al. [3] propose MQTT-G, an extension of the MQTT protocol with Geolocation. While subscribers can define an area of interest to control message distribution, their area definitions are only created once per subscriber rather than for individual subscriptions. In addition, publishers cannot control the matching of messages based on areas defined by them.

Herle et al. [3] also propose to extend the MQTT protocol so that messages can be matched based on spatial geometries appended to published messages and subscriptions [14]. When both geometries overlap, messages are delivered. Their spatial matching, however, does not consider client locations.

Obviously, there is no general understanding of geo-contexts in IoT. Combining all these approaches allows us to identify four geo-context dimensions.

Both data producers and data consumers have a geographic location (**producer location** and **consumer location**), which consists of a latitude and a longitude value. Beyond this, data producers and data consumers have an area of interest, we propose to use geofences[7] to describe these areas. For our purposes, a geofence can have arbitrary shapes and may comprise non-adjacent subareas, e.g., Germany and Italy. The **consumer geofence** ensures that received data originates from an area of interest, i.e., producer locations are inside the consumer geofence. The **producer geofence**, on the other hand, ensures that only clients present in a certain area receive data, i.e., consumer locations are inside the producer geofence. Table 1 summarizes which of the four dimensions are considered by related work. Note, that Frey and Roman [10] only partly consider the location of consumers and producers as they mix it with the geofence.

Table 1. An overview of the geo-context dimensions in related work

Related Work	Location		Geofence	
	Consumer	Producer	Consumer	Producer
Bryce et al. [3]	✗	✓	✓	✗
Chapuis et al. [6]	✗	✗	✓	✓
Chen et al. [7]	✓	✗	✗	✓
Frey and Roman [10]	O	O	✓	✓
Guo et al. [12]	✗	✓	✓	✗
Herle et al. [14]	✗	✗	✓	✓
Li et al. [16]	✗	✓	✓	✗

As in the case of data content described above, producers and consumers can have multiple geo-contexts. For example, in a topic-based pub/sub system, a subscriber (consumer) can create individual subscriptions for different topics. Thus, when also using geo-context, subscribers might specify a geofence per subscription. Likewise, publishers might specify a geofence for every message.

Bringing geofences and locations together, two checks are necessary to decide whether data from a given producer should be sent to a given consumer (Fig. 1). First, from the consumer's perspective with the help of the consumer geofence and the producer location (Consumer GeoCheck) and, second, from the producer's perspective with the help of the producer geofence and the consumer location (Producer GeoCheck).

Figure 2 shows these two concepts by example. Here, a data consumer wants to receive all data from producers located in the northern part of a park (vertical stripes) by using the appropriate consumer geofence. For example, there could be

---

[7] A Geofence is a virtual fences surrounding a defined geographical area. As a usage example, Reclus and Drouard describe a scenario in which such fences are used to notify factory workers about approaching trucks [18].

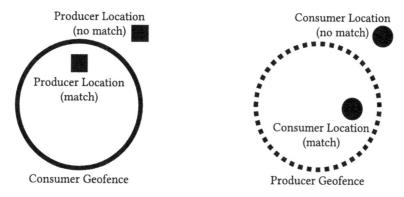

Fig. 1. Consumer GeoCheck (Left) and Producer GeoCheck (Right)

a number of IoT sensors distributed across the park which collect and send information on humidity and other environmental parameters. Each data producer, however, wants to limit access to data consumers located inside an adjacent building (horizontal stripes), e.g., so that sensors do not accidentally expose information on botanical research experiments. Therefore, data producers use the appropriate producer geofence when transmitting data. The data should only be transmitted if the producer location is inside the consumer geofence (Consumer GeoCheck) and if the consumer location is inside the producer geofence (Producer GeoCheck). In the example, this is the case.

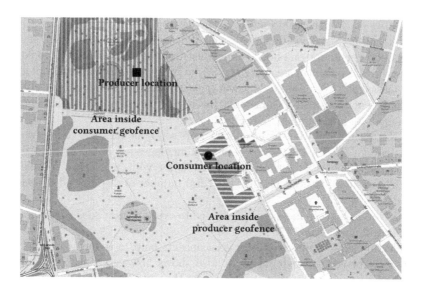

Fig. 2. All GeoChecks are Successful so the Data Consumer Receives Transmissions from the Data Producer. Map data copyrighted by OpenStreetMap contributors and available from https://www.openstreetmap.org

4   Evaluation

In this section, we evaluate the impact of using geo-contexts to control data distribution. We describe a conceivable setup for two of the three scenarios that we introduced in Sect. 2 and calculate the number of messages distributed to consumers when geo-contexts are used (GEO) and not used (NoGEO).

4.1   Local Messaging and Information Sharing

For this scenario, we assume a local messaging service for Central Park in New York City. The goal of this service is to provide a communication platform for visitors of the park while also preventing people outside the park from receiving messages. There is a multitude of different designs for such a service. We assume the following design:

- Clients can connect to the service without having to create an account, only their current location is required.
- Clients can act as data producers and send messages to the service (text, images, videos, etc.).
- Clients can act as data consumers and receive messages from the service.

For our analysis, we distinguish between the two approaches NoGEO and GEO. NoGEO does not consider the geo-context so messages are forwarded to all connected clients. GEO on the other hand, allows producers and consumer to specify geofences.

Central park spans an area of $3.4\,km^2$ and had more than 42 million visitors in 2018 [4]. When assuming an even distribution of visitors across hours, there were about 5000 visitors per hour. Thus, we assume that our service is used by 5000 clients for one hour to demonstrate the effect of using geo-context information. All producer geofences span the whole park (as all visitors should receive messages). We assume, however, that consumer geofences only span 1% of the park each, as visitors are most interested in information that concerns their immediate environment (see Fig. 3).

For the evaluation, we assume that visitors send one message every two minutes on average. This leads to a total of 150k messages per hour. As subscription geofences only span 1% of the park, each visitor will on average receive only 1% of the messages with GEO, thus the total number of distributed messages is $7.5\,m/h$.

With NoGEO, every message is delivered to every visitor, so the total number of distributed messages is $750\,m/h$.

While this shows quite well how geo-contexts help to reduce the number of unnecessary message transmissions, it also shows how geo-context enable new application scenarios. Without geo-contexts, the application would not be useable as each visitor receives 2500 messages a minute, compared to 25 with geo-contexts. Furthermore, the requirement that only people inside the park are allowed to send messages can only be fulfilled with GEO (as long as no one

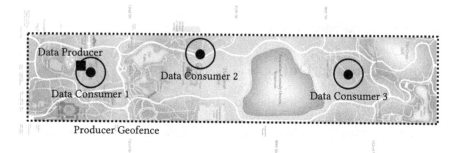

Fig. 3. The Producer Location is inside the Consumer Geofence of Data Consumer 1, so his Messages Get Delivered. All other Data Consumers do not Receive the Producer's Messages, even though their Locations are inside the Producer Geofence. Central Park Map from https://biketourscentralpark.com/central-park-map

spoofs their location). With NoGEO, all users outside of the park would also receive every single message, and every message sent by that user would also be delivered to everyone else.

4.2 Context-Based Data Distribution

For this scenario, we assume a context-based data distribution service for traffic information in the Netherlands. The goal of this service is to distribute measurement data from road side equipment to vehicles (data consumers) based on limitations put into place by the data producers.

In the Netherlands, more than 24 k measurement sites exist which collect data every minute [17]. At the moment, the data is sent to a central database where it is processed before being distributed to data consumers. For this scenario, we propose a different architecture in which data is sent to cars directly so that they can make informed and individual decisions. This would also drastically reduce the latency which is 75 s with the current setup [17].

The Netherlands cover an area of about $42500\,\mathrm{km}^2$. For the GEO evaluation, we assume that each car uses a consumer geofence of the shape and size of the Netherlands. Producer geofences, however, only cover 1% of this area on average and can have very distinct shapes as they are based on the surrounding road network of each measurement site. This enables data producers to control data distribution very accurately and in real-time as geofences can be varied for different data transmissions, e.g., data on severe incidents needs to be send to cars further away while less important information is broadcasted only in the near vicinity.

With NoGEO, every car receives 24 k measurements per minute as the data distribution is not limited. With GEO, every measurements will reach only 1% of the cars on average. Thus, every car only receives $24\,\mathrm{k}*0.01 = 240$ measurements a minute which greatly reduces resource consumption. Similarly, one can easily imagine that even smaller geofence sizes (both consumer and producer) can help to further reduce the number of messages.

5 Conclusion and Outlook

In this paper we proposed to use the geo-contexts associated with IoT devices to control data distribution. We showed that this can help to significantly reduce the amount of transmitted messages for scenarios where geo-context matters while also enabling new (IoT) scenarios that were not possible before. Our definition of geo-context comprises four dimensions: producer location, consumer location, producer geofence, and consumer geofence. We discussed which of these four have been considered by related work and explained why all dimensions are necessary with the help of three scenarios.

In future work, we plan to design a data distribution service based on the pub/sub paradigm that uses the geo-context of publishers and subscribers to control message distribution. For that, we want to use geo-contexts as an additional information input for the matching process which controls the distribution of published messages.

References

1. Nastic, S.: A serverless real-time data analytics platform for edge computing. IEEE Internet Comput. **21**(4), 64–71 (2017)
2. Bellavista, P., Corradi, A., Reale, A.: Quality of service in wide scale publish-subscribe systems. IEEE Commun. Surv. Tutorials **16**(3), 1591–1616 (2014)
3. Bryce, R., Shaw, T., Srivastava, G.: MQTT-g: a publish/subscribe protocol with geolocation. In: 41st International Conference on Telecommunications and Signal Processing. IEEE (2018)
4. Central Park Conservancy Inc.: Central park conservancy annual report 2018 (Rev. 5) (2019). http://www.centralparknyc.org/about/annual-reports.html. Accessed 09 Aug 2019
5. Chapuis, B., Garbinato, B.: Scaling and load testing location-based publish and subscribe. In: IEEE 37th International Conference on Distributed Computing Systems. IEEE (2017)
6. Chapuis, B., Garbinato, B., Mourot, L.: A horizontally scalable and reliable architecture for location-based publish-subscribe. In: IEEE 36th Symposium on Reliable Distributed Systems. IEEE (2017)
7. Chen, X., Chen, Y., Rao, F.: An efficient spatial publish/subscribe system for intelligent location-based services. In: Proceedings of the 2nd International Workshop on Distributed Event-Based Systems. ACM (2003)
8. Dey, A.K.: Understanding and using context. Personal Ubiquitous Comput. **5**(1), 4–7 (2001)
9. Federal Communications Commission: FCC improves wireless emergency alerts (2018). https://www.fcc.gov/document/fcc-improves-wireless-emergency-alerts. Accessed 09 Aug 2019

10. Frey, D., Roman, G.-C.: Context-aware publish subscribe in mobile ad hoc networks. In: Murphy, A.L., Vitek, J. (eds.) COORDINATION 2007. LNCS, vol. 4467, pp. 37–55. Springer, Heidelberg (2007). https://doi.org/10.1007/978-3-540-72794-1_3
11. Guo, L., Chen, L., Zhang, D., Li, G., Tan, K.L., Bao, Z.: Elaps: an efficient location-aware pub/sub system. In: IEEE 31st International Conference on Data Engineering. IEEE (2015)
12. Guo, L., Zhang, D., Li, G., Tan, K.L., Bao, Z.: Location-aware pub/sub system: when continuous moving queries meet dynamic event streams. In: Proceedings of the 2015 ACM SIGMOD International Conference on Management of Data. ACM (2015)
13. Happ, D., Karowski, N., Menzel, T., Handziski, V., Wolisz, A.: Meeting IoT platform requirements with open pub/sub solutions. Ann. Telecommun. **72**, 41–52 (2016). https://doi.org/10.1007/s12243-016-0537-4
14. Herle, S., Becker, R., Blankenbach, J.: Bridging GeoMQTT and REST. In: Proceedings of the Geospatial Sensor Webs Conference (2016)
15. Khelil, A., Soldani, D.: On the suitability of device-to-device communications for road traffic safety. In: IEEE World Forum on Internet of Things. IEEE (2014)
16. Li, G., Wang, Y., Wang, T., Feng, J.: Location-aware publish/subscribe. In: Proceedings of the 19th ACM SIGKDD International Conference on Knowledge Discovery and Data Mining. ACM (2013)
17. National Data Warehouse for Traffic Information: NDW real-time traffic data (2019). https://www.ndw.nu/pagina/en/78/database/79/real-time_traffic_data/. Accessed 09 Aug 2019
18. Reclus, F., Drouard, K.: Geofencing for fleet & freight management. In: 9th International Conference on Intelligent Transport Systems Telecommunications. IEEE (2009)
19. Sanchez, L., et al.: Smartsantander: IoT experimentation over a smart city testbed. Comput. Netw. **61**, 217–238 (2014)
20. Shun, S., Shin, S., Seo, S., Eom, S., Jung, J., Le, K.-H.: A pub/sub-based fog computing architecture for internet-of-vehicles. In: 2016 IEEE International Conference on Cloud Computing Technology and Science (CloudCom) (2016)

A Blockchain Based Solution for Securing Data of IoT Devices

Jaspreet Kaur[✉], Vinayak Singla, and Sumit Kalra

Department of Computer Science and Engineering,
Indian Institute of Technology Jodhpur, Jodhpur, India
kaur.3@iitj.ac.in, singla.1@iitj.ac.in, sumitk@iitj.ac.in

Abstract. In today's time, the number of IoT devices are increasing rapidly. We everyday hear about Amazon echo, Google Mini, Smart watches etc. These devices collect confidential data of a person and as most of these systems follow centralized architecture approach, So most of the data on internet is basically managed by some central authority or organization. Though these organizations have strict policy regarding data misuse or changing of data without consent but one can't overlook the fact that these organizations have the ability to do so. Blockchain helps solve such problem as it is not managed by single party if somebody tries to change data in his Blockchain then the hash of the particular block will no longer match and the particular Blockchain will become invalid and other Blockchain will still be intact and therefore users data won't be compromised. But due to high resource requirement, it becomes problem to run complete Blockchain node on all IoT devices mainly on low power or memory devices. In this paper, we have developed decentralized architecture leveraged from Blockchain technology coupled with an alternative centralized cloud architecture which is a classic client/server architecture with an underlying Blockchain at back-end support with smart contract application written in Solidity language at Ethereum platform. We implement this framework and show how this architecture prevent data misuse by using functionality of Blockchain without requiring the all IoT devices to actually run a Blockchain node. For an end-user experience, it will appear to be same as a normal web app and from the developers perspective, the smart contract application will have similar software design to current web apps thus allowing an easy transition for both of centralized and decentralized methods while still retaining the trust of decentralization.

Keywords: Smart contract · Blockchain node · Private Ethereum blockchain · IoT (Internet of Things) devices · Resource constrained devices · Central authority · Cloud blockchain · Edge blockchain devices

1 Introduction

In today's world, IoT devices have been very popularized in communication domain. They are heterogeneous sensor devices, creates low power lossy networks

© Springer Nature Switzerland AG 2020
S. Yangui et al. (Eds.): ICSOC 2019 Workshops, LNCS 12019, pp. 122–129, 2020.
https://doi.org/10.1007/978-3-030-45989-5_10

for information exchange. Some IoT devices (as smart watch, smart fan etc.) have resource constrained features such as limited memory, limited storage etc. and others are rich in resources as laptops, smart phones etc. Like in the traditional network, these devices and their data also need security such as confidentiality, authenticity, authorization etc. So that, central authorities or intruders cannot disrupt, compromise or misuse any personal confidential data for their own profit. The traditional security approaches as DTLS (Datagram Transport Layer Security), IPSec (Internet Protocol security) and new protocol as Blockchain are the excellent solutions to these problems. But due to high resource requirements and complexities [1], the implementation of these are difficult at resource constrained IoT devices.

Blockchain [7,8] is a new innovative methodology increasingly used by the academia and industry due to their various advantageous features as distributed, decentralized, immutable database or ledger maintained at peer-to-peer network. It takes the concept of smart contract which is self-executing and self-enforcing contract uses the cryptographic techniques that allow digital signing for validation of users data. Blockchain uses the majority voting method for resolving the agreement issues with help of minor nodes and provide incentives or rewards to miners against the resources usage of them. Blockchain has various use cases as crypto-currencies, smart city, smart healthcare, banking etc.

Despite of various advantages, it has various limitations as need high computational resources, high storage space, scalability etc. which hinders the implementation of it in the real world scenario specifically at IoT devices in our case. That's why blockchain is combined with another technologies as cloud computing, edge or fog computing, software defined networking, machine and deep learning algorithms to overcome its limitations. In this paper, we provide a blockchain based solution for securing data of IoT devices while reducing the limitations of blockchain as low as possible.

Rest of the paper is organised as follows: In Sect. 2, we provide some motivation through literature survey or related work. Then this paper is followed by proposed approach along with some preliminary result analysis. Finally conclusion is given followed by future work.

2   Motivation

In literature survey, we have seen that various IoT security issues and their possible solutions [1,12,16–18,20,22] using various technologies as cloud computing, edge or fog computing, machine learning or deep learning methods, SDN (software defined networking) and using various cryptographic primitives. But every solutions have their limits as single point of failure, high complexity and need more resources. So, for reducing these challenges and also maintaining high security to IoT devices, blockchain is prescribe by many of the researchers as a possible solution. But due to the resources constrained nature of some IoT devices or more complex and less scalable nature of blockchain, it is difficult to implement blockchain of things [3,10,11,13–15,19]. Various solutions are also available at web which solve these implementation problems for blockchain of things. They use one or more existing technologies as cloud computing, edge or fog computing etc. or use new framework such as IOTA or use multiple chains for solving these issues. But all of the solutions suggested in the literature have some common problems as:

1. All of the IoT + blockchain solutions those have to be done at cloud infrastructure [4] (centralized or decentralized), again tends to trust on the some centralized authority or creates a single point of failure problem by user end.
2. Some of the researchers use combination of edge and cloud computing platforms for reducing the accessing delay by cloud operations and perform the complex operations of blockchain at cloud [6]. But they again create a more complex system by assuring the security of cloud by adding some another overlay networks and maintain access control list at local blockchain [3]. This solution consider all of the IoT devices are of same type not heterogeneous devices. In another EdgeChain framework [2], They take heterogeneous devices and use edge cloud platform for providing resources to IoT devices by logging IoT devices activities on blockchain. But again, they have not tell about the data security at edge cloud platform and another issue in this paper is key distribution for resource constrained devices.
3. IOTA [5] or other tree like databases have centralized coordinator and theoretical scalable but not fully implemented yet.
4. These solutions also need improvement in Multi-criteria scheduler use for load balancing for incoming transactions of blockchain [6].
5. It also need for collaborative mechanisms or system between different kinds of blockchain's Platform and need to reduce high latency's for cross over multiple chains [6].
6. Key distribution approach for resource constrained IoT devices should be improved [6].
7. Some of the these solutions are specific to the use cases or domain not generalised solution [3,14,19].
8. How accurately and appropriately complex machine and deep learning algorithms are to be helpful for blockchain of things [21].

The above limitations or challenges motivate us for this work at which we choose one common blockchain maintain at centralized cloud architecture with load balancer schedulers along with edge computing devices (high resource IoT devices) to maintaining the decentralized property of blockchain. Low power IoT devices can directly communicate to this blockchain for speed up computation and easier data accessing, it makes proper use of cloud.

3   Proposed Architecture

For performing any data or asset transaction in a decentralized blockchain framework, users or nodes always require a fully synced instance of blockchain node running on their device. But this is problematic to implement at resource constrained IoT devices. So, our proposed architecture constitutes of centralized or third party or cloud blockchain architecture along with edge blockchain methodology for maintaining the decentralization feature of blockchain. We maintain the 50–50% blockchain nodes at both end cloud as well as at edge (making assumption for preventing 51% attack). At centralized cloud, we have X load balanced blockchain nodes always running to divide the incoming request traffic and execute transactions. Now we take 2 types of IoT devices for Blockchain IoT interaction:

Case1: Resource Constrained devices use the web interface to make transactions on Blockchain. Nodes don't need to store blockchain data and run blockchain operations as mining or data storage at that devices. These operations are to be done at central authority blockchain + on edge computing devices. But key generation process are to be done at their end itself.

Case2: High Resource edge IoT devices directly makes transaction on Blockchain via web interface. Node has to run a blockchain process as mining at their own devices and store that blockchain too.

In Both of the IoT devices cases, edge computing is useful for removing the unnecessary data access delay produced by cloud or third party blockchain. The proposed system framework is shown in Fig. 1.

4   Implementation

We create a smart contract application or simulation environment on private Ethereum [9] blockchain network because it is a test network means only we are making transactions on Blockchain, So that changing rate of the blockchain is relatively very less otherwise due to the high read/write requirements of the transactions on HDD storage occurring at public Blockchain becomes a problem for synchronization of Blockchain.

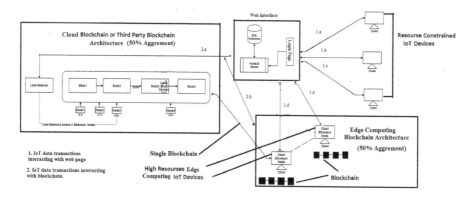

Fig. 1. Proposed approach

Consider a environment, where users or IoT devices are making transactions using both of the case1 and case2. Now central authority can't change or delete data on Blockchain as they can't control all Blockchain nodes and if they change something in their Blockchain out of band. Then, Blockchain will get out of sync with the Blockchain nodes at users edge end and conflict would be identified. Moreover every Blockchain Account has a public-private key pair for signing transactions. These keys are generally stored where the blockchain node is running but we would store these keys on the IoT device for case1 and not on the Blockchain node ran by some 3rd party authority managing servers or not on the any other edge devices. It means every IoT device manages its key generation process by itself. So whenever any transaction has to occur it has to go through IoT device and IoT device will sign the transaction using the private key only then this encrypted transaction can occur in Blockchain and in the case 2, IoT devices already act as a blockchain node. As the data on blockchain is well encrypted and all transactions have to be signed by the account owner for to occur. It ensures that even though data resides with some 3rd party or device they actually don't have the ability to read it or use it without the IoT device holder's permission. So even though, resource constrained IoT devices has no blockchain node running on it still has the ability to completely manage it's blockchain account.

The steps are for Setting a private Ethereum blockchain network, firstly create a genesis file that includes various configuration features such as Difficulty level, Gas Limit and many more of your blockchain. It is used to create the genesis block which is first block of the Blockchain. Smart Contract was developed using solidity language (contract oriented language) at truffle framework (development and testing environment for blockchains using the Ethereum Virtual Machine (EVM)). Finally, we deploy the contract on a private Ethereum Blockchain node simulating third party server and edge server or IoT devices. Then created an interface for its functions on NodeJS server using Web3JS following REST principles allowing to create multiple interfaces like an android app, ios app, web interface all having the same backend with a SQL Database. Note that way of constructing software is similar to what is currently web developers followed.

5   Results and Observations

Our proposed architecture is generalized, it can be applicable where heterogeneous IoT devices data security is challenged as attendance management system, certificate maintenance, Smart home energy management, water supply management etc. We discuss below results for a specific use case of leave application management system. A web app and a smart contract blockchain were created and then deployed. Here, To make transactions we provide each user with some ethers (infinite for the transactions in our work) and for centralized blockchain, we use a very naive load balancer algorithm that is doing mining on some of that x nodes at sign up along with the minors of edge IoT devices (this is done for balancing the power of cloud and edge). In this use case, the ether calculations as below:

Start Amount   = 2.9499991e+20wei
Cost of per transaction = 9.9687e+14wei

Table 1. Transactions results for leave application

Request types	Number of requests	Concurrency	Handled Requests/ Second (RPS)	Time taken(ms) for given percentage of Requests to Complete			
				50	90	95	99
Read	100	10	55	11	19	25	28
	10000	100	1212	74	105	130	207
	10000	500	1317	277	540	1223	1356
	10000	1000	1134	469	1487	1559	3551
Write	100	10	3	3168	5184	5214	5241
	10000	100	23	4114	7225	8520	12353
	10000	500	32	14507	21499	22686	28017
	10000	1000	28	33894	47334	49263	54390

All results are for single Blockchain node running

Above Table 1 shows load testing results for simulation of leave application system on an i7 Intel Processor, 8 GB RAM running NodeJs server with sql database and also maintaining two blockchain instances as centralized blockchain node and edge blockchain Node with multiple blockchain accounts as IoT devices at truffle framework. The results are satisfactory and explainable. Write operations have less RPS as the write has to take place on hard disk storage only after propagation and cryptographic validation of transaction in the network whereas read requires neither of them. One solution to solve high time of write problem is to notify the user immediately that his request has been received and then later on completion of request giving a notification stating the same, this ensures user doesn't have to unnecessarily wait.

6 Conclusion and Future Work

In this paper, we provide a new secure reliable framework for IoT devices based on Blockchain Smart Contract which is a combination of centralized and decentralized architecture. Our architecture is easily scalable, do proper resource utilization, time consuming, no 51% attack, easy to use and more secure. We also simulate our structure and provide some preliminary results those are satisfactory. In future work, we will do some extension to our work as:

1. Every user need some ether values for making transaction irrespective of whether it has blockchain node running on it or not. In our case, we assume that ether value is infinite which is to be given to the all users, but this is not feasible in real practical scenario. So, we will work on with more suitable mining resource distribution algorithm for providing ethers to every client.
2. We will use more suitable software-based load balancer algorithms (machine learning methods) for handling transactions more appropriately.
3. Apply More secure public-private key management at client so that intruder can never access to it.
4. Finally, we apply our framework on real time environment for seeing more implementation challenges.

References

1. Khan, M.A., Salah, K.: IoT security: review, blockchain solutions, and open challenges. Future Gener. Comput. Syst. **82**, 395–411 (2018)
2. Pan, J., et al.: EdgeChain: an edge-IoT framework and prototype based on blockchain and smart contracts. IEEE Internet Things J. **6**(3), 4719–4732 (2018)
3. Dorri, A., Kanhere, S.S., Jurdak, R.: Blockchain in Internet of Things: challenges and solutions. arXiv preprint arXiv:1608.05187 (2016)
4. Fedak, G., Bendella, W., Alves, E.: Blockchain-based decentralized cloud computing. iExec Corporation (2018). https://iex.ec/wp-content/uploads/pdf/iExec-WPv3.0-English.pdf. Accessed 7 Mar 2019
5. Popov, S.: The tangle, 131 (2016)
6. Yang, R., et al.: Integrated blockchain and edge computing systems: a survey, some research issues and challenges. IEEE Commun. Surv. Tutor. **21**(2), 1508–1532 (2019)
7. Nakamoto, S.: A peer-to-peer electronic cash system. Bitcoin (2008). https://bitcoin.org/bitcoin.pdf
8. Zheng, Z., et al.: Blockchain challenges and opportunities: a survey. Work Paper 2016 (2016)
9. Wood, G.: Ethereum: a secure decentralised generalised transaction ledger. Ethereum project yellow paper 151, pp. 1–32 (2014)
10. Ferrag, M.A., et al.: Blockchain technologies for the Internet of Things: research issues and challenges. IEEE Internet Things J. **6**(2), 2188–2204 (2018)
11. Banerjee, M., Lee, J., Choo, K.K.R.: A blockchain future for Internet of Things security: a position paper. Digital Commun. Netw. **4**(3), 149–160 (2018)
12. Raza, S., Wallgren, L., Voigt, T.: SVELTE: real-time intrusion detection in the Internet of Things. Ad Hoc Netw. **11**(8), 2661–2674 (2013)
13. Conoscenti, M., Vetro, A., De Martin, J.C.: Blockchain for the Internet of Things: a systematic literature review. In: 2016 IEEE/ACS 13th International Conference of Computer Systems and Applications (AICCSA). IEEE (2016)
14. Singla, V., et al.: Develop leave application using blockchain smart contract. In: 2019 11th International Conference on Communication Systems & Networks (COMSNETS). IEEE (2019)

15. Samaniego, M., Deters, R.: Blockchain as a service for IoT. In: IEEE International Conference on Internet of Things (iThings) and IEEE GreenComputing and Communications (GreenCom) and IEEE Cyber, Physical and Social Computing (CPSCom) and IEEE Smart Data (SmartData). IEEE (2016)
16. Top IoT Vulnerabilities. In: OWASP, Top IoT Vulnerabilities, May 2016. https://www.owasp.org/index.php/TopIoTVulnerabilities. Accessed 8 Sept 2018
17. Johansson, L., Olsson, O.: Improving intrusion detection for IoT networks-a snort GPGPU modification using OpenCL. Master's thesis 2018, Department of CSE, Chalmers University of Technology and University of Gothenburg, June 2018. https://pdfs.semanticscholar.org/045c/ed267e49cd32dbac61d9ec337e95df88eece.pdf
18. Kaur, J.: A semi supervised hybrid protection for network and host based attacks. J. Eng. Appl. Sci. **12**, 3108–3112 (2017)
19. Qu, C., et al.: Blockchain based credibility verification method for IoT entities. Secur. Commun. Netw **2018**, 1–11 (2018)
20. Al-Garadi, M.A., et al.: A survey of machine and deep learning methods for Internet of Things (IoT) security. arXiv preprint arXiv:1807.11023 (2018)
21. Mohanty, B.: Do we need only AI or IoT or ML or BlockChain or all of them together? February 2019. http://www.bikashmohanty.com/topics/do-we-need-only-ai-or-iot-or-ml-or-blockchain-or-all-of-them-together.html. Accessed 2 Mar 2019
22. Kaur, J.: Wired LAN and wireless LAN attack detection using signature based and machine learning tools. In: Perez, G.M., Mishra, K.K., Tiwari, S., Trivedi, M.C. (eds.) Networking Communication and Data Knowledge Engineering. LNDECT, vol. 3, pp. 15–24. Springer, Singapore (2018). https://doi.org/10.1007/978-981-10-4585-1_2

Toward GDPR Compliance in IoT Systems

Sahar Allegue[1,2]([✉]), Mouna Rhahla[1,2]([✉]), and Takoua Abdellatif[1]([✉])

[1] Polytechnic School of Tunisia, SERCOM, University of Carthage, Carthage, Tunisia
{sahar.allegue,mouna.rhahla,takoua.abdellatif}@ept.rnu.tn
[2] Proxym-Lab, Proxym-IT, Sousse, Tunisia
{sahar.allegue,mouna.rhahla}@proxym-it.com
http://www.proxym-group.com

Abstract. The General Data Protection Regulation (GDPR) allow citizens to control their data. For that, they must define and update their security data policies that are generally more sophisticated and more dynamic than classical access control policies managed by system administrators. Consequently, GDPR implementation in modern scalable and dynamic systems like IoT is still a challenge. We propose a security model for data privacy and an original solution where a GDPR consent manager is integrated using Complex Event Processing (CEP) system and following the edge computing. We show, through a smart home IoT system, the efficiency of our approach in terms of flexibility and scalability.

Keywords: CEP · GDPR and privacy · IoT · Edge computing

1 Introduction

Internet of Things, IoT, consists of several digital devices, individuals, services and other physical objects which have the ability to reliably connect, interact and trade data about themselves and their environment. This makes our lives more straightforward through a digital environment that is sensitive, adaptive and responsive to human needs. For example, smart home [4] sensors collect data that is utilized to monitor users' activities, status and environment to make automated decisions for users' well being. However, a great number of users encounter critical challenges concerning the protection of their personal data. It is crucial today for an individual to be sure that what he has shared is exactly what he wants to be shared, to whom, for what purpose and when. Individuals must have control over their data and can give or revoke permission to access their data for a given service whenever they want. They also have to be notified about illicit access to or unauthorized storage of their data.

These requirements are actually imposed by the recent General Data Protection Regulation (GDPR) [1], which defines the main principles for how organizations can share EU citizens' personal data. Indeed, GDPR compliance imposes

This project is carried out under the MOBIDOC scheme, funded by the EU through the EMORI program and managed by the ANPR.

S. Yangui et al. (Eds.): ICSOC 2019 Workshops, LNCS 12019, pp. 130–141, 2020.
https://doi.org/10.1007/978-3-030-45989-5_11

building solutions to answer *5W* questions: *where* data is going to be stored? *what* personal data is being transferred? *who* has the right to access to the data? *why* those with access have access? and *when* does the transfer take place?

Compliance with GDPR requirements supposes consent managers' implementation as legacy systems to get and oversee suitable user's consent as long as data flows. A data controller determines the purposes, conditions and means of the processing of personal data. Implementing consent managers face the main challenge that consists of shifting the role of data control and management to the data subject. He becomes the administrator of his data in charge of setting and updating his security policies and notified about any security leakage. Many recent solutions to user-centric privacy problems in IoT have been suggested [8–10]. Nevertheless, they fall short in covering GDPR security policies that are more sophisticated than classical role-based access control. They additionally set constraints about access delays and targets. Consequently, a consent manager have to deal with rule-based access control and to continually involve the user informed about his data usage. Furthermore, GDPR consent managers' implementation that introduces data interception and analysis has to be performed without a costly overhead of engineering and system performance.

In this paper, we are interested in providing a GDPR consent manager for modern IoT smart home systems. These systems are based on event-driven processing for event detection and notification [6]. For example, they are used to remotely detect fire, flood, security attacks or health problems [16,18,19]. Central to these systems is the use of Complex Event Processing (CEP) [2] which deals with the detection of complex events based on rules and patterns defined by domain experts. Furthermore, recent smart home systems rely on edge computing to reduce data flow on the network and to be more reactive [20]. The idea is to deploy processing as close as possible to data sources. The classical architecture of a smart home that integrates a CEP engine is shown in Fig. 1. Data flow respects the following steps. First, data is collected from sensors by the GW component that can perform filtering and aggregation processing. Then, the GW sends this data as primary events to a CEP engine that detects more complex events based on a set of predefined CEP rules. Finally, complex events are sent to remote services like Energy service or security service.

Combining CEP and edge computing is very interesting for IoT because it is intended to manage real-time big data. In this context, we build a GDPR consent manager that takes advantage of both these best of breed IoT technology features. The idea is to use CEP as a component that centralizes and controls data dissemination between sensors, services and people. Primary events and user data are annotated at the edge (at the gateway level) following the *5W* GDPR policies defined by the data subject. Security policies are dynamically calculated for complex events based on policies defined for primary events. Our solution is original in that CEP is Commonly used for event processing while we are using it for security data processing. System context and security user preferences are accessed in real-time without performance overhead thanks to the new generation of CEP that allows us to set up dynamic rules and to save

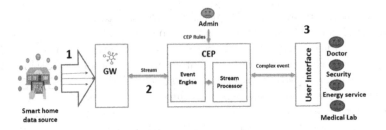

Fig. 1. A smart home use case

system context in dynamic tables [25, 29]. To our knowledge, this is the first work that provides a GDPR consent manager using a CEP engine for private data management. We rely on CEP scalability and efficiency to reduce the consent manager overhead on nominal system processing. In addition to the proposed novel architecture, a main contribution of this work is the security model that takes into account the dependencies and the dynamic state of streaming events. This paper is structured as follows. Section 2 presents some background on CEP and GDPR. In Sect. 3, we describe our security model and we describe our annotation algorithms. The architecture of the GDPR consent manager is presented in Sect. 4. Section 5 describes our first implementation and evaluation results. Section 6 describes the related works. Finally, Sect. 7 gives a summary of the main findings of this paper and highlights new opportunities for future work.

2   Background

In this section, we describe the fields in relation to our contribution, that is CEP and GDPR.

2.1   Complex Event Processing

Complex Event Processing is the technology that interprets and combines streams of primitive events to identify higher-level composite events [2]. CEP has been used in many areas, such as sensor networks for environmental monitoring, continuous analyzing of stocks exchange to detect trends in the financial domains such as stock markets and credit card fraud detection [2]. It relies on several techniques, including Event-pattern detection, Event abstraction, Event filtering, Event aggregation and transformation, modeling event hierarchies and detecting relationships [3]. Nowadays, big data technologies provide a new generation of CEP engines (such as ESPER [21], Apache Flink [25], WSO2 CEP [23]). They open new doors for highly scalable and distributed real-time analytics thanks to the convergence of batch and stream engines and the emergence of state management and stateful stream processing. With the stateful nature of stream processors, Stream SQL statements can be applied directly in the streaming engine and dynamic tables can be created rather than the static tables that represent batch data, dynamic tables which are changing over time.

2.2   General Data Protection Regulation

GDPR [7] sets new rules on security through 99 articles and 173 recitals and aims to protect the rights and freedoms of natural persons. Every organization that deals with data has to comply with GDPR, to protect these rights and to be accountable while improving business models [5]. Accountability aims at demonstrating how controllers comply with data protection principles. In a previous work [17], we defined a framework that allows testing GDPR compliance in Big Data systems. We defined 10 components that need to be implemented to fulfil the GDPR 7 principles: Lawfulness, fairness and transparency, Purpose limitation, Data minimisation, Accuracy, Storage limitation, Integrity and confidentiality and Accountability. This framework is a helpful tool that allows us to evaluate the GDPR compliance of our solution.

3   Security Model

We suppose in our architecture that the communication channel between the GW and the server is secured. We focus on the privacy issue that is the control of data dissemination following the user preferences expressed following $5W$ format. In this section, we describe the used $5W$ labels and then the annotation process. Finally, we present the security checking algorithm.

3.1   5W Labels

A security label provides specific security metadata attached to a data. In our case, events and user profiles represent the data. To express privacy policy, labels are assigned to data to restrict access control to that data and control authorization following the $5W$ constraints. A label general structure is as follows: L = {O:data owner identifier, *who*: "principles having the right to access data", *what*: "data being transferred and processed", *when*: "when the transfer takes place", *where*: "where data is to be stored", *why*: "purpose for collecting data"} where the value is a String and O is the data subject Id. The data subject Id in our case is the concatenation of a unique user ID and the sensor ID. Every W should have a default value. For example, if we take the example of user presence then an example of a label is: L = {O:ID, *who* = {"doctor", "security"}, *what* = {"presence"} *when* = {"15h"}, *where* = {"security-DB", "doctor-DB"}, *why* = {"alert", "diagnostic"}}. Labels are ordered using the no more restrictive than relation, represented by $\subseteq$ symbol. Given two annotation L1 and L2, we have $L1 \subseteq L2$ if and only if owners of L1 are included in L2. The join L of L1 and L2 (written as $L = L1 \cup L2$) represents the least restrictive label that maintains all the flow restrictions specified by L1 and L2. It is constructed so that L owner tag is the union of L1 and L2 owners. We note it: $L.O = L1.O \cup L2.O$. Similarly, we have $L.who = L1.who \cap L2.who$, $L.why = L1.why \cap L2.why$ and $L.where = L1.where \cap L2.where$. Except for *when* requirement, we have $L.when = \text{Min}(L1.when, L2.when)$ and the resulted complex event for the *what* requirement. We provide in the next sub-section an example using the join relation between labels.

3.2 Security Annotation

The annotation process and annotation checking consist in attributing labels to events and user preferences to express privacy constraints. They are formally provided as follows. Let E be the set of events of concern that are stored in the state database: $E = \{e1, e2, \cdots, en\}$, L the set of security annotations (labels) and P the list of user preferences expressed as $5W$ policies. Let S: $P \cup E \rightarrow L$ be a function assigning security annotation to the events and preferences [30].

Security annotation is executed in three cases: (1) at GW level, before sending an event to take into account the user preferences, (2) when a new complex event is calculated at CEP level and (3) when one of the user preferences changes.

We define a dependency relation between events that we denote by $\rightarrow$ symbol. Given two events e1 and e2, we have $e1 \rightarrow e2$ if e2 is calculated from e1. More generally, for a complex event ce calculated from $e1, e2, \cdots, en$, we have for each i in [1..n], $ei \rightarrow ce$. Actually, we generally have an event dependency graph that is built from the $\rightarrow$ causality relationship between events [22]. In this work, we restrict our work to one step relation between events. Indeed, it is sufficient to cover the smart home use case. For a calculated ce from a set of events ei, we have: $S(ce) = \bigcup_{i=0}^{n} S(ei)$. For example, if we consider the real case where we have three events representing respectively temperature, smoke and presence information, the notification about fire is a complex event that is annotated as follows:

- $S(e1 = temperature) = \{ O{:}id1, who = \{ \text{``Security''} \}, what = \{ \text{``temperature''} \}, when = \{ \text{``12h''} \}, where = \{ \text{``security-DB''} \}, why = \{ \text{``alert''} \} \}$.
- $S(e2 = smoke) = \{ O{:}id1, who = \{ \text{``Security''} \}, what = \{ \text{``smoke''} \} when = \{ \text{``12h''} \}, where = \{ \text{``security-DB''} \}, why = \{ \text{``alert''} \} \}$.
- $S(e3 = presence) = \{ O{:}id1, who = \{ \text{``doctor''}, \text{``security''} \}, what = \{ \text{``presence''} \} when = \{ \text{``15h''} \}, where = \{ \text{``security-DB''}, \text{``doctor-DB''} \}, why = \{ \text{``alert''}, \text{``diagnostic''} \} \}$.
- $S(ce = fire) = \{ O{:}id1, who = \{ \text{``Security''} \}, what = \{ \text{``Fire CE''} \}, when = \{ \text{``12h''} \}, where = \{ \text{``security-DB''} \}, why = \{ \text{``alert''} \} \}$.

The annotation of fire notification event authorizes the security service only to access the event and the notification will not be sent to the doctor for instance.

When a user changes his preferences, not only the user events' configuration has to be updated but also the configuration of all the events that are calculated from the user events. We consider the events that are stored in the state database (state DB) that contains the history of streams for a given period and that can be used to calculate future complex events. Algorithm 1 is executed to update an event security configuration. For any event in the state database, the event policies have to be restricted to the user preferences (line 2). In a recursive way, all events depending on the event with updated policies, have their policy updated (line 4–8).

Algorithm 1 Annotation Algorithm

Require: owner O, user preference P and state db D
Ensure: S update calculation
1: foreach $ei \in D$
2: if ei.what== P.what and ei.O==P.O then S(ei)= $S(ei) \cup S(p)$ endif end
3: e=ei
4: while (S changes) do
5:     $\forall ej \in D, e \rightarrow ej$
6:     S(ej)= $S(e) \cup S(ej)$
7:     e = ej
8: End

This dynamic update is essential to maintain a coherent state of the state database that takes into account the last user preferences.

3.3   Security Checking

The security checking aims at preserving users' privacy and then checks that each event (primary or complex) annotation takes into account the user preferences. This task is accomplished each time the server receives an event or each time a new complex event is calculated. Let E be the set of events E = {e1, e2,..,en} and P the set of user preferences in the form of GDPR *5W* stored in the policies database. For an incoming event e which is annotated with the *5W* (*what, who, when, where, why*), the event security configuration is correct if it fulfills the user preference P regarding the same event topic. More formally, the configuration is accepted if we have *e.what==P.what* if S(e) $\subseteq$ S(P). For example if we consider e1 an incoming event that is annotated with the label *S(e1 = Blood pressure)* = {*O:id1, who = "doctor1", what = "blood pressure", when = "12h", where = "doctor1-DB", why = { "diagnostic"}* }. The user preferences for the *what* ="blood pressure" are *S(P.what = Blood pressure)* = {*O:id1, who= { "doctor1, doctor2, doctor3, nurse1"* }, *when = "12h", where = { "doctor1-DB, doctor2-DB, doctor3-DB"}, why = { "diagnostic"}}*. As we see here the S(e1) $\subseteq$ S(P). In the case S(e1) $\not\subseteq$ S(P) a notification is sent to the owner to inform him of an unauthorized access.

4   Architecture

GDPR consent manager architecture is represented in Fig. 2.

A friendly user interface provides the data subject DS with the ability to express his *5W* GDPR preferences and the ability to update them. The Access Handler component translates and stores user preferences in the *5W* policies DB in JSON format. These *5W* policies are used by the Primary event annotator component to annotate events coming from the data source: the smart home sensors. Note that, at GW level, to aggregate and filter data sources, lightweight CEP [36] can be deployed. Like at server side, security annotator is then necessary to calculate the labels of generated events. In this paper, we only consider CEP at server side.

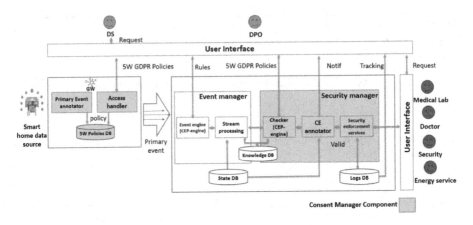

Fig. 2. CEP based smart home security architecture.

The user interface communicates with the server that stores user preferences in the knowledge DB. The server-side software is composed of two main components: the event manager and the security manager. The event manager is responsible for complex event detection and stream processing of received primary events. After processing and detecting complex events, comes the role of the security manager component. Security manager component is the central part of the GDPR consent manager. Based on the proposed security model detailed in Sect. 3, it is in charge of the security checking of complex event annotation. Indeed, the checker component, which is a CEP-engine, executes the security checking algorithm and implements as a rule.

When the security checker (CEP engine) receives an event it extracts the *what* value. Then, it looks, in the knowledge DB, for the values of the other $4W$ preferences of the owner and stores the values of each W in a list. Afterwards, it verifies if the $4W$ of the event are less restrictive than the user preferences using a CEP pattern.

At CE annotator component, the complex event annotation is calculated as mentioned in Sect. 3.2. Finally, before delivering the *ce* to the set of services, it has to be protected by the security enforcement service. In our solution the administrator can act as the data protection officer DPO that evaluates GDPR-Compliance and provides the accountability principle. The provided log DB archives all event history and is used for visualization and data tracking for both data subject and DPO. It keeps a detailed log of all requests and responses of policy setting and updates as well as exchanged data history. The security enforcement service provides a set of services such as cryptography, logs, right to erasure and many other services. As explained in Sect. 5, we use a third party service for security enforcement [35]. The main idea is to use a token that stores the *who* and *when* policies. Tokens are attributed to data consumers (services and persons in our case) to access the events sent by the server. Once the authentication is successful, that is the consumer is the *who* list and the target of processing data is the same as defined by *what* policy, the data consumer receives a token that is unique. The token allows the access to decryption services for the authorized period defined in *when* policy. If this period expires, the encryption keys are revoked and the user can no longer decrypt received events. If the data subject modifies the *who* policy by removing an authorized consumer of his data, the same revocation occurs. A user interface is provided to administrators (DS and DPO) to interact with the consent manager and to receive notifications. Also, it gives the ability to fix or update rules in both event engine and the checker (CEP-engine). In our architecture, we have three databases: policies DB, log DB and state DB. The state can be a dynamic table that contains the history of streams for a given period. This component can be queried to help the CEP component in the annotation process, for example, it can give us the set of events in a chosen window of time to check if event annotations are modified or not. In addition, the state database is used to change the annotation of events if a user updates his preferences which is mentioned in security annotation section.

5   Implementation and Evaluation

This section will describe briefly our first implementation, followed by the evaluation of our solution.

5.1   Implementation

At the GW level, data is annotated in JSON format. As CEP, we used Flink [25] since we take advantage of its CEP engine and its Stream processing features such as the Table API. Dynamic tables are the core concept of Flink Table API and SQL support for streaming data. For the state database, we are essentially building a table from an INSERT-only changelog stream to keep the history of events and maintain a state so to be used and queried for a given window and to check policies update at run time.

We used Hashicorp Vault [35] for the log and security enforcement component. Vault is a tool for securely accessing secrets. A secret is anything that you want to tightly control access to, such as API keys, passwords, certificates, and more. Vault services are accessed through HTTP API. The enforcement component is a particular Vault client that acts as a root asking for tokens in behalf of data consumers (services and persons). Policies, in Vault, can govern what a client is able to do, and they are attached to the token. Tokens also store a bunch of metadata in addition to the policies, so information like the time to live and the duration of the token. In the enforcement component, we translate for each user, the *who*, *where* and *when* policies to Vault token metadata. Tokens are provided to data consumers with authorized *what* policy only for the purpose defined by the user. The *where* policy is translated as a particular data consumer (using data for storage). In addition, we used Vault Encryption as a Service (EaaS) to fortify data during transit and at rest. In our consent manager, we used a java implementation based on Vault Java Driver [31].

Vault encrypts the events so that they are delivered to the right destination and with the constraints defined in the *who* and *when* policies. When, *who* value changes or *when* value expires, the event token will be revoked automatically and data consumers have no longer access to data. Also, the DPO can, dynamically, track data (request and response coming into vault) and receive notification using Kibana [24] visualization interface.

5.2 Evaluation

In a previous work [18], we defined a framework that allows evaluating GDPR compliance in Big Data systems. We used this framework to evaluate GDPR compliance with our solution. The result of the evaluation shows that our solution covers most of the GDPR framework components and principles mentioned in Sect. 2.2. Transparency principle is provided by the user interface component. Since it provides history notification and data tracking based on the logs component. In the GW and security manager components, data minimisation is ensured thanks to *what* policy and purpose limitation is ensured since events are filtered with *why* policy. Encryption enforces the ownership and the *who* policy by providing both integrity and confidentiality principles. Finally, we provided a DPO user interface in which every detail of the system (request/response) is illustrated. In addition to GDPR requirements, our solution provides the data subject and the DPO the flexibility to update their policies dynamically. We rely on Flink for scalability and fault tolerance since it is one of the most robust and scalable big data frameworks. However, we still need to evaluate the overall solution in a more scalable IoT system.

6 Related Works

Related works are classified into two sections: GDPR implementation in IoT systems and CEP usage in smart homes and IoT systems. The review process highlighted that, unlike our work, none of the related works address the all of whole GDPR requirements mainly the *5W* policies. Furthermore, to the best of our knowledge, this is the first work that adopts CEP engines as a GDPR consent manager.

6.1 GDPR Implementation in IoT Systems

In many IoT applications, GDPR implementation has a considerable impact on protecting users' privacy [8]. Nevertheless, current solutions address only partially GDPR requirements. In [9], authors concentrate on profiling. In [10,11], the focus is put on transparency. Like our work, IoT Databox [32] tool provides data access mechanisms at the edge and different API are proposed to allow users to track their data. Nevertheless, the solution is not flexible enough to allow for implementing all GDPR *5W* policies and to allow for dynamic changes. In a previous work [33], we proposed a GDPR consent manager for IoT systems where security, transparency and purpose limitation are implemented but we do not cover all the *5W* policies. In other works [6,34], block-chain technology was adopted to implement users' consent in a distributed environment. In our work, CEP engines represent a centralized hub where all data streams go through but our work can be extended to a distributed CEP.

To express advanced security policies, many standard and policy languages such as XACML [28], SAML [27], P3P [26] and Vault policy [35] are proposed. However, they express only 3 W policies (*who*, *what* and *why*). Also, our work handles the dependencies between events. That is when the user changes his preferences, so all stored events and the events depending on take into account this change.

6.2 CEP in Smart Home and IoT Systems

Like our work, many recent solutions adopt both sCEP and edge computing in smart home IoT systems [12,14,15]. At gateway-side, useful information is extracted from raw data and server-side CEP manages semantic reasoning jobs like correlating between warning messages. In our work, we adopt this approach for privacy data processing in the GDPR context.

Chen et al. [13] use CEP on the server-side for intrusion detection. They detect anomalies by filtering complex events. Policy checking with CEP is more intricate since policies are complex and can be changed dynamically. For this reason, we associate CEP policy checking with stream state queries to take into account policy update at runtime.

7 Conclusion

This paper presents a security model for data privacy respect under GDPR. We introduce a CEP-based architecture that provides GDPR consent manager for modern IoT systems. We show the efficiency of our solution in the context of a smart home. To the best of our knowledge, this is the first work that combines CEP and edge computing features in GDPR context. As future work, we plan to measure in more detail, performance overhead and different intricate cases of policy update and event dependency graphs.

References

1. GDPR. https://gdpr-info.eu/. Acessed 22 Aug 2019
2. Luckham, D.: The power of events: an introduction to complex event processing in distributed enterprise systems. In: Bassiliades, N., Governatori, G., Paschke, A. (eds.) RuleML 2008. LNCS, vol. 5321, p. 3. Springer, Heidelberg (2008). https://doi.org/10.1007/978-3-540-88808-6_2
3. Etzion, O., Niblett, P.: Event Processing in Action, 1st edn. Manning Publications, Greenwich (2010)

4. Verma, H., Jain, M., Goel, K., Vikram, A., Verma, G.: Smart home system based on Internet of Things. In: 3rd International Conference on Computing for Sustainable Global Development (INDIACom), pp. 2073–2075. IEEE, New Delhi (2016)
5. Pham, P.: The applicability of the GDPR to the Internet of Things. J. Data Prot. Priv. **2**(3), 254–263 (2019)
6. Vargas, J.C.: Blockchain-based consent manager for GDPR compliance. In: Open Identity Summit 2019. Gesellschaft für Informatik, Bonn (2019)
7. Regulation (EU) 2016/679 of the European Parliament and of the Council of 27 April 2016 on the protection of natural persons with regard to the processing of personal data and on the free movement of such data, and repealing Directive 95/46/EC (General Data Protection Regulation). Official Journal of the European Union. L119, 1–88 (2016)
8. Seo, J., Kim, K., Park, M., Park, M., Lee, K.: An analysis of economic impact on IoT under GDPR. In: 2017 International Conference on Information and Communication Technology Convergence (ICTC), pp. 879–881. IEEE, Jeju, South Korea (2017)
9. Wachter, S.: Normative challenges of identification in the Internet of Things: privacy, profiling, discrimination, and the GDPR. Comput. Law Secur. Rev. **34**(3), 436–449 (2018)
10. Wachter, S.: The GDPR and the Internet of Things: a three-step transparency model. Law Innov. Technol. **10**(2), 266–294 (2018)
11. Castelluccia, C., Cunche, M., Le Metayer, D., Morel, V.: Enhancing transparency and consent in the IoT. In: 2018 IEEE European Symposium on Security and Privacy Workshops (EuroS&PW), pp. 116–119. IEEE, London, UK (2018)
12. Chen, C., Fu, H., Sung, T., Wang, P., Jou, E., Feng, M.: Complex event processing for the Internet of Things and its applications. In: 2014 IEEE International Conference on Automation Science and Engineering (CASE), pp. 1144–1149. IEEE, Taipei, Taiwan (2014)
13. Jun, C., Chi, C.: Design of complex event-processing IDS in Internet of Things. In: 2014 Sixth International Conference on Measuring Technology and Mechatronics Automation, pp. 226–229. IEEE, Zhangjiajie, China (2014)
14. Kaya, M., Cetin-Kaya, Y.: Complex event processing using IOT devices based on Arduino. Int. J. Cloud Comput. Serv. Architect. IJCCSA **7**, 13–24 (2017)
15. Nocera, F., Di Noia, T., Mongiello, M., Di Sciascio, E.: Semantic IoT middleware-enabled mobile complex event processing for integrated pest management. In: 7th International Conference on Cloud Computing and Services Science (2017)
16. Strohbach, M., Ziekow, H., Gazis, V., Akiva, N.: Towards a big data analytics framework for iot and smart city applications. In: Xhafa, F., Barolli, L., Barolli, A., Papajorgji, P. (eds.) Modeling and Processing for Next-Generation Big-Data Technologies. MOST, vol. 4, pp. 257–282. Springer, Cham (2015). https://doi.org/10.1007/978-3-319-09177-8_11
17. Rhahla, M., Allegue, S., Abdellatif, T.: A framework for GDPR compliance in big data systems. In: Kallel, S., Cuppens, F., Cuppens-Boulahia, N., Hadj Kacem, A. (eds.) CRiSIS 2019. LNCS, vol. 12026, pp. 211–226. Springer, Cham (2020). https://doi.org/10.1007/978-3-030-41568-6_14
18. Boubeta-Puig, J., Ortiz, G., Medina-Bulo, I.: Approaching the Internet of Things through integrating SOA and complex event processing. In: Handbook of Research on Demand-Driven Web Services: Theory, Technologies, and Applications, pp. 304–323. IGI Global (2014)

19. Lan, L., Wang, B., Zhang, L., Shi, R., Li, F.: An event-driven service-oriented architecture for Internet of Things service execution. Int. J. Online Eng. (iJOE) **11**, 4 (2015)
20. Corcoran, P., Datta, K.: Mobile-edge computing and the Internet of Things for consumers: extending cloud computing and services to the edge of the network. IEEE Consum. Electron. Mag. **5**(4), 73–74 (2016)
21. Esper. http://www.espertech.com/. Accessed 19 Aug 2019
22. Flink Gelly API. https://flink.apache.org/news/2015/08/24/introducing-flink-gelly.html. Accessed 29 Aug 2019
23. WSO2 CEP. https://wso2.com/products/complex-event-processor/. Accessed 19 Aug 2019
24. Kibana. https://www.elastic.co/fr/products/kibana. Accessed 19 Aug 2019
25. Apache Flink. https://ci.apache.org/projects/flink/flink-docs-release-1.8/. Accessed 19 Aug 2019
26. Platform for Privacy Preferences (P3P). https://www.w3.org/P3P/. Accessed 26 Aug 2019
27. Security Assertion Markup Language (SAML). http://docs.oasis-open.org/security/saml/Post2.0/sstc-saml-tech-overview-2.0.html. Accessed 26 Aug 2019
28. EXtensible Access Control Markup Language (XACML). http://docs.oasis-open.org/xacml/3.0/xacml-3.0-core-spec-os-en.html. Accessed 26 Aug 2019
29. Dynamic Tables. https://ci.apache.org/projects/flink/flink-docs-stable/dev/table/streaming/dynamic_tables.html. Accessed 27 Aug 2019
30. Abdellatif, T., Bozga, M.: An end-to-end security model for adaptive service-oriented applications. In: Braubach, L., Murillo, J.M., Kaviani, N., Lama, M., Burgueño, L., Moha, N., Oriol, M. (eds.) ICSOC 2017. LNCS, vol. 10797, pp. 43–54. Springer, Cham (2018). https://doi.org/10.1007/978-3-319-91764-1_4
31. Java-vault-driver. https://bettercloud.github.io/vault-java-driver/. Accessed 26 Aug 2019
32. Crabtree, A., et al.: Building accountability into the Internet of Things: the IoT databox model. J. Reliable Intell. Environ. **4**(1), 39–55 (2018). https://doi.org/10.1007/s40860-018-0054-5
33. Rhahla, M., Abdellatif, T., Attia, R., Berrayana, W.: A GDPR controller for IoT systems: application to e-Health. In: 2019 IEEE 28th International Conference on Enabling Technologies: Infrastructure for Collaborative Enterprises (WETICE) (2019)
34. Rantos, K., Drosatos, G., Demertzis, K., Ilioudis, C., Papanikolaou, A., Kritsas, A.: ADvoCATE: a consent management platform for personal data processing in the IoT using blockchain technology. In: Lanet, J.-L., Toma, C. (eds.) SECITC 2018. LNCS, vol. 11359, pp. 300–313. Springer, Cham (2019). https://doi.org/10.1007/978-3-030-12942-2_23
35. Vault. https://www.vaultproject.io. Accessed 01 Aug 2019
36. Dhillon, A., Majumdar, S., St-Hilaire, M., El-Haraki, A.: A mobile complex event processing system for remote patient monitoring. In: IEEE International Congress on Internet of Things (ICIOT) (2018)

A Reconfigurable Microservice-Based Migration Technique for IoT Systems

Chang-ai Sun$^{(\boxtimes)}$, Jing Wang, Jing Guo, Zhen Wang, and Li Duan

School of Computer and Communication Engineering, University of Science and Technology Beijing, Beijing 100083, China
`casun@ustb.edu.cn`

Abstract. An Internet of Things (IoT) system is often an integration of a large number of hardware and software modules, which are expected to be easily replaced or reconfigured in order to cater for quickly-changing environments and requirements. With the popularity of microservices, people have attempted to introduce the microservice architecture to IoT systems, while paid little attention to the connectivity between the decomposed microservices, resulting in poor reconfigurability of the resulting system. In this paper, we propose a reconfigurable microservice-based migration technique for IoT systems, which first decomposes an IoT system as a set of microservices and then introduces variation contexts to make the decomposed microservices reconfigurable. We have conducted a case study on an open-source real-life unmanned aerial vehicle (UAV) system. The results demonstrate that the migrated UAV system can be dynamically reconfigured to handle various run-time changes.

Keywords: Internet of Things (IoT) · Microservices · Migration techniques · Service compositions · Reconfigurable systems

1 Introduction

The Internet of Things (IoT) is the network of devices that contain electronics, software, sensors, actuators, and connectivity which allows these things to connect, interact and exchange data [17]. Due to the rapid development of intelligent devices and mobile networks, IoT systems become pervasive in people's daily life. For instance, a driverless car is a typical IoT system that is capable of sensing its environment and navigating without human intervention. The system integrates a large number of distributed and heterogenous components for data sensing, network communication, computing, and decision making. Considering the component that is responsible for detecting surroundings, it may have different implementations based on radar, lidar, GPS, or more practically, their combinations of all these technologies. Furthermore, the system is continuously running in a dynamic environment which frequently suffers environmental changes (e.g. traffic situations) or requirement changes (e.g. preferred paths). As a result, such an IoT system is expected to be reconfigurable enough.

© Springer Nature Switzerland AG 2020
S. Yangui et al. (Eds.): ICSOC 2019 Workshops, LNCS 12019, pp. 142–155, 2020.
https://doi.org/10.1007/978-3-030-45989-5_12

Recently, people have made efforts to introduce the microservice architecture to IoT systems [11,13,16], or discuss the decomposition of microservices [3,8,12]. However, no efforts have been made to address the connectivity among the decomposed microservices, which is assumed to be defined internally and implicitly. This poses difficulties for inevitable upgrades or extensions. The situations become even worse in the context of continuously-changing environments. For instance, a microservice may become unavailable for some reasons, thus the involved process has to be interrupted and restarting such a process will take a long time. Consequently, the resulting microservice-based IoT systems suffer poor reconfigurability.

To address the reconfigurability of IoT systems, we propose a microservice-based reconfigurable migration technique. Our approach not only introduces the microservice architecture into the IoT systems, but also addresses the reconfigurability of migrated IoT systems, aiming at enabling timely responses to changes from environment or requirements.

1. A microservice-based migration framework for IoT systems was proposed to address the challenges posed by reconfigurable migration of IoT systems.
2. A supporting tool was developed to enable and automate as much as possible the proposed technique.
3. A case study was conducted to comprehensively evaluate the proposed technique using a large-scale open-source unmanned aerial vehicle.

The rest of the paper is organized as follows. Section 2 presents a microservice-based reconfigurable migration technique for IoT systems. Section 3 describes a comprehensive case study which is used to validate the proposed approach. Section 4 introduces related work. Section 5 concludes the paper with future work.

2   Approach

We first give an overview and then discuss the key issues of the proposed approach, followed by a supporting tool.

2.1   Overview of Approach

We propose a microservice-based variation-enabling reconfigurable migration framework for IoT systems, as shown in Fig. 1. The proposed approach works as follows.

First, for a legacy IoT system, our approach decomposes it into a set of microservices with the guidance of various microservice decomposition techniques. Each microservice has a simple structure and functionality that can be independently developed, deployed, and maintained using different techniques [18]. Practically, an IoT system involves a number of intelligent devices which are responsible for sensing surroundings and manifest themselves as hardware modules. Furthermore, these devices normally follow different formats and

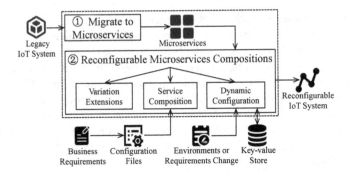

Fig. 1. Reconfigurable microservice-based migration framework for IoT systems

protocols for data transmission. Inspired by the idea of Software Defined Everything (SDX), we add an abstraction layer to mask the heterogeneity. Accordingly, all software and hardware modules are uniformly treated as a set of microservices with RESTful interfaces after the decomposition.

Second, our approach adopts microservices compositions to achieve reconfigurable IoT systems. (i) The microservices are first extended with variability. In this way, the extended microservices can be easily replaced at run-time by modifying variants in the configuration. (ii) We adopt the variation configuration file as a specification for microservices composition. When the system starts, the process information is first loaded and the name of the microservice provider to be invoked is derived according to the configuration. (iii) A dynamic reconfiguration is proposed to support the reconfigurability of the service composition. Since the invocation information between microservices is maintained during the execution, the microservice consumer will be unbound from the original microservice provider and bound to a new microservice provider in case a change occurs. This process corresponds to the variant selection of a variation point in the context of variability management. Consequently, the replacement of microservices in a business process becomes easy and efficient at run-time.

2.2 Details of Approach

(1) Migration to Microservices. The goal is to decompose a legacy IoT system into a set of microservices through analyzing its structure, functionality, business logic, or implementation. The decomposed microservices will be independently deployed and executed, and communicate with each other by lightweight mechanisms. Since the granularity of microservices affects the development and management cost of the migration [15], a key issue is to decide the boundary of microservices [9]. Accordingly, we present the following decomposition principles for the migration to microservices.

- *Domain analysis (P_1)* is a widely used migration principle which determines the granularity of microservices in a top-down manner via domain models [4].

- *Static analysis (P_2)* is a bottom-up migration principle through an analysis of the implementation of a legacy system [7], which can be further classified into *technique analysis, source code analysis, metadata assisted analysis,* and *data analysis.*
- *Hierarchy-aware (P_3)* emphasizes the hierarchy should be carefully considered during the migration to microservices. An IoT system is normally composed of multiple layers. Naturally, the decomposition of microservices should reserve this hierarchy as much as possible. This is particularly important for the migration of the sensing layer to microservices. For those hardware modules, an abstraction layer is necessarily created to mask the heterogeneity of multi-source, heterogeneous, and non-uniformly communicated devices. Furthermore, the abstraction layer should also have a partner microservice in the control layer.
- *Embedded features-aware (P_4)* pays much attention to real-time and reactive features of IoT systems. An IoT system often integrates embedded modules for operation controlling or event triggering. For instance, a driverless car needs to periodically sense its position and surroundings, which is commonly implemented by embedded modules. Furthermore, relevant tasks should be completed in a real-time manner. These features require the preservation of periodical control structures and the abidance of the locality principle during migration to microservices.

(2) Reconfigurable Microservices Compositions. Reconfigurable microservices compositions are shown in Fig. 2. *(i) Variation extensions:* To support dynamic reconfiguration of migrated IoT systems, the decomposed microservices are further extended with variation contexts and registered in the *Registration Center*. Specially, a location where a microservice consumer ("*MS_N*") invokes an external microservice is treated as a variation point, and the potential microservice provider is treated as a variant (for example, "*MS_{M1}*"). In this way, the newly introduced variation contexts make the connectivity between the decomposed microservices explicit and reconfigurable.

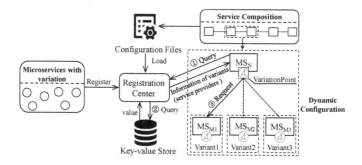

Fig. 2. Reconfigurable microservice-based service compositions

(ii) Service Composition: The decomposed microservices with variation contexts are composed to meet various business requirements. In order to relax the coupling between service consumers and service providers, we introduce a layer of key-value store on top of traditional service discovery. Accordingly, the invocation relationships between microservices are no longer specified internally but kept in a key-value store. In a key-value pair, the "key" corresponds to the microservice consumer indicating the location of the calling external microservices, while the "value" corresponding to the microservice provider indicating the selected microservices. The representation of key-value pairs is shown in Fig. 3.

Key	::= <MicroserviceName> "/VariationPoint" <Index>
Value	::= <MicroserviceName>
MicroserviceName	::= {a|...|z|A|...|Z|0|...|9|_}

Fig. 3. Variation representation based on key-value pairs

(iii) Dynamic Configuration: When an involved microservice of the business process become unavailable due to some reasons such as failures, updates, or network traffic congestion. In our approach, all invocations between microservices have been stored in the key-value store and the status of all involved microservices are monitored in real time. When a microservice becomes unavailable, the value of variant in the key-value pair is updated at run-time through HTTP APIs for key-value updates. Accordingly, the microservice consumer is first unbound from this microservice provider, and then bounded with a new microservice provider candidate returned by the service discovery process. Consequently, the migrated IoT system is able to respond to various run-time changes in an easy and efficient manner.

2.3 Supporting Tool

We have further developed a supporting tool called *CM4MS* to enable and facilitate the proposed migration technique. Its main features include business process representation, microservice management, and dynamic configuration.

As an illustration, Fig. 4 shows a snapshot of business process for the UAV flight control system. The process is represented as a visual flowchart whose nodes represent microservices, while links with directional arrows represent the invocations between microservices. The user can further query the information and status of all involved microservices. Microservices with exceptions are marked pink (blue for normal).

Figure 5 shows a snapshot of dynamic configuration management for the Copter_main in the UAV flight control system. The tool lists all variation points and their associated variants. To change the invocation between microservices, the user enters a variant name in the "invoke" box and then clicks "submit". For instance, the *VariationPoint6* indicates a variant (corresponding to a microservice) is required for positioning. Currently, the involved microservice is based on GPS ("Update_GPS"), and the user just replaces "Update_GPS" with "Update_BEIDOU" in order to switch to a BEIDOU-based microservice ("Update_BEIDOU"). In this way, variation-based business process reconfiguration is supported at run-time.

3   Case Study

In this section, we report a case study to validate the proposed approach.

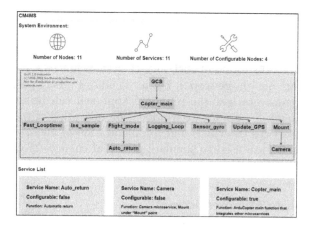

Fig. 4. Business process representation in *CM4MS*

Index	Tag	Invoke	Submit
VariationPoint1	Initialization timer	Fast_Looptimer	Submit
VariationPoint2	Initialize the inertial navigation system	Ins_sample	Submit
VariationPoint3	Current flight mode	Flight_mode	Submit
VariationPoint4	Print log	Logging_Loop	Submit
VariationPoint5	Gyroscope information	Sensor_gyro	Submit
VariationPoint6	GPS positioning service	Update_GPS	Submit
VariationPoint7	Mount the device	Mount	Submit

Variation Points

Fig. 5. Run-time variation configuration in *CM4MS*

3.1 Subject Program and Migration Requirements

We selected an open-source unmanned aerial vehicle (UAV) system (ArduPilot) as subject program which consists about 700,000 lines of code, because UAV has been popularly adopted in various large-scale IoT systems, such as smart cities and intelligent logistics. The system is mainly composed of *simulation plug-ins* (simulation of various sensors and their communications), *flight control* (ArduPilot), and *ground control station*[1]. These modules correspond to the sensing (and transportation), control, and application layer of a hierarchical IoT system, respectively. ArduPilot UAV flight control system supports various aircraft models, such as fixed-wing UAV, multi-rotor UAV, and helicopter.

Obviously, a UAV is expected to provide continuous services, and thus suffers a long-term maintenance. For instance, the flight control system needs to be updated for more stable flight, and some devices need to be replaced or upgraded due to failures. Such extensions or updates are difficult to handle in a large-scale, legacy system with embedded features. In addition, the UAV is running in a reactive manner, the failure of a module may lead to the crash of the system. As a consequence, the refactoring of such an IoT system not only faces a high risk (due to the impact on a large scope), but also endures a long period.

We next demonstrate how the proposed approach can be used to address the above challenges. Especially, we will focus on migration of the flight control system to microservices (Sect. 3.2) and reconfiguration of microservices for various scenarios which are used to simulate potential changes of environment or requirements (Sect. 3.3).

3.2 Migration to Microservices

Following the migration principles, we decompose the UAV flight control system into ten microservices at different layers, as summarized in Table 1. The "Principle" column indicates the principle used for the migration, while the "Microservices" column lists the decomposed microservices of the migration.

Table 1. Migration result of UAV flight control system

Principle	Microservices
P_2	Copter_main
P_3	Sensor_gyro, Update_GPS, Camera, Mount
P_1	Flight_Mode, INS_Sample
P_4	Fast_Looptimer, Logging_Loop, Auto_return

We take "Update_GPS" as an example to illustrate how the above migration of microservices works. The left part in Fig. 6 shows the structure of

---

[1] http://ardupilot.org/dev/docs/learning-ardupilot-introduction.html.

the "Copter::update_GPS ()" module in the legacy system, and this module accordingly calls three functions in the "AP_GPS" module, namely "update ()", "num_sensors ()", and "last_message_time_ms ()". The right part shows the resulting microservice (i.e. "Update_GPS"), including its RESTful APIs, and their description and implementations. "Update_GPS" has three RESTful APIs, namely "GET http://127.0.0.1:8006/v1/gps/update", "GET http://127. 0.0.1:8006/v1/gps/num_sensors", and "GET http://127.0.0.1:8006/v1/gps/last_ message_time_ms/", which corresponds to "update ()", "num_sensors ()", and "last_message_time_ms ()" in "AP_GPS", respectively. In order to implement these interfaces, an "AP_GPS" object is first instantiated, and then the functions in "AP_GPS" are bound to specific URLs. At run-time, "Update_GPS" listens to all invocations on its port and deliver the expected services through its relevant RESTful APIs.

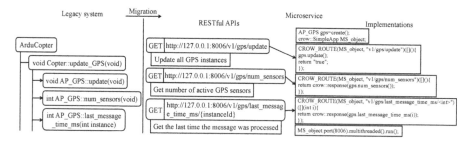

Fig. 6. An illustration of migration to microservices

3.3   Reconfigurability and Performance Evaluation

(1) Handling Environmental Changes. Assume the following scenario (SC_1): During the mission of UAV, GPS signal is suddenly missing due to an environmental exception. Consequently, positioning information is not available, which may lead to a crash of the system. In this regard, one may be interested in evaluating whether the migrated system is able to respond to such an exception. Accordingly, the research question is *"Can the proposed technique effectively deal with this change due to environmental exceptions?"* (RQ_1).

Recall the devices of the system are simulated by *simulation plug-ins*. The GPS exception in SC_1 can be simulated by setting a timed sleep for the "Update_GPS" microservice. When this exception happens, the status of the "Update_GPS" microservice will be detected timely since all microservices of the system are monitored by *CM4MS* at run-time. In the meanwhile, a candidate microservice that provides the similar functionality will be provided through a service discovery process. For instance, the "Update_BEIDOU" microservice is assumed to be an alternative (Note one of multiple service instances can be the alternative in the context of DevOps). Accordingly, a dynamic configuration process is started which will update the value of "Update_GPS" with

"Update_BEIDOU" at the variation point of "Copter_main". As a result, the "Update_GPS" microservice is switched to the "Update_BEIDOU" microservice which hereby provides positioning information. The resulting configuration of the system is shown in Fig. 7. Note that the "GCS" microservice (*ground control station*) is beyond the flight control system.

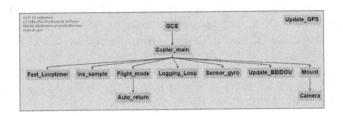

Fig. 7. Switching from "Update_GPS" to "Update_BEIDOU"

Answer to RQ_1: Our approach can effectively deal with run-time changes due to the environmental exceptions by dynamically reconfiguring the microservices. Furthermore, this reconfigurability is useful to avoid expansion of exceptions to the entire system as does in a legacy system.

(2) Handling Requirement Changes. Assume the following scenario (SC_2): As mentioned before, UAV can be mounted with a variety of extra equipments and be customized for the usage in various scenarios. For instance, the original UAV is used for aerial photography, and a new requirement occurs that aerial broadcasting is also supported. One may be interested in evaluating whether the migrated system can be reconfigured to effectively realize this new requirement. Accordingly, the research question is *"Could the proposed approach can be reconfigured to implement new requirements?"* (RQ_2).

To support the new requirement in SC_2, the following refactoring steps are needed: (i) Equip the UAV with a megaphone device; (ii) Create and register three microservices in the Service Registry, namely "Megaphone" (an abstraction of megaphone), "Mount_2" (partner microservice in the control layer), "Flight_mode_2" (for flight mode); (iii) Start a dynamic configuration process which will replace "Camera" with "Megaphone", "Mount" with "Mount_2", and "Flight_mode" with "Flight_mode_2", respectively. After the refactoring, the resulting configuration of microservices is shown in Fig. 8, and the refactored system supports the requirement of aerial broadcasting.

Answer to RQ_2: Our approach can quickly respond to the requirement changes through the reconfiguration and extension of a microservice-based IoT system.

(3) Performance Evaluation. Our approach introduces microservice decomposition and variation contexts in order to deal with run-time changes of environment or requirements, one may be interested in the performance overhead to

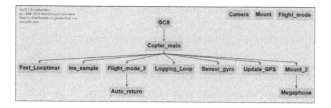

Fig. 8. Configuration of microservices in refactored system supporting aerial broad-casting

achieve the reconfigurability of IoT systems. Accordingly, the research question is *"Does the proposed approach introduce significant performance overhead?"* (RQ_3).

In order to answer RQ_3, we evaluate the run-time performance overhead due to variation configuration, and compare the compilation time and startup time of the system before and after the migration. Note that the both experiments are repeated 10 times and $CM4MS$ is used. We define the following run-time performance metrics: (i) T_{VC} is defined as the time spent on the variation configuration when a microservice is involved; (ii) T_{Res} is defined as the response time of a microservice when it is involved a business scenario. In particular, we consider a real situation as illustrated in SC_2: The flight mode change and the mounted device replacement. Accordingly, SC_2 will involve "Flight_mode" and "Mount" reconfigured.

The evaluation results of run-time performance overhead are summarized as follows: (i) For both two microservices, their T_{VC} are much lower than 1 ms; (ii) T_{Res} of "Flight_mode" varies from 1 to 3 ms, with an average of 1.5 ms when the frequency is 400 Hz; T_{Res} of "Mount" varies from 1 to 19 ms, with an average of 10 ms when the frequency is 50 Hz. We conclude that performance overhead due to the variation configuration could be negligible compared with a relatively long period of response.

The evaluation results of the compilation time and startup time of the system before and after the migration are summarized as follows: (i) Before the migration, the average compilation time is 8.6 s and the average startup time is 3.38 s; (ii) After the migration, the compilation and startup time of each microservice are shown in Table 2; (iii) Both compilation and startup time of each microservice is less than that of the original system. If all the microservices in the migrated system are compiled in a sequential manner, a total of compilation time is about 18 s; Similarly, a total of startup time is about 10.56 s. However, these microservices can be compiled and started in parallel since they are independently deployed and run in a container. In this sense, the compilation time of the migrated system should be up to the maximum of compilation time of all microservices (i.e. 3.85 s); its startup time should be up to the maximum of startup time of all microservices (i.e. 3.46 s).

Table 2. Compilation and startup time of microservices

Microservice	Compilation time (s)			Startup time (s)		
	Min	Max	Avg	Min	Max	Avg
Copter_main	2.98	3.46	3.11	1.03	1.68	1.49
Fast_LoopTimer	0.65	1.58	1.02	0.26	0.55	0.32
Ins_sample	3.52	3.85	3.65	2.14	3.46	2.52
Flight_mode	2.85	3.47	2.93	1.31	2.28	1.93
Logging_Loop	1.57	2.56	1.98	0.61	0.88	0.73
Sensor_gyro	0.48	0.98	0.87	0.19	0.62	0.36
Update_GPS	0.85	1.52	0.96	0.17	0.93	0.51
Mount	0.32	1.64	0.86	0.53	1.26	1.12
Auto_return	1.45	1.98	1.68	0.63	1.58	0.74
Camera	0.51	1.08	0.94	0.35	1.64	0.84

Answer to RQ3: Our approach only introduces very tiny performance overhead due to the variation reconfiguration of microservices. Compared with the original system, the migrated system has a shorter compilation and startup time, indicating a shorter break for the recovery.

4   Related Work

We introduce closely related work in terms of migration to microservices and reconfigurable IoT systems.

4.1   Migration to Microservices

Recently, research efforts have been made on the migration of a legacy system to the microservices architecture due to the popularity of microservices. One category of efforts focus on the automation and standardization of the system migration process. Balalaie et al. [1] summarized the experiences and lessons for the migration to the microservice architecture in the context of DevOps. They further established a pattern repository made of fourteen migration and rearchitecting design patterns, which are derived from industrial-scale software migration projects aiming to improve the efficiency and effectiveness of system migrations [2]. Similarly, Carrasco et al. [5] summarized nine bad smells with their solutions to help identify and correct pitfalls in the migration process.

The other category of efforts focus on microservice decomposition techniques. Baresi et al. [3] presented an automated decomposition approach to identify microservices, which assume the OpenAPI (Swagger) specification of each operation is available and then maps specification into the concepts of a reference vocabulary based on the semantic similarity. This approach relies heavily on well-defined and described interfaces, but this is not always the case. Gysel et al. [8] proposed a structured approach to service decomposition based on 16 coupling criteria which are collected from the literature and industry experience. Levcovitz et al. [12] proposed to extract microservices from a monolithic system based on the dependency graph among facades, business functions, and database tables.

The existing work focuses on microservices identification and decomposition of general systems, while our work addresses the migration of a legacy IoT system into microservices by providing a set of migration principles and further improves the reconfigurability of microservices-based IoT systems.

4.2 Reconfigurable IoT Systems

Most existing work on reconfigurable IoT systems turns to service-oriented architecture (SOA). Issarny et al. [10] proposed a thing-based SOA which consists service discovery, service composition, service access, and thing-based queries, and presented a service-oriented middleware to address the heterogeneity and dynamics of IoT systems. Tiwari et al. [14] proposed a generalized programmable hardware node for all devices that are connected to IoT systems. As an illustration, their approach supports the reconfiguration of the wireless node architecture and addition of devices. Dar et al. [6] proposed a conceptual architectural model that can be used to develop large-scale IoT systems via adaptive service compositions. However, no reference implementation or validation are reported.

Unlike the above work, our approach first decomposes an IoT systems into microservices and then introduces variation contexts to the connectivity of microservices to enable the configurability of IoT systems.

5 Conclusion

We have proposed a microservice-based reconfigurable migration technique for IoT systems. An IoT system is often deployed in a dynamic environment and expected to provide continuous services. Naturally, it is expected be reconfigurable enough to cater for various run-time changes. It is difficult for the legacy architecture to meet such an expectation. The proposed technique overcomes this limitation in two aspects: (i) a legacy IoT system is first migrated into microservices with the guidance of a set of migration principles; (ii) variation contexts are then introduced to the connectivity between the decomposed microservices, which enables the decomposed microservices reconfigurable at run-time. We conducted a case study to comprehensively validate the proposed technique. Experimental results confirmed the improvements on the reconfigurability of the migrated IoT system using our approach.

For future work, we plan to validate our technique with more types of IoT systems, and address the performance requirements during the migration at different levels, such as decomposed microservices, variation points, and configuration patterns.

Acknowledgment. This work is supported by the National Natural Science Foundation of China under Grant No. 61872039 and the Fundamental Research Funds for the Central Universities under Grant No. FRF-GF-19-019B.

References

1. Balalaie, A., Heydarnoori, A., Jamshidi, P.: Microservices architecture enables devops: migration to a cloud-native architecture. IEEE Softw. **33**(3), 42–52 (2016)
2. Balalaie, A., Heydarnoori, A., Jamshidi, P.: Microservices migration patterns. Softw. Pract. Exp. **48**(11), 2019–2042 (2018)
3. Baresi, L., Garriga, M., De Renzis, A.: Microservices identification through interface analysis. In: De Paoli, F., Schulte, S., Broch Johnsen, E. (eds.) ESOCC 2017. LNCS, vol. 10465, pp. 19–33. Springer, Cham (2017). https://doi.org/10.1007/978-3-319-67262-5_2
4. Bucchiarone, A., Dragoni, N., Dustdar, S., et al.: From monolithic to microservices: an experience report from the banking domain. IEEE Softw. **35**(3), 50–55 (2018)
5. Carrasco, A., van Bladel, B., Demeyer, S.: Migrating towards microservices: migration and architecture smells. In: Proceedings of IWOR 2018, pp. 1–6 (2018)
6. Dar, K., Taherkordi, A., Rouvoy, R., et al.: Adaptable service composition for very-large-scale internet of things systems. In: Proceedings of MDS 2011 (2011)
7. Fritzsch, J., Bogner, J., Zimmermann, A., Wagner, S.: From monolith to microservices: a classification of refactoring approaches. In: Bruel, J.-M., Mazzara, M., Meyer, B. (eds.) DEVOPS 2018. LNCS, vol. 11350, pp. 128–141. Springer, Cham (2019). https://doi.org/10.1007/978-3-030-06019-0_10
8. Gysel, M., Kölbener, L., Giersche, W., Zimmermann, O.: Service cutter: a systematic approach to service decomposition. In: Aiello, M., Johnsen, E.B., Dustdar, S., Georgievski, I. (eds.) ESOCC 2016. LNCS, vol. 9846, pp. 185–200. Springer, Cham (2016). https://doi.org/10.1007/978-3-319-44482-6_12
9. Hassan, S., Bahsoon, R.: Microservices and their design trade-offs: a self-adaptive roadmap. In: Proceedings of IEEE SCC 2016, pp. 813–818 (2016)
10. Issarny, V., Bouloukakis, G., Georgantas, N., Billet, B.: Revisiting service-oriented architecture for the IoT: a middleware perspective. In: Sheng, Q.Z., Stroulia, E., Tata, S., Bhiri, S. (eds.) ICSOC 2016. LNCS, vol. 9936, pp. 3–17. Springer, Cham (2016). https://doi.org/10.1007/978-3-319-46295-0_1
11. Krivic, P., Skocir, P., Kusek, M., Jezic, G.: Microservices as agents in iot systems. In: Jezic, G., Kusek, M., Chen-Burger, Y.-H.J., Howlett, R.J., Jain, L.C. (eds.) KES-AMSTA 2017. SIST, vol. 74, pp. 22–31. Springer, Cham (2018). https://doi.org/10.1007/978-3-319-59394-4_3
12. Levcovitz, A., Terra, R., Valente, M.T.: Towards a technique for extracting microservices from monolithic enterprise systems. In: Proceedings of VEM'15. pp. 97–104 (2015)
13. Sun, L., Li, Y., Memon, R.A.: An open IoT framework based on microservices architecture. China Commun. **14**(2), 154–162 (2017)
14. Tiwari, V., Keskar, A.G., Shivaprakash, N.C.: A reconfigurable IoT architecture with energy efficient event-based data traffic reduction scheme. Int. J Online Eng. **13**(2), 34–52 (2017)
15. Villamizar, M., Garces, O., Ochoa, L., et al.: Cost comparison of running web applications in the cloud using monolithic, microservice, and AWS lambda architectures. Serv. Oriented Comput. Appl. **11**(2), 233–247 (2017). https://doi.org/10.1007/s11761-017-0208-y

16. Vresk, T., Cavrak, I.: Architecture of an interoperable IoT platform based on microservices. In: Proceedings of MIPRO 2016, pp. 1196–1201 (2016)
17. Wikipedia: Internet of things. https://en.wikipedia.org/wiki/Internet_of_Things (2019)
18. Yousif, M.: Microservices. IEEE Cloud Comput. **3**(5), 4–5 (2016)

Towards the Creation of Be In/Be Out Model for Smart City with the Use of Internet of Things Concepts

Bartosz Wieczorek and Aneta Poniszewska-Marańda$^{(\boxtimes)}$ (iD)

Institute of Information Technology, Lodz University of Technology, Lodz, Poland
bartosz.wieczorek@edu.p.lodz.pl, aneta.poniszewska-maranda@p.lodz.pl

Abstract. Constantly technological development based on the paradigm of the Internet of Things still gives rise to solutions to many complex problems. This article aims to present an initial concept of the solution to the problem of creating an effective system for the Be-In/Be-Out (BIBO) model. This system is based on technologies originating in the paradigm of the Internet of Things. Most ticket systems use technologies that require many manual interactions from passengers. However, with technological development, the society expects more and more comfort, also in the context of using municipal services. And the SmartCity concept gains in popularity year by year. This study proposes concepts of passenger detection in vehicle based on Bluetooth Low Energy technology combined with the user's smartphone. The paper presents the smartphone- and BLE-based IoT solution for public transportation ticket distribution and fare calculation in the architecture of Be-In/Be-Out model.

Keywords: Internet of Things · Smart city · Smartphone · Bluetooth low energy · Mobile ticketing in public transport

1 Introduction

Since 19th century population of cities is constantly increasing. 55% of the world's population lives in urbanized areas in 2018 and this fraction is expected to increase to 68% by 2050 [1]. Traditional methods of managing constantly growing cities are becoming insufficient due to their inefficiency and costs. Furthermore, increasing demand for fast and reliable urban services available to everyone adds additional difficulties for modern cities. For this reasons, many countries will face issues concerning housing, energy consumption and transportation.

There is already ongoing research on how to ensure a sustainable development of cities and optimizing city management and urban service delivery. In recent years a concept of Smart Cities, which is utilisation of advanced Information and Communication Technology (ICT) to support administration of cities, become

S. Yangui et al. (Eds.): ICSOC 2019 Workshops, LNCS 12019, pp. 156–167, 2020.
https://doi.org/10.1007/978-3-030-45989-5_13

a leading idea for future development of cities. A key concept which enables creation of smart cities is urban Internet of Things (IoT) that is a communication infrastructure, which provides unified access to various public services through deployed digital communication devices deployed within cities [2].

The idea of automating the distribution process in public transportation is being constantly researched. One of the first publications concerning this topic appeared in 2001 and it described EasyRide, a ticketing system utilizing Radio Frequency Identification (RFID) tags to monitor passage access to public transportation, which allowed to record information necessary to calculate and collect fares [3]. Since then, many different RFID-based solutions were created, tested and even used in practice in Germany and Switzerland [16].

In 2010 a new, alternative to RFID, technology was proposed. Bluetooth Low Energy (BLE) is intended as a wireless personal area network with similar communication range as a traditional Bluetooth network but with reduced power consumption and maintenance costs. The technology enables to equip public transportation vehicles with necessary equipment with a minimal overhead. Another advantage of the technology is that almost everyone caries a smartphone and today most of them are able to handle BLE technology.

Ticketing machines confuse travellers with pricing models, force them to study tariffs and require detailed route specifications in order to create a ticket. Be-In/Be-Out (BIBO) systems try to simplify this process by following a basic interaction principle that enables people to seamlessly and implicitly interact with a technical system. Passengers may continue their natural behaviour (i.e. they enter and leave public means of transportation) and automatically execute a pretended incidental but necessary action (i.e. they obtain their tickets and initiate invoicing). There is no need to look at displays or to press buttons distracts them from their focused task or go with a paper ticket or some card to the reader.

The goal of this paper is to describe a concept of smartphone- and BLE-based IoT solution for public transportation ticket distribution and fare calculation. The solution is intended to be Be-In/Be-Out, which means that users of the system use it implicitly without any further activity besides utilizing public transportation.

The remaining parts of the article are divided as follows: Sect. 2 provides backgrounds of Bluetooth Low Energy technology. Section 3 presents the examples of related work in the given domain while Sect. 4 deals with the solution prototype for Be-In/Be-Out model that uses the Internet of Things paradigm and the availability of mobile devices.

2   Bluetooth Low Energy

Bluetooth is a wireless short-range communication solution which goal is to replace cable connections between all kinds of electronic devices. In general, there are two key types of Bluetooth technology [5]:

– Bluetooth Basic Rate,
– Bluetooth Low Energy.

Bluetooth Basic Rate (BBR) operates in a spectrum band in the unlicensed ISM band at 2.4 GHz and uses frequency hopping to counteract interference and fading. BBR is able to transfer 1–3 megabits per second (Mb/s). Bluetooth Low Energy (BLE) operates in the same spectrum as BBR, however, it uses different channels. Furthermore, BLE also utilises frequency hopping, but with different schema. BLE is able to transfer between 125 kilobits per second (kb/s) and 2 megabits per second (Mb/s). It is important to note that both types include device discovery, connection establishment and connection mechanisms. Furthermore, both types are able communicate with each other as long as their respective devices implement either one of them. The main difference is in transmit protocol, which in case of BLE allows only transmission of small packets to save energy [5,6].

BLE devices can be used to create ad-hoc and hands-free (unconscious) interaction between nearby 'smart things' and user, which is the main point of the research about implicit ticket distribution. There exist three models of implicit interactions due to technical alterations and limitations [4]: Be-In/Be-Out, Walk-In/Walk-Out, Check-In/Check-Out.

Be-In/Be-Out (BIBO) interaction is conducted without any input from users, who participate in the interaction just be being within its range. *Walk-In/Walk-Out (WIWO)* is and interaction, which deploys virtual fences that detect users entering and leaving its range [19]. *Check-In/Check-Out (CICO)* interaction requires its participants to show their devices to some form of detectors at entry- and exit points in order to be registered for the interaction. The presented interactions can be mixed to create different variations, for example a Check-In/Be-Out interaction is possible [4]. The system presented in this paper is intended to use Be-In/Be-Out interaction.

3   Related Works

The literature describes three main areas related to the considered problem of creation a Be in/Be out model for intelligent transport. The first area is the concept of IoT and related challenges and problems. We were looking for practices to create the effective systems operating in the environment of IoT. The second area is Bluetooth low energy technology and thus its development as well as its use and potential in solving the contemporary problems. The last area is related to solutions to create an effective system implementing the Be in/Be out model.

Internet of Things is a topic undergoing intensive research. There are numerous publications concerning various aspects of this vast subject. Authors of [7] present an overview of different architectures, taxonomies, requirements and future trends in the IoT field. Furthermore, the authors describe a selection of existing IoT implementations and usages.

Another interesting publication is [9], in which another detailed overview of IoT is presented. The authors focus on architectonic aspects and argue that future development of IoT requires development of a dedicated SOA. The publication presents IoT system structure in great detail. Finally, the authors describe research challenges and future trends of IoT.

In [6] presents Bluetooth Low Energy technology and its usage in IoT, The authors argue that existing mesh topologies for this standard are inadequate and to mitigate that issue, they propose their own improved mesh topology based on CRS Mesh. Paper [10] provides a thorough presentation of the current state of the art in a field of wireless technologies used in IoT. The authors describe Near Field Communication, Visible Light Communication and Bluetooth Low Energy in detail presenting their advantages, disadvantages and current status. Furthermore, the authors argue that BLE allows great opportunities to create indoor/outdoor localization applications, which is closely connected with ticket distribution automation.

[5] is an official documentation provided by Bluetooth Special Interest Group containing a technical description of all Bluetooth technologies and standards. The authors of [4] present a topic of IoT in public transportation ticket distribution and propose their own solution. The described approach is a Be-In/Be-Out system based on BLE technology. The authors present conducted experiments and based on them present a positive conclusion concerning BLE applicability in the context of ticket distribution.

A different approach is used in [11], where the author describes a BLE-based system using a combination of Be-In/Be-Out and Check-In/Check-Out approaches. The presented solution requires its users to conduct a "check-in" procedure from the inside of a given vehicle, however, a "check-out" process is conducted automatically. In [17] authors analyse the current fare collection systems created for integrated transport systems and focus on the possibilities of application of modern fare collection systems in public passenger transport, their subsequent comparison and evaluation. The NFC technology was evaluated as the most suitable variant of fare collection system in integrated transport systems was evaluated.

4   Concept of the Effective Be In/Be Out System Solution

The proposed solution for development of effective Be-In/Be-Out model was based on the paradigm of Internet of Things. According to the statistics, mobile devices are owned by 2/3rds of the population and this market is still growing. Thus, there are many devices in the surroundings generating data or offering certain actions that may be subsequently linked to specific users, like the above-mentioned Beacon used for object identification in space or for data provision for short distances.

4.1   Be In/Be Out System Solution Description

In contrast to the project described in work "Bluetooth Low Energy as Enabling Technology for Be-In/Be-Out Systems" [4], the proposed solution is to assume the existence of at least the beacon identifier of the vehicle in the environment. A beacon is a small Bluetooth radio transmitter. It is like a lighthouse: it repeatedly transmits a single signal that other devices can see. Instead of emitting visible light, though, it broadcasts a radio signal that is made up of a combination of letters and numbers transmitted in a regular interval of approximately 1/10th of a second. A Bluetooth-equipped device like a smartphone can "see" a beacon once it's in range, so it is like sailors looking for a lighthouse to know where they are. The Beacon device will transmit a unique ID number that tells the listening device which beacon is next to. Really, it's just a code name. The beacon sends out its ID numbers about ten times every second (sometimes more, sometimes less, depending on the configuration). A nearby Bluetooth-enabled device (e.g. smartphone) can pick up that signal. When a dedicated mobile application recognizes that signal, it links it to an action or piece of information assigned to this beacon, stored on the server (e.g. located in the cloud) and displays it to the user. A device can be taught how to react to a beacon signal. This is possible due to the creation of appropriate software.

A Beacon, which in this specific case of BIBO system serves as an identifier of an object of municipal infrastructure (e.g. a bus or other transport vehicle) which can be interacted with in the space surrounding a SmartCity user.

Therefore, the solution concept is as follows. As presented in Fig. 1, user P1 remains within the scope of vehicle transmitter T1 and has appropriate software on his mobile device, which enables him to detect intelligent things in the space. The user can make his Sensitive Sensor Data available, thanks to which the collection and analysis of data connected with user behaviour will be possible. The collected data will be used to answer such questions as: when exactly did the user enter and leave the vehicle? How long was he in it and how long did it travel? To answer these questions, during the first stage of data analysis, statistical algorithms will be used to determine the correlation between the data and the attempt to link with an entry/exit vehicle. The next step will be to use artificial neural network algorithms to check the possibility of classifying the user into groups (in the vehicle and outside the vehicle). Because as literature research has shown, relying only on the signal emitted by the vehicle transmitters is insufficient to determine the exact or very close moment of entering and exiting the vehicle.

Sensitive Sensor Data (SSD) is all data that can be gathered in the context of a given user, starting with data originating from a mobile device of a specific user. An example of such data selected as an initial group for analysis of user behaviour is presented in Fig. 2.

Thus, we are dealing with a situation where there are many mobile devices – the users with access to the Internet. What is more, also the use of appropriate software enabling detection and use of intelligent things (i.e. intelligent vehicles, intelligent bus stops or intelligent homes) enables an access to services connected with them. These intelligent things may, but not necessarily do, have access to the Internet in order to transmit the contextual data. Sensor data both from mobile devices and intelligent things is collected in a central or distributed

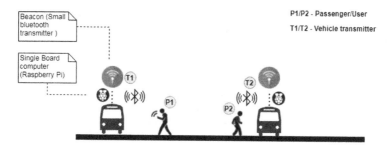

Fig. 1. Visualization of the Be in/Be out model in the context of transport

no.	Sensor data	no.	Sensor data	no.	Sensor data	no.	Sensor data
1	Gyroscope	4	Magnetometer	7	Proximity meter	10	Accelerometer
2	Light sensor	5	Gravity sensor	8	Location data		
3	Sound Level	6	Barometer	9	List of Bluetooth devices nearby	11	The identifier of the nearest object id transmitter

Fig. 2. Examples of user sensory data collected for analysis of user behaviour

database managed by a central system. The central system then provides an access to services executed via specific components or system modules. In the presented concept of the system, the service calculating the probability of user still remaining in the object of SmartCity mobile infrastructure (i.e. intelligent vehicle) is executed via the Machine learning module. Together with information from the vehicle transmitter (Beacon), it unequivocally responds whether the user remains in the vehicle or whether it has just left it, remaining for a short while within the range of the transmitter (Fig. 3).

4.2   Be In/Be Out System Architecture

We propose the following schema to develop the BIBO system based on the Internet of Things paradigm. Initially, it was assumed that the system implementation should contain the elements indicated in Fig. 3. Therefore, the characteristic of these elements is as follows:

1. *Beacon* is the identifier of the intelligent object (i.e. vehicle) with which the user can interact.
2. *Smartphone* performs not only data presentation or system capabilities, for example, information about the route and vehicle or making a complaint, but also the most important source of sensory data in the context of the user. This data is needed for the solution to work.
3. *Single board computer* – its implementation should assume the existence of a vehicle's on-board computer for many reasons: for example with the development of the Internet of Things paradigm, more and more devices, sensors

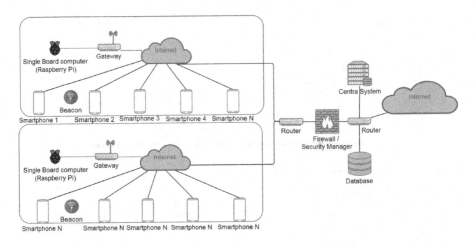

Fig. 3. Deployment concept for BIBO system implementation

that collect data are being created. Next this data can support the decision-making process in the context of the problem of implementing an effective BIBIO system as well as others

Therefore, during the development of the solution concept and building the system prototype, the existence of a micro-computer was taken into account (i.e. Raspberry Pi). The task of the microcomputer is to collect, process and share data downloaded from the sensors connected to it. At the initial stage of the prototype implementation Raspberry Pi will be used to collect location data of the vehicle. These data will be broadcast by the micro-computer operating in the Beacon mode.

So, it is possible to consider two scenarios here: the first one is a situation in which there is a Beacon that serves only as a vehicle identifier; the second one, which assumes the existence of a micro-computer that can work in Beacon mode, that can broadcast not only own ID but also basic sensory data of the vehicle.

4. *Central System* is responsible for providing the services for processing and data collection and performing a key function which is the precise determination of the presence of user in the vehicle.

5. *Database* – as is presented later in the paper, it assumes the existence of many databases (users, vehicles, sensory data), and thus the existence of a component which is the date repository. It is designed to allow an access to collected data.

6. *Gateways and Routers* allow an access to individual elements of the system to the network.

   The presented solution architecture assumes the existence of four logical layers (Fig. 4). The idea of four layers architecture results mainly from good practice consolidated during the recent years on designing the systems executing the paradigm of Internet of Things. It was presented in Sect. 3.

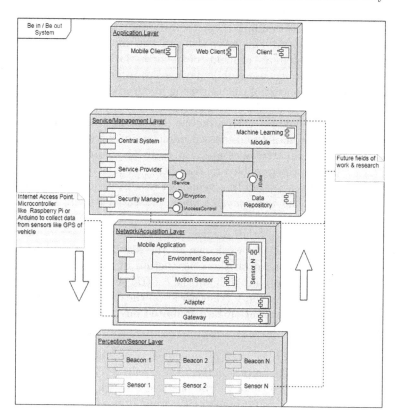

Fig. 4. Architecture of proposed BIBO system with IoT concept

Thus, the first system layer is the *perception layer*, in other words – the *sensor layer*. This layer defines the physical devices and components that generate an identifiable signal via "intelligent" devices (e.g. NFC tags, BLE devices, sensors or widely used minicomputers, such as Raspberry Pi, being specific Gateways for many sensors). The main purpose of this layer is to connect the "intelligent object" of infrastructure, i.e., the above-mentioned devices to the system, and in consequence to download the appropriate data from devices collecting data and/or to execute an appropriate action in the context of a given object. In the discussed Be-In/Be-Out model and in the context of SmartCity, Beacon devices serve as identifiers of smart vehicles. Thanks to the use of Beacon and Bluetooth low energy technology, it is possible to identify the closest intelligent thing (i.e. objects) in the context of which we can start to collect the necessary data to execute a related service. In this specific case – detecting the presence of a passenger in the vehicle will enable charging him for the use of transport and monitoring the passenger flows.

The second layer (*acquisition layer*) is a place where signals emitted from the previous layer are captured. This layer is responsible for downloading data from the lower layer and sending them to the upper layer (i.e. service layer) but in an appropriate form. This layer also contains mobile devices that in the context of the entire system are elements of the first, the second and the last (i.e. application) layers. It is because mobile devices are responsible for downloading the sensor data in the context of the user using integrated sensors. These devices are also a link (Gateway) for data sent from the lower layer, i.e. data generated from devices that can connect with a mobile device via nearby communication networks, such as Beacon or the discussed minicomputer with the GPS module on board the vehicle. Smartphones are also used for communication with the user and for presenting the possible functionalities, such as route preview, travel cost preview or messages related to a vehicle or other intelligent object nearby.

The third layer is the *management layer*, presented e.g. in JSON format. Its main purpose is to store and process the collected data. It also ensures an access to standardised data, other devices and system modules via established interfaces. At this stage of the work, where the solution concept crystallizes and the works are commenced on the construction of the system's prototype, the management layer is based mainly on the central server for simplification of prototype architecture. However, further works on the development of the model must assume a possible application in distributed environment. Therefore, the main responsibility of this layer is:

- *Collection of data sent by user of mobile devices and microcomputers in intelligent objects of the infrastructure.* Data will be collected in dedicated databases. And access to them will be possible through a Data Repository.
- *Making available a module for machine learning.* It assumes the existence of a machine learning component, which based on collected data has to determine if the user made a trip. This module must also fulfil two assumptions. Firstly, it must be able to learn constantly on the data incoming from the sensors. Secondly, because of constantly evolving environment and because we assume the possibility to add the new data types (coming from new sensors), this component should implement a mechanism to consider new data types in the learning process.
- *Ensuring system security implemented through the Security Manager component.* This component will provide encryption of sensitive data, access control to services and resources. During further work on the solution, it also will provide the detection of potentially unwanted behaviours or abuses.
- *Providing contextual services.* Every function of the system, whether it is presenting data on the route of the vehicle, reporting complaints or purchasing a ticket, or even most important in this context, determining the presence of a passenger in the vehicle, will be implemented using a dedicated service that employs other system components. To manage these services, a component named *Service Provider* has been defined.

The last layer is the *application layer*. It uses data and services provided from the lower layer, i.e. service layer, in order to supply the user all the operations and information offered by the system. In other words, it is a layer of applications used by the user, for example, an internet site where he can see his transactions and travelled routes.

Figure 5 presents activity diagram of the system functioning at the level of interaction of the mobile device with the transmitter and the central system. However, before the actions presented in this activity diagram can be realized, it is important to note that the user must have a mobile device using an adequate software permitting detection of intelligent objects (i.e. things). In a given context it will be a vehicle (Beacon). Firstly, this condition is met and the user accepts that the application has access to his *Sensitive Sensory Data* (i.e. *SSD authorization*) and can authorize the communication with intelligent things. In this situation the *Interface for Communication with Intelligent Things* (i.e. *ICIT authorization*) is used. It allows communication with intelligent objects in the background, without user intervention.

Secondly, the transmitter is detected near the user. Then, at the initial stage of beacon recognition process, the algorithm of intelligent object identification will make sure that the currently detected Beacon is the nearest one within the range of the user. Then, when appropriate authorizations have been given, the user data is collected and subsequently sent to the central system.

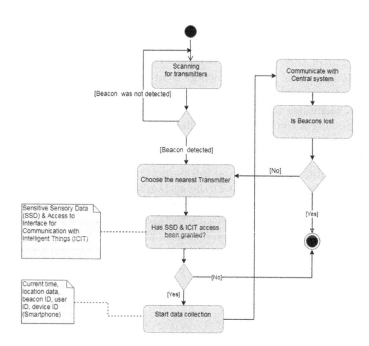

Fig. 5. BIBO system functionality at interaction level of mobile devices with the transmitter and central system

After that via a module based on an artificial neural network (Fig. 4, the data will be used to answer the question whether the user still remains in the object of municipal infrastructure or not. For this purpose the use of model of artificial neural network trained on the basis of this sensory data is proposed. Indication of probability of user presence in a vehicle will permit to increase the efficiency of the entire solution. It will help to eliminate the problem of too early classification of the user as *in the vehicle* upon his entry within the range of the Beacon while the user has not entered to the vehicle yet.

5   Conclusions

Systems based on the paradigm of Internet of Things seem to have a great potential in solution of many complex problems in different areas of our everyday life. One of such areas is constantly evolving ITS (Intelligent Transport System) environment. Such systems are required to provide an automatic price calculation or a pay-as-you-go option for the passengers. In addition they need to serve the more flexible demands depending on the price calculation. These requirements arise from the main problem of using the public transport, such as time consuming tasks of tickets acquiring and checking-in/out tickets or ticket inspector control. Being aware of that, we proposed the prototype of the solution that allows to reduce these problems and simplify all the travel processes.

The presented paper provided the analysis of research on technical possibilities to develop the Be-In/Be-Out model. This model is the basis for the implementation of such concepts as *hands free* and *pay-as-you-go*, which are applicable and required in the transport field and also in the SmartCity approach. It may be used wherever intelligent municipal infrastructure adapts to the user context, facilitates access to services and facilities and eliminates the obstacles, thus ensuring a comfort. The architecture presented in the paper assumes the existence of four logical layers, which include, among others, the elements such as Beacon devices that are small Bluetooth radio transmitters. They can serve as the identifiers of municipal infrastructure objects that the user can be interacted with. Another element of the system is a Smartphone that performs not only data presentation function but also works as source of sensory data in the user's context. The provided architecture also assumes the existence of a machine learning component, which based on the collected data will be used to ensure if the user still remains in the object of municipal infrastructure.

References

1. United Nations Department of Economic and Social Affairs.: 2018 Revision of World Urbanization Prospects. https://www.un.org/development/desa/publications
2. Zanella, A., Bui, N., Castellani, A., Vangelista, L., Zorzi, M.: Internet of Things for smart cities. EEE Internet Things J. 1(1), 22–32 (2014)
3. Gyger, T., Desjeux, O.: EasyRide: active transponders for a fare collection system. IEEE Micro 22(6), 36–42 (2001)

4. Narzt, W., Mayerhofer, S., Weichselbaum, O., Haselböck, S., Höfler, N.: Bluetooth low energy as enabling technology for Be-In/Be-out systems. In: Proceedings of 13th IEEE Annual Consumer Communications & Networking Conference (CCNC) (2016)
5. Bluetooth SIG Inc.: The Bluetooth Core Specification, 17 February 2019. https://www.bluetooth.com/specifications/bluetooth-core-specification
6. Hortelano, D., Olivares, T., Ruiz, M.C., Garrido-Hidalgo, C., López, V.: From sensor networks to Internet of Things. Bluetooth low energy, a standard for this evolution. Sensors J. **17**, 372 (2017)
7. Yaqoob, I., et al.: Internet of Things architecture: recent advances, taxonomy, requirements and open challenges. IEEE Wirel. Commun. **24**(3), 10–16 (2017)
8. Palattella, M.R., et al.: Internet of Things in the 5G era: enablers, architecture, and business models. IEEE J. Sel. Areas Commun. **34**(3), 510–527 (2016)
9. Xu, L.D., He, W., Li, S.: Internet of Things in industries: a survey. IEEE Trans. Ind. Inform. **10**(4), 2233–2243 (2014)
10. García, G.C., Ruiz, I.L., Gómez-Nieto, M.Á.: State of the art, trends and future of bluetooth low energy, near field communication and visible light communication in the development of smart cities. Sens. J. **16**(11), 1968 (2016)
11. Martins, J.G., Mobile ticketing system for public transport based on bluetooth low energy. Master thesis, University of Lisoba, Portugal (2017)
12. Bertoni, G., Daemen, J., Peeters, M., Van Assche, G., Van Keer, R.: Keccak implementation overview (2012). https://keccak.team/files/Keccak-implementation-3.2.pdf. Accessed 4 Mar 2018
13. ISO/IEC: Information technology – Security techniques – Information security management systems – Requirements. In: ISO/IEC 2005 (2005)
14. Vimalachandran, P., Wang, H., Zhang, Y., Heyward, B., Whittaker, F.: Ensuring data integrity in electronic health records: a quality health care implication. In: Proceedings of International Conference on Orange Technologies (ICOT), Australia (2016)
15. Drescher, D.: Blockchain Basics: A Non-Technical Introduction in 25 Steps. Apress, Frankfurt a. M. (2017)
16. Narzt, W., Mayerhofer, S., Weichselbaum, O., Haselböck, S., Höfler, N.: Be-In/Be-Out with bluetooth low energy: Implicit ticketing for public transportation systems. In: Proceedings of IEEE 18th International Conference on Intelligent Transportation Systems, pp. 1551–1556 (2015)
17. Olivková, I.: Comparison and evaluation of fare collection technologies in the public transport. Procedia Eng. **178**, 515–525 (2017)
18. Lahti, J., Heino, I., Kostiainen, J., Siira, E.: Bluetooth beacon enabled mobility services and opportunities in public transit. In: Proceedings of 23rd World Congress on Intelligent Transport Systems, ITS, Australia (2016)
19. Lorenz, H.: Be-In-Be-Out payment systems for public transport. Final report, GWT-TUD GmbH and Department of Transport, London (2009)
20. Atzori, L., Iera, A., Morabito, G.: The Internet of Things: a survey. Comput. Netw. **54**(15), 2787–2805 (2010)
21. Miorandi, D., Sicari, S., De Pellegrini, F., Chlamtac, I.: Internet of Things: vision, applications and research challenges. Ad Hoc Netw. **10**(7), 1497–1516 (2012)
22. Udoh, I.S., Kotonya, G.: Developing IoT applications: challenges and frameworks. IET Cyber-Phys. Syst. Theory Appl. **3**(2), 65–72 (2017)

Ontology for Smart Viticulture: Integrating Inference Rules Based on Sensor Data

Amira Mouakher[1(✉)], Aurélie Bertaux[1(✉)], Ouassila Labbani[1(✉)], Clémentine Hugol-Gential[2(✉)], and Christophe Nicolle[1(✉)]

[1] CIAD, EA 7533, Univ. Bourgogne Franche-Comté, UB, 21000 Dijon, France
{amira.mouakher,aurelie.bertaux,ouassila.narsis,
cnicolle}@u-bourgogne.fr
[2] CIMEOS, EA 4177, Univ. Bourgogne Franche-Comté, UB, 21000 Dijon, France
clementine.hugol-gential@u-bourgogne.fr

Abstract. Smart farming is coming with a clear promise to mitigate the myriad of threatens faced by vineyards. In this respect, relying on sensor data, new challenges are rising in order to proactively warn farmers. In this paper, we introduce the SMARTVINE approach, which extracts knowledge from collected data, converts it into inference rules and integrates them into the reasoning process of the system. In the sake of efficiency, generic bases of association rules are extracted, mapped then to SWRL rules and later used for the enrichment process of the ontology.

Keywords: Smart viticulture · Wireless sensor network · Sensor data · Ontology · Association rule mining

1 Introduction

French viticulture is traditionally a significant economic sector. However, this sector is often threatened by the appearance of numerous events, e.g., diseases, pests, climatic risks, to name but a few. This loss is caused by insects, pathogens and other infectious organisms causing serious damage, including loss of yield and degradation of the quality of the wine. Indeed, humid weather accompanied by high temperatures have factors favoring the development of several diseases. According to the International Organization of Vine and Wine, the French production has fallen by 19% in 2017 due to the vagaries of the vines, which particularly affected strategic regions in the production of wine. Faced with this climate change, the know-how and the expertise of the winemakers remain insufficient to detect in advance all kinds of events that can affect the vines. In order to address this problem, precise farming is emerging as a means to adopt climate-smart farming practices. This new concept offers decision-support to winegrowers through the use of sensors and the Internet of Things paradigm to increase the quality and quantity of their production.

© Springer Nature Switzerland AG 2020
S. Yangui et al. (Eds.): ICSOC 2019 Workshops, LNCS 12019, pp. 168–177, 2020.
https://doi.org/10.1007/978-3-030-45989-5_14

In [10], we proposed a solution that relies on multi-sensor decision support system. The latter solution vehicles a valuable information to winegrowers for real-time event detection and environmental monitoring. This solution mainly focuses on the use of an ontology due to its availability to use a language understandable both by human and machine, to integrate human know-how, to infer (using a reasoning engine based on this human know-how) and to allow to explain its conclusions. In this paper, we drive a step further. Indeed, the knowledge used for reasoning is based only on human know-how. However, this knowledge can variate from an expert to another one. In addition, it closely depends on geographic and meteorologic conditions where his vineyard is located. Thus, this know-how needs to be enriched by a knowledge extracted from data collected by sensors. Indeed, often events such as diseases appear without knowing exactly why. The use of data mining technique can unveil valuable correlations between data to estimate why. Then, these correlations can be transformed into inference rules and can be used for reasoning.

The remainder of the paper is organised as follows: Sect. 2 recalls the pioneering approaches that paid attention to the issue of coupling the ontology with data mining techniques for ontology enrichment. In Sect. 3, we thoroughly describe the architecture of the proposed system called SMARTVINE. Section 4, provides snapshots of the developed prototype as well as a detailed discussion. Section 5 concludes the paper and sketches avenues of future work.

2   Related Work

Among the most powerful tools for knowledge representation, we can cite the ontology which is *a formal and structural way of representing the concepts and relations of a shared conceptualization* [6]. It is often considered a fine source of semantics and interoperability in all artificially smart systems. In parallel, data mining techniques, in particular association rules introduced by AGRAWAL et al. [1], can support the discovery of useful and hidden patterns in the data. Recently, the area of coupling ontology and association rules has attracted the interest of several research. However, most of them were focused on ontology mining which is process for ontology learning [4]. Few researchers have addressed the problem of enriching ontology through supporting the creation of semantic relations between ontology concepts. In this section, we present a quick overview of the most recent approaches.

Paiva et al. introduced an approach to enrich the ontological model with relations between concepts with association rules [12]. The authors use the FP-Growth [7] algorithm which build a tree-like compact structure to discover frequent itemsets from text documents and then generate association rules. These latter are used to learn useful relations in the ontology. In the same trend of works, the author in [11] proposed a novel semi-automatic method for knowledge extraction from unstructured data sources using association rule mining. Relying on FP-Growth algorithm, the work focuses on improving the precision of concept and its semantic relations present in an ontology. Later, IDOUDI et al.

introduced a new approach for evolving the content of an existing mammographic ontology using novel knowledge coming from medical records [8]. For this purpose, they used Apriori algorithm [2] to generate association rules which are then evaluated and classified into three categories: known, unexpected and novel rules. Both of the unexpected and novel rules are considered of great interest to domain experts. The enrichment process of the knowledge base with association between the existing concepts starts once these rules are validated by experts. Recently, the authors in [5] proposed a method for discovering multi-relational association rules from ontological knowledge bases. The discovered rules can be directly integrated within the ontology since they are represented in SWRL. Furthermore, the discovered rules may suggest new axioms.

The scrutiny of the related work unveils the wealthy number of researches on this issue. Nevertheless, common weakness that can be addressed to the above mentioned works stands on the use of traditional frequent pattern mining algorithm such as A-priori or FP-Growth. According to [9], the applicability of these algorithms is limited by the huge number of generated association rules as well as the number of scans to the database. In addition of being a costly process, the complexity of association rule mining increases exponentially with the number of items. Unlike the studied approaches, we are dealing with large volume of sensor data, which are continuously collected from WSNs. In our approach, we rely on deriving a compact set of rules called generic bases of association rules. This minimal set of rules is then mapped into SWRL rules and used for the enrichment process of the ontology.

3   The Proposed Approach

The approach that we introduce in this paper relies on a multi-sensor decision-support viticulture system. Thus, it enters within the scope of precise farming since, the aim is to facilitate accurate and forward-looking decisions to ensure better production, higher profits and a more rational use of chemicals. To do so, the system is based on a network of heterogeneous sensors (on-farm optical sensors or fixed stations in the vineyards, etc.) generating several heterogeneous data streams. Nevertheless, it is of utmost importance to take into consideration the complex nature of these devices, which requires a correct and reliable processing strategy between the generation of information and the representation of knowledge. In this respect, comes to play the main role of the ontology that we use as a model of representation of knowledge to provide a unified terminology. The goal of such knowledge formalization is twofold: (i) represent the tacit knowledge of winegrowers; and (ii) provide an expression language to explain analysis and identify causal relationships in the detected correlations within the sensor lifts. The overall architecture of the system, called SMARTVINE, is glanced by Fig. 1. The system proceeds into two main steps: The first one is the ONTOVINE step which aims to build the ontology based on collecting knowledge from experts. However, there is a lack of genericity in this drawn knowledge. To overcome this downside we suggest to add another step, called VINEMINING, which extracts knowledge from collected data, converts it into inference rules and integrates them into the reasoning process of the system. We thoroughly describe the different stages of this approach in the remainder of this section.

3.1   The OntoVine Step: The Ontology-Based Engine

This step relies on an approach based on the aggregation of refined sensor data into an ontology dedicated to viticulture[1]. Such knowledge modelling aims to allow the system to detect and mitigate the impact of the event's that may occur in the vineyard such as diseases, pests, climate risks, etc.

Thus, the proposed ontology represents a new coupling between the ontologies of the sensors and those dedicated to the events applied to the agricultural sensors. In particular, the ontology combines elements of the W3C SSN ontology[2] coupled with the EVENT ontology[3] as well as the W3C TIME ontology[4]. Two main functions emerge from the construction of this ontology: *(i)* build the links between the main concepts in the above reference ontologies; and *(ii)* extend the ontology to agricultural classes and instantiate it with observational data from agricultural sensors.

The approach starts by collecting knowledge from winegrowers gained through face to face interviews. Then, a knowledge engineering builds the ontology later by combining several ones. Each of them is dedicated to handle the different knowledge collected: event and time. The knowledge is then converted into inference rules aiming the combined ontology to reason.

In parallel data are collected from the vineyard by sensors collecting information such as temperature, humidity, wind, etc. This data is integrated in the system thanks to special SSN ontology for sensor. It allows, at first, to feed a supervision system to give this data to the winegrowers. Furthermore, it allows as well to detect the necessary firing criteria of the inference rules, e.g. temperature greater than 14 °C. Later, this rule is launched. The conclusion part of this rule can be used to warn the winegrower of a the probability of a raising problem and invites him to take the palliating actions.

3.2   The VineMining Step: Building Inference Rules from Data

In this second step, the focus is put on developing a method to enrich existing ontology, through the identification of novel semantic relations between concepts in order to have a better coverage of the domain knowledge. During this phase, a process of raw data analysis is performed in order to extract exploitable knowledge. First, the sensor data is collected in CSV files which are then cleaned and transformed: the valueless records are removed and a multidimensional algorithm MARM [3] is invoked. The latter allows to extract a minimal set of the

---

[1] https://ontology.winecloud.checksem.fr/index-fr.html.
[2] https://www.w3.org/ns/ssn/.
[3] http://purl.org/NET/c4dm/event.owl/.
[4] http://www.w3.org/2006/time/.

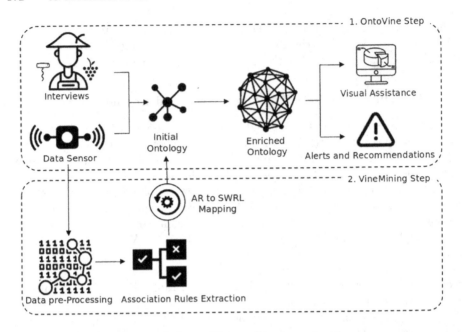

Fig. 1. Overall SMARTVINE architecture at a glance.

most reliable multi-dimensional generic association rules, i.e. allowing to derive all other association rules, from many sources. It is worth mentioning that these rules convey hidden knowledge into the data. Nevertheless, the compelling challenge still lies in the proposal of a very scalable algorithm capable of processing very large amount of data flow. This set of multi-dimensional association rules is later transformed into SWRL (Semantic Web Rule Language) rules, which are injected into the ontology. These SWRL rules can then be used by the inference engine to manage new knowledge related to sensor data.

Extraction of Multidimensional Association Rules. The MARM algorithm (Multidimensional Association Rules Mining) aims to identify a small set of multi-dimensional association rules that allows the derivation of all the other potentially interesting rules in a Boolean tensor. The basics of these association rules are sketched in the following.

Let $\mathcal{D} = \{\mathcal{D}_1, \ldots, \mathcal{D}_n\}$ be a set of n dimensions and $\mathcal{R} \subseteq \mathcal{D}_1 \times \cdots \times \mathcal{D}_n$ an n-ary relation between them. "Association rules" from the tensor $(\mathcal{D}, \mathcal{R})$ involve various dimensions.

Definition 1. *Let $D \subseteq \mathcal{D}$ be a set of dimensions. Let $X_d \subseteq \mathcal{D}_d$, $\mathcal{D}_d \in D$, be a non-empty set of elements of the dimension $\mathcal{D}_d$. The set $\prod_{\mathcal{D}_d \in D} X_d$ is called an association on D and D is called its domain.*

Definition 2. *Let $\mathcal{D}_i$ be a dimension and $X = \prod_{\mathcal{D}_d \in Dom(X)} X_d$ an association. The projection $\pi_{\mathcal{D}_i}(X)$ of X on $\mathcal{D}_i$ is X_i if $\mathcal{D}_i \in Dom(X)$ or $\emptyset$ otherwise.*

Where $Dom(X)$ denotes the domain of an association X.

Definition 3. *A multidimensional association rule is a rule $X \rightarrow Y$ between two associations X and Y. The domain of the rule is the domain of $X \sqcup Y$.*

Definition 4. *The support of an association X with regard to a domain $D \supseteq dom(X)$ is the set $s_D(X) = \{t \in \prod_{\mathcal{D}_d \in \overline{D}} \mathcal{D}_d \mid \exists u \in \prod_{\mathcal{D}_i \in D \setminus dom(X)} \mathcal{D}_i$ such that $\forall x \in X, x.u.t \in \mathcal{R}\}$*

Definition 5. *The natural confidence of the association rule $X \rightarrow Y$ is*

$$conf(X \rightarrow Y) = \frac{|s(X \sqcup Y)|}{|s_{dom(X \sqcup Y)}(X)|}$$

Algorithm 1 computes the set of rules between closed n-sets that are neighbours w.r.t. the inclusion relation on their last $n-1$ components. It transforms the input tensor $\mathcal{T}$ into $\mathcal{T}^\uparrow$ and then computes the closed n-sets. Rules are then constructed either by using the closed n-sets as is or by computing their neighbouring relation w.r.t. the inclusion on their $n-1$ last components.

Association Rules to SWRL Mapping. It is worth mentioning that one of the advantage of these multi-dimensional association rules stands in their inherent similarity with SWRL rules. Indeed, the latter are also of the form *Antecedent $\rightarrow$ Consequent.* Another advantage is the ability to control the number and the quality of the obtained rules through the confidence and the support

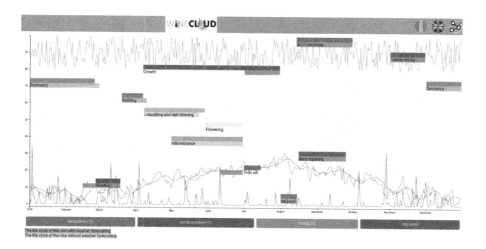

Fig. 2. The different stages of the vine life cycle.

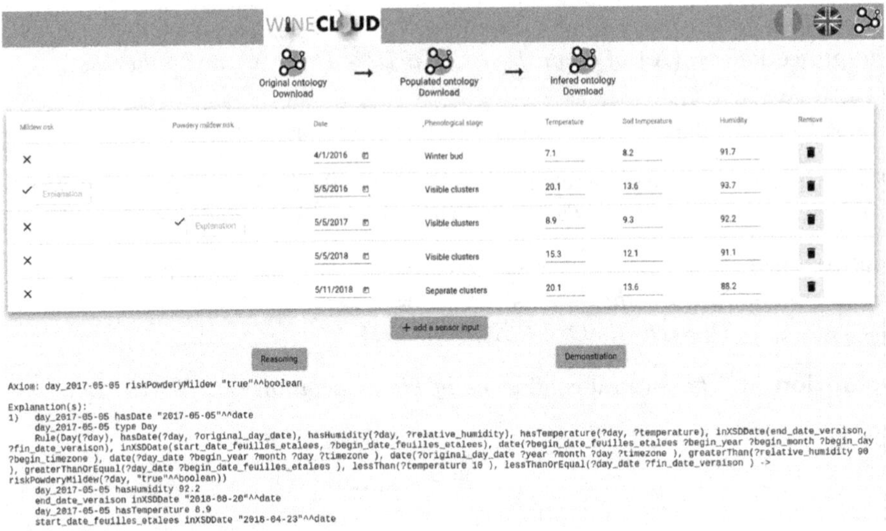

Fig. 3. Detection of vine diseases using SWRL rules.

```
winecloud:WeatherSensor(?weather_sensor) ∧
sosa:madeBySensor(?humidityProperty, ?weather_sensor) ∧
sosa:observedProperty(?humidityProperty, winecloud:RelativeHumidity)∧
sosa:hasSimpleResult(?humidityProperty, ?relative_humidity) ∧
sosa:resultTime(?humidityProperty, ?datetime)∧
sosa:madeBySensor(?soilTemperatureProperty, ?weather_sensor) ∧
sosa:observedProperty(?soilTemperatureProperty,
winecloud:SoilTemperature)∧
sosa:hasSimpleResult(?soilTemperatureProperty, ?soil_temperature)∧
sosa:resultTime(?soilTemperatureProperty, ?datetime)∧
sosa:madeBySensor(?mildiouProperty, ?weather_sensor) ∧
sosa:observedProperty(?mildiouProperty, winecloud:Mildiou) ∧
sosa:resultTime(?mildiouProperty, ?datetime) ∧
swrlb:greaterThan(?soil_temperature, 20)
∧ swrlb:greaterThan(?relative_humidity, 90)
→ sosa:hasSimpleResult(?mildiouProperty, true)
```

Fig. 4. Example of a rule SWRL used for prediction of downy mildew disease.

metrics. However, generating association rules from data is not enough in their raw form, we need to transform them into SWRL rules in order to integrate them in the general context of the ontology. To accomplish the association rules transformation we apply the following steps:

1. Generate semantic classes with bounds for consequents based on the confidence such as: "unlikely" [0;0.30], "conceivable" [0.30;0.60] and "very probable" [0.60;1]

Algorithm 1: COMPUTERULES($\mathcal{T}$)

Input: A tensor $\mathcal{T}$
Output: A base for association rules which domain does not contain $\mathcal{D}_1$
1   $R \leftarrow \emptyset$
2   $\mathcal{T} \leftarrow \mathcal{T}^{\uparrow}$
3   $C \leftarrow ClosedNSets(\mathcal{T})$
4   $R \leftarrow BuildRules(C)$
5   **return** R

---

2. Map the attributes of the antecedent and the consequent to classes in the ontology, generating in the process SWRL rules of the form $C_0 \rightarrow C_1$, where C_0 and C_1 are ontology classes
3. Transform the rules by bringing the consequent to the antecedent side and rely on the confidence metric to select the consequent. For instance, if the confidence for the rules is 75%, then: $C_0 \wedge C_1 \rightarrow very\ probable$.

4   Results and Discussion

The main goal of the SMARTVINE system is to provide winegrowers with a reliable, flexible and "fresh" modular decision support tool that can help them to make the best decisions to fight, reduce and manage diseases and pests while reducing the use of pesticides. The developed prototype is accessible via the following link: https://winecloud.checksem.fr/presentation. The system provides a set of functionalities based on causal reasoning such as the detection of the phases of the vine cycle or the collaborative supervision of events. Although some functionalities are still under development, the system is able to give useful information in the current release. Two main functionalities are identified which are detailed in the following subsections.

4.1   Identifying the Different Stages of the Vine Life Cycle

In addition to the details about the location of the sensors in the vineyards, the SMARTVINE system is able to provide an overview of the vine life cycle including the corresponding dates and characteristics for each stage. Based only on semantic knowledge collected from the carried interviews, the system proposes visual information via the tab "*Cycle of the vine*". Then, real sensor data are added and the obtained results are more accurate. The tab "*Vine life cycle and weather*", of the system, illustrates the influence of weather conditions on the stage duration as well the period (start and end date). These observations are sketched by Fig. 2, which presents a snapshot of this tab. Furthermore, the system is able to explain the reasoning process of the semantic model through the tab "*Explanation cycle of vine + Weather*". For a given date, the corresponding state of the life cycle is displayed and by clicking on the "*Explain reasoning*" button, the system provides the sequence of triples and SWRL rules allowing the ontology to deduce relationship between them.

4.2 Collaborative Event Monitoring

The main purpose of this functionality is the early proactive detection of diseases and pests occurrence. Indeed, these occurrences are considered as events in our predictive model and the SMARTVINE system is able to give an overview about the most critical stages through the tab *"Diseases, Pests"*. This functionality is designed based on the coupling of observations provided by winegrowers as well as hidden knowledge in sensor data discovered from the association rule mining process. Figure 4 illustrates an example of a SWRL rule for the detection of downy mildew disease. Indeed, our predictive model considers precipitation, temperature and humidity as the most relevant factors to disease emergence. For example, the downy mildew which is probably the most dangerous disease producing critical damages during the growing season of grapes, is enhanced by wet weather and high temperature. The *"Disease detection"* tab, given by Fig. 3, illustrates the reasoning process provided by our system to detect downy mildew and powdery mildew. A detailed explanation of the SWRL rule is given whenever one of the disease is detected.

5 Conclusion

This paper presented an upgrade of an ontology-based system aiming at supervising and controlling vineyard to increase the quality and quantity of grapes and wine by detecting different types of risks. This ontology reasoning vehicles a given human know-how, as well as the data collected by sensors placed in the vineyard. However, human knowledge differs from one to another depending on their own vineyard. In addition, in the context of climate change, rules known by winegrowers are disturbed. Then, we propose an upgrade of this system by adding reasoning rules based on data to complete human-based rules. To do so, we focus on data collected by sensors and extract association rules from them. They allow to highlight strong correlations into the data and then generating knowledge. These rules are then automatically transformed into inference SWRL rules and introduced into the reasoning engine.

As a future, we plan to take into consideration the feedback of the winegrowers to validate or not the conclusions of the rules and then generating a dynamic system capable to update itself. In addition, we are looking to mitigate the impact of climate change, which is no longer just an abstract problem. Indeed, the wine culture is threatened by rising global temperatures.

Acknowledgement. This study was conducted as part of the FUI WINECLOUD (https://winecloud.eurestools.eu/.) project. The authors would like to thank the project partners for their valuable contribution, namely: Orange, R-Tech Solutions, The Cave of Lugny and Photon Lines. The authors are also grateful to all the technical team for their collaboration: Nicolas Gros, Marie Simon and Sébastien Gerin.

References

1. Agrawal, R., Imieliński, T., Swami, A.: Mining association rules between sets of items in large databases. SIGMOD Rec. **22**(2), 207–216 (1993)
2. Agrawal, R., Srikant, R.: Fast algorithms for mining association rules in large databases. In: Proceedings of the 20th International Conference on Very Large Data Bases, VLDB 1994, San Francisco, CA, USA, pp. 487–499. Morgan Kaufmann Publishers Inc. (1994)
3. Bazin, A., Gros, N., Bertaux, A., Nicolle, C.: Condensed representations of association rules in n-ary relations. IEEE Trans. Knowl. Data Eng. (TKDE) (2019, to appear)
4. Ben Ahmed, E., Gargouri, F.: Enhanced association rules over ontology resources. IJWA **7**(1), 10–22 (2015)
5. d'Amato, C., Staab, S., Tettamanzi, A.G.B., Minh, T.D., Gandon, F.: Ontology enrichment by discovering multi-relational association rules from ontological knowledge bases. In: Proceedings of the 31st Annual ACM Symposium on Applied Computing, SAC 2016, pp. 333–338. ACM (2016)
6. Gruber, T.R.: A translation approach to portable ontology specifications. Knowl. Acquis. **5**(2), 199–220 (1993)
7. Han, J., Pei, J., Yin, Y.: Mining frequent patterns without candidate generation. SIGMOD Rec. **29**(2), 1–12 (2000)
8. Idoudi, R., Saheb Ettabaâ, K., Solaiman, B., Hamrouni, K., Mnif, N.: Association rules-based ontology enrichment. IJWA **8**, 16–25 (2016)
9. Mahmood, A., Shi, K., Khatoon, S., Xiao, M.: Data mining techniques for wireless sensor networks: a survey. Int. J. Distrib. Sens. Netw. **9**(7), 406316 (2013)
10. Mouakher, A., Belkaroui, R., Bertaux, A., Labbani, O., Hugol-Gential, C., Nicolle, C.: An ontology-based monitoring system in vineyards of the burgundy region. In: Proceedings of the 28th IEEE International Conference on Enabling Technologies: Infrastructure for Collaborative Enterprises, WETICE 2019, Naples, Italy, 12–14 June 2019, pp. 307–312 (2019)
11. Paiva, L.: Semantic relations extraction from unstructured information for domain ontologies enrichment. Ph.D. thesis, Universidade NOVA de Lisboa (2015)
12. Paiva, L., Costa, R., Figueiras, P., Lima, C.: Discovering semantic relations from unstructured data for ontology enrichment: asssociation rules based approach. In: Proceedings of the 9th Iberian Conference on Information Systems and Technologies (CISTI), pp. 1–6 (2014)

TBCE: Towards Blockchain-Based Collaborative Enterprise

Introduction to the First International Workshop on Towards Blockchain-Based Collaborative Enterprise (TBCE 2019)

One of the most promising technologies that can cope with trust and security issues in dynamic collaboration, is distributed ledger technology. However, this technology is, so far, not adapted to the development and the execution of collaborative business processes necessary to meet business needs.

In this workshop, participants tried to answer the question: how to enable distributed ledger based infrastructures so that they can meet collaborative business needs?

Only two papers were accepted.

Layth Sliman

Model-Driven Engineering
for Multi-party Interactions
on a Blockchain – An Example

Gero Dittmann$^{(\boxtimes)}$, Alessandro Sorniotti, and Hagen Völzer$^{(\boxtimes)}$

IBM Research – Zurich, Rüschlikon, Switzerland
{ged,hvo}@zurich.ibm.com

Abstract. Multi-party interactions can be a powerful modeling paradigm for business processes that cross organizational boundaries, but it is typically hard to implement in a distributed setting. Blockchains, however, make such an implementation possible. In a small case study, this paper demonstrates three related approaches how an example taxi dispatcher application involving independent parties can be modeled for implementation on a blockchain: BPMN with an extension for multi-party interactions, synchronized state-machines, and high-level Petri nets, respectively. The three models differ in how well they (a) align with the code in order to support model-driven engineering and (b) support readability of the contractual aspects of the chaincode to business stakeholders. We have implemented and tested the example application as chaincode on Hyperledger Fabric. Our preliminary results suggest that chaincode can be aligned with a high-level model of synchronized state machines which, in turn, can be easily visualized, for example, by an extended BPMN notation.

1 Introduction

A blockchain, or distributed-ledger technology (DLT), combines storage in an immutable, distributed ledger with a *smart contract* defining the transactions that can be invoked to update the ledger. The smart contract is agreed upon beforehand by the partners in the blockchain network. Any update to the distributed ledger, i.e., any transaction must be approved by consensus among a set of partners. The set is defined such that all partners trust the resulting state of the ledger.

This combination of storage, transactions and trust makes a blockchain an ideal platform for automating business processes across organizational boundaries. Business partners that don't trust each others' IT systems can trust a blockchain to execute processes exactly as defined in the smart contract. The ledger gives each partner perfect transparency of the process' progress and history—in some cases subject to privacy domains.

The blockchain concept was introduced by the Bitcoin cryptocurrency network. Many business applications of blockchains, however, do not involve any

© Springer Nature Switzerland AG 2020
S. Yangui et al. (Eds.): ICSOC 2019 Workshops, LNCS 12019, pp. 181–194, 2020.
https://doi.org/10.1007/978-3-030-45989-5_15

cryptocurrency. Some employ *stable coins* for on-chain payments that are backed by fiat currency to inherit its stability and reliability. Other applications don't depend on on-chain payments at all. Instead, they focus on automating business processes to improve operational efficiency while leaving the financial aspects to established invoicing and funds-transfer infrastructures.

Smart contracts are commonly developed by business networks or consortia of multiple parties who need to reach a consensus on the "contract terms". Negotiations of the exact functionality involve not just engineers but business and legal professionals. Those stakeholders would be greatly helped by a graphical representation of the implemented business process, giving parties a more intuitive understanding than source code can.

Existing languages, such as the Business-Process Model and Notation (BPMN) [5], have been successful within corporations but automation of processes spanning multiple organizations has proven difficult and adoption slow. A blockchain can be viewed as a platform on which business processes can run and that is not controlled by an individual party but trusted by all, removing some of the roadblocks to inter-organizational process automation.

In this paper, we report preliminary results from a study how to adapt existing process-modeling notations for business processes across independent organizations and show how to map this notation to a blockchain-based implementation. The approach links the negotiation of functionality in a consortium to its implementation. We demonstrate our approach with the example of a taxi dispatcher application that we have implemented on a permissioned blockchain, Hyperledger Fabric.[1]

A recent book [8] surveys the existing work on model-driven engineering of blockchain applications. For a comprehensive list of related work, we refer to [8, Section 8.5]. In particular, Chap. 8 of that book points out the relevance of models for communicating important aspects of chaincode between business participants. Furthermore, the authors observe that a blockchain can serve as a trusted monitoring facility of all business transactions specified in the chaincode. The same chapter [8, Chapter 8], which extends an earlier paper [7], presents an in-depth supply-chain case study based on traditional BPMN collaboration and choreography diagrams. An implementation in Ethereum is presented, which shows that the message-passing communication mechanism in BPMN collaborations can be mapped to Ethereum chaincode.

We propose an extension of BPMN where participants may communicate using atomic, symmetric multi-party interactions between participants, which is a stronger communication primitive compared to message passing but still easily maps to blockchain transactions.

The case study in [8, Chapter 8] considers also other important aspects of a blockchain application such as privacy, off-chain data storage and non-functional requirements that are out of scope for this paper. An alternative approach to modeling smart contracts using artifact-centric models is presented by Hull et al. [3].

---

[1] As a smart contract for Hyperledger Fabric is also called *chaincode* we use those terms interchangeably.

They focus on conceptual modeling and reasoning over the business logic but do not yet address implementation. Artifacts in artifact-centric models also have an associated state machine, the artifact life cycle, but they use a more explicit and asymmetric communication style between state machines in contrast to the implicit and symmetric style in our approach.

The remainder of this paper is structured as follows. We first introduce an example application in Sect. 2. In Sect. 3, we describe and discuss different process models of our example application. After a brief introduction to Hyperledger Fabric, our implementation platform, in Sect. 4, we describe our blockchain implementation in Sect. 5. We conclude in Sect. 6.

2   An Example Application: A Taxi Dispatcher

To demonstrate our modeling approach, we introduce taxi dispatching as an example application. Many cities are serviced by multiple taxi operators. When a passenger calls a specific operator, an unoccupied taxi might have to be fetched from a distance while another unoccupied taxi from another operator might be much closer. Therefore, a common dispatching service that selects the closest available taxi for a given passenger request, regardless of the operator it belongs to, implements a more efficient allocation that potentially benefits both the taxi operators and passengers.

For taxi operators to engage in such a common dispatching service, they must agree on a dispatching rule, the way it is to be used, and trust its implementation. We believe this makes taxi dispatching a good example of a multi-party application that can benefit from the distributed trust provided by a blockchain.

We consider two actors: taxi drivers and passengers. The blockchain implements the dispatcher. Drivers request a fare (passenger) with the dispatcher, announcing their current location. Likewise, passengers request a ride with the dispatcher, also announcing their location.

To keep the example simple, the dispatching rule matches a new ride request with the closest driver, if any, and each new fare request with the closest passenger, if any. If no match is found, the request is queued. If a match is found, both passenger and driver are notified and the driver is expected to pick up the passenger. When the ride is completed the driver can request the next fare.

3   Process Models for the Example Application

This section presents three alternative approaches to modeling taxi dispatching for a blockchain implementation. The first extends BPMN with multi-party interactions, a powerful modeling paradigm that is also a better representation of blockchain-mediated communication than the standard's message-passing notation. This is followed by proposals based on synchronized state machines and Petri nets, respectively, and a discussion of how the approaches compare.

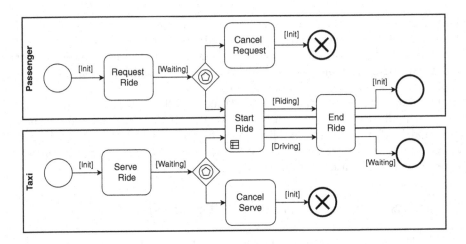

Fig. 1. A process model in an extended BPMN notation

3.1 BPMN with Multi-party Interactions

Figure 1 shows a process model of our taxi dispatching application. This process model represents the smart contract governing interactions between the participants: taxis and passengers. Initially, we consider a single passenger, a single taxi, and their interactions. We discuss later how multiple interacting passengers and taxis can be mapped.

The passenger may request a ride by initiating a transaction *Request Ride* on the blockchain. Such a transaction could be called, for example, from a client on the smartphone of the passenger. We represent the passenger on the blockchain as a state machine that is initially in some generic state *Init* and that moves into the state *Waiting*, which is short for *Passenger.Init* and *Passenger.Waiting*, respectively. This notation is similar to the object life-cycle notation for process models, see for instance [4].

The *Request Ride* transaction registers the passenger ID and location in a waiting list (not shown in this model). Similarly, a taxi can register its availability using the *Serve Ride* transaction. A waiting passenger may cancel her request, and a waiting taxi may withdraw its availability, moving them back to their respective *Init* state.

If a passenger and a taxi are both waiting they can engage in a common taxi ride, provided that they have a *match* which is specified in the business rule (dispatching rule) associated with the *Start Ride* transaction. If the *Start Ride* transaction succeeds the passenger state-machine moves to the *Riding* state and the taxi state-machine proceeds to the *Driving* state. Note that BPMN would require drawing an AND-join in front of both the *Start Ride* and *End Ride* transactions, which we have omitted here by convention for tasks that cross the boundary of pools. The end of a ride is manifested by executing an *End Ride* transaction which moves the state machine of the passenger back to the *Init* state and the taxi state-machine back to the *Waiting* state.

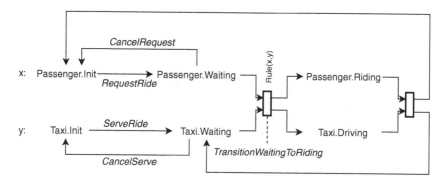

Fig. 2. A synchronized state-machine model

Note that Fig. 1 deviates from, or extends, BPMN in that the participants Passenger and Taxi communicate not by means of message-passing but by means of common transactions. Such transactions are also known as *multi-party interactions* or *multiway rendezvous* and have been studied in various formal languages such as CSP [2]. This interaction paradigm is powerful on a descriptive level in that it can yield very concise system models, but it is typically hard to implement in a distributed setting.

Second generation blockchains, however, make such an implementation possible. Both *Request Ride* and *Serve Ride* invoke the dispatching rule. If the rule finds a match it invokes *Start Ride* on both the passenger and the taxi. *End Ride* is similarly invoked on both.

3.2 Synchronized State Machine

Figure 2 shows a formal model of two synchronized state machines, one for the passenger and one for the taxi. As usual, see for instance UML state charts, a state machine is a connected directed graph that represents a sequential thread of execution. However, the two state machines shown in Fig. 2 are synchronized in two transitions. Each of these two transitions represents the synchronization of their respective inbound transactions. For example, the one labeled *Transition WaitingToRiding* synchronizes the Passenger transition from *Waiting* to *Riding* with the Taxi transition from *Waiting* to *Driving*.

In comparison with Fig. 1, the state-machine model in Fig. 2 reflects more explicitly that each of the two state machines has cycles: the passenger returns to its *Init* state and the taxi returns to its *Waiting* state upon completion of the taxi ride. However, the model in Fig. 2 still refers to two fixed instances of state machines that are synchronized in the entire model, denoted x and y. Note that we also refer to the business rule *Rule(x, y)*, which requires that for the transition *Transition WaitingToRiding* to be successful the dispatching rule is satisfied for x and y, e.g., x is the longest waiting passenger and y the waiting taxi that is closest to x.

3.3   High-Level Petri Net

A process as in Fig. 1 represents only a part of the entire system, namely the interaction of a given pair (x, y) of a passenger x and a taxi y. In the entire system, a taxi y may engage in multiple interactions with different or repeated passengers. Although Figs. 1 and 2 indicate that such repeated interactions are possible by referring to the states of the state machines, the semantics of how multiple such processes may be instantiated and interact with each other is not fully explicit.

To make that semantics explicit, Fig. 3 provides a Petri-net model of the full system with a complete behavioral specification of the entire system. In Fig. 3, P and T represent the set of passengers and taxis, respectively, that have permission for the application. This high-level Petri net has a clear operational semantics—see for instance [6] for a description. It can serve either as code on an abstract machine implemented on the blockchain or as a complete functional specification for blockchain code.

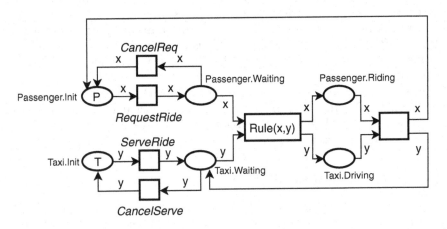

Fig. 3. A high-level Petri-net model of the system

Figure 3 looks similar to both Figs. 1 and 2 but, in contrast to those, Fig. 3 presents all processes simultaneously. Participant instances are now local to a transaction, not fixed for the entire model any longer as in Figs. 1 and 2. This is reflected by pools not being explicit anymore in the Petri-net model. Pools are appealing from a business perspective and they might be useful to represent identity management and authorization aspects of the blockchain application, but they also represent a rigid communication structure—in our example: one instance of a passenger interacts with one instance of a taxi. In more complex applications the communication structure might be more complex and dynamic. For example, multiple passengers could share a ride or passengers could dynamically change from one taxi to another. In such scenarios it becomes difficult to map all interaction details with a fixed set of pools. The Petri-net model overcomes this limitation.

3.4 Discussion

The high-level Petri-net model provides a full specification of the system with full operational semantics that can be directly translated into code. We sketch how such code is structured in Sect. 5. The code structure will resemble most the intermediate model in Fig. 2 of synchronized state machines. The formal description of such a translation is subject of future work. Such a high-level Petri net is not restricted to a fixed set of pools or pool types and can therefore also be used for more complex communication structures.

However, high-level Petri nets do not come with the same tool support as industrial process-modeling languages such as BPMN. Therefore, it is desirable to provide a language that could benefit from existing industry adoption and that is more appealing to business stakeholders. We have argued that BPMN can be extended with multi-party interactions to provide a high-level model of our example that corresponds to the formal high-level Petri net. Again, a formal definition of the BPMN extension and an investigation which existing BPMN constructs should be kept for a blockchain-tailored language are out of the scope of this paper. A definition of such a language will be the subject of future work for which the models in this section can serve as first steps. Such future work should also study how to overcome the limitation of BPMN that result from a fixed set of pools or pool types.

4 Introduction to Hyperledger Fabric

This section introduces a blockchain, Hyperledger Fabric, that we have used to implement the example application. The implementation will be presented in the next section.

Hyperledger Fabric [1], cf. also [8, Sect. 2.3], is a general-purpose distributed operating system providing an execution environment for externally defined programs called *chaincodes*. Its design is based on a set of *organisations* forming a *consortium*: the consortium as a whole defines common rules and policies, e.g. the policy to onboard a new organisation, and defines the shared business logic, i.e. the *chaincodes*. The Fabric network enforces these common rules and policies and maintains the shared *world state*—comprising name, version, and value of all the variables that have been created by all chaincodes—ensuring its consistency.

In order to enforce access-control policies to the functions updating the world state, Fabric is a permissioned blockchain, i.e. a network that only authorized members can join. Each organisation in the consortium acts as an identity management domain and issues identity credentials to its own members.

A Hyperledger Fabric instance consists of two types of nodes: *peers* and *orderers*. The peers' prime responsibility is to manage and execute chaincodes. Peers are also responsible for maintaining the world state. Chaincodes are invoked by fabric *clients*. An invocation, much like a function call, includes a set of arguments; it may read and modify any variable in the system; and it may produce a return value. Successful invocations produce messages called *transactions* that include invocation arguments, return values and world state changes recorded in *read-write sets*. The world state exists in two forms: the *ledger*, which is an append-only log of all transactions, and the *state DB*, which is a snapshot of the current world state. The peer guarantees that the two are kept in sync: as new transactions are appended to the ledger, the state DB is updated to reflect all the variables that have been changed.

The principal role of orderers is to deliver the same set of transactions in the same order to all peers in the system. This is designed to guarantee that ledger and world state of all peers will be identical.

4.1   The Endorser Transaction Protocol

The Endorser Transaction Protocol is the protocol used in Fabric to invoke the business logic defined in one ore more chaincodes. The protocol operates between a client, one ore more endorsers and the ordering service to generate and commit a transaction. The following steps are required to successfully commit a transaction:

Propose Transaction. The application, implemented using a Fabric client SDK, sends a transaction proposal to a selected number of nodes (peers). The transaction proposal specifies the smart contract (chaincode) and the arguments for the chaincode invocation.

Execute Transaction Proposal. The peers that receive the proposal execute the chaincode with the arguments provided in the proposal. They add the outputs of the execution, the return value and a read-write set to the proposal. The read-write set captures the updates to, as well as dependencies on the world state. Note that the world state does not change during the course of a chaincode invocation; proposed changes are merely described in the read-write set. All peers that execute the chaincode sign the output of the execution and send it back to the application. These signatures are called *endorsements*. We sometimes also refer to this step as simulation, since the chaincode is executed but state updates are not immediately applied.

Assemble Transaction. The application bundles all endorsed transaction proposals into a transaction and sends it to the ordering service.

Order Transaction. The ordering service collects incoming transactions and assembles them into blocks based on a consensus algorithm between the orderers. Once a block is complete, the ordering service sends it to the committing peers.

Transaction Validation. When the committing peers receive a new block, they append it to the ledger and validate every transaction in that block. Validation mainly ensures that the endorsements of a transaction satisfy the *endorsement policy* for that chaincode, and that the read-write set does not conflict with concurrent updates that were committed before. If a transaction is valid, the world state is updated with the read-write set of the transaction.

4.2   State Machines in Fabric

Fabric lends itself very well to the implementation of state machines owing to its programming model. The business logic may be conveniently split between private logic on the application side and shared logic on the chaincode side. The application side is represented by the client SDK initiating the endorser transaction protocol and invoking chaincodes. The chaincode side is implemented in the chaincode logic which is directly invoked by the peer in response to a chaincode invocation.

A state machine can be implemented in Fabric as follows:

State. The current state of the state machine is stored in the ledger; this way the network as a whole is in agreement about the current state and any node in the network may handle the request for a state transition. If the state is confidential it is possible to use either encryption or the private data feature to limit the set of participants who may access the information.

State transitions may be implemented as chaincode functions. Each function may inspect the ledger to determine the current state, use identity management and access control capabilities to determine the identity and entitlement of a requester. With this information, the chaincode determines whether the transition is allowed and performs the necessary updates to the ledger to reflect the new state.

Atomicity. The atomic nature of fabric transactions ensures that state transitions across multiple state machines happen atomically.

Access Control. Fabric is a permissioned network and so access control is a built-in feature. It is possible to use Fabric access control together with chaincode-level access control to identify clients and determine whether they are entitled to perform the requested action.

While the chaincode implements the rules and persists the state, creating network-wide enforcement for the state-machine logic, the input for state transitions necessarily comes from the end users. The client SDK receives a request from end users to perform a certain action, translates it into a state change request and submits that to peers by initiating the endorser transaction protocol. The client SDK may perform preliminary checks to ensure that the request is legitimate and timely, e.g. that no two conflicting requests have been submitted, or that the same request isn't submitted twice. While this step is useful in reducing unnecessary transactions that would be rejected by the network, it isn't strictly necessary to guarantee the overall correctness: conflicting or duplicate requests would be automatically rejected by the system.

In a blockchain system, we have to account for adversarial behaviour. For example, it may be advantageous for a malicious entity in the system to force a state machine to transition to a specific state, or to violate the transition rules. Fabric gives the implementer of the chaincode (the state machine in this case) the security control of *endorsement policies* to capture the trust relationships in the network. A Fabric network uses the endorsement policy to describe the set of entities that are trusted to uphold the business logic of the associated chaincode.

By defining the endorsement policy they ensure that state changes are allowed only if they are endorsed by the selected peers. In turn, if the selected peers are chosen to ensure the necessary checks and balances to force an honest behaviour, ledger correctness is guaranteed and hence the correctness of the state machine and its transitions.

Finally, the atomicity property ensures that multiple state machines are capable of jointly transitioning across states, ensuring that business processes that affect multiple entities are supported by the platform.

4.3   The Chaincode Interface

A chaincode must implement a fixed interface comprised of two functions: an `Init` function and an `Invoke` function. `Init` is called once when the chaincode is instantiated, whereas `Invoke` is called in response to client transactions. Either function is invoked by a peer and supplied with an implementation of a `shim` interface through which the chaincode may interact with the ledger and other chaincodes. Most notably, the shim gives access to the world state by exposing basic `Put` and `Get` operations on key-value pairs.

5   An Implementation

This section describes our implementation of the sample use-case described in Sects. 2 and 3. The implementation is structured in two layers:

State-Machine Management (SMM). This is the lowest layer in the implementation and makes direct use of the `shim` interface to implement the general-purpose logic related to state-transition management.

State-Machine Logic (SML). This layer is built on top of the previous and makes use of it to implement the logic of the actual state machine at hand—in our case, the state machine related to our use case. The SML includes the definition of the actual states and transitions as well as the transition logic and access control. This layer defines functions to request state transitions that are directly exposed to chaincode invokers.

5.1   Entities

We assume that the different entities in our system (drivers and passengers) are transacting clients in the blockchain network. Since the network is a permissioned one, each entity has an identity credential that they can use to identify and transact. Credentials may also certify attributes of their owner, for instance in our case we assume they certify the role of the entity—driver or passenger. Finally, entities may either transact directly (thus running the client SDK) or proxy their interaction via a browser or mobile app to an application server. We assume each entity has a unique identifier, which we will refer to as the entity's `ID`.

5.2   State-Machine Persistence

In our use case, we instantiate multiple state machines, one per participant: each state-machine instance identifies the current state of the participant it represents.

The current state of each state machine is persisted to the ledger. In the implementation we make use of composite keys, a well-known feature of key-value stores, that structures state keys as a lexicographically sorted tree with the ability to efficiently retrieve groups of keys by prefix. The current state of an entity is stored on a key which is formed as STATE.{ROLE}.{ID} where {ROLE} is instantiated with the role of the entity (driver or passenger) and {ID} is instantiated with the ID of each entity whose state the key refers to. The value associated with the key stores the current state of that entity. Legal states for entities with the passenger role are INIT, WAITING and RIDING, whereas legal states for entities with the driver role are INIT, WAITING and DRIVING. The SMM layer is responsible for creating and updating these keys, on instructions from the SML layer that requests state transitions.

Each state has some state metadata attached to it which is created, marshalled and consumed by the SML layer and only stored as an opaque byte blob by the SMM layer.

5.3   State-Machine Transitions

The chaincode exposes four main functions: INIT, REQUESTRIDE, SERVERIDE and ENDRIDE. When an entity requests a state transition, the chaincode retrieves the entity's ID from the request, retrieves the current state of the entity from the ledger and uses information from the SML layer to determine whether the transition is legal. If so, the SMM layer performs the necessary transition, possibly updating SML state in the ledger. We also expose a STATUS function to permit entities to query the current status of their state machine. This may be required for a web portal or a mobile app to display status information in the user interface.

The main structure of the Invoke function of the chaincode is the following:

```
func (cc *C) Invoke(shim shim.ChaincodeStubInterface) Response {
    fn, args := stub.GetFunctionAndParameters()
    switch fn {
    case INIT:
        // INIT logic
    case REQUESTRIDE:
        // REQUESTRIDE logic
    case SERVERIDE:
        // SERVERIDE logic
    case ENDRIDE:
        // ENDRIDE logic
    case STATUS:
        // STATUS logic
    default:
```

```
        // error
    }
}
```

In the following we describe the implementation of these functions.

INIT. This function is invoked to handle the initial onboarding of each participant and may thus be invoked by both drivers and passengers. The chaincode logic extracts the ID of the entity from the request, checks that the entity doesn't exist in the system and then sets the entity's status to the INIT state.

REQUESTRIDE and SERVERIDE. These two functions are the passenger and driver version, respectively, of the logic required to pair up a driver with a passenger. The function takes as argument a set of coordinates of the entity and the ID of the requester. The implementation checks that the entity is in either the INIT or WAITING state, performs any state-machine transition that may be required (e.g. if the entity was previously in the INIT state) and sets (or updates) the position of the entity. This information is stored in the WAITING.{ROLE}.{ID} key, where {ID} is instantiated with the ID of the entity and {ROLE} with its role.

The function also attempts to match supply with demand as follows: assume REQUESTRIDE is invoked. The chaincode logic uses the shim to scan the range of the world state rooted at WAITING.DRIVER, which will return the IDs of all waiting drivers. The chaincode logic then reads out all positions and selects the closest driver based on the current position of the passenger supplied as argument to the invocation. If one is found, both entities transition from WAITING to DRIVING and RIDING for a driver and a passenger, respectively.

When a match is found, an ID of the match is also generated and stored in the RIDING.{ROLE}.{ID} key, where {ID} is instantiated with the ID of the entity and {ROLE} with its role. This key also stores the identity of both participants, so that by inspecting one key it is possible to retrieve the other participant. The fact that a match was found is signalled by the fact that both driver and passenger have the same ride ID stored in this key. The transition to this state deletes the WAITING.{ROLE}.{ID} key from both the driver and the passenger.

This PoC implementation has ample room for optimisations (which are outside of the scope of the paper): for instance, position keys may be further sorted to avoid having to scan the entire range of keys. The matching function may also be improved to avoid matching a driver–passenger pair if their locations are not within an acceptable distance. Finally, the REQUESTRIDE function should possibly alert drivers.

ENDRIDE. This function signals the end of a ride and may be invoked by either participant to any given ride. The argument to this function is the position where the ride ended, signalling the new position of the driver now in the WAITING state to signal its willingness to pick up new passengers. The passenger goes back to the INIT state instead because it may no longer need to make use of the platform.

The implementation at first checks that the transition is allowed (i.e. that the requester is in the `DRIVING` or `RIDING` state), determines the ride identifier and the `ID` of the other party to the ride from the `RIDING.{ROLE}.{ID}` key and transitions both participants to the new state, with the new information attached to the state wherever appropriate.

5.4 Testing

We have developed the chaincode logic in `golang` and tested it against Hyperledger Fabric version 2.0.0 alpha. Instead of deploying a full network we have tested the chaincode using the unit test environment with the mock version of the shim interface[2]. In our test runs we exercised the entire functionality of the state machine with the following scenarios: (i) passenger requests a ride, no taxi available; driver later concludes previous ride and now offers a ride to the passenger; (ii) driver is ready to serve a ride at a location but no passenger requires it; later a passenger requests a ride and gets one from the waiting driver; (iii) multiple drivers compete for a passenger, the nearest one serves the passenger; (iv) after concluding a ride, the driver picks up a new passenger that was previously waiting. Our implementation passes all tests.

6 Conclusion and Future Work

We have presented an implementation of a blockchain application whose code is structured along a model of synchronized state machines. Each blockchain transaction moves one or more state machines from one state to one of their potential successor states. Such a set of synchronized state machines can be fully specified by a high-level Petri net. Abstractions that are easier to read are state-machine diagrams and an extended BPMN diagram. We have argued that a useful extension to BPMN are multi-party interactions between participants that can be mapped to blockchain transactions that synchronize multiple state machines.

Note that equally important is an easily readable specification of the business rules—in our example the one that defines how taxis are matched to passenger requests. As with traditional BPMN implementations we propose to specify such business rules in a dedicated rule language such as DMN and encapsulate the corresponding code.

Future work should establish a tighter relationship between model and code in general blockchain applications. This could be achieved either by formal code generation from the process model or by implementing a process engine in chaincode that executes the process model as high-level code. The Petri-net model can serve as a guiding intermediate model between the code and the extended BPMN model. Likewise, code could be generated from a business-rule description or a dedicated rule engine could be implemented on the blockchain.

---

[2] Available   at   https://github.com/hyperledger/fabric/blob/v2.0.0-alpha/core/chaincode/shim/mockstub.go.

Furthermore, it is worth studying how the extended BPMN model can be generalized to express communication patterns between process participants that are more complex than just two static pools. Model-driven engineering also needs extensions, i.e., integrated high-level models, for additional aspects of a blockchain application such as role-based access control and privacy domains.

References

1. Androulaki, E., et al.: Hyperledger Fabric: A distributed operating system for permissioned blockchains. In: Oliveira, R., Felber, P., Hu, Y.C. (eds.) Proceedings of the Thirteenth EuroSys Conference, EuroSys 2018, Porto, Portugal, 23–26 April 2018, pp. 30:1–30:15. ACM (2018). https://doi.org/10.1145/3190508.3190538
2. Hoare, C.A.R.: Communicating Sequential Processes. Prentice-Hall, Upper Saddle River (1985)
3. Hull, R., Batra, V.S., Chen, Y.-M., Deutsch, A., Heath III, F.F.T., Vianu, V.: Towards a shared ledger business collaboration language based on data-aware processes. In: Sheng, Q.Z., Stroulia, E., Tata, S., Bhiri, S. (eds.) ICSOC 2016. LNCS, vol. 9936, pp. 18–36. Springer, Cham (2016). https://doi.org/10.1007/978-3-319-46295-0_2
4. Küster, J.M., Ryndina, K., Gall, H.: Generation of business process models for object life cycle compliance. In: Alonso, G., Dadam, P., Rosemann, M. (eds.) BPM 2007. LNCS, vol. 4714, pp. 165–181. Springer, Heidelberg (2007). https://doi.org/10.1007/978-3-540-75183-0_13
5. OMG: Business process model and notation (BPMN) version 2.0, OMG document number dtc/2010-05-03. Technical report (2010)
6. Reisig, W.: Elements of Distributed Algorithms: Modeling and Analysis with Petri Nets. Springer, Heidelberg (1998). https://doi.org/10.1007/978-3-662-03687-7
7. Weber, I., Xu, X., Riveret, R., Governatori, G., Ponomarev, A., Mendling, J.: Untrusted business process monitoring and execution using blockchain. In: La Rosa, M., Loos, P., Pastor, O. (eds.) BPM 2016. LNCS, vol. 9850, pp. 329–347. Springer, Cham (2016). https://doi.org/10.1007/978-3-319-45348-4_19
8. Xu, X., Weber, I., Staples, M.: Architecture for Blockchain Applications. Springer, Heidelberg (2019). https://doi.org/10.1007/978-3-030-03035-3

Smart Contract Locator (SCL) and Smart Contract Description Language (SCDL)

Andrea Lamparelli[1]([✉]), Ghareeb Falazi[2][iD], Uwe Breitenbücher[2][iD], Florian Daniel[1][iD], and Frank Leymann[2][iD]

[1] Dipartimento di Elettronica Informazione e Bioingegneria, Politecnico di Milano, Via Ponzio 34/5, 20133 Milano, Italy
andrea.lamparelli@mail.polimi.it, florian.daniel@polimi.it
[2] Institute for Architecture of Application Systems, University of Stuttgart, Universitätsstraße 38, 70569 Stuttgart, Germany
{falazi,breitenbuecher,leymann}@iaas.uni-stuttgart.de

Abstract. Today's blockchain technologies focus mostly on isolated, proprietary technologies, yet there are application scenarios that ask for interoperability, e.g., among blockchains themselves or with external applications. This paper proposes the Smart Contract Locator (SCL) for the unambiguous identification of smart contracts over the Internet and across blockchains, and the Smart Contract Description Language (SCDL) for the abstract description of the external interface of smart contracts. The paper derives a unified metamodel for blockchain smart contract description and equips it with a concrete, JSON-based description language for smart contract search and discovery. The goal of the proposal is to foster smart contract reuse both inside blockchains and through the integration of smart contracts inside enterprise applications. The idea is inspired by the Service-Oriented Architecture (SOA) and aims to provide a high-level, cross-blockchain interoperability layer.

Keywords: Blockchain · Smart contracts · Description · SCDL · SCL

1 Introduction

A *blockchain* is a distributed ledger, that is, a log of transactions that provides for their persistency and verifiability [13]. *Transactions* are cryptographically signed instructions constructed by a user of the blockchain [15] and directed toward other parties in the blockchain network, for example the transfer of cryptocurrency from one account to another. A transaction typically contains a predefined set of metadata and an optional payload. Transactions are grouped into so-called *blocks*; blocks are concatenated chronologically. A new block is added to the blockchain using a hash computed over the last block as a connection link. A *consensus protocol* enables the nodes of the blockchain network to create trust in the state of the log and makes blockchains inherently resistant to tampering [9]. *Smart contracts* [14] extend a blockchain's functionality from storing

© Springer Nature Switzerland AG 2020
S. Yangui et al. (Eds.): ICSOC 2019 Workshops, LNCS 12019, pp. 195–210, 2020.
https://doi.org/10.1007/978-3-030-45989-5_16

transactions to performing also computations, for example, to decide whether to release a given amount of cryptocurrency upon the satisfaction of a condition agreed on by multiple partners.

Blockchains can be broadly categorized into *permissionless* and *permissioned*. Early blockchain platforms, such as Bitcoin [13] and Ethereum [15], were permissionless in the sense that participating in the protocol with any role is open for everyone. These platforms favor absolute decentralization at the cost of having relatively weak privacy and performance capabilities. Therefore, permissioned blockchains, such as Hyperledger Fabric [1], Hyperledger Sawtooth [10] and Corda [3], were introduced as an alternative that guarantees data confidentiality and ensures better performance. However, these desirable properties come with the price of losing some degree of decentralization, since joining the network becomes restricted and under the control of a single entity.

Both kinds of blockchains have their use-cases that can sometimes coincide. For example, in a scenario that involves a consortium of enterprises partially trusting each other, one or more permissioned blockchain networks can be used to guarantee to all participants that the collaborative process itself is being conducted exactly as designed, while ensuring good performance and privacy. However, to provide a similar guarantee to external entities that do not trust the consortium as a whole, such as auditing authorities, it is not enough to use permissioned blockchains, since they favor privacy over transparency and cannot prove that some transactions were not removed from the ledger history due to a malicious agreement between the consortium members. In that case, the additional involvement of permissionless blockchains can provide the desired guarantees. Therefore, we see that there is no single blockchain technology that is capable of solving all potential use-cases, which means that existing and new variations of blockchains would continue to co-exist, and end-users would likely become involved in a mixture of them in relatively complex scenarios [6].

To integrate blockchains into existing processes, using, e.g., business process management systems [5,6], their smart contracts need to be used, since, from an external viewpoint, the public functions of smart contracts are the access-points at which blockchains can be utilized by other systems, i.e., they are the *integration points* of blockchains. However, as mentioned earlier, multiple permissioned and permissionless blockchain platforms might need to be integrated in the same use-case. The problem here is that smart contracts of different blockchains are invoked using different mechanisms, protocols, and data formats, which significantly raises the integration barrier for systems wishing to utilize them, since developers need to be aware of these variations making the integration process time-consuming and error-prone. Furthermore, the specific smart contracts relevant for a given use-case need to be identified, which is not a straightforward task, because information regarding existing smart contracts of various blockchains is not uniformly available for developers.

In this paper, we extend our previous approach [8], which introduced an Ethereum-specific smart contract description format, to a wider set of blockchain technologies. Here, we propose a Service-Oriented Architecture (SOA)-inspired style of integration: We first analyze state-of-the-art blockchain platforms and derive cross-blockchain addressing and description requirements (Sect. 2). Then, we introduce a smart contract addressing format, the *Smart Contract Locator* (SCL), as a specialization of the generic URL scheme that facilitates the unambiguous identification of smart contract functions, both externally over the Internet and internally from within the blockchain network (Sect. 3). Then, we define a unified metamodel capable of describing the public interface of smart contracts of multiple permissioned and pemissionless blockchains; finally, we equip the metamodel with a JSON-based language called the *Smart Contract Description Language* (SCDL) for uniform smart contract descriptors that can be stored in a specialized registry to provide the functionality of smart contract search and discovery (Sect. 4). We close the paper with related works in Sect. 5 and a discussion of our proposal and future works in Sect. 6.

2 Analysis of Smart Contracts

In [4], we analyzed contract types, interaction styles, interaction protocols, data formats and blockchain-internal description formats of smart contracts, and demonstrated the suitability of smart contracts for the implementation of a smart contract-based, service-oriented architecture. Next, we study the specifics of smart contract interfaces for contract description.

2.1 Fundamentals of Smart Contracts

Most blockchain platforms today support different *programming languages* for the implementation of smart contracts, ranging from general-purpose languages like Java, C++, Python, JavaScript, Golang to platform-specific languages like Solidity for Ethereum or Bitcoin Script for Bitcoin [4]. Most of these languages are object-oriented and, hence, a smart contract can be seen as an object that has an identity, a behavior, a state, and events. Typically, smart contracts are executed using a blockchain-specific *virtual machine* that replicates the same "computer" on all nodes of the blockchain network. The most famous and used virtual machine today is the Ethereum Virtual Machine ("EVM", https://py-evm.readthedocs.io) developed by Ethereum and used by several other platforms for smart contract execution. For its execution, a smart contract must be *deployed* on the blockchain and *instantiated* in the virtual machine. This process creates an instance of the contract – along with a unique contract identifier – and initializes its state. After this initialization, the contract becomes accessible to possible clients who can invoke the contract according to its *external interface* (the functions made available) by submitting suitable *transactions* that carry the invocation in their body. Invocations may come from other smart contracts inside the same blockchain or from the outside, e.g., from enterprise applications. How exactly contracts are invoked is, again, platform dependent.

Bringing together the different models of smart contracts that have emerged so far, the most important characteristics can be summarized as follows (we analyze concrete technologies in the next subsection):

- *Identity*: This is typically defined by a specific address that corresponds to the deployment location of the contract. Each platform has its own way to compute this address. In some blockchains contracts are treated like any other account, and the address is an *account identifier*; in other platforms they are considered immutable states (variables) identified by a virtual *memory address*. The address does not only distinguish different contracts from each other, but also different, independent instances of a same contract.
- *State*: This refers to the properties (variables) internal to the contract that are *persistent* across multiple invocations. A contract can be *immutable*, where the state cannot be changed after its initialization, or *mutable*, where the state can be modified during the contract's life. Immutable contracts are typically used as transaction validators that check conditions only; mutable contracts can implement any kind of business logic.
- *Functions*: These implement the operations a contract can perform and, thus, its behavior. A function usually has a *scope* that tells the visibility of the function (e.g., private vs. public or blockchain-internal vs. -external), a *name*, a number of *input* parameters, and optional *return* parameters. A function is called "pure" if return values depend only on input values and it does not produce any side effects on the state; it is called "view" function if it provides read-only access to state. Some blockchain platforms allow the *direct* invocation of functions using their name, others advocate the use of a single *dispatcher* function to forward input values to target functions.
- *Events*: An event occurs when a contract sends a signal that an action or *state change* has taken place upon its invocation. Events allow external applications to monitor the state of the contract, while the blockchain platform allows applications to *subscribe* to or *unsubscribe* from events. Events usually have a *name* and a set of *parameters* that represent the payload of the event. Some platforms generate *system events*, others support developer-defined *custom events*. Custom events may require an explicit declaration of the event and its parameters (the event prototype) and can be launched programmatically; system events are launched automatically. Depending on the platforms *single* or *multiple* events may be launched at a time.
- *Description*: For developers to understand the exact model of a given smart contract, since smart contracts are deployed on the blockchain, the developer could inspect the deployed code, but such is typically a compiled version and, hence, not useful to derive how to interact with it. Some platforms in addition generate descriptive *metadata* at compilation time that may provide both the actual source code and an abstract summary of the external interface of the contract, often called *Application Binary Interface* (ABI).

Ideally, for a given smart contract, all these aspects are specified in a proper descriptor and made accessible online (e.g., Ethereum proposes Swarm, https://ethersphere.github.io/swarm-home/, to host such metadata), yet as of today, there is no commonly used *registry* for storing and indexing metadata or descriptors for smart contracts of various blockchain platforms, let alone a uniform description language.

2.2 Comparison of Blockchain Platforms

In order to understand the state of the art of smart contract support by blockchain platforms, we have selected platforms for comparison from the two major blockchain families, permissionless and permissioned. As mentioned earlier, permissionless blockchains allow anyone to participate and access information stored in the network, whereas permissioned blockchains allow only invited nodes to participate and access data. The selected platforms are:

- *Bitcoin* (https://bitcoin.org), the first permissionless blockchain platform introduced with limited support for smart contracts. Contracts are used as validators, have an immutable state and are used to lock/unlock values only.
- *Ethereum* (https://www.ethereum.org), the permissionless platform that first introduced Turing-complete smart contracts that, in principle, allow the implementation of arbitrary application logic.
- *Hyperledger Fabric* (https://www.hyperledger.org/projects/fabric), a permissioned blockchain platform developed by The Linux Foundation that leverages on container technology to host smart contracts called "chaincode".
- *Neo* (https://neo.org), also known as the "Ethereum of China," with support for multiple digital assets and smart contracts; Neo is permissionless.
- *EOSIO* (https://eos.io), a more recent permissioned/permissionless platform with a special focus on transaction throughput for businesses.
- *Hyperledger Sawtooth* (https://sawtooth.hyperledger.org), another permissioned blockchain platform from the The Linux Foundation that is highly modular and configurable. It introduces *transaction families*, which are pulluggable, user-defined components, as the way to define smart contracts.

Moreover, Ethereum is the "father" of many other blockchain platforms, such as Qtum (https://qtum.org), Ubiq (https://ubiqsmart.com), Rootstock (https://www.rsk.co) and others. We omit them from the comparison, as they all comply with Ethereum's smart contract model and use the EVM.

Table 1 summarizes how the chosen platforms implement smart contracts. For the comparison, we use the smart contract characteristics described earlier; we do not consider aspects like access policy, consensus protocol, performance or similar, as these do not affect smart contracts' external interfaces. The analysis aims to provide a picture that abstracts away from implementation languages and instead emphasizes the addressing and functional interface perspective.

Addressing: Looking at how smart contracts are identified (first dimension), it is evident how contracts are referenced differently across different platforms. While there may be platform-specific reasons for this (e.g., Bitcoin does not have the concept of accounts), conceptually – from an external point of view – it must be possible to do so in an abstract, uniform manner.

Interface: State, if not immutable, is manipulated through functions, which are only visible to consumers if they are public; Ethereum and EOSIO further distinguish between functions that are internal to the blockchain (invocable only by contracts of the same blockchain) and functions that are external

Table 1. Comparison of smart contract support by most representative blockchain platforms from an external perspective.

Platform	Identity	State	Functions	Events	Description
Bitcoin	Contracts specify how *unspent transaction outputs* (UTXO) can be used; identified by UTXO address	Set when instantiating contract; immutable	Public; can be invoked directly	–	–
Ethereum	Contracts implement generic application logic; have own accounts	Stored in contracts; modified using functions	Public/private and blockchain-internal/ -external; invoked directly	Multiple custom events possible; explicit declaration of event prototype	Contract metadata and *Application Binary Interface* (ABI)
Hyperledger Fabric	Contracts (*chaincode*) implement generic application logic and are addressed using an ID	Stored in contracts; modified using functions	Public/private; invoked using dispatcher function	Max one custom event per invocation; no explicit event prototype needed	*Chaincode Interface* (CCI) for language-neutral description
Neo	Contracts implement generic application logic; have own accounts	Stored in contracts; modified using functions	Public/private; invoked either directly or via a dispatcher (recommended)	Multiple custom events possible; no declaration needed	Contract metadata and *Neo ABI*
EOSIO	Generic; hosted by EOSIO accounts (1-to-1 relationship) and identified by human-readable unique string	Stored in the contract, modified using functions (*actions*)	Public/private and blockchain-internal/ -external; invoked using dispatcher func	Multiple system events possible; no custom events	Contract metadata and *EOSIO ABI*
Hyperledge Sawtooth	Contracts (*transaction families*) implement generic application logic; addressed using a 35-byte hex hash of transaction family name	Stored in transaction families, modified using functions	Public; invoked only from external apps via a REST call to custom transaction family processor	Multiple custom events possible; explicit declaration of event prototype	Public interface of a transaction family defined by the developer via a set of *protobuf*[a] message types

[a] https://developers.google.com/protocol-buffers/

(invocable also by agents outside the blockchain). Most of the platforms support launching custom events to communicate with external agents; only Bitcoin and EOSIO support either no events or only system events. From a description point of view, it is interesting to note that most platforms are able to generate some descriptive metadata at compile time, along with an ABI that provides a summary of function prototypes – both however providing different kinds of information and focusing on blockchain-specific aspects. Yet, as the table also shows, there are significant similarities across platforms, which hints at the possibility to abstract external interfaces and uniformly describe them for uniform access.

3 Smart Contract Locator (SCL)

Internally, all platforms provide for smart contract addressing or identification; so, there is no need for intervention. Instead, Fig. 1 (solid, black components on the top) illustrates our minimal, architectural assumptions for the specification of the Smart Contract Locator (SCL), which is our proposal for uniformly addressing smart contracts from the outside of their blockchains: an *external consumer* (e.g., an enterprise application) that wants to invoke a *target smart contract* (e.g., a currency exchange app) deployed inside a *blockchain network* (e.g., Ethereum) to which it does not have own access (it does not own any node of the network) may have to cross the Internet to reach a so-called *gateway*, a web-accessible agent that is able to mediate between the external consumer and the target smart contract. SCL tells the external consumer how to reach that gateway and how to identify the target smart contract.

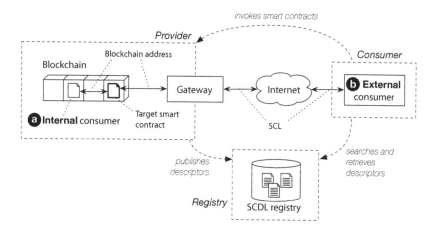

Fig. 1. Conceptual components for smart contract addressing (solid lines) for (a) blockchain-internal consumers and (b) blockchain-external consumers with service-oriented architecture for smart contracts (thin, dashed lines).

We intentionally limit the use of SCL to smart contract addressing only; the identification of the functions to be invoked and the passing of suitable parameter values will be done using the payload of the messages exchanged between consumer and smart contract (e.g., using http POST messages). We assume that the communication channel from the external consumer to the gateway is properly secured using state-of-the-art security mechanisms like https, access control, and encryption.

Now, given the IETF specification of the generic URL format [2]:

```
URL = scheme:[userinfo@]host[:port]path[?query][#fragment]
```

and the preliminary proposal for smart contract addressing in [6] (see Sect. 5), we define an SCL as a specialization of a URL composed of a standard URL (up to the path element included), which identifies the gateway, and of an SCL query, which identifies the target smart contract inside the blockchain network:

```
SCL = scheme:[userinfo@]host[:port]path"?"scl_query
scl_query = "blockchain="bc"&blockchain-id="id"&address="addr

bc = "ethereum" | "bitcoin" | "fabric" | "eosio" | ...

id = NetworkIdentifier              // not further detailed here

addr = eth_addr | bit_addr | fab_addr | eos_addr | ...
eth_addr = 40ByteHexString          // not further detailed here
bit_addr = Bech32Address            // not further detailed here
fab_addr = PathString               // not further detailed here
eos_addr = 12CharacterString        // not further detailed here
```

The SCL extension of URLs thus specifies (i) which type of blockchain is addressed, (ii) which exact blockchain network (there may be more networks accessible through a given gateway), and (iii) the blockchain-internal smart contract address or identifier.

In the following, we list example SCL addresses for a set of the supported blockchains that are accessed using the https scheme via a hypothetical gateway hosted at mygateway.com:

```
* Ethereum:
https://mygateway.com?blockchain=ethereum&blockchain-id=eth-mainnet
    &address=0xa0b73e1ff0b80914ab6fe0444e65848c4c34450b
* Bitcoin:
https://mygateway.com?blockchain=bitcoin&blockchain-id=btc-mainnet
    &address=1Mbk53DzVKCz6MHiBd8ZHkPhsZETo7PtZR
* Hyperledger Fabric:
https://mygateway.com?blockchain=fabric&blockchain-id=part-vendors
    &address=channel1%2Fchaincode1%2Fsmartcontract1
* EOSIO:
https://mygateway.com?blockchain=eos&blockchain-id=eos-mainnet
    &address=myfancyacc05
```

4 Smart Contract Description Language (SCDL)

Looking at the dashed annotations in Fig. 1, we can identify the typical roles of the service-oriented architecture (SOA): a provider, a consumer and a registry [11]. We assume that:

- The **consumer** is represented either by a blockchain-internal entity (a smart contract) or a blockchain-external entity (a software application) – both of them interested in reusing a given target smart contract, e.g., to inherit application logic or to integrate blockchain capabilities into enterprise applications. In order to do so, it is crucial that developers be able to find suitable smart contract descriptions that tell them all they need to know in order to invoke the contract from the inside/outside.
- The **provider** is represented by the operator of the blockchain, who is interested in opening its smart contracts to external entities. The practice is commonly known as Blockchain-as-a-Service (BCaaS [12]) and is pushed by vendors like Amazon (https://aws.amazon.com/managed-blockchain), Upvest (https://upvest.co) or Kaleido (https://kaleido.io). In order to allow external consumers to connect to a hosted blockchain, the provider publishes suitable descriptors and a gateway.
- The **registry** hosts smart contract descriptors and provides consumers with search and retrieval capabilities. The design of this registry is out of the scope of this paper and part of our future work.

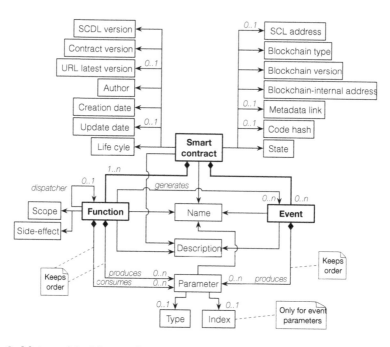

Fig. 2. Metamodel of Smart Contract Description Language (SCDL), version 1.0.

The goal of the Smart Contract Description Language (SCDL) is now to enable the *abstract, blockchain-independent description of the external interfaces of smart contracts* and to cater to both *internal and external consumers*. The language should further provide for the *extensibility* to allow developers to include blockchain-, contract- or application-specific metadata if needed.

4.1 Language Metamodel

Given these requirements and the results of Sect. 2, which analyzed state-of-the-art support for smart contracts, Fig. 2 illustrates the metamodel of SCDL; furthermore, the left half of Table 2 explains each of the entities in the metamodel. According to the metamodel, a smart contract can be seen as a blockchain- or web-accessible entity that is characterized by a set of descriptive metadata elements, a set of functions and a set of events.

Typical *metadata* are generic attributes like contract name, description, author and version, but also access-oriented attributes like the SCL address for external consumers and the blockchain type, version and internal address for internal consumers. Where available (e.g., for Ethereum smart contracts) publicly accessible metadata can be linked and a hash of the contract's code can be added to allow developers to check if a descriptor is up to date. *Functions*, too, have a name and a description and are characterized by the set of input and return parameters they consume/produce; parameter lists are ordered (the order is needed for some platforms to be able to properly invoke functions). Functions may further produce events, e.g., for the implementation of asynchronous communication with consumers, have a scope (e.g., public vs. private), produce or not side-effects (change or not the state), and specify a dispatcher function for those platforms where functions are not invoked directly (e.g., Hyperledger Fabric). *Events* have a name, a description and an ordered list of output parameters. *Parameters* have a name, an abstract data type (external consumers) that allows the derivation of a blockchain-specific, native data type (internal consumers) and may be indexed to enable consumers to query events on the blockchain.

The metamodel does not explicitly provide any extensibility points. It represents the minimum set of properties that allow a provider to describe any of the smart contracts studied in Sect. 2. For Bitcoin scripts, we can interpret clauses as functions and describe how to trigger them by means of the parameters needed to make them true. If additional properties are needed, these can simply be added as properties to the composite objects of the language, i.e., smart contract, function, event, parameter. For instance, if a provider wants to explicitly mention the programming language of a given smart contract, this could be achieved by adding a language property to the smart contract object.

For simplicity, in this paper we assume that there exists a suitable agreement between the provider and the consumer regarding the *costs* the provider may incur when executing smart contracts on behalf of the external consumer (internal consumers are charged directly by the blockchain platform).

4.2 SCDL JSON Syntax

We propose to equip the metamodel with a concrete syntax based on JSON, which is supported by multiple blockchain platforms (e.g., Ethereum, Hyperledger Fabric) and, hence, maintains consistency with existing conventions.

The translation of the metamodel to a concrete syntax follows few simple rules: *entities with associated properties* produce JSON objects with properties;

Table 2. SCDL 1.0 constructs with concrete syntax and domains of values. Mandatory elements are the minimum information needed to uniquely characterize smart contracts.

Construct	Description	Syntax element	Type of $value
Smart contract			
✘ SCDL version	Version of SCDL used; in this paper the version is 1.0	`scdl_version : $value`	`String`
✘ Name	Expressive name of contract	`name : $value`	`String`
✘ Contract version	Version of smart contract	`version : $value`	`String`
☐ URL latest version	Optional URL to latest descriptor	`latest_URL: $value`	`URL`
☐ Description	Free text description of contract	`description : $value`	`String`
✘ Author	Developer name of contract	`author : $value`	`String`
✘ Creation date	Date the descriptor was created	`created_on : $value`	`Date`
☐ Update date	Date the descriptor was updated	`updated_on : $value`	`Date`
☐ Lifecycle	Lifecycle state of contract	`lifecycle : $value`	`"ready"	"destroyed"`
☐ SCL address	SCL address of possible smart contract gateway	`scl : $value`	`SCL address, see Section 3`
✘ Blockchain type	Name of the blockchain platform	`blockchain_type : $value`	`"ethereum"	"bitcoin"	"fabric"	"neo"`
✘ Blockchain version	Version of the blockchain platform the contract runs on	`blockchain_version : $value`	`String`
✘ Blockchain-internal address	Blockchain-internal address of smart contract, e.g., Ethereum accout	`internal_address : $value`	`String`
☐ Metadata link	Link to external metadata of contract, if available	`metadata : $value`	`URL`
☐ Code hash	SHA256 hash of contract code	`hash : $value`	`String`
✘ State	Tells if the contract maintains internal state of not	`is_stateful : $value`	`Boolean`
✘ Functions	List of functions provided by contract	`functions : [Function, Function,...]`	`Array of Function`
☐ Events	List of events generated by contract	`events : [Event, Event,...]`	`Array of Event`
Function			
✘ Name	Contract-wide unique name of function	`name : $value`	`String`
☐ Description	Free text description of function	`description : $value`	`String`
✘ Scope	Visibility of function	`scope : $value`	`"public"	"private"	"internal"	"external"`
✘ Side-effect	Tells whether the function as side-effects on state or not	`has_side_effects : $value`	`Boolean`
☐ Dispatcher	Name of dispatcher function to use for function invocation	`dispatcher : $value`	`String`
✘ Input parameters	List of input parameters	`inputs : [Parameter, Parameter,...]`	`Array of Parameter`
✘ Output parameters	List of output parameters	`outputs : [Parameter, Parameter,...]`	`Array of Parameter`
☐ Events generated	List of names of events generated by function	`events : [String, String,...]`	`Array of String`
Event			
✘ Name	Contract-wide unique event name	`name : $value`	`String`
☐ Description	Free text description of event	`description : $value`	`String`
✘ Output parameters	List of output parameters	`outputs : [Parameter, Parameter,...]`	`Array of Parameter`
Parameter			
✘ Name	Unique parameter name	`name : $value`	`String`
✘ Type	Abstract, blockchain-indepdendent data type of parameter	`type : $value`	`String`
☐ Index	Tells if parameter is indexed and therefore searchable	`is_indexed : $value`	`Boolean`

✘ Mandatory element   ☐ Optional element

composition relationships are translated to JSON arrays; the *order* of parameters of functions or events is expressed by their order inside their respective arrays; *abstract data types* of parameters are expressed using JSON Schema (https://json-schema.org)[1]. The right half of Table 2 defines each individual language construct in detail and equips it with a respective domain of possible values. The general structure of a SCDL descriptor is organized as shown in Fig. 3.

```
{"scdl_version" : "1.0.0",              // generic smart contract properties
  "name" : "TokenConversion", ...
  "functions" : [
    { "name" : "convert", ...           // function properties
      "inputs" : [
        { "name"    : "amount",
          "type"    : "number"
        }, ...                          // list of parameters
      ],
      "outputs" : [...],                // list of parameters
      "events"  : [...]                 // list of parameters
    }, ...                              //  list of functions
  ],
  "events" : [
    { "name"    : "...", ...            //    event properties
      "outputs" : [...],               // list of parameters
    }, ...                             //    list of events
  ]
}
```

Fig. 3. General structure of SCDL descriptor

Next to JSON, also formats like XML, YAML or similar are compatible with the metamodel. We propose the use of JSON Schema to express abstract data types in order to enable external consumers (e.g., a business process engine connected to a blockchain via a gateway) to understand basic data types without the need for blockchain-specific knowledge.

4.3   Example: ZilliqaToken Contract

As an example, let's consider the ZilliqaToken contract deployed on Ethereum by the Zilliqa Team; the deployed contract and its code can be inspected at https://bit.ly/2GBajXC. The contract follows the ERC20 standard (https://theethereum.wiki/w/index.php/ERC20_Token_Standard) for the implementation of the ZIL token in Ethereum. The contract allows its users to check their token balance, transfer tokens among accounts, approve others to spend tokens, etc.

Figure 4 provides an excerpt from a possible SCDL descriptor of the contract (core metadata, one function and one correlated event). Next to the name and

---

[1] For mappings see https://github.com/floriandanielit/scdl#data-encoding.

a short description, the descriptor provides the external consumer with the SCL address of the contract and the internal consumers with the `internal_address`. As we chose the latest version of the contract, there is no link to any newer version of the contract, and the source code is linked using the `metadata` link. The contract is stateful, as it tracks token balances. The function `transfer` allows the user to transfer a given `_value` to a receiver `_to`. The function can be invoked directly using its name and generates the event `Transfer` with parameters `from`, `to`, `value` upon completion of the transfer. The parameters `from` and `to` are indexed and can thus be used for fast search of token transfers among accounts. The description of the complete contract is linked in the caption of Fig. 4.

5 Related Work

The problem of describing the external interface of software components is not new and has gained particular attention with the advent of the service-oriented architecture. Two core service models have emerged: SOAP web services [11] and RESTful APIs [7], the former equipped with description languages like WSDL (https://www.w3.org/TR/2007/REC-wsdl20-20070626) and WSDL-S (https://www.w3.org/Submission/WSDL-S), the latter with languages like WADL (https://www.w3.org/Submission/wadl) and Swagger/OpenAPI (https://swagger.io). WADL and Swagger/OpenAPI are oriented toward stateless resources and are, hence, out of scope. The metamodels of WSDL and WSDL-S are generic, that of SCDL is smart contract specific (e.g., it expresses relationships between functions and events and identifies indexed parameters).

The first approach to describing smart contracts in a blockchain-familiar fashion (JSON) is introduced in [8], where we suggested a SOA-based approach that allows one to uniformly describe Ethereum smart contracts and to store the resulting descriptions in a specialized registry that facilitates reuse. Compared to that work, the SCDL we propose here goes beyond Ethereum to a wider set of permissioned and permissionless blockchains. Furthermore, we also target developers of external applications by differentiating between internal, blockchain-specific smart contract addresses, and external, uniform addresses, i.e., SCLs, which can be used over the Internet.

In previous work [6], we instead focused on the process-based composition of heterogeneous smart contracts. The approach uses an extension of BPMN that allows invocations to permissioned and permissionless smart contract functions from standard business processes that can be executed by regular process engines. To allow for technology-agnostic models, the process engine utilizes an extensible middleware component called Blockchain Access Layer (BAL), which translates the calls it receives from external applications, e.g., the process engine, into blockchain-specific invocations. To identify the smart contract function that needs to be invoked, the BAL used a non URL-compatible URI scheme.

The SCL addressing scheme presented in this paper allows external applications to address heterogeneous smart contract functions across the Internet by utilizing the concept of a gateway that provides access to one or more blockchain

```
{ "scdl_version" : "1.0",
  "name" : "ZilliqaToken",
  "version" : "^0.4.18",
  "latest_url" : null,
  "author" : "0xBfE4aA5c37D223EEBe0A1F7111556Ae49bE0dcD2",
  "description" : "Contract token implementation following the ERC20 standard, the new created
      token is called ZIL",
  "created_on" : "Jan-12-2018 09:44:42 AM +UTC",
  "updated_on" : "Jan-12-2018 09:44:42 AM +UTC",
  "scl" : "https://mygateway.com?blockchain=ethereum&blockchain-id=eth-
      mainnet&address=0x05f4a42e251f2d52b8ed15E9FEdAacFcEF1FAD27",
  "internal_address" : "0x05f4a42e251f2d52b8ed15E9FEdAacFcEF1FAD27",
  "blockchain_type" : "ethereum",
  "blockchain_version" : "v0.4.18+commit.9cf6e910",
  "metadata" : "https://etherscan.io/address/0x05f4a42e251f2d52b8ed15e9fedaacfcef1fad27#code",
  "hash" : "b311edaec5a164050cede3219bf28cc6ce4c0ca43b8bf34d6fd309fb60c4d1d8   -",
  "is_stateful" : true,
  "lifecycle" : "ready",
  "functions" : [
      { "name" : "transfer",
        "description" : "* @dev transfer
        token for a specified address.
        @param _to The address to transfer
        to. @param _value Amount to be transf."
        "scope" : "public",
        "has_side_effects" : true,
        "inputs" : [
            {    "name" : "_to",
                 "type" : "string"
                 "pattern" : "^0x[a-fA-F0-9]{40}$"

            {    "name" : "_value",
                 "type" : "number"
                 "minimum" : "0"
                 "maximum" : "2^256-1"
            }
        ],
        "outputs" : [
            {    "name" : null,
                 "type" : "boolean"
            }
        ],
        "events" : ["Transfer"],
        "dispatcher" : null
      }, ...
],
```

```
"events" : [
    {    "name" : "Transfer",
         "description" : "Triggered when
         tokens are transferred",
         "outputs" : [
             {    "name" : "from",
                  "type" : "string",
                  "pattern" :
                      "^0x[a-fA-F0-9]{40}$"
                  "is_indexed" : true
             },
             {    "name" : "to",
                  "type" : "string",
                  "pattern" :
                      "^0x[a-fA-F0-9]{40}$"
                  "is_indexed" : true
             },
             {    "name" : "value",
                  "type" : "number"
                  "minimum" : "0"
                  "maximum" : "2^256-1"
                  "is_indexed" : false
             }
         ]
    }, ...
]
```
continues

Fig. 4. JSON-based SCDL descriptor of ZilliqaToken smart contract with hypothetical SCL address. For brevity, we report here only one function and one connected event; the full descriptor can be inspected online via https://bit.ly/2LRy9Tb.

platforms. This decouples the external consumers from the middleware that facilitates the communication with blockchain platforms.

6   Discussion and Outlook

This paper advances the state of the art in blockchain technology with two proposals of abstraction, i.e., the Smart Contract Locator (SCL) for cross-blockchain addressing of smart contracts and the Smart Contract Description Language (SCDL) for the abstract description of smart contracts. We consider both as founding ingredients for the development of a service-oriented architecture that is based on smart contracts and enables a service-like integration of blockchains into generic software applications. Commercial Blockchain-as-a-Service providers like Amazon, Upvest and Kaleido are evidence that the market is ready, yet this paper claims that suitable abstractions and middleware support are still missing.

In this respect, SCL and SCDL do not just want to advance that state of the art but they also want to stimulate the discussion.

The proposal of SCL is compliant with standard URLs, which makes it natively ready for the Internet. The examples in this paper use a scheme binding of "http" or "https", but nothing prohibits the use of SMTP or any other transport protocol. Similarly, SCDL is proposed with a JSON binding for serialization. This choice was driven by the observation that most blockchain platforms analyzed already make large use of JSON, e.g., for the invocation of functions, and hence aims to keep consistency. However, given the metadmodel of SCDL, alternative bindings can be defined for XML, YAML, WSDL or others.

The next step of our work will concentrate on the specification of a smart contract invocation protocol to rule the communication between external consumers and gateways, as well as on the implementation of a reference architecture for gateways able to provide access to different blockchain technologies. In terms of SCDL, the next version of the language will provide for the description of non-functional aspects like service-level agreements and payments – one feature where smart contracts excel compared to SOAP/REST services. SCDL will also be equipped with a suitable, open registry able to host descriptors and to provide for search and retrieval of smart contracts.

We intend to use GitHub to evolve the proposals of SCL (https://github.com/ghareeb-falazi/scl) and SCDL (https://github.com/floriandanielit/scdl) with help from the community.

Acknowledgements. This work was supported by the European Union's Horizon 2020 research and innovation programme, project DITAS, grant agreement RIA 731945.

References

1. Androulaki, E., et al.: Hyperledger fabric. In: EuroSys 2018, pp. 1–15. ACM Press (2018). https://doi.org/10.1145/3190508.3190538
2. Berners-Lee, T., Masinter, L., McCahill, M.: Uniform Resource Locators (URL) (1994). https://www.ietf.org/rfc/rfc1738.txt
3. Brown, R.G.: The Corda Platform: An Introduction. Corda Platform Whitepaper, pp. 1–21 (2018). https://www.corda.net/content/corda-platform-whitepaper.pdf
4. Daniel, F., Guida, L.: A service-oriented perspective on blockchain smart contracts. IEEE Internet Comput. **23**(1), 46–53 (2019)
5. Falazi, G., Hahn, M., Breitenbücher, U., Leymann, F.: Modeling and execution of blockchain-aware business processes. SICS Softw. Intensiv. Cyber Phys. Syst. **34**(2), 105–116 (2019). https://doi.org/10.1007/s00450-019-00399-5
6. Falazi, G., Hahn, M., Breitenbücher, U., Leymann, F.: Process-based composition of permissioned and permissionless blockchain smart contracts. In: EDOC 2019 (2019, to appear)
7. Fielding, R.: Representational state transfer. Architectural Styles and the Design of Network-based Software Architecture, pp. 76–85 (2000)
8. Guida, L., Daniel, F.: Supporting reuse of smart contracts through service orientation and assisted development. In: IEEE DappCon 2019, pp. 59–68 (2019)

9. Mingxiao, D., Xiaofeng, M., Zhe, Z., Xiangwei, W., Qijun, C.: A review on consensus algorithm of blockchain. In: SMC 2017, pp. 2567–2572. IEEE (2017)
10. Olson, K., Bowman, M., Mitchell, J., Amundson, S., Middleton, D., Montgomery, C.: Sawtooth: An Introduction. Hyperledger Sawtooth Whitepaper, pp. 1–7 (2018). https://www.hyperledger.org/wp-content/uploads/2018/01/Hyperledger_Sawtooth_WhitePaper.pdf
11. Papazoglou, M.P., Georgakopoulos, D.: Service-oriented computing. Commun. ACM 46(10), 25–28 (2003)
12. Samaniego, M., Deters, R.: Blockchain as a service for IoT. In: 2016 IEEE iThings/GreenCom/CPSCom/SmartData, pp. 433–436. IEEE (2016)
13. Satoshi, N.: Bitcoin: A Peer-to-Peer Electronic Cash System (2008). https://bitcoin.org/bitcoin.pdf
14. Szabo, N.: Smart contracts: building blocks for digital markets. EXTROPY J. Transhumanist Thought (16), 18, 2 (1996)
15. Wood, G.: Ethereum: a secure decentralised generalised transaction ledger. Ethereum Proj. Yellow Pap. 151, 1–32 (2014)

STRAPS: Smart daTa integRation And Processing on Service Based Environments

Introduction to the First International Workshop on Smart daTa integRation And Processing on Service Based Environments (STRAPS 2019)

Massive heterogeneous data integration is part of a continuum that starts with data, goes through sources, and lands in knowledge extraction and decision making processes. New applications require solving even more complex queries, including millions of sources and data with high levels of volume and variety. Thus, reducing the cost of data integration by efficiently evaluating queries is an important challenge, given that today the economic cost in computing cycles (see your cloud invoice), in energy consumption, and the performance required for some critical tasks have become increasingly important. Despite the proposal of academic and industrial research and consolidated results, data integration is still an important topic with open issues like data quality, trusted data, data providers, and processing operations; trusted infrastructures deal with data which differs according to data consumer requirements and different understandings of what are trust, quality, and acceptable levels of such properties. These new challenges call for intelligent processes that can learn from previous experiences, as well as be adaptable to changing requirements and dynamic execution contexts.

STRAPS aims at promoting scientific discussion on the way data stemming from different providers and produced under different conditions can be efficiently integrated to answer simple, relational, analytical queries ensuring providers, algorithms, and data trust.

The first edition of the workshop accepted three full research papers (an acceptance rate 40%) focusing on important and timely research problems, and one invited paper on "Constructing a secured, reactive & scalable data platform for a better exploitation of rich data assets in the tourism industry." Papers were evaluated under a blind evaluation process by three experts in the domain: members of the workshop Program Committee. Papers reported experience reports in real-life application settings addressing large scale data integration issues guided by SLA, quality, trust, privacy, and performed through services/microservices based systems on cloud and multi-cloud architectures.

Genoveva Vargas-Solar
Chirine Ghedira Guegan
Nadia Bennani

Measuring the Quality of Life
in "La Condesa"
Activating Mexico City Neighbourhood Economy While Maximising Well-Being

Ana-Sagrario Castillo-Camporro[1], José-Luis Zechinelli-Martini[2,3(✉)], and Javier A. Espinosa-Oviedo[3,4]

[1] Universidad Nacional Autónoma de México, Mexico City, Mexico
sagrariocastillo@hotmail.com
[2] Fundación Universidad de las Américas, Puebla, Mexico
joseluis.zechinelli@udlap.mx
[3] French-Mexican Laboratory of Informatics and Automatic Control, Mexico City, Mexico
javier.espinosa@tudelft.nl
[4] Delft University of Technology, Delft, The Netherlands

Abstract. Mexico City government has promoted central and historical areas by applying public policies intended to activate their economy. This is the case of the neighbourhood "La Condesa" located 4 km. from the Historical Downtown Area of Mexico City. Yet, beyond activating the economy, promoting massive tourism, leisure activities and business life, these policies have had questionable social implications. For example, valuing spaces for the benefit of the real estate investors that do not live in the areas and that promote non-permanent lodging; franchises that do not promote authentic services and products. Thus, it seems that the growth in economy with this approach is not compatible with human development, with the cultural benefit and the conservation of the green areas of the territory.

This paper presents our approach for computing the index of quality of life considering quantitative and qualitative measures seeking to maximise a holistic return of investment. Our notion of return of investment is holistic because it considers both quantitative and qualitative variables calibrated to find and "optimum" of economic and well-being benefit. Our proposal combines different data collections provided by the Mexican National Institute of Statistics and Geography (INEGI) that feed a novel mathematical model proposed for computing determining the elasticity of the index of quality of life. Given the volume of data sets about Mexico City and its inhabitants it has been necessary to use adapted computational methods to model urban phenomena happening in the area "La Condesa" in Mexico City. We have applied data analytics computational techniques based on mathematical methods, statistics and knowledge discovery to find patterns within data sets that represent the behaviour of quality of life as a social phenomenon measure.

© Springer Nature Switzerland AG 2020
S. Yangui et al. (Eds.): ICSOC 2019 Workshops, LNCS 12019, pp. 213–223, 2020.
https://doi.org/10.1007/978-3-030-45989-5_17

1   Context and Motivation

Contemporary urbanism addresses the relationship between qualities of urban and regional environments with the social, economic and environmental performance of societies, and the well-being of citizens. Yet, some regions have proposed public policies that go against this vision. During the last decade, the economic growth of the real estate market and tourism has been achieved through the revaluation of historical downtown areas and towns. Revaluation is the result of urban processes achieved through public policies aimed at bringing about changes in the territory. In Mexico, for example, the ministry of tourism has implemented public policies intended to activate the economy in small villages and historical downtown quarters.

Yet, beyond the activation of economy, promoting massive tourism, leisure activities and business life, these policies have had questionable social implications. For example, valuing spaces for the benefit of the real estate investors that do not live in the areas and that promote non-permanent lodging; franchises that do not promote authentic services and products. Thus, it seems that the growth in economy with this approach is not compatible with human development, with the cultural benefit and the conservation of the green areas of the territory. For example, in Europe, Barcelona is an example of a city that implemented public policies applied in historical areas for the benefit of the tourism and real estate sectors. Public authorities have promoted the city as a product. The consequence has been the emergence of mobility conflicts, increased pollution, increased consumption of water and energy, dispossession of public spaces and denial of the basic right to housing.

The problem, in our opinion, is that public policies are often designed empirically without defining quantitative and qualitative objectives and quantitative measures to assess them. In the case of the strategies applied to activate the economy of urban areas, the quality of life index can be an immediate and "natural" assessment strategy. Quality of life is defined as a "multidimensional index that measures good living conditions and degree of well-being. It also includes the collective satisfaction of needs obtain through social policies" [7]. Different mathematical models have been proposed for measuring quality of life [1,3,8]. Some consider measurable variables often based on economic indices. Others adopt an holistic approach and consider qualitative variables such as happiness, quality of experience and stress. Other visions like the theory of utilitarianism by Jeremy Bentham, define quality of life as the maximum well-being for the maximum number to act in a way that produces greater benefit to a greater number of people. This goes beyond the measurement of an index but it seeks to define a point within a spectrum where economic and well-being benefits searched by public policies are optimised. In any case, the challenge is to choose the variables that determine quality of life and then collect meaningful and objective data that can be used for computing them.

This paper presents our approach for computing the index of quality of life considering quantitative and qualitative measures seeking to maximise an holistic hybrid return of investment. Our notion of return of investment is hybrid because considers both quantitative and qualitative variables calibrated to find and optimum of economic and well-being benefit. Therefore our proposal combines different data collections that feed a novel mathematical model proposed for computing determining the elasticity of the index of quality of life. Given the volume of data sets about the city and its inhabitants it has been necessary to use adapted computational methods to model urban phenomena. We have applied data analytics computational techniques that apply mathematical methods, statistics and knowledge discovery to find patterns within data sets that represent the behaviour of certain phenomena. Accordingly the remainder of the paper is organised as follows. Section 2 introduces our proposal of data based quality index, defines the measures that compose it and discusses the analytics approach proposed for computing it. Section 2.3 describes our experiment setting and results. Section 3 synthesises and compares different projects and approaches based on collected data for computing quality of life indexes in projects aiming to revitalise historical spaces in different regions of the world. Section 4 concludes the paper and discusses future work.

2 Holistic Approach for Measuring Quality of Life in La Condesa

Mexico City promotes central and historical spaces applying public policies intended to activate the economy of these areas. Public policies implement actions in urban areas that affect the daily life of people. This is the case of the quarter "La Condesa" located 4 Km from the Historical Downtown Area of Mexico City (cf. Fig. 1).

1. Mexico City Boroughs   2. Cuauhtémoc's Neighborhoods   3. La Condesa

Fig. 1. Urban distribution of Mexico City boroughs and location of La Condesa neighbourhood

"La Condesa" was founded in the early twentieth century. Today it has an area of 450,320.02 square meters organised into 62 blocks [2] (cf. Figs. 1, 2 and 3), and since its foundation, there are 40% of green areas.

Along the decades, "La Condesa" has had different transformations. During the 1970s, the country's political and social effervescence led to first urban changes seeking economic activation. The government built new urban areas outside downtown for middle and upper classes. Thus, this policy caused the migration of inhabitants from central spaces to the new areas. Later, the 1985 earthquake caused the decrease of the value of properties in central areas such as "La Condesa". This accelerated the decline of this area with problems such as subsidence, depopulation and wide spread deterioration due to lack of maintenance and investment. In the early 2000's the governmental program "Bando 22" activated again the area of "La Condesa". The government promoted projects to activate the real estate sector. As a result, the use of the land, the economic activity and the so called *vie de quartier* changed dramatically. The occupation of the buildings changed from housing to commercial and administrative activities. The socio-economical level of the inhabitants that could live in the area changed too and with this started the desertification of the area. As shown in [2], La Condesa hosted 688 commercial points in only 68 blocks. From 2000 to 2010 (INEGI) there was a decrease in the number of inhabitants from 15,916 to 11,792. The same happened in the number of inhabited houses, with 5,350 existing housing, 4,508 were classified as habitable and the remaining 842 are classified under "other uses". All these changes caused an increase in the price of the land, which went from $21,960.00 in 2012 to $27,500.00 in 2015.

The question is to which extent have these public policies been adequate? Did they result in an improvement in the quality if life of inhabitants? Are segregation, exclusion, changes in land use, lack of water, over population, desertification beneficial to economy and acceptable for the area? These changes transform quality of life standards. Modern urbanism promotes the balance between economic development and quality of life. The current characterisation of central spaces in cities and particularly in "La Condesa" call for an analysis of quality of life measures to study the way these changes have modified the daily life of inhabitants and to which extent this balance is respected?

We propose the "Quality of Life Elasticity Index". We define elasticity in urban terms establishing a relationship between the quality of life of the inhabitants in the territory with respect to the variables that effect welfare behaviour, whether positive or negative. Elasticity is introduced in the qualitative and quantitative estimation of quality of life. The result is an index that uses a range of every day living permissible in a territory.

2.1 Quality of Life Index

Quality of life is an index that can be mathematically modelled by combining variables. The selection criteria for calculating and combining them are based on economic and political trends.

We adopted the mathematical model proposed by Puskoruis [9] for measuring quality of life, based on studies by [10]. We chose this model as basis for introducing our urban elasticity notion because it considers economic variables together with variables that reflect the quality of human life. Thus, quality of life index is given by the following formula:

$$I = \sum_{i=1}^{10} a_i b_i \tag{1}$$

The index results of the summation of 10 pondered indicators. Weights used to ponder indicators are represented by a_i terms.

- b_1 - health
- b_2 - employment and occupation
- b_3 - quality of time at work
- b_4 - income status
- b_5 - consumption
- b_6 - environment and accommodation
- b_7 - population's education
- b_8 - law, security, order and corruption levels of the population
- b_9 - ethics-morality, spirituality, value of culture and leisure of the population
- b_{10} - population's gender equality indicator

2.2 Elasticity in Quality of Life

We believe that together, qualitative and quantitative variables generate a more inclusive assessments of quality of life. Existing mathematical models defining the quality of life index do not consider the point of no return in quality of life. That is, they do not measure to which extent it is possible to have a satisfactory quality of life in a territory where specific public policies are applied.

The economic term "elasticity of demand" can be introduced into quality of life index models. In Economy, elasticity is defined as the relationship between the percentage change in the quality demanded or offered and the percentage change in price.

$$E_p = \frac{\Delta Quantity}{\Delta Price} = \frac{\frac{(P_1)+P_2}{2}}{\frac{(Q_1)+Q_2}{I_{12}}} \tag{2}$$

We define elasticity in urban terms we will see that there is a relationship between the quality of life of the inhabitants in the territory with respect to the variables that effect welfare behaviour.

2.3 Experimental Setting

The collection of information and the analysis of the data becomes essential to obtain reliable and representative results. In Mexico, we used data from the National Institute of Statistics and Geography (INEGI[1]) that provides statistics from the national census of different years. Most of the indicators chosen for computing the quality of life index were already computed for Mexico City so we filtered them for computing the quality of life index for different years and first results on elasticity. Next we describe the data collections.

---

[1] http://www3.inegi.org.mx/sistemas/TabuladosBasicos/Default.aspx?c=27302.

Data Collections. We used a twelve data sets for computing quality of life. Each data set provides also aggregated data used by international organisations for measuring different indicators. We filtered data for observing the indicators in Mexico City and then in the area corresponding to "La Condesa".

Table 1. Well being indicators provided by the INEGI database

	Well being dimension	Indicators
1	Accessibility to services	(1.1) access to health services,
		(1.2) houses with high speed Internet connection,
		(1.3) houses with access to basic services
2	Community	(2.1) quality of the support social network
3	Education	(3.1) dropping out of school, (3.2) years in school
4	Balance life-work	(4.1) satisfaction w.r.t leisure time,
		(4.2) people working more than 48 hours
5	Income	(5.1) gini family income per capita,
		(5.2) family income,
		(5.3) people in poverty,
		(5.4) people in extreme poverty
6	Environment	(6.1) air quality,
		(6.2) waste products
7	Civic compromise and governance	(7.1) civic and political participation,
		(7.2) electoral participation,
		(7.3) confidence in justice/law,
		(7.4) perception of corruption in the juridic system,
		(7.5) confidence on judges
8	Health	(8.1) living newborns expectation,
		(8.2) health control,
		(8.3) obesity rate, (8.4) motherhood mortality
		(8.5) children mortality,
		(8.6) mother deaths/100 alive newborns
9	Life satisfaction	(9.1) idem
10	Security	(10.1) homicides rate,
		(10.2) confidence in police,
		(10.3) insecurity perception,
		(10.4) criminal rate
11	Employment	(11.1) occupation index,
		(11.2) informal jobs rate,
		(11.3) unemployment rate,
		(11.4) economic contribution
12	Housing	(12.1) rooms/person,
		(12.2) solid construction rate

The *well-being indicators database* provides 35 indicators defined by the OCDE. The indicators are used for computing the better life index based on the notion of well-being and progress. The indicators are grouped into 12 dimensions (see Table 1): accessibility to services, community (social relations), education, balance life-work, income, environment, civic compromise and governance, health, satisfaction, security, employment, housing. Data collected for computing these indicators are a snapshot of the years 2010–2015. For our study, we did not use the aggregated indicators but the full data regarding the indicator required for computing the quality of life index introduced in the previous section.

Sheet 2

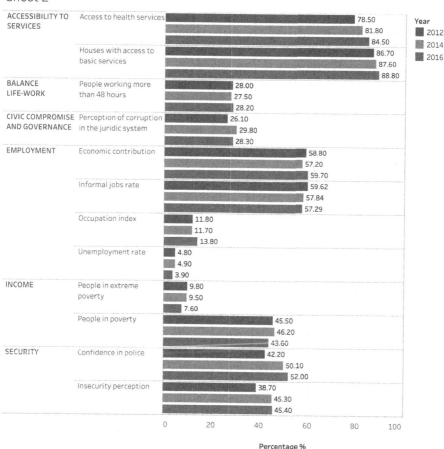

Fig. 2. General overview of the distribution of the data of the indicators

Computing Quantitative and Qualitative Measures. Data sets regarding quality of life indicators that have been exported by the INEGI correspond to census done every two years since 2010. We remarked that not all indicators were collected in every exported data set and those of 2018 are still not available. Thus, for our experiment we first computed the quality of life index in Mexico for three years 2012, 2014, 2016. After analysing the distribution of the indicators values we saw that some were expressed as percentages of the population that answered the census others as interval values and ad hoc measures like for the quality of air. Since we did not have the raw data for the last ones, we decided to exclude them from the computation. Therefore, we decided to use the most homogeneous measures in order to ensure the precision of our computations (see Fig. 2).

As shown in the figure our experiment considered six dimensions namely, accessibility to services, balance life-work, income, civic compromise and governance, security and employment. For every dimension we chose those sub-dimensions that were expressed as percentages from the whole number of participants of the census. Given that these census are promoted by the government and are considered a civic commitment a representative amount of the population participates in this task.

According to the quality of life formula that we adopted we pondered indicators according to the knowledge of the domain of our colleagues experts in urbanism. We privileged those concerning qualitative perceptions like security and we gave less importance to those concerning economic measures. This is because our study wants to have a picture of the perception of population about their quality of life in La Condesa neighbourhood. The resulting revisited formula is given as follows:

$$I = \sum_{i=1}^{12} a_i b_i \tag{3}$$

It considers 12 measures from the chosen groups of indicators shown in Fig. 2, where accessibility to services and income (a_1, a_2, a_4, a_5) were pondered with 0,08; balance life-work (a_3) and employment were pondered with 0,04 (a_9–a_{12}); and civic compromise and governance and security with 0,16 (a_6–a_8).

As seen in Fig. 3, the quality of life index shows that quality of life as perceived by citizens is not very high. This means that they consider that life is acceptable but still services, security, income need public policies that can make life better. As shown in the figure quality of life has become better comparing 2012 and 2016, but the increase between 2014 and 2016 was not very significant. Our first perception through the evaluation of quality of life index, validates our hypothesis that other strategies are required to measure it. Combining quantitative and qualitative indicators is a first step to provide a more representative view of quality of life. Yet it is not correlated with the type of policies applied that have been applied and how they are related to indicators. Our current work is devoted to study this aspect.

We also want to use information from a project started by the Mexican INEGI willing to measure the mood of Twitter users in Mexico City. INEGI in

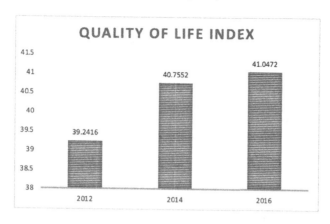

Fig. 3. Index of quality of life 2012–2016 in La Condesa

collaboration with Twitter is making roads into data base applications to solve urban problems with technology applied to Big Data. Considering the mood of privileged citizens having access to social networks for measuring quality of life index considering socioeconomic aspects can give a more representative measure.

3 Related Work

Measuring the quality of life of inhabitants in urban or rural areas has been discussed and studied by international forums and commissions (Beyond GDP was held in November 2008. For example, the study "How is life?" [5] proposes 11 quantitative and qualitative variables. The Human Development Index (HID) proposed by [6] includes three main variables health, education and living standards.

The European Parliament, the OECD and the WWF have been seeking to develop indices based on accurate measurements that model daily life, poverty, inequality and the needs of the inhabitants in specific areas. The Commission on the Measurement of Economic Development and Social Progress (CMPEPS) created in 2008 in France defined new measures to evaluate social progress. The National Institute of Statistics (ISTAT) defined 12 variables for evaluating progress that included economic, social and environment aspects. The study proposed by National Statistics Institute in Spain defined a quality of life index based on different studies like Eurostat which includes qualitative measures. In 2016 the Stiglitz-Sen-Fitoussi report included a new section on multidimensional analysis introducing welfare components. This measurement made by the Quality of Life Export Working Group includes 9 dimensions. Data are collected through surveys answered by individuals. Other data are gathered from the Living Conditions Survey (LCS) and the Economically Active Population Survey (EAPS).

The Quality of Life (NPQV) research core (Mackenzie Presbyterian University, located in Sao Paolo, Brazil) proposed a quality index that includes variables like transport, visual pollution and noise. These variables are pondered with different weights when they are combined to define the quality of like index. Data used for computing these variables are collected by the Brazilian Institute of Geography and Statistics and the national survey for housing sampling.

The project "Quality of life in Argentina"[2] proposes a ranking approach of well-being by department. It identifies different strategies for measuring poverty and quality of life. Poverty is defined as a measure of deprivation including those who do not reach and established minimum threshold. Quality of life is defined as an optimum economic level. The measures are defined by socioeconomic and environmental variables. The data used for computing these measures are gathered in census information, statistical sources, satellite images and field surveys. To measure the quality of life index, the study uses a quantitative and qualitative variables to asses personal satisfaction.

In Mexico, the welfare index named National Index of Quality of life (INCAVI) proposed by the University of Monterrey 2011 uses seven classes of measures each divided into different qualitative and quantitative values variables. The National Institute of Statistics and Geography (INEGI) proposed the BIARE index (self-report of well-being) used to measure the way people experience their own quality of life. It is based on measuring the subjective dimension of well-being and conforms to the OECD guidelines. This index is associated with the survey ENGASTE 2012, ENCO 2013, MCS 2014 and 2015.

Quality of life indexes proposed in Hong Kong include personal, social, political, cultural, economic and environmental measures, along with 21 indicators classified into three groups: social, economic and environmental. It introduces variables such as degree of press freedom and stress.

The Paradise of Michalos [4] recognises that people living in the same area can have different points of view concerning the conditions of life. He proposes a matrix where he identifies (i) the paradise of the fools (ii) the real paradise (iii) the real hell and (iv) the hell of the fools. In these spaces the perception of life depends on the perception of the people who live there. He underlines the importance of the conditions in which surveys are applied to gather the perception of people about their quality of life. The sequence of the questions, the working are factors that strongly influence the answers of to a survey.

According to existing approaches for measuring quality of life, must include both quantitative and qualitative measures. We also underline the importance of the quality of data used for computing the different variables. This quality includes the provenance, the choice of the population interviewed for collecting data (socio-economic level, education, age, gender), the reliability of the data, the freshness, etc.

---

[2] https://teleport.org/cities/buenos-aires/.

4   Conclusions and Future Work

In this research we proposed a first approach for computing the elasticity of quality of life index. In addition to quantitative measures, qualitative measures are used, as representative indicators of the life experience of an individual in a territory.

The study was based on the use of technology and computational tools (Big Data Analytics) and data science (statistical methods and know ledge discovery) to manipulate and combine different data collections. We used descriptive statistical to compute quality of life. The interest of computing the quality of life index is that it can help to design public policies that can revitalise urban spaces for empowering economy without scarifying citizens well being. This can be used for computing the elasticity of the quality of life but this corresponds to our future work.

References

1. García, JdJ: Hacia un nuevo sistema de indicadores de bienestar. Revista internacional de estadística y geografía **2**(1), 78–95 (2011)
2. INEGI: Mexican census of poblacion y vivienda 2010 (2010). https://www.inegi.org.mx/programas/ccpv/2010/. Accessed 26 Dec 2018
3. López Santillán, R.: Lo bonito, limpio y seguro: usos del espacio de la ciudad de méxico por una fracción de clase media. Alteridades **17**(34), 9–25 (2007)
4. Michalos, A.C.: Essays on the Quality of Life, vol. 19. Springer, Dordrecht (2013). https://doi.org/10.1007/978-94-017-0389-5
5. The Organisation for Economic Co-operation and Development: How's Life? 2015: Measuring Well-being. OECD, Paris (2015)
6. ONU: Human development index. http://hdr.undp.org/en/content/human-development-index-hdi. Accessed 26 Dec 2018
7. Palomba, R.: Calidad de vida: Conceptos y medidas concepto de calidad de vida. Calidad de Vida: Conceptos Y Medidas, pp. 1–12 (2002)
8. Puskorius, S.: The methodology of calculation the quality of life index. Int. J. Inf. Educ. Technol. **5**(2), 156 (2015)
9. Puškorius, S.: Theoretical model of estimating the quality of life index (2015)
10. Stiglitz, J.E., Sen, A., Fitoussi, J.P.: Measurement of economic performance and social progress. http://bit.ly/JTwmG. Accessed 26 June 2012 (2009)

Adaptive Agent-Based Architecture for Health Data Integration

Ibtihel Selmi[1]([✉]), Nadia Kabachi[2], Sana Ben Abdalah Ben Lamine[1], and Hajer Baazaoui Zghal[1]

[1] ENSI, Riadi Laboratory, University of Manouba, Manouba, Tunisia
selmiibtihel7@gmail.com
[2] ERIC Laboratory, University of Lyon, University of Claude Bernard Lyon 1, 3083 Villeurbanne, EA, France

Abstract. The work presented in this paper is developed in the context of the "PersoDiagMedi" project which is Franco-Tunisian cooperation between laboratories' multidisciplinary programs in the fields of computer science and health-care. In the health-care domain, Artificial Intelligence (AI) provides multiple technologies that allow machines to learn, act and make decisions autonomously. In this sense, AI helps experts and doctors in diseases' diagnosis and the detection of emerging diseases' presence. However, the medical data come from multiple sources: doctors, biologists, meteorological specialists, and environmental organizations. The difficulty of the epidemic state's surveillance lies in the conciliation between the search for the largest number of relevant signals and their treatments. In this paper, we propose the project's general architecture that facilitates medical data integration and data processing to detect unusual facts and to prevent the presence of emergent diseases. In this proposed data integration architecture, we present the different functionalities, describe its layers and components as well as present an adaptive multi-agent system for the unusual facts' detection. To this end, the feasibility of our proposal is first proven and later two use cases are presented to cover users' needs.

Keywords: Health-care · Multi-agent system · OLAP · Artificial Intelligence · Unusual facts detection

1 Introduction

Modern medicine is one of the most sophisticated areas of scientific activities, whose main challenge is to develop effective diagnostic systems for the various health-care problems. On the other hand, this area is marked by its complex communication and coordination between the different health-care actors. Usually,

Supported by the SCUSI (Coopérations scientifiques et académiques internationales) program of the region Auvergne Rhône-Alpes in France for the project "PersoDiagMedi", Number 1700938003.

S. Yangui et al. (Eds.): ICSOC 2019 Workshops, LNCS 12019, pp. 224–235, 2020.
https://doi.org/10.1007/978-3-030-45989-5_18

health data are obtained from different sources that are heterogeneous, multi-spectral and incomplete observations. Indeed, large health data is essentially complex data sets that are specified with unique characteristics that complicate the process of extracting exploitable knowledge about any given phenomenon. The intervention of AI has become a necessity since human capacities are becoming more and more limited compared to the exponential data growth generating Big Data. The primary objective of the AI in the health-care domain is to module intelligent computer systems that can process and reason efficiently to improve the quality of distributed large scale data-provisioning services in this field. Therefore, AI contributions in the healthcare domain have proven to enhance the performance of the medical systems particularly in the context of Big Data. Several studies have been carried out to show the contribution of AI in the medical field by treating various problematics such as medical data processing, diseases' diagnostic and the effective detection of emergent diseases, it is in this context that the PersoDiagMedi project fits. The aim of this project is developing a framework that can provide numerous medical data integration and processing services, to ensure early detection of emerging disease and to help experts in the medical field monitoring the epidemic. In this paper, we present the architecture of this framework and then prove its technical feasibility and test its efficiency. The ambition of this work is not to focus on each part of the proposed architecture but it aims to test the proper process of the whole system. Since this is a first step of this project, the goal is simply to develop a coherent system. The work presented in this paper is organized as follows: Sect. 2 presents an overview of the researches that have been conducted around intelligent systems in the health-care domain. Section 3 introduces our proposed architecture as well as describes functions of the various components of our approach. We illustrate and discuss the experimental results obtained at this stage in Sect. 4. Finally, we conclude and present our future work in Sect. 5.

2   Background and Related Work

2.1   Theoretical Basis

For a better understanding of our project and related works, we first describe the main theoretical basis that is relevant to our work: OLAP cubes, multi-agent systems, and adaptive agents.

OLAP Cubes: The data warehouse is designed to facilitate data analysis and data querying. Users can exploit the data warehouse through the combination of multiple dimensions and corresponding hierarchies. The execution of queries on very large data is both expensive and requires a long response time [13]. To remedy this problem, a new concept is introduced, which is data cubes (also called OLAP cube). An OLAP cube is used to calculate and map all possible combinations and to store them to facilitate their subsequent exploitation. So with this tool, the users' queries become easier since data is already calculated and stored.

Multi-agent Systems: Multi-agent systems are computer systems composed of several heterogeneous entities that communicate and cooperate for problem resolution [15]. These entities are also called agents which is *a real or virtual entity that offers services, that are able to act in an environment, communicate directly with other agents and that has skills* [4]. These agents can then perform the actions and perceive their environments and they are also able to make decisions independently [15]. Agents are mainly classified in four classes: Cognitive agent which is an intelligent agent who has a knowledge base with which he can accomplish his task and manage his actions and intersections, BDI agent who is based on three concepts: belief, desire, and intent, and reactive Agent which is unlike the cognitive agent, he has no representation of the environment, and requires no memory since it does not keep its past [4].

Adaptive Multi-agent Systems: The adaptation in multi-agent systems can be implemented in two different ways, either an individual adaptation (of a single agent) or The adaptation in multi-agent systems can be implemented in two different ways, either an individual adaptation (of a single agent) or a collective adaptation (of all the set of agents) [14]. The adaptive agent can learn from the environment while adapting to the changes of the environment and can communicate and cooperate with other agents. The contribution of adaptation to multi-agent systems is that the system will be able to react to a new situation and therefore to a changing environment, it can also decide what is the most appropriate behavior on its own. With the machine learning, the agent becomes able to learn without being explicitly programmed. There are three classifications of learning techniques: supervised learning, unsupervised learning and reinforcement learning [14]. The reinforcement learning is a learning method that does not require knowledge of the system and is based on a satisfaction criterion called "reinforcement". This method allows the agent to perform actions and reactions without specifying how the action should be performed. Among the reinforcement learning algorithms, we quote the Q-learning algorithm that we will present further in this paper [2].

2.2   Related Work

Extracting effective knowledge from a mass of medical data is one of the most challenging areas of research. To explore this data, it is necessary to offer powerful data processing and analysis systems and to propose approaches that will aim to ameliorate the adaptive capacity of these systems with environmental changes. In this context, several approaches have been proposed since 1970 [6].

One of the first diagnosis systems in this literature was Internist-I and Internist-II [1], this system treated over 70% of possible diagnoses in internal medicine. It operated on a single disease. Because of its long training, the interaction with users took up to 90 min. DXplain (87) is a decision-making system that acts on a set of clinical data to produce a classified list of diagnoses that can illustrate clinical manifestations. This system is similar to Internist but it added hierarchical lexicon results [5].

Iliad (94) [3] is an expert diagnostic system, it adjoined the probability to healthcare system reasoning, it can be useful as a healthcare provider and as a personal consultant as well. This system provided diagnosis and advice on balanced and effective cost strategies.

Isabel [8] is a web-based diagnostic decision support system, created in 2001 by physicians to provide diagnostic decision support in the field of healthcare. Isabel has been widely proven to enhance the clinician's cognitive skills and thereby improve patients' safety and the quality of their heath. The difficulty of surveillance lies in the conciliation between the search for the largest number of relevant signals on the one hand and their treatments on the other hand. Researchers have continued to improve the medical systems and found new solutions. Indeed, they had involved AI technologies to improve the adaptability to environmental changes and systems learning [17]. Adaptive multi-agent systems represent one of the most important solutions of AI [16]; Indeed, they are intelligent computer systems whose processing is assigned to several software or physical entities, called adaptive agents that can adapt to environmental changes [10,12]. Thanks to their problem-solving efficiency, adaptive multi-agent systems are being used more and more in the health-care field [11,14]. The authors in [9] designed an adaptive Agent module that consists of four main modules: Perception Unit, Decision Unit, Behavior Set and Effectors.

In [10], the purpose was to build processes, tools, and services for agent-based software maintenance. To build and run the multi-agent environment, the authors of the article used the Jade platform. The services provided by the system proposed by the authors are Tele-medicine, Patient monitoring, Disaster Management, Communication between patients and medical staff. The ultimate goal of this system is to monitor and control the patients' health through verifying medical reports and providing a competent medical service with the assistance of the medical personnel.

In [7], the authors proposed a multi-agent system architecture for telemedicine that designed to simulate a module for the categorization of cancer. In this system, each different medical problem is provided with a distinct agent and that what makes the autonomy increase, the communication and the reaction ability possible. The communication between the agents is done via an audio-video communication system. The different agents proposed in this article are Initial agent: interacts with the system user, Coordinator Agent: Mediator Agent, Agent assistant which is preceded by the problem detection, it, therefore, acts without being explicitly programmed. The implementation of machine learning in multi-agent systems improves agent and system performance [19]. Concerning multi-agent systems, they illustrate the most efficient solution for distributed data processing, for distributed computing and for finding a solution for sophisticated problems as well. It is acknowledged that there is no existing medical system in which we interrogate the data in the form of OLAP cubes via adaptive agents. Compared to existing work, we aim to integrate all these technologies and put them end to end and to test the interoperability of the whole system in order to take advantage of all of its benefits at the same time.

On that account, the purpose of this work is to propound an approach that will be applied in the medical field and that will aid experts to detect the emerging diseases and explore the medical data more expeditiously and efficiently. Hence, the need is to integrate the heterogeneous data stored in a NoSQL database and processed with the notion of OLAP and to design and adaptive multi-agent systems in a Big Data context.

3   PersoDiagMedi Architecture

3.1   General Architecture

We introduce in this paper a preliminary work in the context of the Franco-Tunisian project entitled "PersoDiagMedi: Service-oriented collaborative platform for the personalization of the medical service and the early detection of emerging diseases". The main objectives of this project are the integration of structured and unstructured medical data into a repository, the design of a medical ontology and the development of a reasoning and detection module. In this section, we propose our global architecture of the PersoDiagMedi project that is composed of four layers as depicted in Fig. 1:

(1) *Data layer*: this layer represents the different data sources. Data may be pharmaceutical, medical, meteorological or social media data;

(2) *Collection, organization and data storage layer*: this layer is responsible for the integration of the data which arises from the data layer, the construction of a medical ontology, the storage of the data in a database and the mapping between the data and the designed ontology;

(3) *Reasoning, detection, and alert layer*: this layer represents the intelligent part of our proposition. It is in charge of the OLAP cubes building from the Database built-in the precedent layer, the OLAP cubes interrogation and the detection of emerging diseases through an adaptive multi-agent system);

(4) *Graphical User Interface layer*: this layer allows the user to pilot and interrogate the architecture.

The architecture is composed of two main parts: *A semantic-based data integration system* which collects and stores heterogeneous and multi-source data in a NoSQL database (layers 1 and 2) and *an Agent-based Data Query system* which allows the interception of the NoSQL database in order to analyze the data and trigger alerts if necessary (layers 3 and 4).

The semantic-based data integration system allows the storage of multi-source and heterogeneous data on a domain ontology-based database. Indeed, the medical data comes from multiple sources and in different forms structured (such as excel, tables, structured DB), semi-structured (XML, CSV, ..) and unstructured (such as tweets, images) one of the main functionalities of this system is to allow the database loading, which is the data integration system's principal phase, guaranteeing the data's protection and the mapping between the data and the medical ontology that we'd designed for this purpose, this ontology is based

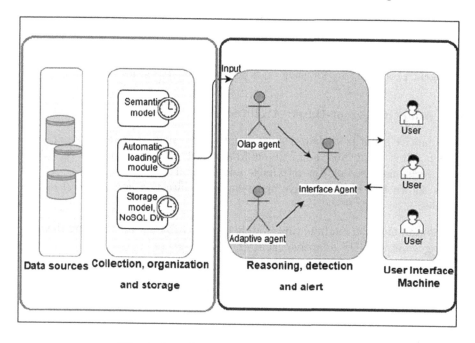

Fig. 1. PersoDiagMedi: General architecture.

on medical expert's knowledge. In [18], the system is detailed and evaluated and its different components are described.

After integrating and storing the data in a NoSQL Database, we focus in this paper on testing if the whole process can be functional and we detail the agent-based data query system. The aim of the adaptive agent-based approach for cubes interrogation is to enhance the medical system management and to facilitate the data interrogation using OLAP queries. The approach is mainly represented by the third and fourth layers (Fig. 1). There are several types of users and that can manage our system such as the experts in the health domain that can, interrogate the data and receive responses. Surveillance organizations can monitor the epidemiological state and consult the analyzes and statistics. The users can manage and interrogate the system through a graphical interface that represents the user interface machine layer. The features offered to those users are provided from reasoning detection and alert layer which represents the functional part of our architecture. As discussed in [18], the third layer takes the data stored in the NoSQL database as input. This layer is an adaptive multiagent system that aims to promote access to stored data, minimize time responses, and to handle users' requests and also to provide responses and notifications as results. The main challenge of this intelligent system is to perform analyzes to detect unusual facts. This adaptive multiagent system has essentially two main objectives: The first consists of building OLAP cubes based on the NoSQL database (the output of the semantic-based data integration system). As for the second, it consists of designing an adaptive agent that allows monitoring the epidemiological state and detecting the presence of unusual facts to alert stakeholders in case of emerging diseases. In the next section, we will itemize the intelligent processing by focusing on adaptive agent-based architecture.

3.2 Adaptive Agent-Based Architecture

The adaptive agent is in charge of emergent disease detection and sending alerts to users. This agent must adapt to environmental' changes and must be able to make decisions based on his knowledge and previous experiences.

As shown in Fig. 2, adaptive agent-based architecture is composed of four modules:

(1) Communication module: this module is responsible for interpreting the messages between the adaptive agent and other agents;
(2) Cognitive module: this module contains facts, meta-rules, rules, and uncertainties. It ensures the agent knowledge enrichment;
(3) Perception module: the instances of this module trigger the reasoning module if they note the existence of a peak in the indicators states;
(4) Reasoning module: this module is in charge of processing. To program this module, we used the reinforcement learning technique by adapting the Q-Learning algorithm.

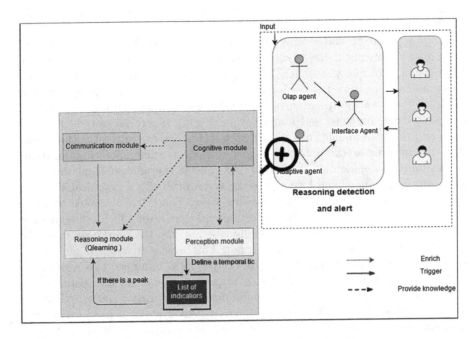

Fig. 2. PersoDiagMedi: Adaptive agent-based architecture

Adaptation of the 'Q-Learning' Algorithm

As this work is preliminary, we worked with the Q-learning algorithm. In future work, we intend to use different algorithms and compare results.

The Q-Learning is an automatic control method that does not require an initial knowledge of the model, but rather it depends on satisfaction criteria. With this algorithm, the agent can learn the optimal policy from its history. This method is one of the machine learning techniques that allow systems to adapt to the environment's changes that do not require any initial model of the environment. To adapt this algorithm to our work, we included rules into a class responsible for learning agents. In this class, we have defined facts as attributes whose values are retrieved from the OLAP cube or entered by the user. The state S is represented by a list of indicators I_n and attributes Att_n; $S = \{I_0, I_1, .., I_i\} \wedge \{Att_0, Att_1, .., Att_i\}$; The actions A are in the form of textual notifications sent to the final users; Reward is a function that returns the evaluation of the action chosen by the algorithm. In this function, we check if the agent has chosen the right action by comparing this action with the action we get when we process the algorithm (Fig. 3).

```
Algorithm 1 Q-Learning
    Input :  State s, Action a
2:  Output :  Decision
    Begin
4:      Q(s, a) ← 0
        CurrentState ← IntialState
6:      Repeat
            Choose action a using a decision policy
8:          Take action a
            Observe reward r
10:         S ← NewState
            Update Q(s,a) S ← S'
12: a ← a'
14: End
```

Fig. 3. Q-Learning algorithm [2]

4 Experimentation

To test the feasibility of our solution and the functionality of our proposed system, we made some experimentation. First, we prepared the development environment. To do so, we used an ASUS laptop (I5 processor, 8G Ram) configured using UBUNTU 14.04 OS. Then, we installed the necessary software applications and frameworks for Big Data processing including Apache Hadoop[1]; Apache Hive; Apache Spark[2]. The reason we used this type of applications is because we need to process large health data volumes. Hadoop is used to guarantee and to improve the data security which is essential for management systems in the medical field. As for spark, it provides a learning library *MLLIB* as well as guarantees fast processing in memory of large data. The integration of these two frameworks is then the most suitable solution to develop our agents. As for the

---

[1] https://hadoop.apache.org/.
[2] https://spark.apache.org/.

Olap cubes' construction, we have used Apache Kylin[3] which is an open-source software that supports extremely large datasets. The generated OLAP cubes are stored in Hbase[4] a system of storage and database management on Hadoop.

4.1 Data Description

The medical data comes from multiple sources: doctors, biologists, meteorological specialists, and environmental organizations. The available data are initially structured, semi-structured, and unstructured data. The structured data is provided from the ONMNE. This data has approximately 50,000 patient records. It summarizes information on flu between the years 2009–2010 and the year 2016–2017. This data is cleaned and stored in a NoSQL database because it provides a simple and flexible structure when it comes to unstructured data and it is easier to scale up. Then, this data is exported in JSON and CSV formats. The data can be classified by Consultants age: Three classes ([0–5],[5–16],[16,+oo]); Region: the region where the consultation has been done. A region represents one of the twenty-four Tunisian governance; Period: represented by the year and the month of the consultation.

As the adaptive agent needs to find quick results to make a quick decision and as we are in a context of detection and alert system, we've built an OLAP cube because the data multidimensional modeling (OLAP) facilitates the analytic. With OLAP modeling, we can focus for example on all the consultations in a specific region and year of infected patients. We can also simply present the consultations of infected patients that have the same age and in a specific region. With the use of OLAP cubes, we can manipulate aggregated data according to multiple dimensions that make the data interrogation faster and more efficient.

Parameters and Alert Scenarios: To implement the adaptive agent, we have to understand how epidemic diseases spread and what are the factors that we have to consider. Therefore, we asked for the help of experts in the healthcare domain to precise the parameters and to define the different scenarios that allow us to efficiently detect unusual facts. In the following, we quote a list of parameters that we have chosen so that we can simulate use cases that we will present, and this is to detect unusual facts (the abnormal facts) and to trigger alerts. The indicators are infection rate (by region, sex, age...), stocks of Medicines (by region), number of patients with a contagious disease declared by the medical profession and death mortality caused by an illness. An alert scenario is a use case where the system detects an abnormal sign whose detection requires the urgent intervention of experts in the field. Our partners in the health field propose these scenarios to allow us to validate our preliminary tests: The first alert scenario is the nominal scenario in which all the indicators mentioned above did not exceed the specified thresholds. In this case, the system has nothing to trigger, the second alert scenario is that one of the indicators: Infection Rate or Drugs' stocks (or both) exceed the indicated threshold. In this case, the system

---

[3] http://kylin.apache.org/.

[4] https://hbase.apache.org/.

must send a notification to the specialists so that they can study the situation. As for the third alert scenario, it is identified if all the indicators studied exceed their thresholds. At this time, the system must urgently trigger an alert to those responsible for reacting urgently.

4.2 Use Cases

In this section, we present two use cases of the proposed architecture. The first use case is the OLAP cube queries' use case and the second is the unusual fact detection use case.

We must first clarify what an abnormal condition implies in the context of epidemics in order to better understand how our alert system operate. An unusual fact, in fact, is a critical concept and hard to describe. To better understand **the first use case**, we introduce some of the proposed OLAP requests. The OLAP requests are organized according to the number of the used dimensions. OLAP agent (Fig. 2) is in charge of handling the requests of two types: users' requests or intelligent agents' requests. The pursuit of this agent is to interrogate the OLAP cube and obtain responses that have already been aggregated and calculated according to the users' needs (Fig. 4).

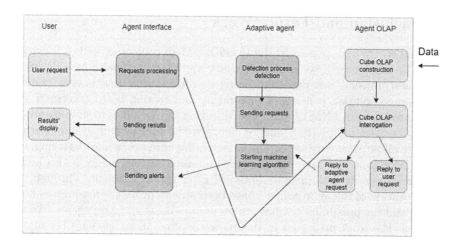

Fig. 4. Use cases diagram

To test the second scenario, we have changed the threshold values defined in the Q-Learning algorithm so that we can know if the agent can detect the change and send the appropriate notification to the user. For example, if the agent detects that the infection's rate exceed the 0.1[5], it has to alert the end users that there is an unusual fact. In fact, we injected erroneous data in order

---

[5] This value was provided from the project partners (OMNE).

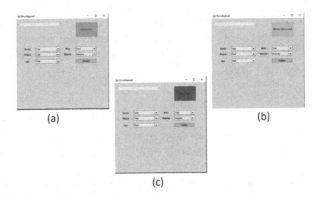

Fig. 5. Second use case results

to test the efficiency of the agent and prove that it is able to detect changes in the data. As mentioned above, the indicators and thresholds we used to test our approach were provided from the project partners in the healthcare domain; In Fig. 5, we notice that our adaptive agent was able to detect the change in the data and was able to alert the user of the different situations.

5   Conclusion and Future Work

In this paper, we have presented the PersoDiagMedi project as well as its architecture. In this context, we proposed a new approach for health-care decision-making and unusual fact detection based on an adaptive multi-agent system. Our proposed solution consists of integrating and storing both structured and unstructured data in a NoSQL database, querying OLAP cubes to simplify access to pre-calculated information and to improve the multi-agent system performance to allow the early detection of emerging diseases while detecting the unusual facts from the data. We have also detailed two use cases of this architecture and presented the results obtained after the experiment. Through the implementation of the approach, we have been able to prove the feasibility of our proposal and the possibility to query cubes of data using adaptive agents. We are aware that the work presented in this paper requires many changes because it is a preliminary work that has to be improved. Being reassured that our system can be performing, we plan to formalize the proposed architecture and detail each part and define the scientific locks for every architecture's component. We are currently working on further development of the approach on real-time data processing and to improve the adaptive agent intelligent reasoning by implementing it with deep learning. Subsequently, we plan to integrate pharmaceutical and meteorological databases, to improve use case scenarios and include a module for medical diagnosis, prediction and decisions' recommendation. For the fault tolerance, we are planning to clone our most important agent "adaptive agent" and put it in standby. If the first fails, the other is automatically activated following a message from the system.

References

1. Miller, R.A., et al.: INTERNIST-1: an experimental computer-based diagnostic consultant for general internal medicine. N. Engl. J. Med. **307**(5), 468–476 (1982)
2. Watkins, C.J.C.H., Dayan, P.: Q-learning. Mach. Learn. **8**, 279–292 (1992). https://doi.org/10.1007/BF00992698
3. Warner Jr., H.R., et al.: Innovation review: Iliad-a medical diagnostic support program. Top Health Inf. Manage. **14**(4), 51–58 (1994)
4. Ferber, J.: Les systémes multi-agents: Vers une intelligence collective. InterEditions (1995)
5. Barnett, G.O., Famiglietti, K.T., Kim, R.J., Hoffer, E.P., Feldman, M.J.: DXplain on the Internet. In: Proceedings of the AMIA Symposium, pp. 607–611 (1998)
6. Chan, A.S., et al.: Evaluating provider adherence in a trial of a guideline-based decision support system for hypertension. In: Medinfo, pp. 125–129 (1998)
7. Han, B.M., Song, S.J., Lee, K.M., Jang, K.S., Shin, D.R.: Multi agent system based efficient healthcare service. In: 8th International Conference Advanced Communication Technology, pp. 89–551 (2006)
8. Ramnarayan, P., et al.: Assessment of the potential impact of a reminder system on the reduction of diagnostic errors: a quasi-experimental study. BMC Med. Inform. Decis. Mak. **6**(1), 22 (2006)
9. Chaw, E.: Naïve Bayesian learning based multi agent architecture for telemedicine. Int. J. Innov. Appl. Stud. **2**, 412–422 (2013)
10. Zhang, M.-E.: Adaptive system construction of medical knowledge agent learning technology. IEEE (2017)
11. Min, C., Yixue, H., Kai, H., Lu, W., Lin, W.: Disease prediction by machine learning over big data from healthcare communities. IEEE Access **8**, 8869–8879 (2017)
12. Nicolas, R., Jeremy, B., Julien, N., Dorian, D., Marie-Pierre, G.: Lifelong machine learning with adaptive multi-agent systems (2017)
13. El Malki, M., Ben Hamadou, H., Chevalier, M., Péninou, A., Teste, O.: Querying heterogeneous data in graph-oriented noSQL systems. In: Ordonez, C., Bellatreche, L. (eds.) DaWaK 2018. LNCS, vol. 11031, pp. 289–301. Springer, Cham (2018). https://doi.org/10.1007/978-3-319-98539-8_22
14. Anju, A.: Machine learning based system health check analyzer for energy components (2018).http://hdl.handle.net/11250/2564383. Accessed 3 Aug 2019
15. Julian, V., Botti, V.: Multi-agent systems. Appl. Sci. **9**(7), 1402 (2019)
16. Becker, Colja A., Timm, Ingo J.: Planning and scheduling for cooperative concurrent agents with different qualifications in the domain of home health care management. Association for the Advancement of Artificial Intelligence (2019)
17. Kuziemsky, C.E., Harris, A.: An agent based framework for healthcare teamwork. Association for Computing Machinery (2019)
18. Raddaoui, M., Ben Abdallah Ben Lamine, S., Zghal Baazaoui, H., Ghédira Guegan, CH., Kabachi, N.: Knowledge guided integration of structured and unstructured data in health decision process. In: 28th International Conference On Information Systems Development, vol. 28 (2019)
19. Amanda, R., et al.: A mobile-based deep learning model for cassava disease diagnosis. Front. Plant Sci. **10**, 272 (2019)

Constructing a Secured, Reactive and Scalable Data Platform for a Better Exploitation of Rich Data Assets in the Tourism Industry

Fanjuan Shi[✉]

IAE Lyon, University of Jean Moulin Lyon 3, Lyon, France
shifanjun@gmail.com

Abstract. This paper presents our endeavor to construct a secured, reactive and scalable data platform as a response to the increasing needs for reliable, real-time, and actionable insights that are refined from data. The adventure starts with the design and share of a business-driven data platform implementation strategy by several business and IT teams. Based on that, we demonstrate the main functions and features of this platform and justify the reason for which we had selected a virtual private cloud solution. Then, we described the types of ingested data and our data ingestion method. We further discussed several business & engineering problems and our method to solve them. Finally, we present our prospection of future efforts to improve our data platform at the end of this paper.

Keywords: Data platform · Data ingestion · Universal dataset · Analytics · Machine learning

1 Context

C-GROUP is the leader for constructing and operating hotel facilities and resorts in Europe. The group has over 100 hotels and holiday villages in Europe. Each year, these facilities accommodates more than 5 million visitors all over the world and provides them with memorable holiday experience.

Over the past few years, a worldwide digitalization trend has fundamentally changed the behaviors of both consumers and companies in the tourism industry [1]. To better understand, reach, serve, and interact with its prospects and customers, C-GROUP needs to tackle a series of new challenges that are associated with the capability to produce reliable, real-time and actionable insights from data.

1.1 Omni-Channel Customer Knowledge and Marketing Actions

C-GROUP sells vacation products through its own sales channels (website, call center) and those of its business partners (online travel agencies, tour operators, member clubs, worker councils...). Meanwhile, consumers use different devices (mobile phones, computers, tablets) and ways (phone call, e-booking) to interact with these sales channels. As a result, C-GROUP has to deal with consumer information that is

© Springer Nature Switzerland AG 2020
S. Yangui et al. (Eds.): ICSOC 2019 Workshops, LNCS 12019, pp. 236–244, 2020.
https://doi.org/10.1007/978-3-030-45989-5_19

scattered in different touchpoints. To boost the chance of sales conversion, C-GROUP has to find a way to rebuild a (somehow) complete customer journey using these fragments so that it will be able to take into account all the recent changes of consumer intents and behaviors.

1.2 Personalization

There is an increasing number of consumers expect a brand to propose the most relevant tourism products (accommodations & nearby activities and services) to their tastes & needs out of thousands of choices [2]. In order to maximize the chance of sales conversion, C-GROUP should also consider using the most preferred communication channels and moments of each consumer [3]. To perform such a task simultaneously for thousands of consumers, C-GROUP not only needs to remember the taste of many consumers but also to have the powerful computational capability so that recommender systems based on collaborative filtering or deep learning algorithms can quickly find relevant recommendations and their probability of acceptance.

1.3 Performance Reporting and Analysis

C-GROUP needs to keep track of all the ongoing sales initiatives using data. The firm believes in the notion that all teams shall base their analysis on the same source of data and the same business rules so as to avoid any divergence or misinterpretation of conclusion due to the quality and consistency of data and its processing rules. The firm calls for a centralized and shared platform to bridge data silos and share information.

1.4 Personal Data Protection

Due to the rapid growth of volume and variety of data generated by consumers and collected by C-GROUP, it becomes increasingly important for the firm to establish rules, processes and mechanisms to prevent such sensitive information from being abused. This requires the capability to track the use of sensitive personal data throughout its lifecycle and anonymize such data when necessary.

2 Data Platform: Challenging Business Objectives

The above-mentioned challenges bring to a decision of the C-GROUP top management in late 2018 to forge a secured, reliable, and scalable data platform for both data storage and computation use cases in the sales and marketing domain. Meanwhile, the top management required the project task force to achieve two challenging business objectives:

(1) 12 months after the project kick-off, the data platform must generate revenue
(2) 24 months after the project kick-off, the data platform must generate profit

3   Conquer the Challenges Using a Business-Driven Approach

Conventional approaches will not allow us to achieve these challenging business objectives. This is due to the fact that these approaches usually require months of work of design (functions, architecture, applications, hardware & software interfaces, and policies security), solution evaluation and selection, development & implementation (platform construction & configuration, interaction sockets & protocols with existing information systems, security policies), functional test (capability, performance & stability), and validation. After that, we have to spend months to map different data sources, ingest them, and industrialize the update processes. Depending on the quality of the data, we will also have to design and perform data pre-processing tasks so that the raw data would be transformed into an exploitable status. All these tasks present complicated dependencies and uncertainties, which can easily delay the project for months. This is not to mention the time necessary for data analysts and machine learning engineers to work on data, develop models that can create business value, test & optimize them, and deploy them to the real production environment.

3.1   Creating More Value Within the Same Period of Time

Due to the above analysis, we decided to parallelize the development of IT capabilities (data platform & infrastructure), exploitable resources (data), and business solutions (analysis and models), illustrated in Fig. 1.

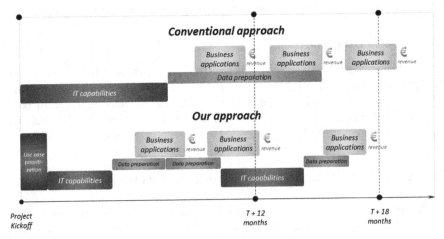

Fig. 1. Parallelization of developments reduces the time to market and allows for a faster revenue generation using same project resources.

Before designing our data platform, we spent time analyzing our internal needs for data analysis and machine learning use cases. By estimating their potential business values and technical efforts, we prioritized the use cases and identified the indispensable data platform features and data assets in short, middle, and long term. Based on this knowledge, we designed the data platform architecture and an implementation roadmap that can accelerate value creation.

The first phase (V1) aimed at providing indispensable data ingestion, storage, transformation and transmission capabilities for use cases that require batch data processing capabilities (Fig. 2). We limited our needs for analysis and modeling to a minimal level (i.e. to handle batch data analysis and Python script execution) to reduce the complexity and development time of the first version of the data platform. Since the first users of this data platforms were experienced machine learning engineers, such limitations had not brought to them any inconvenience.

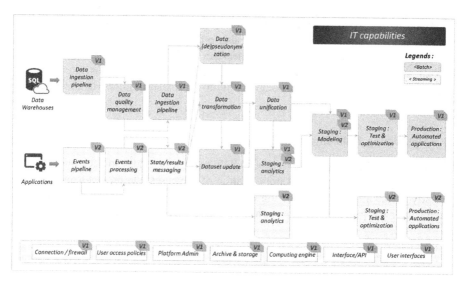

Fig. 2. This chart illustrates how data moves through different functional modules of the data platform. The development of these features was split into two phases (V1 and V2).

The second phase (V2) aimed at providing data processing capabilities for use cases requiring real-time calculation (Fig. 2). The integration of advanced data analysis and visualization features was also carried out during this phase. As the data platform was made accessible to data analysts and business analysts, these more user friendly (code-light or code-free) applications accelerated the user adoption of the new tool.

3.2 Solution Selection: Minimize Time to Market

We based our data platform selection criteria on the business needs to minimize time to market while keeping the exigences for security, performance, and reliability.

On-premises development was the first to be excluded. This was due to our concerns for the excessive time, human resources and budget spent on creating and maintaining big data frameworks, services, data access, development environments and libraries. The project team had only two data engineers for this project. We preferred to allocate them to more important tasks (data ingestion, automation, and application deployment).

In-the-cloud solutions have quite a few obvious advantages. (1) We can save a lot of time that would have been spent on technical details as the management and maintenance of the infrastructure and platform are taken care of by a vendor. (2) We can start with a small platform and scale it up easily when we need to. (3) The pay-by-usage pricing strategy reduces the initial investment in the project. Meanwhile, users of a cloud data solution need to pay attention to the brand new pricing scheme and have frequent and profound discussions with the service vendor to apply best practices to the platform setting up starting from day one.

Among all the virtual private cloud vendors, we have chosen Google Cloud Platform (GCP) as the solution to our data platform. Whereas we recognized that solutions like Amazon AWS and Microsoft Azure also offered competitive Infrastructure as a Service (e.g. networking, storage, firewall services, virtualization technologies etc.) and Platform as a Service (e.g. runtime, middleware, operating systems etc.), we had chosen GCP because of its better compatibility to our existing infrastructures and data assets.

3.3 Optimizing Data Ingestion Tasks for Quicker Value Delivery

As many large international firms, C-GROUP has a lot of data sources available for ingestion. Thanks to the previous prioritization of use cases, the project team was able to clearly define and follow a data ingestion roadmap that could ensure a fast delivery of use cases. We present the data sources in Table 1 and their descriptions.

Table 1. Example of data sources.

Priority	Category	Type	Update	Ingestion strategy
1	Media reach log	Semi-structured	D + 1	Increment/batch
2	Web navigation log	Semi-structured	H + 4/real-time	Incremental/batch + streaming
3	CRM data	Structured	W + 1	Replacement/batch
4	User opt-in	Structured	Real-time	Replacement/streaming
5	Transaction log	Semi-structured	D + 1	Replacement/batch
6	Product catalog	Structured	D + 1	Replacement/batch
7	Call center log	Semi-structured	D + 1	Increment/batch
8	References	Semi-structured	D + 1	Replacement/batch
9	Email campaign log	Semi-structured	W + 1	Increment/batch
10	Search query logs	Semi-structured	D + 1	Increment/batch
11	Customer survey	Semi-structured	W + 1	Increment/batch
12	Social media events	Semi-structured	H + 4	Increment/batch
13	Call records	Non-structured	W + 1	Increment/batch
14	Customer complaints	Non-structured	D + 1	Increment/batch
15	Mobile App events	Semi-structured	H + 4/real-time	Incremental/batch + streaming
16	Open data	Structured	Depends	Depends

Media reach log records the type of contents that are exposed to each known and unknown consumers and their feedback to the contents.

Web navigation log records consumers' behaviors and their analytics on our e-commerce websites.

CRM data records customers' background information, their recent interactions with C-Group their consumption history, and their value potential.

User opt-in records consumers' decision to accept or refuse our proactive contacts from different touchpoints.

Transaction log records all the detailed information of a confirmed, canceled or pending customer order, including rich quantitative and qualitative information.

Product catalog records all information related to our hundreds of thousands of vacation products and offers.

Call center log records the key information related to an inbound or outbound consumer call.

References record various business rules and configurations.

Email campaign log records the contents of different campaigns, target consumer audience, and their reaction to the email.

Search query log records keywords queried by consumers and their reactions to the provided search results.

Customer survey provides quantitative and qualitative customer feedback to our products and services.

Social media events record the interactions between consumers and social media accounts of C-GROUP.

Call records provide original and complete information of an inbound or outbound consumer call.

Customer complaints records the qualitative information of customer dissatisfaction.

Mobile App events record the behaviors and their analytics of consumers who use our mobile Apps.

Open data is information that could be useful for our analysis and modeling. Examples include weather condition and social-economic data.

We split the data ingestion tasks into three waves. Each wave aimed at ingesting indispensable data sources for the subsequent analysis or machine learning use cases.

The data ingestion task was composed of the following steps: (1) define and validate the interface contract between the source and the destination datasets and data fields; (2) set up SFTP in the data platform and define repositories in SFTP; (3) create Talend workflow to extract data and send it to SFTP repositories; (4) set up configuration table and test the ETL workflow; (5) create data catalog and dictionary with descriptions and examples; (6) define repositories for arriving data cache, raw data storage, and data archive; (7) develop and test scripts to move data files from arriving data cache to raw data repository and to archive; (8) develop and test scripts to execute pre-defined data processing rules; (9) develop and test scripts to pseudonymize and depseudonymize data fields that contain recognizable personal data.

3.4   Enriching the Value of Data Through Blending and Connecting

In many data labs and data warehouse, the job of a data engineer is limited to the data sources ingestion & automation, as is mentioned above. In our data platform project, we encouraged data engineers to do more than that because we believed that connected data were much more valuable than siloed data.

This additional task is to connect siloed datasets and automate the process. If ingesting data can be regarded as mining iron ore, connecting data can be considered as making "crude steel", which is an intermediary product that can be used for many manufacturing and construction purposes (Fig. 3).

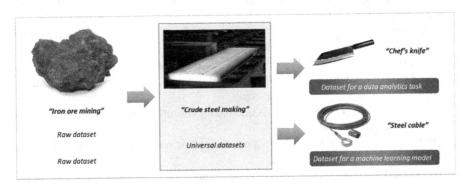

Fig. 3. "Connecting siloed datasets" aims at creating universal datasets ("crude steel") that can be used for various types of data analysis and machine learning projects.

In our project, data engineers who carried out the data connecting jobs performed the following tasks. (1) discuss with data analysts and machine learning engineers to identify the data sources that can be connected; (2) identify the data fields to be kept in each dataset; (3) identify common data fields to connect data sources; (4) define rules to connect datasets – for datasets that have different data granularity, define the rules of aggregation; (5) develop and test the script to automate the data connecting job; (6) create, name and move new data files to the raw data and archive repository; (7) create data catalog and dictionary for new users.

To forge universal datasets for different analysis and machine learning purposes, we organized data connecting workshops where data analysts, machine learning engineers, and other key data users sat together to analyze, consolidate, and validate business needs. Knowledge obtained in these workshops allowed us to identify datasets to be connected (based on the frequency of usage), the data fields to be kept, and the types/rules of data aggregation to be applied.

There are five benefits to create universal datasets by data engineers. (1) Universal datasets significantly reduced recurrent & unnecessary data connecting efforts of data analysts and machine learning engineers, enabling them to focus on their analytics and machine learning use cases; (2) a centralized production and maintenance of universal datasets assured the consistency of raw data processing and avoided data quality and reliability issues resulting from misinterpretation of data processing rules; (3) a centralized production of universal datasets minimized the waste of computing resources & budget resulting from repeated data connecting by downstream users. (4) universal datasets enabled data engineers to participate in business analysis or machine learning projects in an earlier stage, facilitating the subsequent industrialization tasks; (5) universal datasets and their data catalog/dictionary are much more user-friendly to new users who have few analytical backgrounds.

3.5   Governance of the Data Platform

A data platform is a complex research, development and production environment that involves stakeholders from many business and IT teams. In order to assure well-functioning and governance of this community, we defined clear roles, access permissions, and responsibilities for platform administrators and users.

Based on the RACI model, we defined four data platform roles: (1) *"responsible"* refers to persons who carry out actual tasks to solve a problem; (2) *"accountable"* refers to persons who approve/authorize the execution of tasks; (3) *"consulted"* refers to persons who provide information useful or necessary to execute tasks; (4) *"informed"* refers to persons who should only be informed of the results of tasks.

We further clarified 10 categories of responsibilities. (1) network: assure good and sustainable functioning of connection between the data platform and existing information systems; (2) infrastructure: assure good and sustainable functioning of such infrastructures as servers, operating systems, database, and middleware; (3) applications: installation and maintenance of applications for job management (Airflow), code maintenance and integration (Gitlab, Jenkins), applications monitoring (InfluxDb), information visualization (Grafana), and so on; (4) service continuity: define and assure service continuity and restore services when there is an incident; (5) security: supervise system vulnerability and attacks (e.g. DDoS), manage certificates; (6) access and administration: manage service accounts and access to data platform console, create, modify and delete accounts, manage the usage of the data platform in terms of storage and computing resources, manage the billing; (7) data ingestion: create, monitor and maintain data ingestion jobs, create and update data catalog, and perform data pseudonymization and depseudonymization jobs; (8) data connecting: create and maintain universal datasets and their data catalogs, create and maintain references; (9) data analysis: create and maintain project-level datasets, produce analytical products, manage the consumption of storage and computing resources; (10) modeling: create and maintain project-level datasets, create, maintain and deploy machine learning models, manage the consumption of storage and computing resources.

By crossing the roles and the responsibilities, we created a responsibility assignment matrix to specify the requirements for each user. Relevant KPIs and dashboards were also created for the data platform manager to keep track of the good governance of the community.

4   Discussion and Prospection

Since the project kick off in Feb 2019, we succeeded in delivering the first version of the data platform features and datasets in 5 months. We industrialized the first use case in 6 months (personalized activation email based on recent consumer intent) and obtain incremental revenue. Meanwhile, the second use case (recommender system of services to consumers) has passed the offline blind test in June and was scheduled for a subsequent online AB test.

For the next step, we want to put our efforts on the following subjects.

(1) The first priority is to keep the momentum of data ingestion and data connecting tasks as they are the fundamental of our subsequent analytics and machine learning tasks. For the moment, we have had ingested and connected media, web, CRM, transaction, user opt-in, and product data, it enable us to perform use cases like personalized emailing and recommender systems. The subsequent focus is to ingest call center data so as to better orchestrate call center staffing with an aim to maximize revenue creation.

(2) The second priority is to integrate more user-friendly analytics features for citizen business analysts. Intuitive and code-light analytics solutions like BigQuery and Dataiku makes sophisticated statistical analysis more intuitive to users. By integrating these features, we will be able to increase the adoption rate of the data platform within our organization.

(3) The third priority is to plan for the integration of real-time data processing and dispatching capability. As more and more consumers require for personalized tourism product shopping experience, we need to create user scoring and interaction applications that take into account consumers' intents and behaviors in real time.

(4) Finally, we should start exploring the capability to process and exploit non-structured data such as voice record and images because these data sources usually contain richer consumer information that structured and semi-structured data cannot provide. Use cases such as conversation pain point analysis and user intent/interest analysis rely on such capability. Nowadays, cloud solution providers have made available various computer vision and voice recognition solutions (e.g. deep learning frameworks, pretrained models, and packaged APIs). We need to evaluate them and chose the ones that cater to our needs and context.

References

1. Gretzel, U., Sigala, M., Xiang, Z., Koo, C.: Smart tourism: foundations and developments. Electron. Mark. 25(3), 179–188 (2015). https://doi.org/10.1007/s12525-015-0196-8. Author, F., Author, S.: Title of a proceedings paper. In: Editor, F., Editor, S. (eds.) CONFERENCE 2016, LNCS, vol. 9999, pp. 1–13. Springer, Heidelberg (2016)
2. Lu, J., et al.: Recommender system application developments: a survey. Decis. Support Syst. 74, 12–32 (2015)
3. Melero, I., Sese, F.J., Verhoef, P.C.: Recasting the customer experience in today's omni-channel environment. Univ. Bus. Rev. 50, 18–37 (2016)

Towards Multi-level Trust-Driven Data Integration in Multi-cloud Environments

Senda Romdhani[✉]

University of Lyon, CNRS, University of Lyon 3, LIRIS, Lyon, France
senda.romdhani@univ-lyon3.fr

Abstract. The service composition process in multi-cloud environments is emerging as a promising approach to integrate data made available through different sources w.r.t user's requirements and quality conditions. In this approach, individual cloud services with different offers and quality aspects are federated into composite data-provisioning cloud services with few fine control about the conditions in which they are implemented and provided. In this work, we aim to guide the data integration process in multi-cloud by adding a trust dimension as quality warranty taking into account user's preferences and Service Level Agreement. Accordingly, our contribution consists in defining a data integration trust-aware workflow in multi-cloud by computing trust scores of all entities implied in the integration process.

Keywords: Trust · Multi-cloud · Data integration · Composite service · Service level agreement

1 Introduction

Nowadays, with the advances of the cloud computing, individual people and organizations can obtain and process data from different sources. Putting in place an accurate and reliable data integration process to ensure that the most trustworthy data are made available and delivered to end users is becoming of paramount importance. A key step in the integration process is to select participating data-provisioning cloud services. However, reliance on services for data provisioning requires them to be trustworthy and of good quality.

Since the offered QoS specified in SLAs is unreliable and generally fluctuates due to the dynamics of the cloud and due to the possible presence of malicious data sources and cloud resources, we deem necessary evaluating the trustworthiness of cloud data-provisioning services participating in the integration process. Our work aims at guiding data integration process in multi-cloud environments by adding a trust dimension. The objective being to select the most suitable data composite services for clients with respect to their requirements using multiple

This work has been done in the context of the project SUMMIT (http://summit.imag.fr) funded by the Auvergne Rhone Alpes region.

cloud services and data with different provenance. To build such trust model, we take into account various aspects that may affect the trustworthiness of the data. Usually, the trustworthiness of the data depends on the trustworthiness of the data sources and on the parties that process the data. In this context, data is likely to be true if it is provided by trustworthy data sources, cloud and services. Due to such inter-dependency between them, we deem necessary developing a procedure to compute the trust scores of those entities so we can identify them and avoid any untrustworthy or misleading data.

To illustrate this need, let us suppose that for a surgery preparation, a doctor requires some important and sensitive information about his patient's health record. This information includes but not limited to blood pressure history, DNA information and pills subscriptions over the years that can be provided by different actors involved in the patient's medical control (e.g. cardiologist, personal smart devices, hospitals. etc.). Assume that these actors can store and give access to their data using different clouds (private cloud used by hospitals/cardiologist and public cloud used by smart devices.). Besides, assume that the doctor has several preferences regarding data (e.g. he requires data timeliness and availability, he wants good security measures etc.) and also has requirements regarding the integration process (e.g. integration with minimal cost and fast response time) expressed through SLA. In this case, several data-provisioning cloud services with different QoS can be composed to participate to integrate data for the doctor. Differentiating those services using a trust score may help selecting the most trustworthy composite service that best cope with doctor's requirements.

While there have been some efforts to evaluate the trustworthiness of cloud resources, the problem of trusted data integration in multi-cloud has not been widely investigated [15]. Previous solutions have either evaluated the trustworthiness of cloud resources individually or presented some guidelines for quality dimensions and standardization efforts. However, even though those solutions are important, they do not address the question on whether one can truly trust a composite multi-cloud data-provisioning service [14].

To this end, this paper aims to formulate the problem of data integration in multi-cloud environments, to revisit previous trust evaluation solutions in cloud environments in order to adapt them to our context, and finally this paper proposes a trust-aware data integration workflow. The remainder of this paper is organized as follows: Sect. 2 presents trusted data integration challenges and defines the quality criteria used for data-provisioning service selection and explains how values of these criteria can be computed for each integration entity. Section 3 presents our trust-aware data integration workflow. Section 4 concludes the paper and presents future work.

2   Trusted Data Integration on Multi-cloud Environments

Evaluating the trustworthiness of composite cloud services requires a mathematical model in which all aspects, parameters and user requirements are investigated. In this section, we shed light on (multi)-cloud computing and trust by discussing their definitions as well as formulating data integration trust computation challenges. Afterwards, we present the trust assessment criteria for the different data integration entities namely data, service and cloud according to standards and those presented in research works.

2.1 Preliminary Definitions

Commonly agreed definitions for trust and (multi)-cloud does not exist. Thus, we present hereafter those that are deemed relevant for our work.

Cloud Computing: also the pay-as-you-go model, is a model for enabling on-demand network access to a shared pool of configurable computing resources that can be rapidly provisioned and released with minimal management effort [24].

Multi-Cloud: This term denotes the usage of multiple cloud service providers by a client. This strategy is adopted to take advantage of the best offered services of each service provider with minimal cost in order to develop a solution that is perfectly tailored to the client's needs. Multi-Cloud allows end users to avoid vendor lock-in and offers better flexibility. It also offer the possibility to benefit from the advantageous prices and from the unlimited scalability of the cloud.

Trust: The concept of trust has first showed in sociological environment. It is a relationship built over time between two individuals which is affected positively or negatively by their previous experiences and memories. In the information technology area, trust is a complex notion and its definition is not unique, it may vary depending on the where and what context it is going to be employed. For cloud computing we provide the following trust definition: trust is the belief that a cloud resource is going to perform as the client's expectations, preferences and quality requirements presented in their SLAs. Trust can be regarded from multiple aspects- based on multiple sources and perspectives [1,6]. Considering data integration context in multi-cloud environment, the notion of trust becomes even more and more fuzzier.

For example, in Fig. 1, a user asks for some information that is composed of data **d1**, data **d2** and data **d3** using the composite service **cs**. The user has also asked for this data to be fresh (up to date), complete and there are security measures. The user's trust in composite service **cs**, implies his trust in **d1**, **d2** and **d3**. Data **d1** can be provided by service **s1** which is deployed on cloud **c1** and cloud **c2**, **d2** can be provided either by service **s2** deployed on cloud **c1** or service **s4** deployed on cloud **c3**. For data **d3**, we only have the service **s3** deployed on **c2**. As a result, to be able to trust the output data delivered by **cs**, we also need to establish trust with the other participating entities in the data integration (cloud, service) with the trust score TL_{ei} (e denotes the entity and i denotes the entity's number). An association of entities form a *path* with a trust value TL_j resulting from the aggregation of the entities trust levels (j denotes the path number). In this case, the data integration process needs to compute individual TL_{ri} then TL_j, and selects a path for each desired data by comparing the different obtained TL_j. Later, we need to compose those services' paths and evaluate their composite trust in the aim to find the best data-provisioning service composition for the end user. These goals can be achieved using a multi-level trust solution.

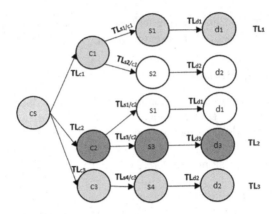

Fig. 1. An example to illustrate data integration trust computation challenges

To evaluate the trustworthiness of the participating services, we need to answer *questions concerning data* like "Where did the data come from? How trustworthy is the original data source?", *questions concerning the cloud and services that deliver the data* like "Who is authorized to modify the data? Is data protected from malicious access?" and finally *questions concerning the composition process* like "how to ensure that the process considers trust requirements? Which technique to use to evaluate composite trust? Do we start by evaluating the cloud or the services they host? Is data trust more important than the service trust? Are we going to find the information we need for this evaluation?" etc.

During the trust computation phase, multiple attributes need to be taken into account to ensure reliable decision making in the cloud computing [20]. We believe that it is vital to identify trust assessment criteria for the different cloud resources in order have insights on the best way to evaluate them. Nevertheless, such process generally lacks comprehensiveness and guidance. In the next section, we are going to discuss the different trust assessment criteria.

2.2 Criteria for Trust Assessments in Cloud Computing

In this section, we present the state of the art of trust assessment criteria used for each entity implied in the data integration process namely data trust assessment criteria and cloud service trust assessment criteria.

Data Trust Assessment Criteria
In order to identify the relevant criteria for data trustworthiness assessment, we referred to papers that discuss data quality dimensions and considered influential by the scientific community [2,7,8]. We summarize below in Table 1 these dimensions, their quality indicators and some possible assessment methods.

Cloud Service Trust Assessment Criteria
QoS has been discussed a lot in the literature and seen as a major criteria for evaluating the trustworthiness of cloud services. QoS is defined in various ways

Table 1. Data quality dimensions

Dimensions	Definition	Indicators	Assessment
Accessibility	The extent to which data is available reflecting ease of data attainability	Whether a data access interface is provided	*Min or Max operation*: This metric trades off the time interval over which the user needs data against the time it takes to deliver data. It is defined as the maximum value of two terms: 0 or one minus the time interval from request by user to delivery to user divided by the time interval from request by user to the point at which data is no longer useful
Timeliness	The extent to which data is sufficiently up to date. It reflects how up-to-date the data is with respect to the task it's used for	Whether data are regularly updated	*Min or Max operation*[2]: Measured as the maximum of one of two terms: 0 and one minus the ratio of currency to volatility. Here, currency is defined as the age plus the delivery time minus the input time. Volatility refers to the length of time data remains valid; delivery time refers to when data is delivered to the user; input time refers to when data is received by the system; and age refers to the age of the data when first received by the system.
Completeness	The extent to which data is not missing and is of sufficient for the task at hand	Whether the deficiency of a component will impact data accuracy and integrity	*At the data level*, one can define column completeness as a function of the missing values in a column of a table. This measurement corresponds to Codd's column integrity [25]
Interpretability	The extent to which data is in appropriate languages, symbols, and units and the definition are clear	Data description, classification, and coding content satisfy specification and are easy to understand	Verifying its meta-data
Free-of-Error	The extent to which data is correct and reliable	Data provided are accurate OR Data and the data from other data sources are consistent or verifiable	*Simple ratio*: the number of data units in error divided by the total number of data units subtracted from 1
Security	The extent to which access to data is restricted appropriately to maintain its security	Authentication and Authorization type AND/OR certifications	The better the authentication and authorization type, the better the data quality AND/OR Verifying certifications validity and provenance

Table 2. Cloud service trust quality dimensions

Dimensions	Definition	Factors & Metrics	Assessment
Capability	Specific functionality relating to the cloud service	Mean time to recovery/Mean time to failure/Failure handling (backup frequency)	Can be obtained directly from the service provider or from SLA
Capacity	Maximum amount of some property of a cloud service	Maximum resource capacity: e.g. CPU capacity, Memory size, Network bandwidth, Service throughput, Storage capacity, number of parallel sessions	Can be obtained directly from the service provider or from SLA
Performance	Information is obtained through resource auditing and monitoring	**(i) Availability**: being accessible and usable upon demand by an authorized entity	(i) Current (CPU-memory-bandwidth) utilization rate, Percentage of successful requests, Percentage of downtime/uptime
		(ii) Time efficiency	(ii) Ratio of the number of times the cloud provider is time effective to the number of service requests successfully completed
		(iii) Data integrity	(iii) Ratio of the number of times the data integrity is preserved to the number of service requests successfully completed)
		(iv) Response time	(iv) Average
		(v) Task success ratio or **Cost**	(v) Average
Security & Privacy	Information about employed security and privacy measures can be fixed and obtained through SLAs, through Standards such as NIST [3], ISO/IEC [4], and SMI [17], and through Certifications which are generally provided by cloud service providers. A certified resource should have a more chance to give a better quality of service	**(i)Authentication type** (Simple password, X.509, Kerbeos), **(ii)Authorization type** (Simple password, Identity-based authorization, Role-based authorization), **(iii)Self Security competence** (Malware/Firewall protection, Intrusion detection system, the number of malicious access), **(iv) Mean time required to revoke user access (v)service reliability** (property to function correctly without failure)	Comparison to the security and privacy terms fixed through policies or performing security controls: e.g. continuity management and disaster recovery etc. (vi) Frequency of scanning of important ports

and measured by different metrics, which causes confusion sometimes. After examining existing trust solutions research efforts in the area of cloud computing, we identify three trust assessment approaches for cloud services including:

Capacities/Capabilities Assessment: In this approach, user's preferences and requirements are mapped to different capabilities of the offered cloud resources. In this sense, the offer that best suits the user is the most trustworthy.

Performance Monitoring and Auditing: It is performed through SLA of cloud resources before or during service usage. In the first case, data collected from previous experiences are used to measure the degree of SLA fulfilment. If the SLA is satisfied, then the cloud resource is considered as trustworthy and vise versa. In the second case, SLA is monitored during service usage to detect violations. In case of violation, the service is either penalized or abandoned and replaced by another one.

Security & Privacy Assessment: This approach consists of verifying security and/or privacy measures of cloud resources.

The different trust evaluation dimensions are presented in details in Table 2 hereafter. We assign trust factors and metrics for each dimension as well as presenting guidelines for their assessment.

In Table 3, we present the studied research work and their adopted trust assessment dimensions.

3 Trust-Aware Data Integration Workflow in Multi-cloud

Selecting and optimizing data-provisioning composite services in multi-cloud environments are some of the most interesting challenges at present. The optimization challenge has been partially addressed previously in the work [16]. Their main objective was to compose data services in multi-cloud according to user's requirements and quality aspects using SLAs. In our present work, we are developing a solution that focuses on the selection's challenge by extending the solution in [16] adding a multi-level trust dimension.

In this section, we present the proposed multi-level trust-aware data integration workflow. We are using the e-health scenario presented in Sect. 1 to describe it. We suppose that, when the process starts, the trust levels of data, cloud and service are already evaluated and that they remain constant during the integration. Please note that the trust evaluation approach as well as the algorithm that allows to produce selection plans guided by dimensions presented in Sect. 2 are not addressed in this paper and are among our future work.

As illustrated in Fig. 2, the main entities in our workflow are: *the user* (doctor), the *profile extractor*, the *service selection and composition manager* (developed in [16]), the *service directory manager*, and finally the *trust manager*.

Profile Extractor: Parameters extraction involves careful analysis of user's request to learn his integration requirements and quality preference. This entity supplies the extracted requirements and preferences as input parameters required for rewriting queries in the data integration process.

Service Selection and Composition Manager: Data integration is generally realized in two steps including *service selection* and *service composition*. The first step is about matching user's request to existing services to extract those capable of executing it or part of it. Service Composition is about finding the best composition for selected services in the previous step to deliver requested information to the end user.

Service Directory Manager: This entity has access to the list of the available cloud services across the multi-cloud environment. If the *Service selection and composition manager* launches a service discovery request, the *service directory manager* is able to provide him with the list of the available and suitable ones. Any new service in the environment is added to the list of available services and their related documents and SLAs are extracted. We suppose that these documents contain information about the delivered data, about the cloud that hosts the service and information about the service itself.

Trust Manager: This is the module that has control over the trust computation of cloud resources implied in the integration process. It uses the infor-

Table 3. Cloud service trust assessment works

Paper	Applicability	SLA	Trust dimensions
Manuel (2009) [5]	All services	No	**Security:** Authentication type, Authorization type, Self security competence, **Performance:** Processor speed, Free ram size, Network Parameters (bandwidth, latency)
Chakraborty et al. [21] (2012)	All services	Yes	**Capacity/Capability:** CPU capacity, Memory size, Storage capacity, Number of parallel sessions, Failure handling (backup frequency, mean time to recovery), Average throughput
Lu et al. (2015) [22]	All services	No	**Security/Performance:** Passing delay, Passing packets quantity
Xiaoyong et al. (2015) [9]	IaaS	Yes	**Capacity/Capability:** CPU frequency, memory size, hard disk capacity and network bandwidth/**Performance:** Availability, Average response time, average task success ratio, and the number of malicious access.
Mrabet et al. (2016) [18]	All services	Yes	**Performance:** Availability (% accepted requests), Reliability (% requests successfully completed), Time efficiency, Data integrity

Table 3. (*continued*)

Paper	Applicability	SLA	Trust dimensions
Liao et al. (2016) [19]	All services	No	**Performance:** Generic/**Certifications**
Chiregi et al. (2016) [11]	All services	No	**Capability:** Processor speed, Memory speed, and Network (latency and bandwidth)/**Performance:** Availability, Reliability (task success ratio), data integrity (includes privacy and data accuracy)/**Security** identity (it is the weighted sum of Authorization level, Security level, Entity Protection level and Recovery level)
Singh et al. (2017) [12]	All services	Yes	**Performance:** Data processing accuracy, Data privacy, Data storage success, data transmission (% of success), and data security. Availability, Reliability, Turnaround time and service use factor of the service (related to the number of users that uses the service)
Saxena et al. (2018) [23]	IaaS	Yes	**Security:** standards, Guidelines and Certifications
Bao et al. (2018) [13]	All services	Yes	**Security:** Prevention of unauthorized access/**Performance:** Reliability (average response time, average task success ratio), Availability
Xiaoyong et al. (2018) [10]	All services	Yes	**Security:** Authentication type, Authorization type, Self-security competence/**Performance:** Availability, Average response time, Average task success ratio

mation provided by the *service directory manager* to extract trust scores of all data, service and cloud and then compute the path's overall trustworthiness.

Working principle of our trusted data integration workflow works as follows:

- *Step 1.* The doctor logs into the data integration interface and submits his request along with his requirements and quality preferences.
- *Step 2.* The *profile extractor* analyze the request in order to extract these requirements and preferences. Requirements are stored in a vector $\mathbf{RQ} = \{RQ_{kl}\}$ and quality preferences are also stored in $\mathbf{QP} = \{QP_{ql}\}$ (k denotes the kth requirement, q denotes the qth preference and l identify the user's request).
- *Step 3.* These vectors are used by the *service selection and composition manager* to rewrite the query and determine services needed for the composition. To do so, the manager runs the vectors and try to match them with services that can contribute to produce the final result. Therefore, he sends a request to the *service directory manager* to screen for available services.

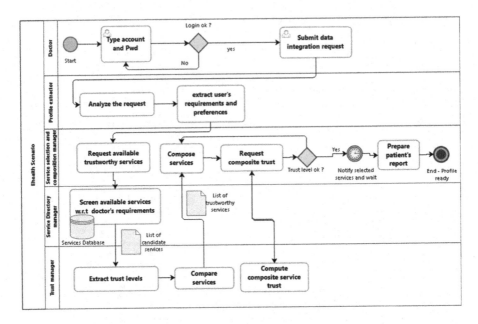

Fig. 2. Trusted data integration workflow: E-health scenario

- *Step 4.* The *service directory manager* uses SLAs and other available documents to find available cloud services that best cope to the request. The resulted list is then sent to the *trust manager* for computation of trust scores that will help identify the most trustworthy services.
- *Step 5.* The list of trustworthy services is sent back to the *service selection and composition manager* which will use it to compose services.
- *Step 6.* Finally, to find the best service composition, the *service selection and composition manager* sends a request to the *trust manager* to compute trust scores of composite services. The most trustworthy composite service is chosen and then concerned services are notified.

4   Conclusion and Future Work

The issue of trusting data-provisioning services in multi-cloud environments when integrating data has become of paramount concern. Multiple entities from different levels participate into the integration process including data with different provenance and quality conditions (freshness, timeliness..), cloud providers with different deployment models (private, public..) and data-provisioning services with different quality of services (security, availability..).

To this end, to avoid malicious data manipulations as well as to select the most suitable provisioning services for a given service composition, we believe it is important to put in place a mechanism to compute trust scores of data, cloud and service. Therefore, the aim of this work is to develop a multi-level trust model for data integration in multi-cloud environments. In this paper, we propose a trust-aware data integration workflow adapted to multi-cloud environments. In order to move towards a multi-level trust evaluation model, we reviewed some trust assessment criteria for the different entities implied in the data integration process namely cloud, service and data. This is a work in progress. Currently we are formalizing ways to compute the trust scores of each integration entity and the multi-cloud composite services. After the multi-level trust computation model being formalized, the next step would be to formalize an SLA for data integration taking into account our multi-level trust model.

References

1. Mohannad, A., Bertok, P., Tari, Z.: Trusting cloud service providers: trust phases and a taxonomy of trust factors. IEEE Cloud Comput. 4(1), 44–54 (2017)
2. Ballou, D.P., Pazer, H.L.: Modeling data and process quality in multi-input, multi-output information systems. Manage. Sci. 31(2), 150–162 (1985)
3. Wayne, J., Grance, T.: Draft NIST special publication guidelines on security and privacy in public Cloud computing. Computer Security (2011)
4. Saint-Germain, R.: Information security management best practice based on ISO/IEC 17799. Inf. Manag. J. Prairie Village 39(4), 60 (2005)
5. Manuel, P.: A trust model of cloud computing based on Quality of Service. Ann. Oper. Res. 233(1), 281–292 (2013). https://doi.org/10.1007/s10479-013-1380-x
6. Jin-Hee, C., Chan, K., Adali, S.: A survey on trust modeling. ACM Comput. Surv. 48(2), 28 (2015)
7. Pipino, L.L., Yang, W.L., Richard, Y.W.: Data quality assessment. Commun. ACM 45(4), 211–218 (2002)
8. Cai, L., Zhu, Y.: The challenges of data quality and data quality assessment in the big data era. Data sci. J. 14, 1–10 (2015)
9. Li, X., Ma, H., Yao, W., Xiaolin, G.: Data-driven and feedback-enhanced trust computing pattern for large-scale multi-cloud collaborative services. IEEE Trans. Serv. Comput. 11(4), 671–684 (2018)
10. Li, X., Yuan, J., Ma, H., Yao, W.: Fast and parallel trust computing scheme based on big data analysis for collaboration cloud service. IEEE Trans. Inf. Forensics Secur. 13(8), 1917–1931 (2018)
11. Chiregi, M., Navimipour, N.J.: A new method for trust and reputation evaluation in the cloud environments using the recommendations of opinion leaders' entities and removing the effect of troll entities. Comput. Hum. Behav. 60, 280–292 (2016)
12. Singh, S., Sidhu, J.: Compliance-based multi-dimensional trust evaluation system for determining trustworthiness of cloud service providers. Future Gener. Comput. Syst. 67, 109–132 (2017)
13. Bao, L.: QoS-based trust computing scheme for SLA guarantee in cloud computing system. In: 2017 International Conference on Computing Intelligence and Information System (CIIS), Nanjing, pp. 236–240 (2017)
14. Carvalho, D.A.S., Neto, P.A.S., Vargas-Solar, G., Bennani, N., Ghedira, C.: Can data integration quality be enhanced on multi-cloud using SLA? In: Chen, Q., Hameurlain, A., Toumani, F., Wagner, R., Decker, H. (eds.) DEXA 2015. LNCS, vol. 9262, pp. 145–152. Springer, Cham (2015). https://doi.org/10.1007/978-3-319-22852-5_13

15. Romdhani, S., Bennani, N., Ghedira-Guegan, C., Vargas-Solar, G.: Trusted data integration in service environments: a systematic mapping. In: Yangui, S., Bouassida Rodriguez, I., Drira, K., Tari, Z. (eds.) ICSOC 2019. LNCS, vol. 11895, pp. 237–242. Springer, Cham (2019). https://doi.org/10.1007/978-3-030-33702-5_18

16. Carvalho, D.A.S., Souza Neto, P.A., Ghedira-Guegan, C., Bennani, N., Vargas-Solar, G.: *Rhone*: a quality-based query rewriting algorithm for data integration. In: Ivanović, M., et al. (eds.) ADBIS 2016. CCIS, vol. 637, pp. 80–87. Springer, Cham (2016). https://doi.org/10.1007/978-3-319-44066-8_9

17. Jane, S., Jeff, P.: Cloud services measures for global use: the service measurement index (SMI). In: Annual SRII Global Conference, USA, pp. 411–415. IEEE (2012)

18. Mrabet, M., ben Saied, Y., Saidane, L.: Modeling correlation between QoS attributes for trust computation in cloud computing environments. In: 17th IEEE/ACM International Symposium on Cluster, Cloud and Grid Computing, Spain, pp. 488–497. IEEE Press (2017)

19. Liao, L., Bixin, L., Chao, L.: A model to evaluate the credibility of service in cloud computing environment. In: 14th International Conference on Dependable, Autonomic and Secure Computing, 14th International Conference on Pervasive Intelligence and Computing, 2nd International Conference on Big Data Intelligence and Computing and Cyber Science and Technology Congress, Auckland, pp. 294–301. IEEE (2016)

20. Habib, S.M., Sebastian, R., Max, M.: Towards a trust management system for cloud computing. In: 10th International Conference on Trust, Security and Privacy in Computing and Communications, Changsha, pp. 933–939. IEEE (2011)

21. Sudip, C., Roy, K.: An SLA-based framework for estimating trustworthiness of a cloud. In: 11th International Conference on Trust, Security and Privacy in Computing and Communications, Liverpool, pp. 937–942. IEEE (2012)

22. Lu, K., Jiang, H., Li, M., Zhao, S., Ma, J.: Resources collaborative scheduling model based on trust mechanism in cloud. In: 11th International Conference on Trust, Security and Privacy in Computing and Communications, Liverpool, pp. 863–868. IEEE (2012)

23. Saxena, A.B., Meenu, D.: IAAS trust in public domain: evaluative framework for service provider. In: 18th International Conference on Advanced Learning Technologies, India, pp. 458–460. IEEE (2018)

24. Peter, M., Tim G.: The NIST definition of cloud computing (2011)

25. Codd, E.F.: The 1981 ACM Turing Award Lecture. Communications (1982)

PhD Symposium

User-Oriented Description of Emerging Services in Ambient Systems

Maroun Koussaifi[(✉)]

University of Toulouse/IRIT, Toulouse, France
maroun.koussaifi@irit.fr

Abstract. Ambient intelligence aims at providing users the right services at the right time. Our solution composes software components and their services, automatically and on the fly, and makes composite services emerge from the environment. An important question is their intelligible presentation to an average user (not a service composition expert). Our approach consists in the automatic generation of user-oriented descriptions from unit descriptions of components and services. For that, we propose a domain-specific language for component and service descriptions and a combining method.

1 Introduction

Applications of the Internet of Things, ambient and cyber-physical systems consist of fixed or mobile connected devices. Devices host independently developed and managed software components that provide services specified by interfaces and, in turn, may require other services [8]. Components are building blocks that can be assembled by binding required and provided services to build composite applications. Due to mobility and separate management, devices and software components may appear and disappear without this dynamics being foreseen.

Humans are at the core of these dynamic and open systems. Ambient intelligence aims at offering them a personalized environment adapted to the current situation, anticipating their needs and providing them the right applications at the right time with the least effort possible.

We are currently exploring and designing a solution in which components are dynamically and automatically assembled to build new composite applications and so customize the environment at runtime. Our approach is quite disruptive: unlike the traditional goal-directed top-down mode, applications are built on the fly in bottom-up mode from the components that are present and available at the time, without user needs being made explicit, and without relying on predefined plans. That way, composite applications continuously emerge from the environment, taking advantage of opportunities as they arise: for example, a slider on a smartphone, a software adapter, and a connected lamp can opportunely be composed to provide the user with a lighting service when entering a room.

Supervisors—J.-P. Arcangeli, J.-M. Bruel and S. Trouilhet.

© Springer Nature Switzerland AG 2020
S. Yangui et al. (Eds.): ICSOC 2019 Workshops, LNCS 12019, pp. 259–265, 2020.
https://doi.org/10.1007/978-3-030-45989-5_21

Composition is automated by an *opportunistic composition engine* (OCE), in line with the principles of autonomic computing [4]. OCE senses the existing components and proactively makes the connections. The heart of OCE is a multi-agent system where agents manage the services and their connections [10]. To make the right decisions and build relevant applications, the agents learn online and by reinforcement.

OCE behavior and decisions are out of the scope of this paper, which focuses on placing the user in control of the deployment of emerging applications [6]. First of all, she/he must be informed of an emerging, possibly unexpected, application. Then, depending on its interest, she/he must be able to accept or reject it, or possibly modify it (provided that she/he has the required skills). For that, an editor displays the component-based architecture of the application, and allows modification [6]. However, such representation is only accessible to experts in component-based programming. Moreover, it does not explain the service that is offered. It is then essential to assist the user in the appropriation of the applications pushed by the engine. For that, they must be described in a useful and understandable way. This is especially important since the user's reactions are the sources of feedback for learning: based on them, OCE builds and updates a model of the user's preferences and habits.

This paper focuses on a solution to provide the user with an intelligible description of emerging composite applications. Section 2 states the problem and the requirements; Sect. 3 analyzes the state of the art; Sect. 4 describes the solution and preliminary results; Sect. 5 concludes and outlines the main perspectives.

2   Problem Statement and Requirements

In the absence of prior specification, emerging applications may be unknown and possibly surprising for the user. Thus, the way new applications are presented is critical. The purpose of the application must be explicit [R1-Semantics] (e.g. "The application allows to light up the lamp"), and how to use the application must be explicit too [R2-Usage] (e.g. "Press the switch to turn ON/OFF the light"). The description must also be understandable [R3-Intelligibility]: here, we target average users that are not familiar with programming or computer science (e.g. the inhabitant of a smart house or a public transport traveller in a smart city). Moreover, the description should remain intelligible even if the application consists of one to a few dozen components [R4-Scalability].

Henceforth, the problem is to build and display user-oriented understandable descriptions. As applications are automatically assembled, the descriptions of the services they provide must be computed automatically from the descriptions of their components and services [R5-Automation]. Besides, the language that supports the description of components and services should be expressive and easy-to-use for engineers that provide them [R6-Expressiveness].

3   Related Work

There exists many solutions for functional and extrafunctional service description. They are mainly used to support automated service discovery and selection in a top-down composition approach, that tends to build a complex service from unit ones. However, there exists no solution which aims at combining descriptions to build the description of a composite service to be presented to the user. To the best of our knowledge, there is no work that meets our requirements, mainly those concerning usage, intelligibility, and automated processing, in the context of bottom-up and goal-free application construction. In the following, we synthesize the related work.

For Whom and Why Describing a Service? Basically, service description is used as documentation for developers. It allows services to be located and used, as it is the case with WSDL. In Web service composition, the required services are specified explicitly. Then, in a more or less automatic approach [7], they are discovered and selected, based on their similarity with the expected ones, then assembled together. Hence, this consists in a top-down mode approach where the service description are no longer necessary in the composition phase. In [9], authors propose a user-centric composition platform: end-users first specify their goals using keywords, then the editor present the possible services that answer his/her needs, and suggest possible and user-changeable processes.

How to Describe a Service? In automated service composition approaches, the description of services varies according to the requirements of the discovery and selection steps. The different solutions for service description have been classified [3]. Descriptions may be limited to a syntactic way. For example, in object-oriented middleware (e.g. Java RMI), services are located only through a name. Otherwise, descriptions may be functional. It can have the form of signature with inputs and outputs, likely completed by preconditions and effects [5]. However, signature is not enough because their might be different functions with the same signature or even two services with the same function but with different quality levels. Therefore, a service description should include extrafunctional characteristics that is QoS-related properties. According to [3], OWL-S has become a standard for industrial service composition. OWL-S is an ontology-based language for describing semantic Web services that enables their automated discovery, composition and use. Ontology-driven description of services have proved to be efficient for selection and composition [9].

4   Proposition

Building the description of a composite application consists in combining unit descriptions of the components and their services. For that, we propose *(i)* a domain-specific description language and *(ii)* a combination method. Due to space limitation, we do not detail our solution here (see [1]). The idea is to describe both the services and the components with their services and possibly their states. Descriptions mainly rely on logical rules which state how services interact and transform data, and how the user can use the interactive components. Engineers that develop components provide component and service descriptions. In addition, the latter are completed by the engine with the emerging bindings. Then, the rules are combined to produce application-level rules.

In order to validate our approach, we have developed a prototype solution and tested it on several use cases, with different component assembly topologies. In the following, we present two of them.

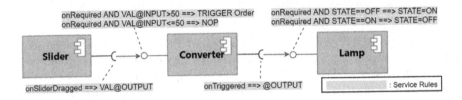

Fig. 1. Structural representation of the lighting service

Lighting Service. The application (see Fig. 1) consists of three components assembled in pipeline mode: a slider, a converter and a lamp. The slider acts as a switch. It requires the *Process Value* service. The converter provides the *Transform* service (that subsumes the *Process Value* service): it receives a value and, if greater than 50, transforms it into an command for the lamp through the *Order* required service. The lamp provides the *OnOff* service (that subsumes the *Order* service). Fig. 2 shows the rules resulting from the combination of the service rules highlighted in Fig. 1. Rules are then translated into a more intelligible version of the supplied service (see Fig. 3).

```
IF onSliderDragged AND VAL@INPUT<=50 THEN   NOP
IF onSliderDragged AND VAL@INPUT>50 AND Lamp:STATE==ON
        THEN Lamp:STATE=OFF
IF onSliderDragged AND VAL@INPUT>50 AND Lamp:STATE==OFF
        THEN Lamp:STATE=ON
```

Fig. 2. Description rules of the lighting service

```
onSliderDragged of Slider IMPLIES
Turn OFF the Lamp IF VAL >50 AND Lamp is ON
Turn ON the Lamp IF VAL >50 AND Lamp is OFF
```

Fig. 3. User-oriented textual description of the lighting service

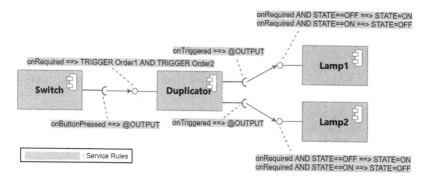

Fig. 4. Structural representation of the multiple lighting service

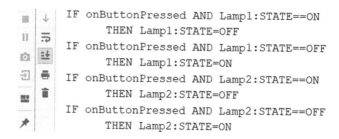

```
IF onButtonPressed AND Lamp1:STATE==ON
      THEN Lamp1:STATE=OFF
IF onButtonPressed AND Lamp1:STATE==OFF
      THEN Lamp1:STATE=ON
IF onButtonPressed AND Lamp2:STATE==ON
      THEN Lamp2:STATE=OFF
IF onButtonPressed AND Lamp2:STATE==OFF
      THEN Lamp2:STATE=ON
```

Fig. 5. Description rules of the multiple lighting service

```
onButtonPressed of Button IMPLIES
Turn OFF the Lamp IF Lamp1 is ON
Turn ON the Lamp IF Lamp1 is OFF
Turn OFF the Lamp IF Lamp2 is ON
Turn ON the Lamp IF Lamp2 is OFF
```

Fig. 6. User-oriented textual description of the multiple lighting service

Multiple Lighting Service. The application (see Fig. 4) uses a wall switch and a component responsible of controlling two lamps at the same time, assembled in a star topology. Figure 5 shows the rules resulting from the combination of the rules highlighted in Fig. 4. Figure 6 shows the same rules but in a user-oriented intelligible version.

In this example, the lamps are commanded in parallel. Note that our solution supports other types of composition operators, e.g. a sequence operator.

5   Conclusion and Perspectives

In this paper, we have exposed an approach that aims to answer most of the identified requirements (see Sect. 2): [**R5-Automation**] by automatically generating user-oriented descriptions; [**R1-Semantics**] by the description of the behaviour of the assembly by explicit rules; [R2-Usage] by integrating dedicated operators in the language description; and [R3-Intelligibility] by making the descriptions intelligible thanks to functions combination algorithms and generation of descriptions in natural language. We have experimented several use cases with standard topologies that show that our approach can meet those requirements.

At this point of our work, through user-oriented textual descriptions, average users can be informed and understand the service that is offered by emerging composite applications. Further experiments must now be carried out on more complex applications and topologies to address the missing requirement: [R4-Scalability]. In addition, real users should be involved in the experiments to improve and validate intelligibility and scalability of the presentation.

Our description language being a domain-specific language, and the input assembly being a model, Model-Driven Engineering (MDE) which has been proved useful in this particular case [2] will allow us to define transformation between assemblies and their descriptions. In order to easily upgrade and extend our description language, we intend to fully use the power of MDE approaches and tools to support the automatic generation of combination algorithms from the description language definition itself. In addition, using MDE to manipulate (e.g. fold/unfold) the descriptions should help to address the scalability issue [R4-Scalability].

Finally, we plan to investigate the use of ontologies to help in the combination process, in order to provide more intelligible descriptions (e.g. by aligning heterogeneous but related service concepts). This should limit the risk of rejection of the service by the end-user due to misdescription of emerging applications.

References

1. Component and service description language for automated description of composite applications. https://www.researchgate.net/publication/333675107_Component_and_service_description_language_for_automated_description_of_composite_applications. Accessed 10 June 2019
2. Bruneliere, H., et al.: Model-driven engineering for design-runtime interaction in complex systems: scientific challenges and roadmap. In: Mazzara, M., Ober, I., Salaün, G. (eds.) STAF 2018. LNCS, vol. 11176, pp. 536–543. Springer, Cham (2018). https://doi.org/10.1007/978-3-030-04771-9_40
3. Fanjiang, Y., Syu, Y., Ma, S., Kuo, J.: An overview and classification of service description approaches in automated service composition research. IEEE Trans. Serv. Comput. 10(2), 176–189 (2017). https://doi.org/10.1109/TSC.2015.2461538
4. Kephart, J.O., Chess, D.M.: The vision of autonomic computing. Computer 36(1), 41–50 (2003). https://doi.org/10.1109/MC.2003.1160055
5. Klusch, M.: Semantic web service description. In: CASCOM: Intelligent Service Coordination in the Semantic Web, pp. 31–57. Birkhäuser Basel, Basel (2008)
6. Koussaifi, M., Trouilhet, S., Arcangeli, J.-P., Bruel, J.-M.: Ambient intelligence users in the loop: towards a model-driven approach. In: Mazzara, M., Ober, I., Salaün, G. (eds.) STAF 2018. LNCS, vol. 11176, pp. 558–572. Springer, Cham (2018). https://doi.org/10.1007/978-3-030-04771-9_42

7. Sheng, Q.Z., Qiao, X., Vasilakos, A.V., Szabo, C., Bourne, S., Xu, X.: Web services composition: a Decade's overview. Inf. Sci. **280**, 218–238 (2014). https://doi.org/10.1016/j.ins.2014.04.054

8. Sommerville, I.: Component-based software engineering. In: Software Engineering, 10 edn., pp. 464–489. Pearson Education (2016). Chap. 16

9. Xiao, H., Zou, Y., Tang, R., Ng, J., Nigul, L.: Ontology-driven service composition for end-users. SOCA **5**(3), 159 (2011). https://doi.org/10.1007/s11761-011-0081-z

10. Younes, W., Trouilhet, S., Adreit, F., Arcangeli, J.P.: Towards an intelligent user-oriented middleware for opportunistic composition of services in ambient spaces. In: Proceedings of the 5th Workshop on Middleware and Applications for the Internet of Things, pp. 25–30. ACM, New York (2018). https://doi.org/10.1145/3286719.3286725

A Web-Component-Based Cross-Platform Mobile Application Development Environment for Ordinary Users

Zhaoning Wang[✉]

State Key Laboratory of Networking and Switching Technology,
Beijing University of Posts and Telecommunications, Beijing, China
asimoo@bupt.edu.cn

Abstract. The rapid progress of the mobile internet has been promoting the popularity of mobile devices, and mobile application development is getting more pervasive. However, state of the art development environments have a high learning barrier for ordinary users. In this paper, we take consideration of ordinary users' requirements and propose a WYSIWYG cross-platform web-component-based mobile applications creation environment for ordinary users. This environment has a WYSIWYG visual editor with drag-and-drop web component. A web component library model is proposed to standardize customized libraries. A cross-platform application model based on composite web components is imported to implement a rapid application build approach with one-click buttons, which helps ordinary users generate installing packages within simple operations for multiple platforms. A native plugin model is proposed to assist web components to invoke native functionalities. The experiment result shows that ordinary users could easily start to create mobile applications in our environment.

Keywords: Web component · Cross-platform · Mobile application · Mobile service

1 Introduction

The rapid evolution of mobile technologies has made mobile devices become an irreplaceable part of daily lives, therefore mobile application development is becoming familiar to ordinary users who do not have programming skills. Historically, traditional development environments are designed following programmers' habits lack of features supporting ordinary users, which has become an invisible obstacle for ordinary users to realize their innovative ideas. Another crucial challenge for ordinary users in mobile development is cross-platform. Mainstream mobile platforms, iOS, Android and Windows Phone, correspond to completely different frameworks incompatible for each other requiring specified

Supervised by Bo Cheng.

software and hardware. However, most traditional development environments only support single frameworks. What ordinary users need is an environment isolating the heterogeneous frameworks and adapting to any platforms freely as their wills.

2   Related Work

2.1   Graphical Development Environment

Several solutions have been proposed to improve traditional development environments. A visual designer is a graphical drag-and-drop tool or plugin which has been widely used in multiple mobile development environments to facilitate the GUI designing process. Current graphical development products use a visual component as a basic designing unit to make up an application. Plenty of practical research achievements have been proposed around graphical development environments. [1] implements MashMaker, a graphical service orchestration tools. [2] proposed a semantic-based composition platform of heterogeneous services and applications. [3] implements a service creation environment on mobile devices named MicroApp. MIT App Inventor [4] is a visual programming environment that allows everyone to build fully functional applications for Android smartphones. These products have common problems unsolved. Firstly, only single specific platforms are supported. Secondly, functionalities of visual components are limited in GUI designing.

2.2   Cross-Platform

Web components are custom, reusable, encapsulated HTML tags to use in web pages and web applications. Custom components will work across modern browsers, and can be used with any JavaScript library or framework that works with HTML. A web application is a kind of mobile application based on pure web technologies running in a browser to simulate native application known as Native developed following the traditional framework. The web application is a popular solution to cross-platform. AppGyver Composer [5] is an online web application development tool which combines graphical programming and web application development. Web components and applications have weaknesses in the native functionality invocation since the inherent limitation of web technologies.

3   Motivation Scenarios

A representative scenario we have considered is designers who could participate in the designing procedure in the traditional development process. Designers or product managers are responsible for designing work lack of concerning implementation. They use image tools like PhotoShop and deliver prototypes to developers. As a consequence, these prototypes may include inenarrable functionalities leading to difficulties in the implementation phase, namely the final products are worse than expectations. This gap between designing and implementing has prevented innovative ideas transforming to actual applications. Another typical scenario is beginners in development education. Learning is a smoothly growing process from easy to difficult, especially when people first get to know a field as complicated as application development. Traditional development environments directly bring programming knowledge to beginners lack of a reasonable learning curve, which persuades beginners before further understanding. Our proposed environment solve these problems in multiple perspectives. Graphical integrated development tools and drag-n-drop operation pattern lower learning obstacles for ordinary users like designers and beginners. Visually native functionality invocation, multi-platform support, and automatic application creation help users generate executable mobile applications isolating platform differences.

4   Contributions

In this paper, we propose a WYSIWYG web-component-based cross-platform mobile application development environment. The main contributions of us are:

(1) We identify the present problems of mobile development for ordinary users and specify requirements which are graphical development, automatic tools, and cross-platform.
(2) We propose the cross-platform mobile development environment based on web component assemble and relative models to address these issues. The visual editor helps users assemble and configure web components visually. A novel web component library model is included. The native plugin model supports invoking native functionalities of operating systems. The application creation approach supports users rapidly building applications for multiple platforms.
(3) We conduct preliminary experiments in a group of ordinary users and the results show the outperforming usability and convenience of our environments.

5   Proposed Environment and Models

5.1   Architecture Overview

The proposed environment is developed as a web application that could be accessed on any devices with browsers. Figure 1 shows the architecture divided into three functional components: library repository, visual IDE layer, and server module based on the OSGi framework which is a dynamic module system for Java.

5.2   Visual Editor

The visual IDE component provides a drag-and-drop development environment where web components assemble. The visual editor provides a WYSIWYG working area. Each time users create a new project, the visual editor generates an app container to establish an execution environment for a user's application parsing web components composition result to runtime images. Users could drag chosen web components to the app container and visually modify their position and size to design their appearances. The app container provides an event engine with a set of pub/sub interface for web components to send or monitor events The palette provides a toolkit that allows ordinary users to visually configure native plugins. The file operation provides a series of visual tools to operate users' project files including native plugin uploading, and application build.

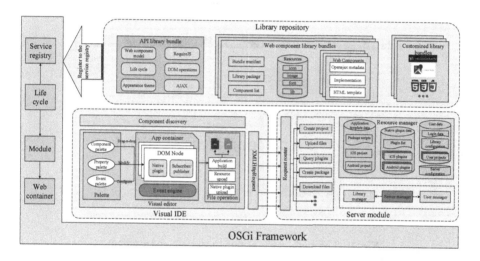

Fig. 1. The architecture of the environment

5.3   Web Component Library Model

A web component is implemented via web technologies instantiated as a customized reusable DOM node, namely an HTML tag, running in the web browser environment standardized by W3C through all platforms, from desktops to mobile devices, therefore it is the foundation of cross-platform development. A typical web component in our environment consists of an openajax metadata (OAM) file, an implementation file, and HTML templates. The OAM represents a set of industry-standard metadata defined by the OpenAjax Alliance that enhances interoperability across AJAX toolkits and Ajax products. The OAM file describes the essential information of a web component, including a unique ID, library name, requiring files, context, and other optional properties. The implementation file is a JavaScript AMD (Asynchronous Module Definition) module inherited the web component model in the API library. A web component library is characterized as a container of web components encapsulated in a OSGi bundle, an independent component of the OSGi framework, maintaining the essential data and resources that define a web component collection. Figure 1 shows a standard web component library model. All available library bundles are dynamically loaded by the OSGi framework and register library interfaces to the service registry.

5.4   Native Plugin Model

A native plugin is an extension helping web components communicate with mobile operating system. Native plugins provide interfaces to web components, while have a channel accessing OS service interfaces, which set up a bridge between web components and native functionalities.

Fig. 2. The main page of our proposed environment

5.5   Application Creation Approach

The application build service is encapsulated in the server side transparent for users. We define a application template as a collection of essential files to assist application creation. Resource manager in the server side maintains application templates and corresponding package scripts for different platforms. Users send requests via GUI controls in the file operation area. When a request is received, the create package handler in the server side resolve parameters and the app container is copied from the user's directory to the corresponding application template. Meanwhile, a native plugin list maintained by the app container recording applied native plugins in the project is read and the corresponding resources of native plugins are copied to the native plugin library maintained by the template. Configuration file and dependencies of the app container are imported into the application template. The corresponding package script is executed to generate the apk or ipa file that is responded to the client.

6   Demonstration and Evaluation

Figure 2 shows the main page of the environment. We create an application as an example in the video on YouTube (https://youtu.be/hYSrv_EWEtg). To evaluate the usability, we have an experiment compared with MIT App Inventor. We organized 20 users without programming expertise from Beijing University of Posts and Telecommunications. We show them tutorials and let them try two environments. A questionnaire about three aspects shown in the note of Fig. 3 is asked to filled after trials. The result shown in Fig. 3 indicate our proposed environment obtain more scores in users' reviews.

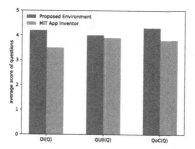

Fig. 3. The comparison result of questionnaire *(Note: OI represents the overall impression. GUII represents GUI operation impression. QoC represents quality of components.)*

7   Conclusion

This paper proposes a WYSIWYG cross-platform mobile applications development environment for ordinary users. We describe the architecture and models in detail. It provides users an easy-operating visual editor, abundant web component libraries, native plugins, and an application creation approach. Summarizing above, our proposed environment has learned from traditional development environments and improved the functionalities to be more friendly to ordinary users. In the future we are looking forwarding to optimizing application performance in mobile cloud environment.

References

1. Ennals, R.J., Garofalakis, M.N.: MashMaker: mashups for the masses. In: Proceedings of the 2007 ACM SIGMOD International Conference on Management of Data, SIGMOD 2007, pp. 1116–1118. ACM, New York (2007)
2. Ngu, A.H.H., Carlson, M.P., Sheng, Q.Z., Paik, H.: Semantic-based mashup of composite applications. IEEE Trans. Serv. Comput. **3**(1), 2–15 (2010)

3. Francese, R., Risi, M., Tortora, G., Tucci, M.: Visual mobile computing for mobile end-users. IEEE Trans. Mob. Comput. **15**, 1033–1046 (2016)
4. Pokress, S.C., Veiga, J.J.D.: MIT app inventor: enabling personal mobile computing (2013)
5. AppGyver composer. Apparchitect.com (2019). http://www.apparchitect.com/

OSPAci: Online Sentiment-Preference Analysis of User Reviews for Continues App Improvement

Jianmao Xiao[✉]

College of Intelligence and Computing, Tianjin University, Tianjin, China
zt_xjm@tju.edu.cn

Abstract. Detecting user's sentiment and preference (e.g., complain or new feature wanted) timely and precisely is crucial for developers to improve their apps correspondingly to win the competitive mobile-app market. In this paper, we propose a novel and automated framework OSPAci, which aims to identify user's sentiment and preference effectively based on online user reviews. OSPAci uses sentiment analysis and natural language processing techniques to obtain sentence-level sentiment scores and fine-grained user preference from mobile app reviews. Then, it analysis the evolution of user's sentiment trend and preference. Finally, the user sentiment trend and preference correlation is analyzed along the time dimension, thus this model can be used to monitor user's sentiment tendency and preference almost in time. We evaluate the feasibility and performance of OSPAci by using real Google play's user reviews. The experimental results show that OSPAci can effectively and efficiently identify the user's sentiment tendency and detect user preference timely and precisely.

Keywords: User review · Sentiment trend · Preference feature · Time series · Evolution

1 Introduction

App stores are digital distribution platforms that allow users submit feedback on downloaded apps by rating or text review, which explicitly or implicitly expresses the user's potential sentiment and preferences for the app. Sentiment can represents the user's attitude towards the app and the preference express the user's intention of the app. User's preference can be expressed by the user's review feature (referred as preference feature). To keep track of the user's sentiment and preference features of the app timely and precisely can greatly improve and help the app provider to improve subsequent versions of the app, such as bug fixes, feature refining, or adding new features.

Supervised by Shizhan Chen, College of Intelligence and Computing, Tianjin University, China, shizhan@tju.edu.cn, Shiping Chen, CSIRO Data61, Australia, Shiping.Chen@csiro.au, Xiao Xue, College of Intelligence and Computing, Tianjin University, China, Zhiyong Feng, College of Intelligence and Computing, Tianjin University, China, zyfeng@tju.edu.cn

© Springer Nature Switzerland AG 2020
S. Yangui et al. (Eds.): ICSOC 2019 Workshops, LNCS 12019, pp. 273–279, 2020.
https://doi.org/10.1007/978-3-030-45989-5_23

User reviews are direct feedback from the users who have experienced the apps, and reflect the instant user experience [1]. Recent empirical studies [2] are focused on mining features in app reviews and classify them into different category, analyze user interest features in apps, identify emerging app issues [3], etc. However, these studies did not consider the changes in the user's sentiment and preference features of the app over time. In fact, due to the internal factors (e.g., new bugs) or external environment (e.g, new competitors) of the app change over time, the user's sentiment and preference will change dynamically. Therefore, detecting and understanding of the user's possible sentiment and preference features timely and precisely is of great significance to app providers.

We propose a novel framework named OSPAci to detect the sentiment and preference of the app from user reviews timely. OSPAci takes user reviews as input. Then, it use NLP and collocation finding techniques [4] mining the fine-grained preference features from user reviews. Finally, it realize the mapping relationship between user sentiment and preference features over time.

The remainder of the paper is structured as follows. Section 2 outlines the overall picture and details each step involved in the framework. Section 3 describes the experiments and results. Section 4 is the conclusions and future work.

2   Methodology

2.1   Overview

Our main purpose is to analyze the correlations of user's sentiment and preference over a continuous time slice based on user review information, it including data mining and sentiment analysis techniques in the process. Figure 1 shows an overview of the OSPAci. First, OSPAci extract the review sentiment and review preference from user reviews based on the NLP technology and the sentiment analysis respectively. Then, the review sentiment and the preference evolution are analyzed based on time series. Finally we establish a mapping relationship between sentiment tendency and preference features along the time dimension and analysis their correlations, which can help the app provider to keep track of the user's sentiment and preference in time and realize app improvement continuously.

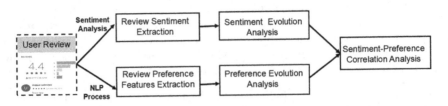

Fig. 1. Overview of the OSPAci

2.2   Sentiment and Preference Extraction

Review Text Processing. Reviews submitted by users through mobile terminals generally contain a lot of noise data, such as repeated words, misspelled words and non-English words, etc., which will seriously affect the fine-grained preference feature extraction from the user review. Therefore, we have do four additional steps to processing the review data first. Include filter non-English review, part of speech extraction, noise word (include stop words) removal and lemmatization. Through these processes, the obtained review information has basically eliminated most of the noise interference.

Review Sentiment Extraction. Sentiment analysis is the process of assigning a quantitative value of each positive or negative for each review [5]. To analyze the sentiment in user reviews, we use SentiStrength [4], a lexical sentiment extraction tool to implement sentiment for user review sentiment analysis. SentiStrength can divide the review information into sentence levels and assign corresponding positive or negative values. The value range is $[-5, 5]$, where $+5$ indicates very positive sentiment, and -5 indicates very negative sentiment.

Review Preference Extraction. To obtain a fine-grained user preference feature, we further use the sentiment dictionary provided by HowNet[1] to remove the interference of emotional words in this process and manually filter such as "app", "please", "android", "google" and other effects words according to the characteristics of the app. Finally, we use the collocation search algorithm of NLTK to extract the fine-grained features in the user review.

Meanwhile, to implement preference feature weight analysis, we also calculate the scores of the fine-grained preference features according to the principles: if the preference feature appears in the review, its sentiment score is equal to the positive or negative score of the sentence in which it is located.

2.3   Sentiment and Preference Evolution Analysis

Time Series Sentiment Evolution. We take the average sentiment score $ARS(\text{score})$ as the users sentiment score, and the calculation formula is as follows:

$$ARS(\text{score}) = \frac{1}{n} \sum_{\substack{j=1 \\ i \in T(t_1, t_2, \ldots, t_m)}}^{n} RS_{i,j} \tag{1}$$

$T(t_1, t_2, \ldots, t_m)$ represents m consecutive but non-overlapping time slice with equal lengths, $RS_{i,j}$ is expressed as the jth review sentiment score of the app in the T_i, n represents the number of reviews within T_i time slice.

Time Series Preference Evolution. In order to figure out the fine-grained preference feature score during different time slices. For each app, we construct a matrix to represent the distribution of fine-grained preference feature score by

---

[1] http://www.keenage.com/html/c_bulletin_2007.htm.

all users on each feature over a time slice. It is called Time-Series Preference Feature Score Matrix TSPFS.

Table 1. Time-series preference feature score matrix (TSPFS)

	T_1	T_2	...	T_m
PF_1	$PFS_{1,1}$	$PFS_{1,2}$	...	$PFS_{1,m}$
PF_2	$PFS_{2,1}$	$PFS_{2,2}$	...	$PFS_{2,m}$
...	...	...	...	...
PF_n	$PFS_{n,1}$	$PFS_{n,2}$	...	$PFS_{n,m}$

Table 1 shows the visual form of TSPFS. The row of the matrix indicates that n fine-grained preference features, and columns are m consecutive but non-overlapping time slice with equal lengths (i.e., $T_1, T_2, \ldots, T_m$), T_i represents the ith time slice. $PFS_{i,j}$ is expressed as the overall score of the preference feature j of the app during the ith time slice, and the calculated formula as (2):

$$PFS_{i,j} = \sum_{\substack{k=1 \\ i \in T(T_1, T_2, \ldots, T_m)}}^{n} FRS_{i,j,k} \tag{2}$$

where n indicates the number of times that feature j appears during the ith time slice, $FRS_{i,j,k}$ is the score of feature j in review k in the slice T_i.

2.4 Sentiment-Preference Correlations Analysis

User's sentiment would continues change dynamically over time due to the app version updates, unpredictable security issues in apps, etc., and it will resulting in the user's sentiment trend would appear crest and trough. So in our work, we establish the mapping relationship between sentiment and preference features along the time dimension. i.e., at different time slices, when the user sentiment changes, the preferences we mining from user reviews also change in real time. During our work, we mainly focus on the user's sentiment in crest and troughs, which are more likely to express the user's preference features.

3 Experiments

3.1 DataSet

To ensure that the app has enough review data, we crawled the review data with more popular and include different types of apps from Googleplay. Overall, we obtain 82,595 reviews from November 9th, 2018 to January 24, 2019 under four apps (Facebook, Uber, ManFIT and YouTube Music). With multiple categories, the generalization of OSPAci can ensured to some extent.

3.2 Results

In order to reflect OSPAci timely, we set the time period for user review of each app under different categories to span 1–2 months due to the app reviews number is different under different categories. We divide the time into 20 time slice, i.e., each time slice include 1 to 3 days since the number of reviews and the user review time is different under different app.

Sentiment Evolution Analysis. Figure 2 shows the evolution trends of single app Facebook and Uber. The history of user's sentiment score changes from Nov. 2018 to Jan.2019 is visualized by line charts. We can see that the user express a quit diversified changing trends for different category app. In addition, apart from a stable sentiment trend, the user's sentiment will rise or fall rapidly during different time slice, resulting in trends such as crests and troughs, e.g., Uber.

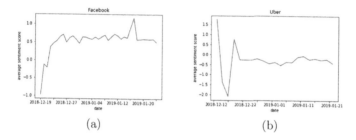

(a)   (b)

Fig. 2. ARS (score) evolution under a single app

Preference Evolution Analysis. During different time slices, the user's preference are dynamically changed, the evolution of preference reflects the user intent changes directly. As we see in Fig. 3, the user's preference feature are "customer service" and "waiting time", their score is −19, −6 respectively under the time slice of December 16, 2018. However, at January 3, 2019, the user's preference feature are "payment method" and "credit card", and the similar for other time slices. Here we mainly focus on the new appearance features and low sentiment score since it is more likely to express the user's significant intention.

Sentiment-Preference Correlation Analysis. Figure 3 visualizes the dynamic mapping of Uber in terms of sentiment tendency and preference features. For example, on December 16, 2018, the sentiment trend is in the trough. The user's overall sentiment score is −2.08. The preference features are "customer service" and "waiting time", their sentiment scores are −19, and −6. However, the sentiment trend reaches a Crest by December 18, 2018, and the preference feature is "waiting time" and "customer service", their sentiment scores become −9, and −12. At this time, the order of preference features and the sentiment score changes, which indicates that the importance of the preference features to the user changes.

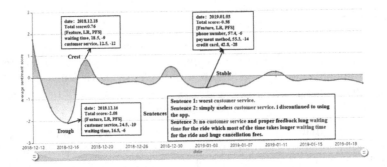

Fig. 3. Sentiment-preference features mapping along time dimension of Uber

Furthermore, OSPAci also can dynamically locate the specific review sentences in which these preference features are located. As show in Fig. 3, in the trough, the sentence in which the user's preference feature is located can be displayed in real time by clicking on the feature on the page. This can ensure that the developer can track the user's true intention timely and precisely.

4   Conclusion and Future Work

Timely and effectively detecting user's sentiment tendency and preference is crucial for app providers in terms of mobile app's maintenance and evolution and make it competitive. We propose OSPAci, a novel framework for automatically detect user's sentiment and preference from user reviews timely and precisely. In the future, we will refine OSPAci such as considering topic clustering model to achieve higher-dimensional feature topic and make OSPAci to be a real useful tool applied to the industry field.

Acknowledgements. This work is supported by the National Key R&D Program of China grant No. 2017YFB1401201, the National Natural Science Foundation of China grant No. 61572350, the National Natural Science Key Foundation of China grant No. 61832014 and the Shenzhen Science and Technology Foundation (JCYJ20170816093943197).

References

1. Nguyen, T.-S., Lauw, H.W., Tsaparas, P.: Review synthesis for micro-review summarization. In: Proceedings of the Eighth ACM International Conference on Web Search and Data Mining, pp. 169–178. ACM (2015)
2. Di Sorbo, A., et al.: What would users change in my app? Summarizing app reviews for recommending software changes. In: Proceedings of the 2016 24th ACM SIGSOFT International Symposium on Foundations of Software Engineering, pp. 499–510. ACM (2016)

3. Gao, C., Zeng, J., Lyu, M.R., King, I.: Online app review analysis for identifying emerging issues. In: 2018 IEEE/ACM 40th International Conference on Software Engineering (ICSE), pp. 48–58. IEEE (2018)

4. Manning, C.D., Schütze, H.: Foundations of Statistical Natural Language Processing. MIT Press, Cambridge (1999)

5. Kucuktunc, O., Barla Cambazoglu, B., Weber, I., Ferhatosmanoglu, H.: A large-scale sentiment analysis for Yahoo! answers. In: Proceedings of the Fifth ACM International Conference on Web Search and Data Mining, pp. 633–642. ACM (2012)

ADS4all: Democratizing Authenticated Data Structures

Nasser Alzahrani[✉], Ibrhaim Khalil, and Xun Yi

RMIT University, Melbourne, Australia
s3297335@student.rmit.edu.au, {ibrahim.khalil,xun.yi}@rmit.edu.au

Abstract. Bitcoin and Merkle trees are instances of Authenticated data structures (ADS). Unfortunately, such ADS's are not widely used although they provide enormous security benefits for many distributed systems. This is because current tools and methods are not easy to use for system engineers. We present our ongoing work to create *ADS4all*, a framework that allows for the design and implementation of ADS's that are tailored to specific domains.

1 Introduction

ADS are data structures that allow an untrusted prover to provide the operations of these data structures which can be verified by some verifier to check its authenticity. For instance, ADS can be used to improve the security of some distributed systems such as the cloud. The client asks for an answer and the server provides the answer together with a proof that the client may be able to verify. If the proof doesn't verify, then the client has the evidence that the result is not authentic. Another example of ADS is that of a blockchain. It is helpful to think of blockchain as linked lists where the pointers are authenticated. Such linked lists are known as Merkle list.

It has always been the case that designing new ADS is not a straight forward procedure. The steps needed in order to design and implement a new ADS include inventing new authentication mechanism, then proving the correctness of the authentication, and finally, prove the correctness of the implementation. On the other hand, Bitcoin ADS can be modeled with our proposed framework *ADS4all* using Haskell programming language [21] as easily as:

```
type Ledger = Set
data Block = Genesis | Block (Auth Block) (Auth Transaction)
```

That is, a block in a blockchain is either Genesis (the first block) or it is recursive block of another block together with a transaction object. The ledger is represented by the *Set* data type. Furthermore, if for some reason the performance of *Set* turned out to be suboptimal, we can easily change the underlying data structure such as Red-black trees.

To mitigate the problems associated with inventing new ADS, Miller [15] introduced *LambdaAuth*, a programming language which includes a special syntax for creating ADS. This allows for easier development of new ADS's. However,

© Springer Nature Switzerland AG 2020
S. Yangui et al. (Eds.): ICSOC 2019 Workshops, LNCS 12019, pp. 280–286, 2020.
https://doi.org/10.1007/978-3-030-45989-5_24

one still has to create a new programming language and then try to convince people to use it which makes it difficult to have an impact. Therefore, we develop *ADS4all* based on the semantics of *LambdaAuth* using the Haskell programming language. ADS4all can also be developed for other programming languages provided that these languages have powerful type systems. The core of *ADS4all* is category-theoretic interfaces that allowed the interpretation of *LambdaAuth* denotational semantics.

The Haskell programming language [21] is used to implement *ADS4all* for the following reasons. First, Haskell is a functional language which is based on $\lambda - calculus$. This helps in the interpretation of *LambdaAuth* which is also based on $\lambda - calculus$. Secondly, Haskell has *higher-kinded* types which consequently makes the translation from category-theoretic interfaces to Haskell proceeds in a straightforward manner. Thirdly, Haskell is mainstream language and it has been widely used in many industrial and research applications. Haskell allows for equational reasoning which is crucial in proving the correctness of the implemented framework. The main contribution of this paper is that we present category-theoretic interfaces to interpret the semantics of *LambdaAuth* making it easy to use in main-stream langauges such as *Haskell*.

2   Authenticated Data Structures

ADS's are used in many applications. For instance, trustworthy duplication of data, GPG keyservers, Tor relay directories, Tahoe-LAFS mutable files, and many more other applications. Figure 1 shows one application of using ADS. The data can be mirrored across different servers reducing contention on the data. The client can communicate securely with untrusted servers since it has the root hash from the trusted server which can be used to verify responses from the untrusted servers.

One very well known example of ADS is that of Merkle trees [14]. Merkle trees are the bases for many distributed systems such as *peer to peer* networks and the Blockchain [18]. Other examples of ADS include: skip lists [9], authenticated graphs [10], Binary trees [17]. All of these versions of ADS had to be designed and implemented then proved to be correct from scratch for every single one of them. That is, there is no common framework that encompasses all of them under well defined interfaces. This shortcoming is due to the lack of a general model that can abstract the differences. This shortcoming was mitigated by *LambdaAuth* [15] based our work on to create *ADS4all*.

3   Framework: *ADS4all*

Category theory formalizes mathematical structures in terms of a labelled directed graph called a category, whose nodes are called objects, and whose labelled directed edges are called morphisms. In our work, we utilize Category-theoretic [4] interfaces to design our framework. More precisely, in our work, we design authenticated data structures generically using Monads and Kleisley category [4]. Monads are algebras that are equipped with certain operations obeying

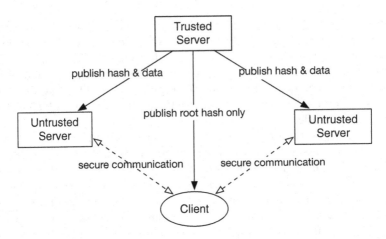

Fig. 1. A typical application of ADS: secure computation is distributed across the network. The trusted server can only be contacted when data has changed to get the updated root hash. This reduces the load on the central trusted server which consequently improves the performance of the network

some laws (the Monad laws). We assume some familiarity with the Monadic representation in programming languages such as Haskell. For more background material regarding monads and category theory in general, please refer to [4]. As a refresher, a Monad M is an endofunctor together with a unit operator, $return : a \to Ma$ and the *bind* operator, $(>>=) : Ma \to (a \to Mb) \to Mb$. In our framework we utilize two Monads, the Writer and the Reader Monads.

In *ADS4all*, the Writer Monad implements the Prover functionality. In Haskell Writer Monad is given by:

```
class (Monoid w, Monad m) => MonadWriter w m | m -> w
```

And the state monad implements the Verifier which verifies the proof produced by the server:

```
class Monad m => MonadState s m | m -> s
```

The *Writer* monad represents the computation at the server and *state* monad represents the computation at the client. This allows a system engineer codes up any supported data structure and tag where he/she wants the authentication to take place. The framework will then have two versions of the same code: one for the server and one for the client. Although they look exactly the same, the code is interpreted differently depending on the mode being either *Prover* (server) or *Verifier* (client). For instance, the following computation:

```
unauth (auth (auth 9)) >>= unauth
```

Authenticates the number 9, then authenticate the authentication itself. After that, one level of un-authentication takes place followed by another un-authentication. The use of auth and unauth vocabulary is to be consistent with the language of the semantics given by *LambdaAuth*. This code produces the following output at the server (prover):

```
(9, [String "0ade7c2cf97f75d009975f4d720d1fa6c19f4897",Number 9.0])
```

That is, it produces the number 9 together with the evidence that it has accumulated while traversing the tree structure. It is worth noting that the authentication of an authenticated value is only the hash. The code, however, has different interpretation and therefore different output at the client (verifier):

```
Just 9
```

That is, the client successfully was able to compute the result (9 in this case) based on the evidence-list that was returned by the server (*Just* is a type constructor for the *Maybe* type in *Haskell*). Had the evidence failed to verify, the computation would have returned *Nothing* value instead. *ADS4all* can be used to implement authenticated versions of skip-lists, binary search trees, red-black trees and others.

3.1 Examples of ADS Using *ADS4all*

Now we present some examples of increasing complexity. Example 1 also serve as a vehicle to understand how the same computation is interpreted differently depending on the mode.

Example 1. Authenticated one cell database The *Maybe* type in Haskell has two values constructors, *Nothing* and *Just a*. Therefore, it can be thought of as a one-element list where *Nothing* denotes empty list and *Just a* is the singleton list. The *Maybe* type in Haskell without the use of authentication is as follows:

```
data Maybe a = Nothing | Just a
```

The data declaration is how one introduces new algebraic data types in Haskell. The vertical bar is read 'or'. A value of type *Maybe a* either contains a value of type a (represented as Just a), or it is empty (represented as Nothing). Using Maybe is the default way to deal with failures or exceptions in Haskell. Modeling the Maybe type to be authenticated using *ADS4all* can be achieved using the following code:

```
data AuthMaybe a = Nothing | Just (Auth a)
```

Example 2. Merkle tree This ADS can be modeled in one line of code using *ADS4all*:

```
data Merkle a = Root | Bin (Auth Merkle a) a (Auth Merkle a)
```

This code states that a Merkle tree is either a root or binary of two authenticated Merkle sub-trees. One advantage of designing ADS's using *ADS4all* is that we can tag where we want the authentication to happen. For instance, we could have another authenticated version of Merkle trees simply by:

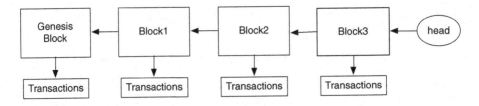

Fig. 2. Bitcoin ADS: every block holds on to a set of transactions

```
data Merkle a = Root | Bin (Merkle a) (Auth a) (Merkle a)
```

In this case, only the trees in *Bin* value are authenticated and not the sub-trees.

Example 3. Bitcoin in *ADS4all* Bitcoin is peer to peer system which uses a form of ADS to confirm authenticity of transaction over global ledger that contains the bitcoin transactions as shown in Fig. 2. Transactions remove or add coins and they are only valid if they spend existing coins and create new ones. Coins are associated with a quantity and a public key. Bitcoin can be written as follows:

```
type CoinsToRemove = Int
type CoinsToAdd = Int
type Ledger = Set

data Transaction = Tx [CoinsToRemove] [CoinsToAdd]
data Block = Genesis | Block (Auth Block) (Auth Transaction)
```

The first three lines are just type-synonyms. The first one models the spent coins in a transaction while the second one models coins to be added to the blockchain. The ledger is just a built-in *Set* type. A transaction is a data type that wraps the lists of *CoinsToRemove* and *CoinsToAdd*. Finally, a block is either *Genesis* (root block) or a recursive block containing authenticated blocks and authenticated transactions.

4   Related Work

One proposed solution for easily creating ADS is [15] which provides semantics for a programming language that supports ADS called *LambdaAuth*. However, as mentioned in this paper, one still has to create a new programming language and convince people to use it which is less likely to be widely spread among engineers and is difficult to have an impact. Our main contribution is Category-theoretic interfaces for ADS and therefore, creating a new language is not needed in any language that has a powerful type system. And even for languages that lack such powerful systems, we are investigating a solution to this problem (see Sect. 5).

Category theory has been used both to design and implement algorithms and frameworks in various domains. For example, [8] realises backprop algorithm (used to train Neural networks) as a Functor which leads to a generalization of the algorithm and as a consequence allows for applying Backpropagation algorithm in different settings. Another example where category theory inspired the design of a novel library is in [7] where the author describes the essence of automatic differentiation. His work involves creating correct by construction learning algorithms. He also showed that Backpropagation algorithm is just an instance of the general idea of AD which facilitates creating parallel learning algorithms. In [11], the author presents a category-theoretic (string diagrams) way to compose monads in programming. In [3], the author uses similar methods to compose electrical circuits. In previous work [2] and [1], we used CT as a formal specification for our proposed framework which was about combining some formal methods with property-based testing in software engineering.

5   Future Work

To reach a larger user base, we plan to implement *ADS4all* in main stream used languages that lack the needed expressiveness in their type systems. For example languages such as java, swift, kotlin and many others can implement *ADS4all* using [23]. ADS deals mainly with the issue of integrity and they have little to say about the issue of privacy. *Zero-Knowledge Proofs* can be used to help in the privacy of ADS. We plan to extend *ADS4all* to research private ADS's. In addition, for privacy-preserving smart contracts, *ADS4all* can be extended to implement frameworks similar to [12], [6] and [19].

6   Conclusions

In this paper, we presented our ongoing work on *ADS4all*, a framework that allows system engineers to easily create authenticated data structures such as Merkel trees, Bitcoin and other custom ones. Our work is based on *LambdaAuth* for which we provide monadic interfaces. We believe that such tools are important to the security of many systems that require them.

References

1. Alzahrani, N., Spichkova, M., Blech, J.O.: Spatio-temporal models for formal analysis and property-based testing. In: Milazzo, P., Varró, D., Wimmer, M. (eds.) STAF 2016. LNCS, vol. 9946, pp. 196–206. Springer, Cham (2016). https://doi.org/10.1007/978-3-319-50230-4_14
2. Alzahrani, N., Spichkova, M., Blech, J.O.: From temporal models to property-based testing. arXiv preprint arXiv:1705.10032 (2017)
3. Baez, J.C., Fong, B.: A compositional framework for passive linear networks. arXiv preprint arXiv:1504.05625 (2015)
4. Barr, M., Wells, C.: Category Theory for Computing Science, vol. 49. Prentice Hall, New York (1990)
5. Bove, A., Dybjer, P., Norell, U.: A brief overview of Agda – a functional language with dependent types. In: Berghofer, S., Nipkow, T., Urban, C., Wenzel, M. (eds.) TPHOLs 2009. LNCS, vol. 5674, pp. 73–78. Springer, Heidelberg (2009). https://doi.org/10.1007/978-3-642-03359-9_6

6. Bowe, S., Chiesa, A., Green, M., Miers, I., Mishra, P., Wu, H.: ZEXE: enabling decentralized private computation. IACR ePrint 962 (2018)

7. Elliott, C.: The simple essence of automatic differentiation. In: Proceedings of the ACM on Programming Languages 2(ICFP), 70 (2018)

8. Fong, B., Spivak, D.I., Tuyéras, R.: Backprop as functor: a compositional perspective on supervised learning. arXiv preprint arXiv:1711.10455 (2017)

9. Goodrich, M.T., Papamanthou, C., Tamassia, R.: On the cost of persistence and authentication in skip lists. In: Demetrescu, C. (ed.) WEA 2007. LNCS, vol. 4525, pp. 94–107. Springer, Heidelberg (2007). https://doi.org/10.1007/978-3-540-72845-0_8

10. Goodrich, M.T., Tamassia, R., Triandopoulos, N.: Efficient authenticated data structures for graph connectivity and geometric search problems. Algorithmica 60(3), 505–552 (2011)

11. Hinze, R., Marsden, D.: Equational reasoning with lollipops, forks, cups, caps, snakes, and speedometers. J. Log. Algebr. Methods Program. 85(5), 931–951 (2016)

12. Kosba, A., Miller, A., Shi, E., Wen, Z., Papamanthou, C.: Hawk: the blockchain model of cryptography and privacy-preserving smart contracts. In: 2016 IEEE Symposium on Security and Privacy (SP), pp. 839–858. IEEE (2016)

13. Leroy, X., Doligez, D., Frisch, A., Garrigue, J., Rémy, D., Vouillon, J.: The OCaml system release 4.02. Institut National de Recherche en Informatique et en Automatique 54 (2014)

14. Merkle, R.C.: A digital signature based on a conventional encryption function. In: Pomerance, C. (ed.) CRYPTO 1987. LNCS, vol. 293, pp. 369–378. Springer, Heidelberg (1988). https://doi.org/10.1007/3-540-48184-2_32

15. Miller, A., Hicks, M., Katz, J., Shi, E.: Authenticated data structures, generically. ACM SIGPLAN Notices 49(1), 411–423 (2014)

16. Moggi, E.: Notions of computation and monads. Inf. Comput. 93(1), 55–92 (1991)

17. Mykletun, E., Narasimha, M., Tsudik, G.: Authentication and integrity in outsourced databases. ACM Trans. Storage (TOS) 2(2), 107–138 (2006)

18. Nakamoto, S., et al.: Bitcoin: A Peer-to-Peer Electronic Cash System (2008)

19. Sasson, E.B., et al.: Zerocash: decentralized anonymous payments from bitcoin. In: 2014 IEEE Symposium on Security and Privacy, pp. 459–474. IEEE (2014)

20. Sørensen, M.H., Urzyczyn, P.: Lectures on the Curry-Howard Isomorphism, vol. 149. Elsevier, Amsterdam (2006)

21. Thompson, S.: Haskell: The Craft of Functional Programming, vol. 2. Addison-Wesley, Boston (2011)

22. Wadler, P.: Monads for functional programming. In: Jeuring, J., Meijer, E. (eds.) AFP 1995. LNCS, vol. 925, pp. 24–52. Springer, Heidelberg (1995). https://doi.org/10.1007/3-540-59451-5_2

23. Yallop, J., White, L.: Lightweight higher-kinded polymorphism. In: Codish, M., Sumii, E. (eds.) FLOPS 2014. LNCS, vol. 8475, pp. 119–135. Springer, Cham (2014). https://doi.org/10.1007/978-3-319-07151-0_8

Demonstrations

ProMoEE - A Lightweight Web Editor Supporting Study Research on Process Models

Michael Winter$^{(\boxtimes)}$ (iD), Rüdiger Pryss (iD), and Manfred Reichert (iD)

Institute of Databases and Information Systems, Ulm University, Ulm, Germany
{michael.winter,ruediger.pryss,manfred.reichert}@uni-ulm.de

Abstract. Process models are not only used for the sole documentation of the numerous processes in an organization. Among others, they are essential artifacts in the context of service-oriented computing. Hence, high quality process models are the enabler for streamlining, prediction, and automation in many fields (e.g., industrial production). Therefore, a proper and effective comprehension of process models and knowledge about factors influencing the creation of such models constitutes a key criterion for this endeavor. The collection and analysis of data in scientific studies help to understand the objective and subjective factors influencing process model creation and comprehension. This work presents an editor for the definition, execution, and analysis of studies in the context of process model creation and comprehension. The editor features a clean design and allows for a fast implementation for conducting and reporting study research, while ensuring the collection of high-quality data.

Keywords: Study research · Experimental web editor · Process models

1 Introduction

Graphical workflows (i.e., process models) are key artifacts for the descriptive representation of business tasks, logistical steps, or sophisticated algorithms. For instance, as a centerpiece of the Business Process Management (BPM) domain [7], it must be ensured that business process models are created and comprehended in such a way that practitioners can apply them correctly for their purposes. Moreover, in the context of service-orientation, process models integrate a multitude of essential functions, such as the definition of service mechanisms, allocation of responsibilities, and the formulation of effective routines [2]. Research on process models has unraveled numerous factors that influence the creation of process models as well as factors fostering model comprehension [3]. However, there are still many not known or not adequately known factors (e.g., especially from a cognitive point of view) influencing the process model creation as well as the comprehension. Consequently, it poses a challenge to bring those factors into the light. One promising approach for coping with this challenge is

© Springer Nature Switzerland AG 2020
S. Yangui et al. (Eds.): ICSOC 2019 Workshops, LNCS 12019, pp. 289–293, 2020.
https://doi.org/10.1007/978-3-030-45989-5_25

to conduct studies in order to develop a deeper understanding of the essential factors in this context [9]. Following this, the work at hand presents the Process Modeling Experimental Editor (ProMoEE)[1]. ProMoEE is a lightweight web editor enabling academics as well as professionals to get a swift, intuitive, and clean way to conduct studies aiming at process model creation and comprehension. In the long term, ProMoEE shall improve our general understanding of working with process models in different domains (e.g., service-orientation).

The structure of this paper is as follows: Sect. 2 introduces ProMoEE. In Sect. 3, related work is discussed and, finally, Sect. 4 summarizes the paper.

2 Process Modeling Experimental Editor

The emphasis of the Process Modeling Experimental Editor (ProMoEE) is to foster study research on the creation as well as comprehension of process models. Thereby, the editor supports the following three mandatory stages in study research, i.e., *Definition* ①, *Execution* ②, and *Analysis* ③.

Regarding *Definition* ①, Fig. 1 presents the graphical user interface for the definition of a study in ProMoEE. Thereby, the editor relies on the concept of questionnaires. More specifically, a study and its progression are defined in a structure known from questionnaires (see Fig. 1(A)). Thereby, each questionnaire contains an unique key to identify the correct study. A questionnaire has at least one page (see Fig. 1(B)) and a page can be defined with the following types: *Question, Comprehension,* and *Creation.* In the *Question* section (see Fig. 1(C)), questions (e.g., demographics) can be created with different response options (e.g., text field, single-/multi-choice). In the *Comprehension* section (see Fig. 1(D)), a predefined process model expressed in terms of the Business Process Model and Notation (BPMN) 2.0 is provided in order to evaluate the aspects of process model comprehension [5]. Therefore, specific questions emphasizing model comprehension can be created to the user's need. Finally, in the *Creation* section, an environment is provided that allows for the creation of process models in BPMN 2.0. In addition, a predefined process model can be specified in the environment as well, which can be then adapted.

Regarding *Execution* ②, to participate in a study, the unique key defined in *Definition* ① must be entered in the start screen. Here, as a major advantage, ProMoEE can be accessed via web browser from anywhere with any computer device (e.g., laptop, tablet). After entering the unique key, study participants complete the study based on the defined questionnaire structure in *Definition* ①. Thereby, questions types like *mandatory* or *restricted* (e.g., integers only) ensure that there are no missing or inconsistent values. Moreover, participants are able to scroll (e.g., back) between the pages and, in case the study is canceled very early, no data will be stored. At the end, participants are able to leave feedback.

In *Analysis* ③, the originator of a study is able to analyze the obtained data with a set of empirical and statistical methods. Therefore, all types of

---

[1] Demonstration video of ProMoEE: https://tinyurl.com/y2hbvm99.

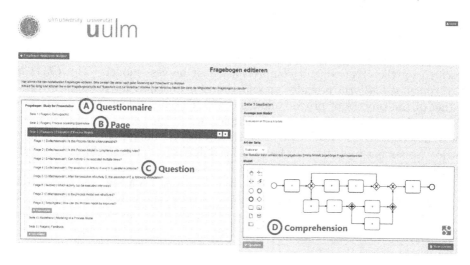

Fig. 1. Definition of a study in ProMoEE

different data (e.g., timestamps) are stored in a database during the execution of a study. In a specific analysis view, ProMoEE allows for a fine-grained analysis; the obtained answers can be aggregated as well as visualized with different techniques (e.g., pie chart). Moreover, on the created or comprehended process models, numerous quantitative metrics as well as customized process model inspectors (e.g., syntactical compliance, semantic completeness) can be applied. In addition, ProMoEE offers an export of data in an Excel file. Therefore, the editor generates an adapted file (e.g., colored separation) for further usage in other applications (e.g., SPSS). Finally, ProMoEE includes an identity and access management, in which three different account types can be utilized (i.e., *Admin* Ⓐ, *User* Ⓑ, and *Participant* Ⓒ).

Altogether, ProMoEE supports research in the definition, execution, and analysis of studies in the context of process model creation as well as comprehension. The editor provides a standardized and intuitive procedure for study research to support academics or professionals in this context. For example, ProMoEE mitigates threats towards data validity and pursues the collection of high-quality data. Further, ProMoEE can be accessed with any computer device (e.g., smartphone), only by the use of a web browser. Due to the use of latest technologies (i.e., backend is implemented with PHP, frontend is implemented using current web technologies), ProMoEE can be enriched with additional features. Finally, the lightweight characteristics of ProMoEE allow for a fast and clean implementation as well as execution of studies. Generally, ProMoEE might be applied in various studies to gain a better understanding of working with process models.

3   Related Work

Various tools exist for the implementation of studies that can be employed for research on the creation and comprehension of process models. The *Cheetah Experimental Platform* provides an experimental workflow for research investigating of the process of process modeling [6]. The authors in [8] demonstrate a powerful configurator for designing studies, which, in turn, may also be used for similar settings as ProMoEE. [1] presents a highly configurable smart mobile device assessment tool that can be used for different visual tasks in the context of process model comprehension. The application in [4] offers similar features for collecting and sharing data from surveys. Summarizing, ProMoEE was developed for empirical research in the domain of BPM to study especially cognitive aspects (e.g., decision-making) and, hence, none of the discussed approaches combines such functionality with lightweight characteristics like ProMoEE does.

4   Summary and Outlook

This paper presented the Process Modeling Experimental Editor (ProMoEE) empowering researchers to define, execute, and analyze studies in the context of process model creation as well as comprehension in an intuitive, clean, and fast manner. Thus, the insights obtained with ProMoEE may be used, inter alia, to improve the business processes of an organization. Currently, ProMoEE is used in different studies in order to evaluate user acceptance, usability, and performance, especially in large-scale studies. Furthermore, ProMoEE is used in various studies in the context of a conceptual framework to foster process model comprehension from a cognitive viewpoint [10]. In future, ProMoEE will be enriched with additional features (e.g., multi-process notation support), metrics, and statistical methods (e.g., significance tests) to increase its applicability.

References

1. Andrews, K., et al.: A smart mobile assessment tool for collecting data in large-scale educational studies. In: 15th International Conference on MobiSPC 2018, pp. 67–74 (2018)
2. Deng, S., et al.: Computation offloading for service workflow in mobile cloud computing. IEEE Trans. Parallel Distrib. Syst. **26**(12), 3317–3329 (2014)
3. Figl, K.: Comprehension of procedural visual business process models - a literature review. Bus. Inf. Syst. Eng. **59**(1), 41–67 (2017)
4. Google: Google Forms (2019). https://www.google.com/forms/about. Accessed 27 Sept 2019
5. OMG: Object Management Group Specification. Business Process Model & Notation 2.0 (2019). https://www.bpmn.org. Accessed 20 Sept 2019
6. Pinggera, J., et al.: Investigating the process of process modeling with cheetah experimental platform. In: 1st International Workshop on ER-POIS 2010, pp. 13–18 (2010)

7. Rosemann, M., vom Brocke, J.: The six core elements of business process management. In: vom Brocke, J., Rosemann, M. (eds.) Handbook on Business Process Management 1. IHIS, pp. 105–122. Springer, Heidelberg (2015). https://doi.org/10.1007/978-3-642-45100-3_5

8. Schobel, J., et al.: A configurator component for end-user defined mobile data collection processes. In: 14th International Conference on ICSOC 2016, pp. 216–219 (2016)

9. Tallon, M., et al.: Comprehension of business process models: insight into cognitive strategies via eye tracking. Expert Syst. Appl. **136**, 145–158 (2019)

10. Zimoch, M., Pryss, R., Probst, T., Schlee, W., Reichert, M.: Cognitive insights into business process model comprehension: preliminary results for experienced and inexperienced individuals. In: Reinhartz-Berger, I., Gulden, J., Nurcan, S., Guédria, W., Bera, P. (eds.) BPMDS/EMMSAD -2017. LNBIP, vol. 287, pp. 137–152. Springer, Cham (2017). https://doi.org/10.1007/978-3-319-59466-8_9

The EDMM Modeling and Transformation System

Michael Wurster[1]($\boxtimes$), Uwe Breitenbücher[1], Antonio Brogi[2], Ghareeb Falazi[1],
Lukas Harzenetter[1], Frank Leymann[1], Jacopo Soldani[2],
and Vladimir Yussupov[1]

[1] Institute of Architecture of Application Systems,
University of Stuttgart, Stuttgart, Germany
{wurster,breitenbuecher,falazi,harzenetter,leymann,
yussupov}@iaas.uni-stuttgart.de
[2] Department of Computer Science, University of Pisa, Pisa, Italy
{brogi,soldani}@di.unipi.it

Abstract. Since deployment automation technologies are heterogeneous regarding their supported features and modeling languages, selecting a concrete technology is difficult and can result in a lock-in. Therefore, we presented the Essential Deployment Metamodel (EDMM) in previous work that abstracts from concrete technologies and provides a normalized metamodel for creating technology-independent deployment models. In this demonstration, we present tool support for EDMM in the form of the EDMM Modeling and Transformation System, which enables (i) creating EDMM models graphically and (ii) automatically transforming them into models supported by concrete deployment automation technologies.

Keywords: Deployment modeling · Automation · Transformation · Tool

1 Motivation: The Deployment Technology Lock-In

An integral aspect of efficient application deployment processes is that they must be highly automated: Manually deploying applications consisting of multiple components is complex, time-consuming, error-prone, and, moreover, requires immense technical expertise to execute the technical deployment tasks. Therefore, several *deployment automation technologies* have been developed in the past years that are actively used by industry and research. Deployment technologies are usually offered as a software system or service that can deploy applications fully automatically by processing so-called *deployment models*. Deployment models can be categorized into two types: (i) imperative models and (ii) declarative models [1]. The main idea of imperative models is to describe a detailed, executable process specifying all necessary technical tasks to be executed, their implementations, and their order. In contrast, declarative models only describe

S. Yangui et al. (Eds.): ICSOC 2019 Workshops, LNCS 12019, pp. 294–298, 2020.
https://doi.org/10.1007/978-3-030-45989-5_26

the components to be deployed, their configurations, and the relations between them, but hardly provide technical execution details. Declarative models, hence, need to be interpreted by a deployment automation technology that derives the technical deployment instructions while an imperative model can be directly executed as-is. Since our previous work [3] has shown that 13 of the most important deployment technologies are either declarative by nature or support declarative deployment modeling, we focus on declarative deployment models in this work.

However, the available deployment technologies are heterogeneous regarding their features and supported modeling languages. Thus, deciding for a specific technology quickly results in a *Deployment Technology Lock-In*, which means that it is hard to exchange the technology later. The main reasons for this lock-in result from (i) the deep technical expertise that needs to be acquired to work with such a technology and (ii) the need to rewrite all deployment models that are currently in use. Therefore, we introduced the *Essential Deployment Meta-model (EDMM)* in previous work [3], which abstracts from concrete technologies and provides a normalized metamodel that only supports commonalities of the 13 most important technologies. Thereby, it enables to create *deployment technology-agnostic EDMM models* that can be translated into each of the 13 technologies following the translation guidelines we presented in Wurster et al. [3]. However, this translation is currently a manual, time-consuming, and error-prone approach.

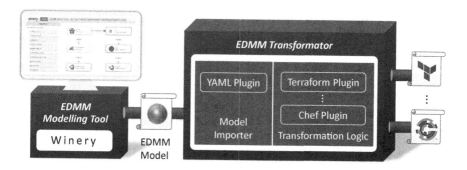

Fig. 1. EDMM modeling and transformation system architecture.

2   The EDMM Modeling and Transformation System

To tackle this issue, in this demonstration, we present the *EDMM Modeling and Transformation System* shown in Fig. 1, which consists of (i) the *EDMM Modeling Tool* and (ii) the *EDMM Transformation Framework*. Using the EDMM Modeling Tool, a user is able to graphically model the deployment of an application in the form of an EDMM model that describes the components to be deployed, their configurations, their implementations, and their relations. The resulting EDMM model is independent of concrete deployment technologies and can be exported as a file. This EDMM model file can be fed into the EDMM Transformation Framework, which offers a command-line interface (CLI) that can be either used directly by the user or integrated into any automation work-flow. Using the CLI, the desired target deployment technology in which the EDMM model should be transformed can be selected. The output is an exe-cutable, technology-specific deployment model, which can be executed using the selected technology. Our prototype[1], as well as a video demonstrating the sys-tem, are available on GitHub.

EDMM Modeling Tool

The EDMM Modeling Tool has been developed by extending Eclipse Winery [2], which is a web-based environment to graphically model TOSCA-based applica-tion topologies. It includes (i) a *back-end* to manage component and relation types, their properties, and artifacts and (ii) a *Topology Modeler* that enables to graphically compose application components and specify configuration proper-ties. Since EDMM can be mapped to TOSCA [3], Winery has been extended by providing an export plugin to transform its internal TOSCA-based data model to the YAML format defined by EDMM. The EDMM export functionality was developed for the Java back-end and is merged to Winery's official *master* branch. Further, an administration component in the Angular user-interface has been added to specify custom type mappings between the maintained TOSCA node types and the built-in EDMM types. The Topology Modeler itself did not need an extension as we fully rely on Winery's internal data model during modeling.

EDMM Transformation Framework

The EDMM Transformation Framework provides a CLI for transforming EDMM models into technology-specific deployment models. At this stage, the framework supports YAML files as input according to the published EDMM YAML spec-ification[2]. All components, as well as their component types, must be provided in a single EDMM model file at the time of writing.

We designed the framework to employ a plugin architecture that supports integrating various deployment technologies in an extensible and pluggable way. Each plugin defines an identifier and a corresponding display name, e.g., the "kubernetes" plugin is implemented to transform EDMM-based models into "Kubernetes" resource files. The transformation can be started by using the `transform` command of the CLI: The user has to specify the EDMM model file and the identifier of the target deployment technology. For the framework, we use Java with Spring and Spring Boot to build the CLI as well as to load the plugins dynamically once they are registered in a configuration file. Each

---

[1] https://github.com/UST-EDMM/transformation-framework.
[2] https://github.com/UST-EDMM/spec-yaml.

plugin must implement a `transform()` method to execute the required transformation logic. Further, a plugin may implement different lifecycle methods: (i) `checkModel()` to indicate whether a model can be transformed by a plugin, (ii) `prepare()` to execute preparation activities prior to the transformation, e.g., download external files, and (iii) `cleanup()` to execute clean up activities after the transformation.

The internal data model of the EDMM Transformation Framework is based on and represented as a graph using the Java library JGraphT. By employing a graph, also for the reason that the component structure in an EDMM-based model naturally forms a graph, the plugins are able to efficiently traverse the data model to apply the respective transformation logic. Plugins may apply arbitrary graph algorithms, e.g., topological sorting of components to traverse the graph in a certain way. Further, this also enables to make use of the visitor pattern to add or extend new plugin logic without modifying the graph structure.

Developed Plugins and Supported Component Types

Currently, the framework supports all 13 deployment technologies which were systematically selected and reviewed by Wurster et al. [3]. Details of the plugins' implementations and the transformation rules can be found in the documentation. Please note: In this demonstration, we only focus on deployments that are based on virtual compute resources, i.e., operating systems, virtual machines, or containers, and on the software that needs to be deployed on them including their configuration and orchestration[3]. Therefore, we introduce a couple of built-in EDMM component types as modeling baseline. The base of all supported deployments is represented by the *Compute* component type that permits modeling a virtual compute resource, which can be then transformed by a plugin into a virtual machine or container, respectively, depending on the target technology's capabilities. For example, a Compute component gets transformed into a virtual machine for OpenStack Heat, while it is transformed into a container for Kubernetes. We also defined several software component types that can be installed on Compute components, e.g., a MySQL database. To install such components, either the plugin (i) contains built-in logic to translate a certain component type into the corresponding modeling element in the target model or (ii) it uses *EDMM Operations*, which provide generic plug-points in EDMM models to specify installation scripts for components that can be injected into the target model by the plugin. Also, the orchestration of components is supported, e.g., to connect an application to its database (possibly hosted on different Compute components), plugins inject the properties of the target component, e.g., IP address, as environment variable into the source component, which enables using them, for example, in installation scripts. In future work, we plan to extend the plugins for other types of components, e.g., PaaS, FaaS, and other Cloud services.

---

[3] An example that is supported by all developed plugins can be found here: https://github.com/UST-EDMM/getting-started.

Acknowledgments. This work is partially funded by the European Union's Horizon 2020 research and innovation project *RADON* (825040), the DFG project *SustainLife* (379522012), and the projects *AMaCA* (POR-FSE) and *DECLware* (University of Pisa, PRA_2018_66).

References

1. Endres, C., et al.: Declarative vs. imperative: two modeling patterns for the automated deployment of applications. In: Proceedings of the 9th International Conference on Pervasive Patterns and Applications. Xpert Publishing Services (2017)
2. Kopp, O., Binz, T., Breitenbücher, U., Leymann, F.: Winery – a modeling tool for TOSCA-based cloud applications. In: Basu, S., Pautasso, C., Zhang, L., Fu, X. (eds.) ICSOC 2013. LNCS, vol. 8274, pp. 700–704. Springer, Heidelberg (2013). https://doi.org/10.1007/978-3-642-45005-1_64
3. Wurster, M., et al.: The essential deployment metamodel: a systematic review of deployment automation technologies. SICS Softw.-Inensiv. Cyber-Phys (2019). https://doi.org/10.1007/s00450-019-00412-x

BlockMeds: A Blockchain-Based Online Prescription System with Privacy Protection

Minhua He, Xu Han, Frank Jiang$^{(\boxtimes)}$, Rongbai Zhang, Xingzi Liu, and Xiao Liu

School of Information Technology, Centre for Cyber Security Research and Innovation (CSRI), Deakin University, Geelong, Australia
{frank.jiang,xiao.liu}@deakin.edu.au

Abstract. Since the authentication of digital prescription is a lengthy and error-prone process by pharmacy employees, nowadays in many countries around the world, the paper-based prescription is still the only valid document for patients to purchase their prescribed medication from a pharmacy. Moreover, as a prescription can contain a lot of private information about the patients and their illness, the security and privacy issues in using digital prescription also raise big concerns. Recently, Blockchain has been widely regarded as a promising technology to secure online business data and transactions. In this paper, we present BlockMeds, a Blockchain based online prescription system which enables the authentication of digital prescriptions. Meanwhile, to address the privacy issue during the authentication and transaction for buying the medication, a privacy protection strategy is also implemented in the system. BlockMeds provides the proof of concept for a Blockchain based online prescription system. It also demonstrates the need for privacy protection which is often overlooked in a Blockchain-based system. BlockMeds can be used as a prototype system by both researchers and industrial practitioners who are interested in Blockchain-based medical service systems.

Keywords: Blockchain · Online prescription system · Privacy protection · Medical service

1 Introduction

Nowadays, despite the wide popularity of online shopping, paper-based prescriptions are still required to buy prescribed medication from a pharmacy. Digital prescriptions (namely prescriptions in an electronic file format such as jpg, pdf and html) cannot be used directly. For example, Chemist Warehouse[1] offers online shopping for prescribed medication. However, customers will still need to send their original prescriptions in the mail after purchase. In some places, digital prescriptions can be used in emergency

---

[1] https://www.chemistwarehouse.com.au/prescriptions.

S. Yangui et al. (Eds.): ICSOC 2019 Workshops, LNCS 12019, pp. 299–303, 2020.
https://doi.org/10.1007/978-3-030-45989-5_27

supply of medicines, but a pharmacist may provide only up to three days' emergency supply under government regulations[2]. Clearly, digital prescriptions can only be used in very limited occasions. One of the critical challenges for replacing paper-based prescriptions is that the authentication of digital prescriptions is very difficult by pharmacy employees. In addition, it is difficult to change the remaining amount of medications on a digital prescription for repeated prescriptions if there is no online system to manage these digital documents.

Blockchain is an emerging technology that suits the decentralized application environment with the need of the distributed consensus [1]. Blockchains have been adopted or considered by various industries. The main driving force of using Blockchains in these applications is the introduction of digital identification, distributed security, intelligent contracts and micro metrology through the distributed Blockchain ledger [2, 3]. Under the protection of Blockchain technology, data cannot be easily tampered by attackers. Such an encryption feature can enable multiple service providers to jointly maintain the same user account information. A user only needs to maintain the account information on the ledger to complete all the identity authentication on different services, which can bring more efficiency.

Even though a Blockchain based system can theoretically ensure the security of the online business data and transactions, there still exists the risk for privacy information leakage. For example, during the process for authentication of digital descriptions and the purchase of medications in the pharmacy, information about the patients and their illness can be breached if no privacy protection strategy is in place. Therefore, it is very important to enhance the Blockchain based systems with privacy protection.

In this paper, we present BlockMeds which is a Blockchain based online prescription system with the privacy protection. BlockMeds provides the proof of concept for a Blockchain based online prescription system which can provide the secured storage, authentication and access of online prescriptions. In addition, to ensure the privacy protection during the transactions for purchasing prescribed medications, a data anonymisation algorithm is implemented and running on the servers of participating pharmacies. BlockMeds can be used as a prototype system by both researchers and practitioners who have the endeavour in Blockchain based medical service systems.

2   BlockMeds

In this section, we introduce the detailed business process for **BlockMeds**[3], its Blockchain architecture and key services. In our work, we assume BlockMeds is used by a hospital of a medium size city and hundreds of participating pharmacies. The business process for a typical blockchain based online prescription system is depicted in Fig. 1, specifically it consists of three major stakeholders - hospitals, pharmacy stores and online pharmacies.

---

[2] https://ww2.health.wa.gov.au/Articles/A_E/Emergency-supply-of-medicines.

[3] https://youtu.be/jtCS33S6pQA .

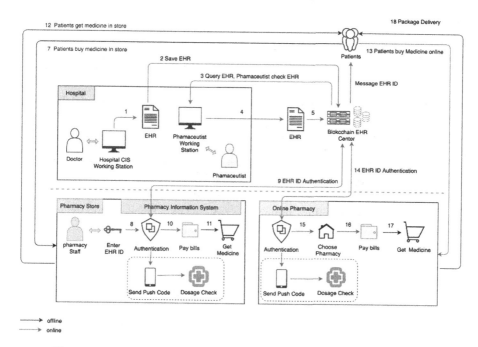

Fig. 1. The business process of a blockchain based online prescription system

In the Hospital: all EHRs (Electronic Health Records) are stored in the Blockchain EHR centre. Firstly, a doctor creates or edits an EHR with the prescription details and then send it to a pharmacist for approval. Once the request is received, the pharmacist approves or rejects the prescriptions and save the results back to the Blockchain EHR centre. Once it is approved, the patient will obtain the EHR id with a link to the digital prescription via a mobile message which will be used later to buy their prescribed medications in store or online.

In a Pharmacy Store: a staff of a participating pharmacy enters the EHR id provided by the patient. To authenticate the prescription and his/her identity, push codes will be sent to both the pharmacy information system and the patient's mobile phone. If these two push codes match, the details of the digital prescription will be shown in the pharmacy information system. The patient can buy the medications within the valid dosage listed on the prescription. Once the payment is confirmed, the amount of available dosage will be updated in the prescription and save back to the Blockchain.

In the Online Pharmacy: the patient enters the EHR id. For authentication, a push code will be sent to the patient's mobile phone. Once the push code is verified, the details of the digital prescription will be shown in the online shopping cart. After the valid amount of dosage is selected and the payment is confirmed, the digital prescription will be updated and saved back to the Blockchain.

It should be noted that as a common business requirement, for every successful purchase using the digital prescription, the transaction information including the patient's personal information and the purchased medications will be stored in the database of the participating pharmacies. Therefore, there is a serious risk for privacy breaches. To address this problem, we enforce all participating pharmacies to run a privacy protection algorithm in their database server. For proof-of-concept purpose, we employ Datafly which is a greedy heuristic algorithm providing anonymity to medical data that satisfies k-anonymity [5, 6]. We assume that in the pharmacy database, for each transaction record, there are 8 attributes including 2 key attributes named *EHR ID, NAME*, 2 quasi identifiers which are *AGE, GENDER* and 4 sensitive attributes which are *PRODUCT_NAME, PRICE, QUANTITY* and *TRANSACTION_DATE*. For each key attribute and Quasi Identifier attribute, they are specified by a corresponding Domain Generalization Hierarchy (DGH), which is used to generalize the attribute values. With Datafly, the values of the key attributes and the *GENDER* attribute are replaced by '*'. The values of the quasi identifier attribute are replaced by a broader category while the sensitive attributes remain public.

The architecture of BlockMeds is depicted in Fig. 2. BlockMeds is implemented using the IBM hyperledger fabric framework [4] and we use the embedded functions of channel controls to manage the information confidentiality within different organizations. Figure 2 depicts the architecture of the Blockchain system with three parts (i.e., part1, part2 and part3) and the details about the peers in the public and private channel (part4 and part5). The Blockchain EHR centre subsystem consists of three types of peers: (1) the order peers which are responsible for the distribution of messages to other nodes; (2) the private peers of the hospital which can only be accessed internally. These peers contain private patient and medical information which can only be accessed by doctors and pharmacists in the hospital; (3) the public peers of the hospital which can be accessed by external pharmacies. These peers facilitate the authentication of digital prescriptions and update the amount of dosage after purchase.

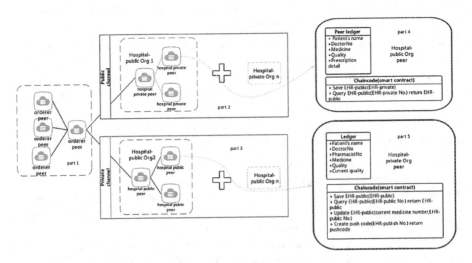

Fig. 2. The architecture of a blockchain based online prescription system.

The management of digital prescriptions in the hospital is implemented by the smart contracts of the private peers. The smart contract is an agreement within the different stakeholders. Specifically, the public peers of the hospital conduct the authentication of digital prescriptions and update the amount of purchased dosage for each transaction. The smart contract can verify the EHR id and send the push code to both pharmacies and patients for the identity verification. The smart contract will check for the valid amount of dosage before transaction and update the remained amount of dosage on the digital prescriptions after each successful transaction.

3   Discussion

BlockMeds provides an extensible platform for the research of Blockchain based e-health systems. Two of the immediate research directions which we are planning to investigate based on BlockMeds include:

(1) The scalability issue of the blockchain based e-health system. In the current demo, we only include one hospital with two roles (doctor and pharmacist) and some participating pharmacies. However, the target for BlockMeds is to serve as a city-level online prescription system. In the future, we are planning to include more hospitals and their specific departments, and much more participating pharmacies. In such a case, the scalability of BlockMeds will become a challenging issue. To address this issue, we are investigating the hyperledger fabric's capabilities in handling large volumes of requests.

(2) The privacy preserved medical data sharing and mining. Prescription is one of the most important type of EHRs. Participating hospitals of BlockMeds can share the prescriptions and other associated EHRs for medical data mining purpose. In such a case, the ability of privacy preservation will become a challenging issue. To address this issue, we are investigating and implementing more advanced privacy preservation strategies in BlockMeds such as Differential Privacy and Federated Learning.

References

1. Panarello, A., Tapas, N., Merlino, G., Longo, F., Puliafito, A.J.S.: Blockchain and IoT integration: a systematic survey. Sensors (Basel) **18**(8), 2575 (2018). https://doi.org/10.3390/s18082575
2. Singh, R., Singh, J., Singh, R.: TBSD: a defend against sybil attack in wireless sensor networks. Int. J. Comput. Sci. Netw. Secur. **16**(11), 90–99 (2016)
3. Casadei, R., Fortino, G., Pianini, D., Russo, W., Savaglio, C., Viroli, M.: A development approach for collective opportunistic edge-of-things services. Inf. Sci. **498**, 154–169 (2019)
4. IBM Hyperledger. https://www.ibm.com/blockchain/hyperledger. Accessed 3 Mar 2019
5. Gao, Y., Luo, T., Li, J., Wang, C.: Research on K anonymity algorithm based on association analysis of data utility. In: 2017 IEEE 2nd Advanced Information Technology, Electronic Automation Control Conference (IAEAC) (2017). https://doi.org/10.1109/IAEAC.2017.8054050
6. Vierti, A.: Python Datafly. https://github.com/alessiovierti/python-datafly. Accessed 21 Mar 2019

Janus: A Tool to Modernize Legacy Applications to Containers

Hoang Ho[1], Daniel Gordon[2], Anup Kalia[3(✉)], Jin Xiao[3], and Maja Vukovic[3]

[1] University of Massachusetts, Amherst, MA, USA
[2] University of the West Indies, St. Augustine, Trinidad and Tobago
[3] IBM T.J. Watson, Yorktown Heights, New York, USA
anup.kalia@ibm.com

Abstract. Modernizing a legacy application to a set of containers is highly desirable as containers are agile, scalable, and can be easily tested and deployed on any cloud environment. In this paper, we propose Janus, a modernization tool that helps architects and developers to transform a legacy application into a set of containers. Janus realizes two capabilities: one, it automatically discovers configurations and dependencies needed to create docker artifacts, with prior rules and knowledge mined from similar legacy applications; two, it provides a dynamic web interface to interact with architect/developer to verify the discovered configurations and dependencies and guide users in acquiring missing information. We provide a demonstration of Janus on a legacy application.

1 Introduction

Containers offer a logical packaging mechanism with which applications can be abstracted from the running environment. This decoupling allows container-based applications to be deployed more easily and consistently, on top of many hosting environment including on the Cloud infrastructure. This degree of agility and scalability is much sought after by today's enterprise IT who have significant portions of their applications running on J2EE, .NET, and COBOL. There is an ongoing effort in the industry to modernize these legacy applications to containers such that they can be deployed onto the Cloud. However, much of the existing effort relies on manual work. Often times, the lack of prior updated business or implementation documents about the applications makes the task even more difficult.

To help scale up the modernization activities, we propose Janus. Janus provides a process that has three phases: *discovery, validation,* and *generation.*

In the *discovery* phase, Janus discovers an application's configurations and dependencies and extracts them based on an existing knowledge base and rules. Manually, this task is quite difficult and time consuming, taking days to weeks depending on the size of the application. In the *validation* phase, Janus validates discovered configurations and dependencies toward container artifacts generation. Current manual efforts at times generate incomplete or inconsistent configuration information, that need to be evaluated and reviewed by hand

© Springer Nature Switzerland AG 2020
S. Yangui et al. (Eds.): ICSOC 2019 Workshops, LNCS 12019, pp. 304–307, 2020.
https://doi.org/10.1007/978-3-030-45989-5_28

post-discovery and it is difficult to obtain completeness and correctness with complex applications. In the *generation* phase, Janus generates container artifacts such as *Dockerfiles, docker-compose.yml*, and an application bundle ready for deployment.

Among all the phases, the discovery phase is the most important and challenging phase considering the complexity and diversity of legacy applications. For example consider the examples of the database configurations such as the database URL specification from two J2EE applications as shown in Fig. 1.

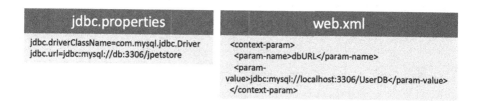

Fig. 1. The database configurations for two J2EE applications, respectively.

In the configuration file *jdbc.properties*, the pattern for extracting the database URL significantly differs from that in *web.xml* file. Based on nature of such specifications, it gets extremely difficult to generalize such rules. Thus, Janus applies a meta-model driven approach that has a set of meta-concepts, a set of concepts within a meta-concept, and attributes within a concept. Under each attribute, Janus provides a list of predefined rules. In addition to predefined rules, Janus creates a dynamic web interface based on meta-concepts, concepts, and attributes to obtain feedback from users thereby learning the ground truth directly from users and creating additional rules. Janus further enhances the meta-model based on new types of applications and their configurations and dependencies.

Janus is similar to Meng et al.'s [1] approach of discovering configurations using an ontology, however, the ontology they consider is predefined and may not be flexible to accommodate changes. Further, their approach requires users to manually annotate configurations rather than providing guidance to obtain appropriate configurations. Also their approach does not generate target code such as container artifacts.

2   The Janus Architecture

We provide the underlying details of Janus in its architecture as shown in Fig. 2. Janus is developed using Python. In the architecture Janus has four components: *configurations and dependencies extractor, dynamic web interface (GUI) for user feedback, docker setup configurations validator*, and *application bundle generator*.

At the center of Janus is a *universal meta-model* that learns from representative legacy applications what configurations and dependencies are required for

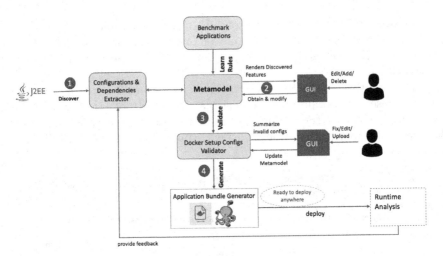

Fig. 2. The Janus tool process flow

container artifacts generation and the various forms and contexts of how they are specified in legacy applications. The meta-model has three components: one, the meta-concepts that capture different key components within an application such as application server, database, and middleware; two, the concepts that are within a meta-concept and capture specific instances of a meta-concepts e.g., DB2, MySQL, SQL SERVER, ORACLE instances under the concept 'database'; three, the attributes that are within a concept and capture different properties of a concept e.g., hostname, username, password, port number, and URL properties under the instance MySQL. Under each attribute, Janus has a set of predefined rules that are primarily written using regex pattern-matching rules as shown in Listing 1.1.

Listing 1.1. A snippet of Janus' metamodel.

```
1    "database": [{
2        "instance": "mysql",
3        "attributes": {
4            "DBNAME": [{
5            "type": "regex",
6            "pattern":"jdbc:mysql://.+/([a-zA-Z]+)"
7            }}
```

A modernization request is triggered from end user with an application archive e.g., WARs or EARs, a choice of deployment, and an application server archive e.g., Apache Tomcat or IBM Websphere-Liberty. In *discovery phase*, Janus decompresses the application and application server archives, scans through all uncompressed files, and then applies regex based pattern-matching rules from the universal meta-model to extract relevant data. From the data, Janus generates an instance-level meta-model, that maps the configurations and dependencies of the uploaded application to their corresponding specifications and values. For example, as shown in Listing 1.1, Janus can extract the required MySQL database names based on the pattern 'jdbc:mysql://.+/([a-zA-Z]+)'. Because the universal Meta-model may not have complete knowledge of all representation forms and contexts of configurations, Janus' dynamic web interface (GUI) guides user to make changes to the instance Meta-model: add new or delete existing configurations & dependencies, or change the values or specifications

Then, in the *validation phase*, Janus utilizes docker setup configuration validator to scan through the instance-level meta-model to make sure all the required specifications for container artifacts are valid. If the specifications are invalid, Janus requests valid input from user via the dynamic web interface (GUI). Once the user provides feedback either by editing the exiting attributes or by uploading required files, Janus re-validates until all validations are passed.

The final version of instance-level meta-model is passed to application bundle generator. Finally, in the *generation phase*, using data from instance-level meta-model, the generator repackages input application and application server archives, and generates Dockerfiles, docker-compose.yml and an application bundle that is ready to deploy to a target cloud environment.

3   Demonstration

We demonstrate Janus on *Jpetstore*, a well-known e-commerce based J2EE application. To trigger a modernization request, we provide a Jpetstore application WAR file and an appserver archieve i.e., Tomcat.

4   How to Watch the Video?

The demo file is titled "Janus DEMO ICSOC 2019.mp4". It is a MP4 video format, no sound, any MP4 viewer should be able to play this video. It can be found in the following link: https://ibm.box.com/s/k28mdcxa7z2gu0dr-ymh9nk6dahse8d5n

Reference

1. Meng, F.J., et al.: A generic framework for application configuration discovery with pluggable knowledge. In: IEEE Sixth International Conference on Cloud Computing, pp. 236–243. IEEE, June 2013

A Programming Framework for People as a Service

David Bandera$^{(\boxtimes)}$, Alejandro Pérez-Vereda$^{(\boxtimes)}$, Carlos Canal$^{(\boxtimes)}$,
and Ernesto Pimentel$^{(\boxtimes)}$

Department of Computer Science, University of Malaga, Málaga, Spain
{dbandera,apvereda,canal}@lcc.uma.es, epimentel@uma.es
http://scenic.uma.es/

Abstract. The number of devices connected to the internet is constantly growing, which implies an increased complexity when interacting with so many heterogeneous devices. Automating this process is key to keep up with this growth. This People as a Service model works towards developing virtual profiles for every user in their own mobile devices and under their full control. These profiles allow to establish user preferences and predefined parameters, which are then applied by the devices they connect to. By integrating both the information in the virtual profiles and these devices, we can create a context in which to make smart decisions and apply them automatically, all of this in a decentralised way. In order to show our proposal in action, we have developed a treasure hunting game as a proof of concept to bring to the spotlight the utility of an environment with programmatically adapted devices.

Keywords: People as a Service · PeaaS · Beacons · Virtual profile · IoT

1 Introduction

The increase in the capabilities of smart devices has brought a growth in the amount of embedded systems and devices we can find everywhere. However, these devices are highly heterogeneous, which causes an increase in difficulty and complexity of intercommunication between them, and an increase in security threats [1]. To help alleviate this issue, we need to work towards automating the task of configuring multiple devices and interacting with them in an easy and personalised way for each user.

For this purpose we have adopted the People as a Service (PeaaS) model [2]. The idea behind PeaaS is to give the users a way to offer as a service a virtual profile with personal-related information. The virtual profile can be accessed by the devices the user interacts with, but at the same time giving the user full control over their data. Not only that, smart devices must be able to adapt to

This work has been funded by the Spanish Government under grant PGC2018-094905-B-100.

the user's situation. This would be achieved by modifying the virtual profiles in a programmatic way.

As a proof of concept, in this work we have developed a treasure hunting game. Treasures will be represented by Eddystone beacons. These simple devices can be easily deployed, require very little maintenance and can be programmatically adjusted. The same approach can then be extrapolated to other areas of application, such as smart cities. For example, for informing the users of how long the bus will take to arrive, to detect how many people are waiting at the bus stop, and from that inferring if an extra bus would be needed.

This paper is structured as follows. Section 2 explains how the system was implemented and the technologies involved. Section 3 presents the treasure hunt game as a proof of concept of the proposal. Finally, Sect. 4 summarises the conclusions and possible utilities of this work, along with future work. A more detailed description of the proposal can be found in [3].

2 Overview of the Proposal

Our goal is to develop a framework that implements the PeaaS model. PeaaS implies a shift from a server-centric structure to a distributed environment, where the smartphones are the focus of the system and becomes an interface through which the virtual profile is accessed, via an specific API.

The framework allows to develop generic mobile and server applications that download and run the scripts provided by the devices and interact with the profile. This allows dynamically updating the user's virtual profiles and modifying the behaviour of the devices, building this way a context of the situation the user is currently in.

In this scenario, the functionality of the system can be updated by modifying the script, without the need to deploy new applications on the server and mobile layers, or to change the settings of the deployed IoT devices. Scripts can be also modified by user's interaction. Depending on their virtual profile and context, some variables of the script can be updated to change how the device behaves. This way, devices automatically adapt to suit the users' needs in a seamless way.

In this work we present a treasure hunt game to show a working example of our proposal, and highlight the advantages and disadvantages we found.

3 Motivating Scenario: A Treasure Hunt

The framework is composed of three elements, the mobile application, the server, and the beacons (Fig. 1). In the treasure hunt, the players look for treasures hidden around the city by following a set of hints, and each treasure found gives a new hint to figure out the location of the next one. The treasures are represented by Eddystone beacons, small devices that broadcast Bluetooth packets, allowing nearby devices to connect to them.

To find the treasures, players employ a mobile application which acts both as the platform where the game is played, detecting and interacting with the beacons, and as an entrance point to their virtual profile for the elements involved in the game, via an API.

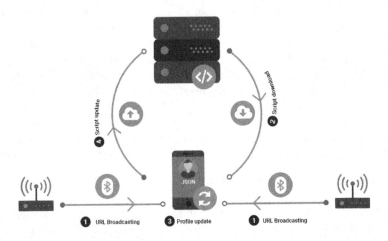

Fig. 1. Dynamic programming framework

Beanshell (http://www.beanshell.org) is a simple Java interpreter capable of uploading and executing code during runtime. It allows us to write simple scripts for querying and updating the virtual profile, as well as to display notifications and messages.

The server is a Node.js server written in JavaScript, using Express as the framework for the server API. It hosts the scripts and the information needed to keep all the players synchronised, and it is accessed by the mobile devices.

The information about the treasures and the available hints is kept in a MongoDB database. We keep track of which player has visited each treasure in order to inform others users of how many players have already visited the treasure they just found.

Each beacon holds the shortened URL linking to the location of a script on the server. When a player accesses it, the server sends the Beanshell script to the mobile device. The script is interpreted and run locally on the player's device.

We have developed one single script that works the same for all the treasures, but it could be possible to have specific scripts for different types of beacons, so they behave in a different way. The variables of the script are set up each time it is downloaded with the relevant values, based on the current user and context.

The mobile application has been developed for Android. It's purpose is to hold the player's virtual profile, to communicate with the beacons and the server as well as provide access to the virtual profile to other devices, and to execute the Beanshell scripts holding the logic of the game.

The application downloads and execute the scripts in a controlled fashion, accessing the user profile through the API, updating the information contained to add the treasure and the new hint just found. Once one player finds the last treasure, she will be informed of being the winner, and the rest of the players will receive a notification of the game ending and the name of the winner the next time they find a treasure.

The functionality of the script is as follows. First, it will check if the treasure was already found by the user to avoid giving more than one hint per treasure. This is done by looking for treasure ID in the player's virtual profile, in which case it will inform the user that they already obtained this particular treasure. If the treasure is a new one, the script connects to the server and informs that the player has found this treasure, in order to update the database. The server will then send a response with the current state of the game. If the game had already finished, the player will receive a notification informing them about it and the name of the winner. Otherwise, the script will try to give the user a new hint. If the user already has all the hints, a message will appear congratulating them for having won the game, while at the same time connecting to the server to declare them as the winner to set the game as finished.

In the case where the player still hasn't finished the game, the script displays the new hint.

4   Conclusions

The ability to infer virtual profiles of people according to their daily routines and activities is a key element to create a world where technology adapts to the people in a seamlessly way [4]. In this work we have presented a working example of a system able to adapt to the user based on their virtual profile in an automated way. Using Bluetooth devices give us a high degree of flexibility when developing these systems. There are many types of devices with different characteristics available on the market, allowing for a more complex behaviour. By replacing the beacons we used in our system by devices with more capabilities, we can extend the functionality of the system, taking advantage of the extra processing and qualities they offer. This would also allow to have a more interactive system where the different devices share information to work towards a common goal, improving the quality of the solutions obtained.

References

1. Covington, M.J., Carskadden, R.: Threat implications of the Internet of Things. In: 2013 5th International Conference on Cyber Conflict (CYCON 2013), pp. 1–12. IEEE (2013)
2. Guillen, J., Miranda, J., Berrocal, J., Garcia-Alonso, J., Murillo, J.M., Canal, C.: People as a Service: a mobile-centric model for providing collective sociological profiles. IEEE Softw. **31**(2), 48–53 (2014)

3. Pérez-Vereda, A., Flores-Martín, D., Canal, C., Murillo, J.M.: Towards dynamically programmable devices using beacons. In: Pautasso, C., Sánchez-Figueroa, F., Systä, K., Murillo Rodríguez, J.M. (eds.) ICWE 2018. LNCS, vol. 11153, pp. 49–58. Springer, Cham (2018). https://doi.org/10.1007/978-3-030-03056-8_5
4. Sadeeq, M.A., Zeebaree, S.R., Qashi, R., Ahmed, S.H., Jacksi, K.: Internet of Things security: a survey. In: 2018 International Conference on Advanced Science and Engineering (ICOASE), pp. 162–166. IEEE (2018)

Author Index

Printed in the United States
By Bookmasters